5 language
VISUAL
dictionary

5 language

VISUAL

dictionary

A DK PUBLISHING BOOK

London, New York, Munich, Melbourne, and Delhi

Senior Editor Angeles Gavira
Senior Art Editor Ina Stradins
US Editors Margaret Parrish, Christine Heilman
DTP Designer Rajen Shah
Production Controller Melanie Dowland
Picture Researcher Anna Grapes
Managing Editor Liz Wheeler
Managing Art Editor Phil Ormerod
Category Publisher Jonathan Metcalf

Designed for Dorling Kindersley by WaltonCreative.com
Art Editor Colin Walton, assisted by Tracy Musson
Designers Peter Radcliffe, Earl Neish, Ann Cannings
Picture Research Marissa Keating

Language content for Dorling Kindersley by
g-and-w PUBLISHING
Managed by Jane Wightwick, assisted by Ana Bremón
Translation and editing by Ana Bremón, Renate Betson,
Marc Vitale, Christine Arthur
Additional input by Dr. Arturo Pretel, Martin Prill,
Frédéric Monteil, Meinrad Prill, Mari Bremón,
Oscar Bremón, Anunchi Bremón, Leila Gaafar

First American Edition, 2003
03 04 05 06 07 10 9 8 7 6 5 4 3 2 1

Published in the United States by
DK Publishing, Inc.
375 Hudson Street
New York, New York 10014

Copyright © 2003 Dorling Kindersley Limited

A Cataloging-in-Publication record is available from the
Library of Congress

ISBN 0-7894-8439-0

Color reproduction by Colourscan, Singapore
Printed and bound by Mohndruck, Germany

See our complete product line at www.dk.com

contents
table des matières
Inhalt
contenido
sommario

about the dictionary

The use of pictures is proven to aid understanding and the retention of information. Working on this principle, this highly-illustrated multilingual dictionary presents a large range of useful current vocabulary in five European languages.

The dictionary is divided thematically and covers most aspects of the everyday world in detail, from the restaurant to the gym, the home to the workplace, outer space to the animal kingdom. You will also find additional words and phrases for conversational use and for extending your vocabulary.

This is an essential reference tool for anyone interested in languages - practical, stimulating, and easy-to-use.

A few things to note
The five languages are always presented in the same order - English, French, German, Spanish, and Italian.

Other than in English, nouns are given with their definite articles reflecting the gender (masculine, feminine, or neuter) and number (singular or plural), for example:

seed   almonds
la graine   les amandes
der Samen   die Mandeln
la semilla   las almendras
il seme   le mandorle

Verbs are indicated by a (v) after the English, for example:

harvest (v) • récolter • ernten • recolectar • raccogliere

Each language also has its own index at the back of the book. Here you can look up a word in any of the five languages and be referred to the page number(s) where it appears. The gender is shown using the following abbreviations:

m = masculine
f = feminine
n = neuter

à propos du dictionnaire

Il est bien connu que les illustrations nous aident à comprendre et retenir l'information. Fondé sur ce principe, ce dictionnaire multilingue richement illustré présente un large éventail de vocabulaire courant et utile dans cinq langues européennes.

Le dictionnaire est divisé de façon thématique et couvre en détail la plupart des aspects du monde quotidien, du restaurant au gymnase, de la maison au lieu de travail, de l'espace au monde animal. Vous y trouverez également des mots et expressions supplémentaires pour la conversation et pour enrichir votre vocabulaire.

Il s'agit d'un outil de référence essentiel pour tous ceux qui s'intéressent aux langues – pratique, stimulant et d'emploi facile.

Quelques points à noter
Les cinq langues sont toujours présentées dans le même ordre – anglais, français, allemand, espagnol et italien.

Sauf en anglais, les noms sont donnés avec leurs articles définis qui indiquent leur genre (masculin, féminin ou neutre) et leur nombre (singulier ou pluriel):

seed   almonds
la graine   les amandes
der Samen   die Mandeln
la semilla   las almendras
il seme   le mandorle

Les verbes sont indiqués par un (v) après l'anglais, par exemple:

harvest (v) • récolter • ernten • recolectar • raccogliere

Chaque langue a également son propre index à la fin du livre. Vous pourrez y vérifier un mot dans n'importe laquelle des cinq langues et vous serez renvoyé au(x) numéro(s) de(s) page(s) où il figure. Le genre est indiqué par les abréviations suivantes:

m = masculin
f = féminin
n = neutre

über das Wörterbuch

Bilder helfen erwiesenermaßen, Informationen zu verstehen und zu behalten. Dieses mehrsprachige Wörterbuch enthält eine Fülle von Illustrationen und präsentiert gleichzeitig ein umfangreiches aktuelles Vokabular in fünf europäischen Sprachen.

Das Wörterbuch ist thematisch gegliedert und behandelt eingehend die meisten Bereiche des heutigen Alltags, vom Restaurant und Fitnesscenter, Heim und Arbeitsplatz bis zum Tierreich und Weltraum. Es enthält außerdem Wörter und Redewendungen, die für die Unterhaltung nützlich sind und das Vokabular erweitern.

Dies ist ein wichtiges Nachschlagewerk für jeden, der sich für Sprachen interessiert – es ist praktisch, anregend und leicht zu benutzen.

Einige Anmerkungen
Die fünf Sprachen werden immer in der gleichen Reihenfolge aufgeführt – Englisch, Französisch, Deutsch, Spanisch und Italienisch.

Außer für Englisch werden Substantive mit den bestimmten Artikeln, die das Geschlecht (Maskulinum, Femininum oder Neutrum) und den Numerus (Singular oder Plural) ausdrücken, angegeben, zum Beispiel:

seed   almonds
la graine   les amandes
der Samen   die Mandeln
la semilla   las almendras
il seme   le mandorle

Die Verben sind durch ein (v) nach dem englischen Wort gekennzeichnet:

harvest (v) • récolter • ernten • recolectar • raccogliere

Am Ende des Buchs befinden sich Register für jede Sprache. Sie können dort ein Wort in einer der fünf Sprachen und die jeweilige Seitenzahl nachsehen. Die Geschlechtsangabe erfolgt mit folgenden Abkürzungen:

m = Maskulinum
f = Femininum
n = Neutrum

sobre el diccionario

Está comprobado que el empleo de fotografías ayuda a la comprensión y a la retención de información. Basados en este principio, este diccionario plurilíngüe y altamente ilustrado exhibe un amplio registro de vocabulario útil y actual en cinco idiomas europeos.

El diccionario aparece dividido según su temática y abarca la mayoría de los aspectos del mundo cotidiano con detalle, desde el restaurante al gimnasio, la casa al lugar de trabajo, el espacio al reino animal. Encontrará también palabras y frases adicionales para su uso en conversación y para ampliar su vocabulario.

Este diccionario es un instrumento de referencia esencial para todo aquél que esté interesado en los idiomas; es práctico, estimulante y fácil de usar.

Algunos puntos a observar

Los cinco idiomas se presentan siempre en el mismo orden: inglés, francés, alemán, español e italiano.

A excepción del inglés, los sustantivos se muestran con sus artículos definidos reflejando el género (masculino, femenino o neutro) y el número (singular/plural):

seed	almonds
la graine	les amandes
der Samen	die Mandeln
la semilla	las almendras
il seme	le mandorle

Los verbos se indican con una (v) después del inglés:

harvest (*v*) • récolter • ernten • recolectar • raccogliere

Cada idioma tiene su propio índice. Aquí podrá mirar una palabra en cualquiera de los cinco idiomas y se le indicará el número de la página donde aparece. El género se indica utilizando las siguientes abreviaturas:

m = masculino
f = femenino
n = neutro

informazioni sul dizionario

È dimostrato che l'uso di immagini aiuti a capire e memorizzare le informazioni. Applicando tale principio, abbiamo realizzato questo dizionario multilingue, corredato da numerosissime illustrazioni, che presenta un ampio ventaglio di vocaboli utili in cinque lingue europee.

Il dizionario è diviso in vari argomenti ed esamina dettagliatamente molti aspetti del mondo moderno, dal ristorante alla palestra, dalla casa all'ufficio, dallo spazio al regno animale. L'opera contiene inoltre frasi e vocaboli utili per conversare e per estendere il proprio vocabolario.

È un'opera di consultazione essenziale per tutti gli appassionati delle lingue – pratica, stimolante e facile da usare.

Indicazioni

Le cinque lingue vengono presentate sempre nello stesso ordine: inglese, francese, tedesco, spagnolo e italiano.

In tutte le lingue, tranne l'inglese, i sostantivi vengono riportati con il relativo articolo determinativo, che indica il genere (maschile, femminile o neutro) e il numero (singolare o plurale), come ad esempio:

seed	almonds
la graine	les amandes
der Samen	die Mandeln
la semilla	las almendras
il seme	le mandorle

I verbi sono contraddistinti da una (v) dopo il vocabolo inglese, come ad esempio:

harvest (*v*) • récolter • ernten • recolectar • raccogliere

Alla fine del libro ogni lingua ha inoltre il proprio indice, che consente di cercare un vocabolo in una qualsiasi delle cinque lingue e di trovare il rimando alla pagina che gli corrisponde. Il genere è indicato dalle seguenti abbreviazioni:

m = maschile
f = femminile
n = neutro

how to use this book

Whether you are learning a new language for business, pleasure, or in preparation for a vacation abroad, or are hoping to extend your vocabulary in an already familiar language, this dictionary is a valuable learning tool which you can use in a number of different ways.

When learning a new language, look out for cognates (words that are alike in different languages) and false friends (words that *look* alike but carry significantly different meanings). You can also see where the languages have influenced each other. For example, English has imported many terms for food from other European languages but, in turn, exported terms used in technology and popular culture.

You can compare two or three languages or all five, depending on how wide your interests are.

Practical learning activities
• As you move around your home, workplace, or school, try looking at the pages which cover that setting. You could then close the book, look around you and see how many of the objects and features you can name.

• Challenge yourself to write a story, letter, or dialogue using as many of the terms on a particular page as possible. This will help you retain the vocabulary and remember the spelling. If you want to build up to writing a longer text, start with sentences incorporating 2–3 words.

• If you have a very visual memory, try drawing or tracing items from the book onto a piece of paper, then close the book and fill in the words below the picture.

• Once you are more confident, pick out words in a foreign-language index and see if you know what they mean before turning to the relevant page to check if you were right.

comment utiliser ce livre

Que vous appreniez une nouvelle langue pour les affaires, le plaisir ou pour préparer vos vacances, ou encore si vous espérez élargir votre vocabulaire dans une langue qui vous est déjà familière, ce dictionnaire sera pour vous un outil d'apprentissage précieux que vous pourrez utiliser de plusieurs manières.

Lorsque vous apprenez une nouvelle langue, recherchez les mots apparentés (mots qui se ressemblent dans différentes langues) et les faux amis (mots qui se ressemblent mais ont des significations nettement différentes). Vous pouvez aussi voir comment les langues se sont influencées. Par exemple, l'anglais a importé des autres langues européennes de nombreux termes désignant la nourriture mais, en retour, exporté des termes employés dans le domaine de la technologie et de la culture populaire.

Vous pouvez comparer deux ou trois langues ou bien toutes les cinq, selon votre intérêt.

Activités pratiques d'apprentissage
• Lorsque vous vous déplacez dans votre maison, au travail ou à l'université, essayez de regarder les pages qui correspondent à ce contexte. Vous pouvez ensuite fermer le livre, regarder autour de vous et voir combien d'objets vous pouvez nommer.

• Forcez-vous à écrire une histoire, une lettre ou un dialogue en employant le plus de termes possibles choisis dans une page. Ceci vous aidera à retenir le vocabulaire et son orthographe. Si vous souhaitez pouvoir écrire un texte plus long, commencez par des phrases qui incorporent 2 à 3 mots.

• Si vous avez une mémoire très visuelle, essayez de dessiner ou de décalquer des objets du livre sur une feuille de papier, puis fermez le livre et inscrivez les mots sous l'image.

• Une fois que vous serez plus sûr de vous, choisissez des mots dans l'index de la langue étrangère et essayez de voir si vous en connaissez le sens avant de vous reporter à la page correspondante pour vérifier.

die Benutzung des Buchs

Ganz gleich, ob Sie eine Sprache aus Geschäftsgründen, zum Vergnügen oder als Vorbereitung für einen Auslandsurlaub lernen, oder Ihr Vokabular in einer Ihnen bereits vertrauten Sprache erweitern möchten, dieses Wörterbuch ist ein wertvolles Lernmittel, das Sie auf vielfältige Art und Weise benutzen können.

Wenn Sie eine neue Sprache lernen, achten Sie auf Wörter, die in verschiedenen Sprachen ähnlich sind sowie auf falsche Freunde (Wörter, die ähnlich aussehen aber wesentlich andere Bedeutungen haben). Sie können ebenfalls feststellen, wie die Sprachen einander beeinflusst haben. Englisch hat zum Beispiel viele Ausdrücke für Nahrungs-mittel aus anderen europäischen Sprachen übernommen und andererseits viele Begriffe aus der Technik und Popkultur ausgeführt.

Sie können je nach Ihrem Interesse zwei oder drei, oder auch alle fünf Sprachen miteinander vergleichen.

Praktische Übungen
• Versuchen Sie sich zu Hause, am Arbeits- oder Studienplatz den Inhalt der Seiten einzuprägen, die Ihre Umgebung behandeln. Schließen Sie dann das Buch und prüfen Sie, wie viele Gegenstände Sie in den anderen Sprachen sagen können.

• Schreiben Sie eine Geschichte, einen Brief oder Dialog und benutzen Sie dabei möglichst viele Ausdrücke von einer bestimmten Seite des Wörterbuchs. Dies ist eine gute Methode, sich das Vokabular und die Schreibweise einzuprägen. Sie können mit kurzen Sätzen von zwei bis drei Worten anfangen und dann nach und nach längere Texte schreiben.

• Wenn Sie ein visuelles Gedächtnis haben, können Sie Gegenstände aus dem Buch abzeichnen oder abpausen. Schließen Sie dann das Buch und schreiben Sie die passenden Wörter unter die Bilder.

• Wenn Sie mehr Sicherheit haben, können Sie Wörter aus einem der Fremdsprachen-register aussuchen und deren Bedeutung aufschreiben, bevor Sie auf der entsprechenden Seite nachsehen.

cómo utilizar este libro

Ya se encuentre aprendiendo un idioma nuevo por motivos de trabajo, placer, o para preparar sus vacaciones al extranjero, o ya quiera ampliar su vocabulario en un idioma que ya conoce, este diccionario es un instrumento muy valioso que podrá utilizar de distintas maneras.

Cuando esté aprendiendo un idioma nuevo, busque palabras similares en distintos idiomas y palabras que parecen similares pero que poseen significados totalmente distintos. También podrá observar cómo los idiomas se influyen unos a otros. Por ejemplo, la lengua inglesa ha importado muchos términos de comida de otras lenguas pero, a cambio, ha exportado términos empleados en tecnología y cultura popular.

Podrá comparar dos o tres idiomas o los cinco, dependiendo de cómo de amplios sean sus intereses.

Actividades prácticas de aprendizaje
• Mientras se desplaza por su casa, lugar de trabajo o colegio, intente mirar las páginas que se refieren a ese lugar. Podrá entonces cerrar el libro, mirar a su alrededor y ver cuántos objetos o características puede nombrar.

• Desafíese a usted mismo a escribir una historia, carta o diálogo empleando tantos términos de una página concreta como le sea posible. Esto le ayudará a retener vocabulario y recordar la ortografía. Si quiere ir progresando para poder escribir un texto más largo, comience con frases que incorporen 2 ó 3 palabras.

• Si tiene buena memoria visual, intente dibujar o calcar objetos del libro; luego cierre el libro y escriba las palabras correspondientes debajo del dibujo.

• Cuando se sienta más seguro, escoja palabras del índice de uno de los idiomas y vea si sabe lo que significan antes de consultar la página correspondiente para comprobarlo.

come usare questo libro

Che stiate imparando una lingua nuova a scopo di lavoro, per diletto o in preparazione per una vacanza all'estero, o desideriate estendere il vostro vocabolario in una lingua che vi è già familiare, questo dizionario è uno strumento di apprendimento prezioso che potete usare in vari modi diversi.

Quando imparate una lingua nuova, cercate le parole affini per origine (che sono quindi simili nelle varie lingue) ma occhio alle false analogie (vocaboli che sembrano uguali ma hanno significati molto diversi). Questo dizionario mostra inoltre come le lingue hanno influito l'una sull'altra (l'inglese, per esempio, ha importato dalle altre lingue europee molti vocaboli relativi agli alimenti ma ne ha esportati molti altri relativi alla tecnologia e alla cultura popolare) e vi consente di confrontare due, tre o anche tutte e cinque le lingue, a seconda di quelle che vi interessano.

Attività pratiche di apprendimento
• Girando per casa, in ufficio, a scuola, guardate le pagine relative all'ambiente in cui vi trovate, poi chiudete il libro, guardatevi attorno e cercate di ricordare il nome del maggior numero possibile di oggetti e strutture.

• Provate a scrivere un racconto, una lettera o un dialogo usando il maggior numero possibile dei vocaboli riportati su di una pagina in particolare. Vi aiuterà a memorizzare i vocaboli e a ricordare come si scrivono. Se volete scrivere testi più lunghi, cominciate con delle frasi che comprendano 2 o 3 delle parole.

• Se avete una memoria molto visiva, prendete un foglio di carta e disegnatevi o ricopiatevi le immagini che appaiono nel libro, quindi chiudete il libro e scrivete le parole sotto alle immagini.

• Quando vi sentite più sicuri, scegliete dei vocaboli dall'indice di una lingua straniera e cercate di ricordarne i significati, trovando poi le pagine corrispondenti per verificare che siano giusti.

people
les gens
die Menschen
la gente
le persone

body • le corps • der Körper • el cuerpo • il corpo

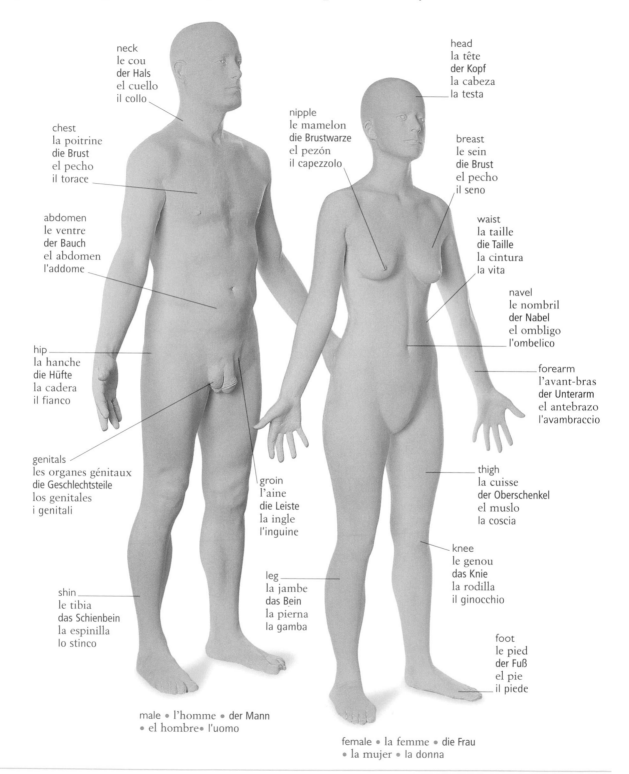

neck
le cou
der Hals
el cuello
il collo

head
la tête
der Kopf
la cabeza
la testa

nipple
le mamelon
die Brustwarze
el pezón
il capezzolo

breast
le sein
die Brust
el pecho
il seno

chest
la poitrine
die Brust
el pecho
il torace

waist
la taille
die Taille
la cintura
la vita

abdomen
le ventre
der Bauch
el abdomen
l'addome

navel
le nombril
der Nabel
el ombligo
l'ombelico

forearm
l'avant-bras
der Unterarm
el antebrazo
l'avambraccio

hip
la hanche
die Hüfte
la cadera
il fianco

genitals
les organes génitaux
die Geschlechtsteile
los genitales
i genitali

thigh
la cuisse
der Oberschenkel
el muslo
la coscia

groin
l'aine
die Leiste
la ingle
l'inguine

knee
le genou
das Knie
la rodilla
il ginocchio

shin
le tibia
das Schienbein
la espinilla
lo stinco

leg
la jambe
das Bein
la pierna
la gamba

foot
le pied
der Fuß
el pie
il piede

male • l'homme • der Mann
• el hombre• l'uomo

female • la femme • die Frau
• la mujer • la donna

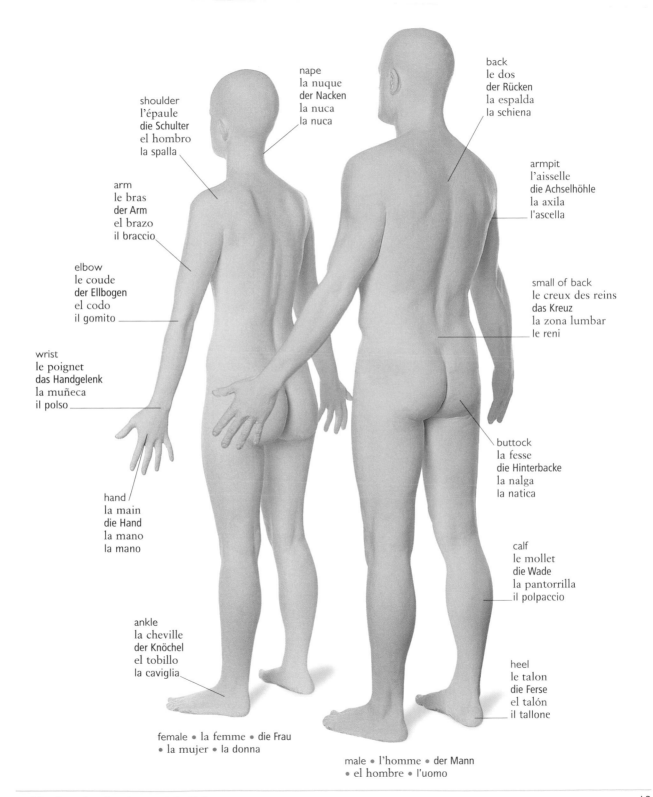

shoulder
l'épaule
die Schulter
el hombro
la spalla

nape
la nuque
der Nacken
la nuca
la nuca

back
le dos
der Rücken
la espalda
la schiena

arm
le bras
der Arm
el brazo
il braccio

armpit
l'aisselle
die Achselhöhle
la axila
l'ascella

elbow
le coude
der Ellbogen
el codo
il gomito

small of back
le creux des reins
das Kreuz
la zona lumbar
le reni

wrist
le poignet
das Handgelenk
la muñeca
il polso

buttock
la fesse
die Hinterbacke
la nalga
la natica

hand
la main
die Hand
la mano
la mano

calf
le mollet
die Wade
la pantorrilla
il polpaccio

ankle
la cheville
der Knöchel
el tobillo
la caviglia

heel
le talon
die Ferse
el talón
il tallone

female • la femme • die Frau
• la mujer • la donna

male • l'homme • der Mann
• el hombre • l'uomo

face • le visage • das Gesicht • la cara • la faccia

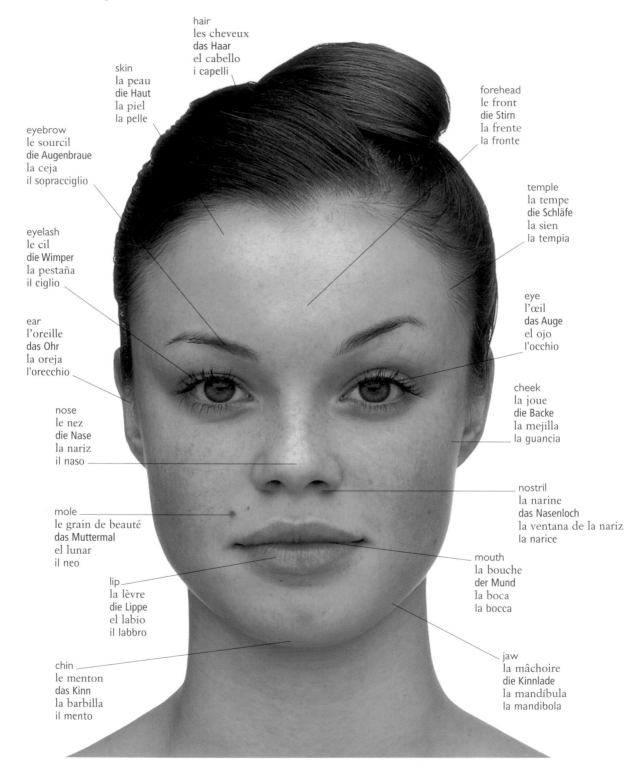

hair
les cheveux
das Haar
el cabello
i capelli

skin
la peau
die Haut
la piel
la pelle

forehead
le front
die Stirn
la frente
la fronte

eyebrow
le sourcil
die Augenbraue
la ceja
il sopracciglio

temple
la tempe
die Schläfe
la sien
la tempia

eyelash
le cil
die Wimper
la pestaña
il ciglio

eye
l'œil
das Auge
el ojo
l'occhio

ear
l'oreille
das Ohr
la oreja
l'orecchio

cheek
la joue
die Backe
la mejilla
la guancia

nose
le nez
die Nase
la nariz
il naso

nostril
la narine
das Nasenloch
la ventana de la nariz
la narice

mole
le grain de beauté
das Muttermal
el lunar
il neo

mouth
la bouche
der Mund
la boca
la bocca

lip
la lèvre
die Lippe
el labio
il labbro

jaw
la mâchoire
die Kinnlade
la mandíbula
la mandibola

chin
le menton
das Kinn
la barbilla
il mento

wrinkle • la ride • die Falte
• la arruga • la ruga

freckle • la tache de rousseur
• die Sommersprosse •
la peca • la lentiggine

pore • le pore • die Pore
• el poro • il poro

dimple • la fossette
• das Grübchen • el hoyuelo
• la fossetta

hand • la main • die Hand • la mano • la mano

ring finger
l'annulaire
der Ringfinger
el anular
l'anulare

middle finger • le majeur
• der Mittelfinger • el dedo
corazón • il medio

index finger • l'index
• der Zeigefinger • el
índice • l'indice

little finger
l'auriculaire
der kleine Finger
el meñique
il mignolo

wrist
le poignet
das Handgelenk
la muñeca
il polso

palm
la paume
die Handfläche
la palma de
la mano
il palmo

thumb
le pouce
der Daumen
el pulgar
il pollice

nail • l'ongle • der Fingernagel
• la uña • l'unghia

cuticle
la cuticule
die Nagelhaut
la cutícula
la pellicina

knuckle
le nœud de
l'articulation
der Handknöchel
el nudillo
la nocca

fist • le poing
• die Faust • el puño
• il pugno

foot • le pied • der Fuß • el pie • il piede

ball
l'avant-pied
der Ballen
el juanete
l'avampiede

toe
l'orteil
der Zeh
el dedo del pie
il dito del piede

heel
le talon
die Ferse
el talón
il tallone

sole
la plante du pied
die Fußsohle
la planta del pie
la pianta del piede

instep
le cou-de-pied
der Spann
la parte interna del pie
il collo del piede

arch
la cambrure
das Gewölbe
el arco plantar
l'arco plantare

big toe
le gros orteil
der große Zeh
el dedo gordo
del pie
l'alluce

bridge
le dos du pied
der Fußrücken
el empeine
il dorso del
piede

toenail
l'ongle du pied
der Zehennagel
la uña del pie
l'unghia del piede

little toe
le petit orteil
der kleine Zeh
el dedo pequeño
del pie
il mignolo del
piede

ankle
la cheville
der Knöchel
el tobillo
la caviglia

muscles • les muscles • die Muskeln • los músculos • i muscoli

frontal
le frontal
der Stirnmuskel
el frontal
il frontale

pectoral
le pectoral
der Brustmuskel
el pectoral
il pettorale

deltoid
le deltoïde
der Deltamuskel
el deltoideo
il deltoide

trapezius
le trapèze
der Kapuzenmuskel
el trapecio
il trapezio

intercostal
l'intercostal
der Zwischenrippenmuskel
el intercostal
l'intercostale

latissimus dorsi
le dorsal
der Rückenmuskel
el dorsal
il dorsale

biceps
le biceps
der Bizeps
el bíceps
il bicipite

triceps
le triceps
der Trizeps
el tríceps
il tricipite

abdominals
les abdominaux
die Bauchmuskeln
el abdominal
gli addominali

hamstring
• le tendon du
jarret • der
Kniesehnenstrang
• el tendón de
la corva
• il tendine

buttock
le fessier
der Gesäßmuskel
el glúteo
la natica

quadriceps
les quadriceps
die Oberschenkelmuskeln
el cuádriceps
il quadricipite

Achilles tendon
• le tendon
d'Achille
• die Achillessehne
• el tendón de
Aquiles • il tendine
di achille

calf
les muscles
jumeaux
der Wadenmuskel
los gemelos
il polpaccio

skeleton • le squelette • das Skelett • el esqueleto • lo scheletro

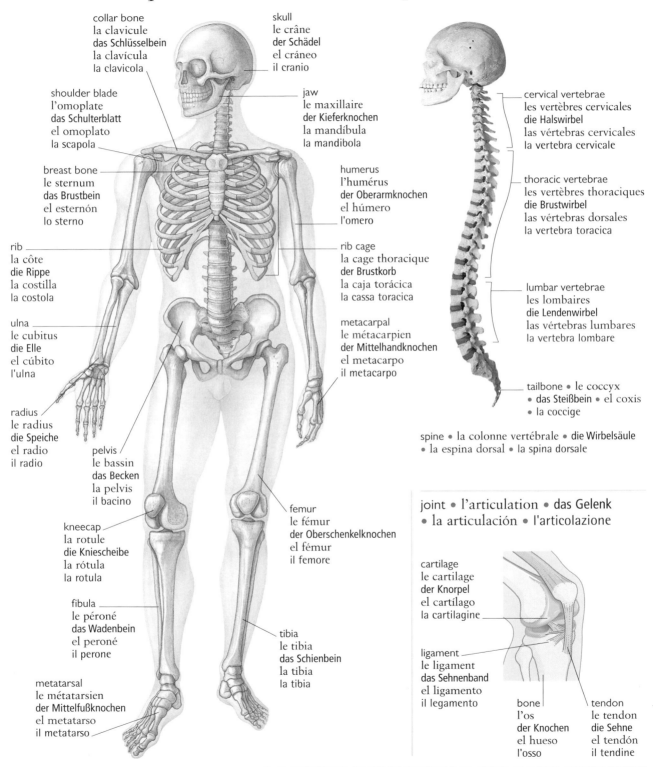

collar bone
la clavicule
das Schlüsselbein
la clavícula
la clavicola

skull
le crâne
der Schädel
el cráneo
il cranio

shoulder blade
l'omoplate
das Schulterblatt
el omoplato
la scapola

jaw
le maxillaire
der Kieferknochen
la mandíbula
la mandibola

breast bone
le sternum
das Brustbein
el esternón
lo sterno

humerus
l'humérus
der Oberarmknochen
el húmero
l'omero

rib
la côte
die Rippe
la costilla
la costola

rib cage
la cage thoracique
der Brustkorb
la caja torácica
la cassa toracica

ulna
le cubitus
die Elle
el cúbito
l'ulna

metacarpal
le métacarpien
der Mittelhandknochen
el metacarpo
il metacarpo

radius
le radius
die Speiche
el radio
il radio

pelvis
le bassin
das Becken
la pelvis
il bacino

kneecap
la rotule
die Kniescheibe
la rótula
la rotula

femur
le fémur
der Oberschenkelknochen
el fémur
il femore

fibula
le péroné
das Wadenbein
el peroné
il perone

tibia
le tibia
das Schienbein
la tibia
la tibia

metatarsal
le métatarsien
der Mittelfußknochen
el metatarso
il metatarso

cervical vertebrae
les vertèbres cervicales
die Halswirbel
las vértebras cervicales
la vertebra cervicale

thoracic vertebrae
les vertèbres thoraciques
die Brustwirbel
las vértebras dorsales
la vertebra toracica

lumbar vertebrae
les lombaires
die Lendenwirbel
las vértebras lumbares
la vertebra lombare

tailbone • le coccyx
• **das Steißbein** • el coxis
• la coccige

spine • la colonne vertébrale • **die Wirbelsäule**
• la espina dorsal • la spina dorsale

joint • l'articulation • das Gelenk • la articulación • l'articolazione

cartilage
le cartilage
der Knorpel
el cartílago
la cartilagine

ligament
le ligament
das Sehnenband
el ligamento
il legamento

bone
l'os
der Knochen
el hueso
l'osso

tendon
le tendon
die Sehne
el tendón
il tendine

internal organs • les organes internes • die inneren Organe • los órganos internos • gli organi interni

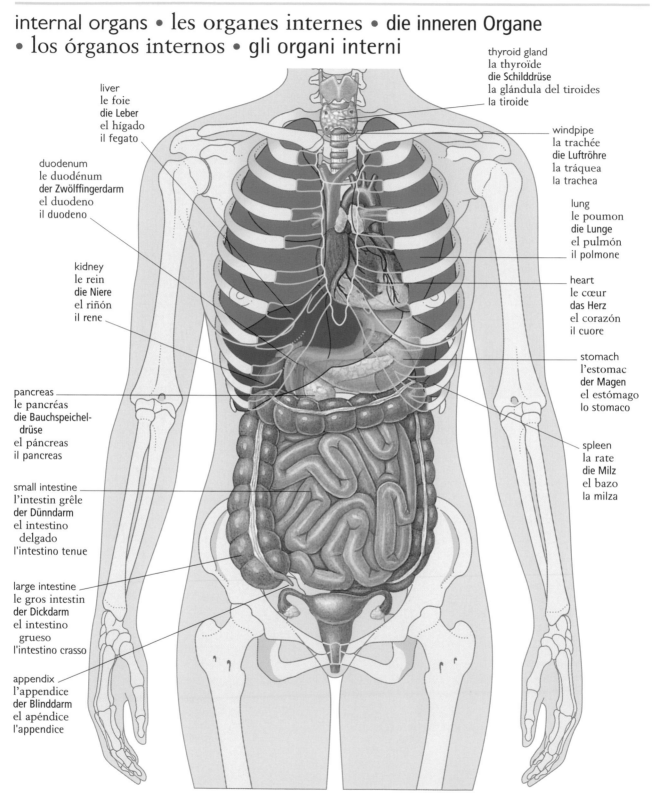

thyroid gland
la thyroïde
die Schilddrüse
la glándula del tiroides
la tiroide

liver
le foie
die Leber
el hígado
il fegato

windpipe
la trachée
die Luftröhre
la tráquea
la trachea

duodenum
le duodénum
der Zwölffingerdarm
el duodeno
il duodeno

lung
le poumon
die Lunge
el pulmón
il polmone

kidney
le rein
die Niere
el riñón
il rene

heart
le cœur
das Herz
el corazón
il cuore

stomach
l'estomac
der Magen
el estómago
lo stomaco

pancreas
le pancréas
**die Bauchspeichel-
drüse**
el páncreas
il pancreas

spleen
la rate
die Milz
el bazo
la milza

small intestine
l'intestin grêle
der Dünndarm
el intestino
 delgado
l'intestino tenue

large intestine
le gros intestin
der Dickdarm
el intestino
 grueso
l'intestino crasso

appendix
l'appendice
der Blinddarm
el apéndice
l'appendice

head • la tête • **der Kopf** • la cabeza • la testa

sinus • le sinus • **der Sinus** • el seno • il seno

palate • le palais • **der Gaumen** • el paladar • il palato

tongue • la langue • **die Zunge** • la lengua • la lingua

larynx • le larynx • **der Kehlkopf** • la laringe • la laringe

Adam's apple • la pomme d'Adam • **der Adamsapfel** • la manzana de Adán • il pomo di Adamo

vocal cords • les cordes vocales • **die Stimmbänder** • las cuerdas vocales • le corde vocali

brain le cerveau **das Gehirn** el cerebro il cervello

pharynx le pharynx **der Rachen** la faringe la faringe

epiglottis • l'épiglotte • **der Kehldeckel** • la epiglotis • l'epiglottide

esophagus • l'œsophage • **die Speiseröhre** • el esófago • l'esofago

throat • la gorge • **die Kehle** • la garganta • la gola

body systems • les systèmes du corps • **die Körpersysteme** • los sistemas • i sistemi corporali

diaphragm le diaphragme **das Zwerchfell** el diafragma il diaframma

respiratory • respiratoire • **das Atmungssystem** • respiratorio • respiratorio

digestive • digestif • **das Verdauungssystem** • digestivo • digestivo

vein la veine **die Vene** la vena la vena

artery l'artère **die Arterie** la arteria l'arteria

cardiovascular • cardio-vasculaire • **das Herz- und Gefäßsystem** • cardiovascular • cardiovascolare

lymphatic • lymphatique • **das lymphatische System** • linfático • linfatico

gland la glande **die Drüse** la glándula la ghiandola

urinary • urinaire • **das Harnsystem** • urinario • urinario

endocrine • endocrine • **das endokrine System** • endocrino • endocrino

nerve le nerf **der Nerv** el nervio il nervo

nervous • nerveux • **das Nervensystem** • nervioso • nervoso

reproductive • reproducteur • **das Fortpflanzungssystem** • reproductor • riproduttivo

reproductive organs • les organes de reproduction • die Fortpflanzungsorgane • los órganos reproductores • gli organi riproduttivi

fallopian tube
la trompe de Fallope
der Eileiter
la trompa de Falopio
il tubo di Fallopio

ovary
l'ovaire
der Eierstock
el ovario
l'ovaia

uterus
l'utérus
die Gebärmutter
el útero
l'utero

cervix
le col de l'utérus
der Gebärmutterhals
el cuello uterino
il collo dell'utero

vagina
le vagin
die Scheide
la vagina
la vagina

follicle
le follicule
der Follikel
el folículo
il follicolo

bladder
la vessie
die Blase
la vejiga
la vescica

clitoris
le clitoris
die Klitoris
el clítoris
il clitoride

urethra
l'urètre
die Harnröhre
la uretra
l'uretra

labia
les lèvres
die Schamlippen
los labios
le labbra

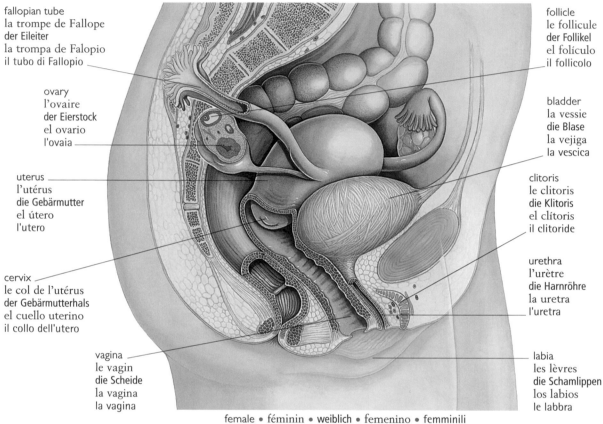

female • féminin • weiblich • femenino • femminili

reproduction • la reproduction • die Fortpflanzung • la reproducción • la riproduzione

sperm
le sperme
das Spermium
el esperma
lo sperma

egg
l'ovule
das Ei
el óvulo
l'ovulo

fertilization • la fertilisation • die Befruchtung • la fertilización • la fertilizzazione

hormone	impotent	menstruation
l'hormone	impuissant	les règles
das Hormon	impotent	die Menstruation
la hormona	impotente	la menstruación
l'ormone	impotente	la mestruazione
ovulation	fertile	intercourse
l'ovulation	fécond	les rapports sexuels
der Eisprung	fruchtbar	der Geschlechtsverkehr
la ovulación	fértil	el coito
l'ovulazione	fecondo	il coito
infertile	conceive	sexually transmitted disease
stérile	concevoir	la maladie sexuellement transmissible
steril	empfangen	die Geschlechtskrankheit
estéril	concebir	la enfermedad de transmisión sexual
sterile	concepire	la malattia trasmissibile per via sessuale

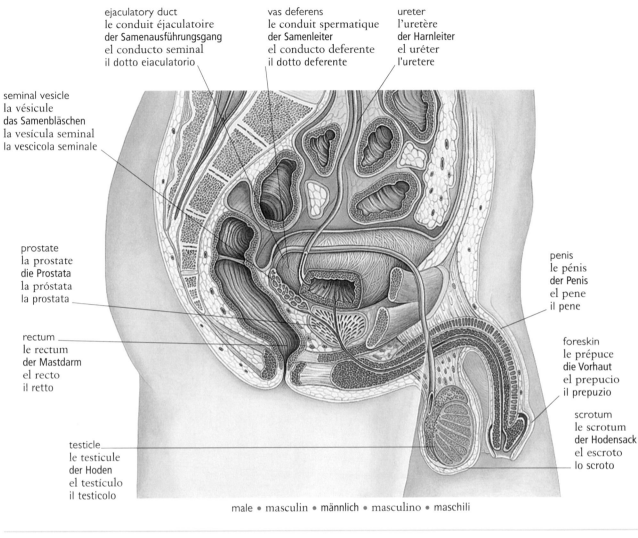

ejaculatory duct
le conduit éjaculatoire
der Samenausführungsgang
el conducto seminal
il dotto eiaculatorio

vas deferens
le conduit spermatique
der Samenleiter
el conducto deferente
il dotto deferente

ureter
l'uretère
der Harnleiter
el uréter
l'uretere

seminal vesicle
la vésicule
das Samenbläschen
la vesícula seminal
la vescicola seminale

prostate
la prostate
die Prostata
la próstata
la prostata

rectum
le rectum
der Mastdarm
el recto
il retto

testicle
le testicule
der Hoden
el testículo
il testicolo

penis
le pénis
der Penis
el pene
il pene

foreskin
le prépuce
die Vorhaut
el prepucio
il prepuzio

scrotum
le scrotum
der Hodensack
el escroto
lo scroto

male • masculin • männlich • masculino • maschili

contraception • la contraception • die Empfängnisverhütung
• la anticoncepción • la contraccezione

cap
le pessaire
das Pessar
el anillo cervical
il cappuccio cervicale

diaphragm
le diaphragme
das Diaphragma
el diafragma
il diaframma

condom
le condom
das Kondom
el condón
il preservativo

IUD
le stérilet
die Spirale
el dispositivo intrauterino DIU
il dispositivo intrauterino

pill
la pilule
die Pille
la pastilla
la pillola

family • la famille • die Familie • la familia • la famiglia

grandmother • la grand-mère • die Großmutter • la abuela • la nonna

grandfather • le grand-père • der Großvater • el abuelo • il nonno

uncle • l'oncle • der Onkel • el tío • lo zio

aunt • la tante • die Tante • la tía • la zia

father • le père • der Vater • el padre • il padre

mother • la mère • die Mutter • la madre • la madre

cousin • le cousin • der Cousin • el primo • il cugino

brother • le frère • der Bruder • el hermano • il fratello

sister • la sœur • die Schwester • la hermana • la sorella

wife • la femme • die Ehefrau • la esposa • la moglie

daughter-in-law • la belle-fille • die Schwiegertochter • la nuera • la nuora

son • le fils • der Sohn • el hijo • il figlio

daughter • la fille • die Tochter • la hija • la figlia

son-in-law • le gendre • der Schwiegersohn • el yerno • il genero

grandson • le petit-fils • der Enkel • el nieto • il nipote

granddaughter • la petite-fille • die Enkelin • la nieta • la nipote

husband • le mari • der Ehemann • el esposo • il marito

relatives	parents	grandchildren	stepmother	stepson	generation
les parents	les parents	les petits-enfants	la belle-mère	le beau-fils	la génération
die Verwandten	die Eltern	die Enkelkinder	die Stiefmutter	der Stiefsohn	die Generation
los parientes	los padres	los nietos	la madrastra	el hijastro	la generación
i parenti	i genitori	i nipoti	la matrigna	il figliastro	la generazione
grandparents	children	stepfather	stepdaughter	partner	twins
les grands-parents	les enfants	le beau-père	la belle-fille	le/la partenaire	les jumeaux
die Großeltern	die Kinder	der Stiefvater	die Stieftochter	der Partner/die Partnerin	die Zwillinge
los abuelos	los niños	el padrastro	la hijastra	el/la compañero/-a	los gemelos
i nonni	i bambini	il patrigno	la figliastra	il/la compagno/-a	i gemelli

mother-in-law
• la belle-mère
• die Schwiegermutter
• la suegra • la suocera

father-in-law
• le beau-père
• der Schwiegervater
• el suegro • il suocero

**stages • les stades • die Stadien
• las etapas • le fasi**

baby • le bébé
• das Baby • el bebé
• il bimbo

child • l'enfant
• das Kind • el niño
• il bambino

brother-in-law
• le beau-frère
• der Schwager • el
cuñado • il cognato

sister-in-law • la belle-
sœur • die Schwägerin
• la cuñada
• la cognata

boy • le garçon
• der Junge • el niño
• il ragazzo

girl • la fille
• das Mädchen
• la niña • la ragazza

niece • la nièce
• die Nichte • la
sobrina • la nipote

nephew • le neveu
• der Neffe • el
sobrino • il nipote

Mrs.
Madame
Frau
Señora
Signora

teenager • l'adolescente
• die Jugendliche
• la adolescente
• l'adolescente

adult • l'adulte • der
Erwachsene • el adulto
• l'adulto

**titles • les titres • die Anreden
• los tratamientos • gli appellativi**

Miss	Mr.
Mademoiselle	Monsieur
Fräulein	Herr
Señorita	Señor
Signorina	Signore

man • l'homme
• der Mann
• el hombre • l'uomo

woman • la femme
• die Frau • la mujer
• la donna

relationships • les relations • die Beziehungen • las relaciones • i rapporti

manager
le chef
der Chef
el jefe
il capo

assistant
l'assistante
die Assistentin
la asistente
l'assistente

business partner
l'associée
die Geschäftspartnerin
la socia
il partner di affari

employer
l'employeuse
die Arbeitgeberin
la empresaria
il datore di lavoro

employee
l'employé
der Arbeitnehmer
el empleado
l'impiegato

colleague
le collègue
der Kollege
el compañero
il collega

office • le bureau • das Büro • la oficina • l'ufficio

neighbor • le voisin
• der Nachbar • el vecino
• il vicino

friend • l'ami • der Freund
• el amigo • l'amico

acquaintance • la connaissance
• der Bekannte • el conocido
• il conoscente

pen pal • le correspondant
• der Brieffreund • el amigo
por correspondencia
• l'amico di penna

boyfriend
le petit ami
der Freund
el novio
il ragazzo

girlfriend
la petite amie
die Freundin
la novia
la ragazza

fiancé
le fiancé
der Verlobte
el prometido
il fidanzato

fiancée
la fiancée
die Verlobte
la prometida
la fidanzata

couple • le couple • das Paar • la pareja • la coppia

engaged couple • les fiancés • die Verlobten • la pareja • i fidanzati

emotions • les émotions • die Gefühle • las emociones • le emozioni

smile
le sourire
das Lächeln
la sonrisa
il sorriso

happy • heureux • glücklich
• contento • felice

sad • triste • **traurig** • triste
• triste

excited • excité • **aufgeregt**
• entusiasmado • eccitato

bored • ennuyé • **gelangweilt**
• aburrido • annoiato

surprised • surpris
• **überrascht** • sorprendido
• sorpreso

scared • effrayé • **erschrocken**
• asustado • spaventato

frown • le froncement
de sourcils • **das
Stirnrunzeln** • el ceño
fruncido • aggrottare
le sopracciglia

angry • fâché • **verärgert**
• enfadado • arrabbiato

confused • confus • **verwirrt**
• confuso • confuso

worried • inquiet • **besorgt**
• preocupado • preoccupato

nervous • nerveux • **nervös**
• nervioso • nervoso

proud • fier • **stolz**
• orgulloso • fiero

confident • confiant
• **selbstsicher** • seguro de sí
mismo • fiducioso

embarrassed • gêné
• **verlegen** • avergonzado
• imbarazzato

shy • timide • **schüchtern**
• tímido • timido

upset	laugh (v)	sigh (v)	shout (v)
consterné	rire	soupirer	crier
bestürzt	lachen	seufzen	schreien
triste	reír	suspirar	gritar
turbato	ridere	sospirare	gridare
shocked	cry (v)	faint (v)	yawn (v)
choqué	pleurer	s'évanouir	bâiller
schockiert	weinen	in Ohnmacht fallen	gähnen
horrorizado	llorar	desmayarse	bostezar
scandalizzato	piangere	svenire	sbadigliare

life events • les événements de la vie • die Ereignisse des Lebens • los acontecimientos de una vida • gli avvenimenti della vita

be born (v) • naître • geboren werden • nacer • nascere

start school (v) • commencer à l'école • zur Schule kommen • empezar el colegio • iniziare la scuola

make friends (v) • faire des amis • sich befreunden • hacer amigos • fare amicizia

graduate (v) • obtenir sa licence • graduieren • graduarse • laurearsi

get a job (v) • trouver un emploi • eine Stelle bekommen • conseguir un trabajo • trovare un lavoro

fall in love (v) • tomber amoureux • sich verlieben • enamorarse • innamorarsi

get married (v) • se marier • heiraten • casarse • sposarsi

have a baby (v) • avoir un bébé • ein Baby bekommen • tener un hijo • avere un bambino

wedding • le mariage • die Hochzeit • la boda • il matrimonio

divorce • le divorce • die Scheidung • el divorcio • il divorzio

funeral • l'enterrement • das Begräbnis • el funeral • il funerale

christening le baptême die Taufe el bautizo il battesimo	die (v) mourir sterben morir morire
bar mitzvah la bar-mitsvah die Bar Mizwa el bar mitzvah il bar mitzvah	make a will (v) faire son testament sein Testament machen hacer testamento fare testamento
anniversary l'anniversaire de mariage der Hochzeitstag el aniversario l'anniverario	birth certificate l'acte de naissance die Geburtsurkunde el acta de nacimiento il certificato di nascita
emigrate (v) émigrer emigrieren emigrar emigrare	wedding reception le repas de noces die Hochzeitsfeier el banquete de boda il ricevimento nuziale
retire (v) prendre sa retraite in den Ruhestand treten retirarse andare in pensione	honeymoon le voyage de noces die Hochzeitsreise la luna de miel il viaggio di nozze

celebrations • les fêtes • die Feste • las celebraciones • le celebrazioni

birthday party
la fête
die Geburtstagsfeier
la fiesta de cumpleaños
la festa di compleanno

card
la carte
die Karte
la tarjeta
la cartolina

birthday • l'anniversaire • der Geburtstag • el cumpleaños • il compleanno

present
le cadeau
das Geschenk
el regalo
il regalo

Christmas • le Noël • das Weihnachten • la Navidad • il Natale

Passover • la Pâque • das Passah • la Pascua judía • la Pasqua ebraica

New Year • le Nouvel An • das Neujahr • el Año Nuevo • il Capodanno

carnival • le carnaval • der Karneval • el carnaval • il carnevale

procession
le défilé
der Umzug
el desfile
la processione

Ramadan • le Ramadan • der Ramadan • el Ramadán • il Ramadan

ribbon
le ruban
das Band
la cinta
il nastro

Thanksgiving • la fête de Thanksgiving • der Thanksgiving Day • el día de Acción de Gracias • il giorno del ringraziamento

Easter • Pâques • das Ostern • la Pascua • la Pasqua

Halloween • la veille de la Toussaint • das Halloween • el día de Halloween • la vigilia d'Ognissanti

Diwali • la Diwali • das Diwali • el Diwali • il Diwali

appearance
l'apparence
die äußere Erscheinung
la apariencia
l'aspetto

children's clothing • les vêtements d'enfants • die Kinderkleidung • la ropa de niño • gli abiti da bambino

baby • le bébé • das Baby • el bebé • il bimbo

snowsuit • la combinaison de neige • der Schneeanzug • el traje de invierno • la tutina da neve

undershirt • le tricot de corps • das Hemdchen • la camiseta • la canottiera

snap le bouton-pression der Druckknopf el botón il bottone automatico

onesize • la grenouillère • der Strampelanzug • el mameluco • la tutina

sleeper • le pyjama • der Schlafanzug • el mameluco • il pigiamino

romper suit • la combinaison-short • der Spielanzug • el mameluco sin pies • la tutina senza maniche

bib • le bavoir • das Lätzchen • el babero • il bavaglino

mittens • les moufles • die Babyhandschuhe • los guantes • i guanti

booties • les chaussons • die Babyschuhe • las botas • le scarpette

cloth diaper • la couche éponge • die Stoffwindel • el pañal de felpa • il pannolino di spugna

disposable diaper • la couche jetable • die Wegwerfwindel • el pañal desechable • il pannolino usa e getta

plastic underpants • la culotte en plastique • das Gummihöschen • el calzón de plástico • le mutande di plastica

toddler • le petit enfant • das Kleinkind • el niño pequeño • il bambino piccolo

t-shirt le t-shirt das T-Shirt la playera la maglietta

sun bonnet • le chapeau de soleil • der Sonnenhut • el gorro para el sol • il cappello per il sole

overalls la salopette die Latzhose los panatalones con peto la salopette

apron • le tablier • die Schürze • el delantal • il grembiulino

shorts le bermuda die Shorts los shorts i pantaloncini

skirt la jupe der Rock la falda la gonna

child • l'enfant • das Kind • el niño • il bambino

dress • la robe
• das Kleid • el
vestido • il vestito

hood
la capuche
die Kapuze
la capucha
il cappuccio

jeans
le jean
die Jeans
los jeans
i jeans

sandals
les sandales
die Sandalen
los huaraches
i sandali

summer • l'été • der
Sommer • el verano
• l'estate

raincoat • l'imperméable
• der Regenmantel
• el impermeable
• l'impermeabile

backpack
le sac à dos
der Rucksack
la mochila
lo zaino

toggle
le bouton
der Knebelknopf
el broche
l'olivetta

fall • l'automne
• der Herbst • el otoño
• l'autunno

duffel coat • le duffel-
coat • der Dufflecoat • el
abrigo • il montgomery

scarf
l'écharpe
der Schal
la bufanda
la sciarpa

parka
l'anorak
der Anorak
la chamarra
l'eskimo

galoshes
• les bottes de
caoutchouc
• die Gummistiefel
• las botas de
agua • le galosce

winter • l'hiver • der
Winter • el invierno
• l'inverno

robe
la robe de chambre
der Morgenrock
la bata
la vestaglia

logo
le logo
das Logo
el logotipo
il distintivo

sneakers
les baskets
die Sportschuhe
los tenis
le scarpe da ginnastica

nightgown
la chemise de nuit
das Nachthemd
el camisón
la camicia da notte

slippers
les pantoufles
die Hausschuhe
las pantuflas
le pantofole

soccer uniform • la tenue
de foot • der Fußballdress
• el uniforme del equipo
• la tenuta da calcio

warm-up suit • le
survêtement • der
Trainingsanzug • los
pants • la tuta

leggings • les leggings
• die Leggings • las
mallas • il pantacollant

nightwear • les vêtements de nuit • die Nachtwäsche
• la ropa para dormir • gli indumenti per la notte

natural fiber	Is it machine washable?
la fibre naturelle	C'est lavable en machine?
die Naturfaser	Ist es waschmaschinenfest?
la fibra natural	¿Se puede lavar en lavadora?
la fibra naturale	È lavabile in lavatrice?
synthetic	Will this fit a two-year-old?
synthétique	C'est la taille pour deux ans?
synthetisch	Passt das einem Zweijährigen?
sintético	¿Le quedará a un niño de dos años?
sintetico	È la taglia giusta per un bambino di due anni?

men's clothing • les vêtements pour hommes • die Herrenkleidung • la ropa de caballero • l'abbigliamento da uomo

collar
le col
der Kragen
el cuello
il colletto

tie
la cravate
die Krawatte
la corbata
la cravatta

belt
la ceinture
der Gürtel
el cinturón
la cintura

lapel
le revers
das Revers
la solapa
il risvolto

buttonhole
la boutonnière
das Knopfloch
el ojal
l'asola

jacket
la veste
die Jacke
la chaqueta
la giacca

cuff
la manchette
die Manschette
el puño
il polsino

pocket
la poche
die Tasche
el bolsillo
la tasca

pants
le pantalon
die Hose
el saco
i pantaloni

button
le bouton
der Knopf
el botón
il bottone

business suit • le costume
der Straßenanzug • el traje
• l'abito

coat • le manteau
• der Mantel • la gabardina
• il cappotto

lining
la doublure
das Futter
el forro
la fodera

leather shoes
• les chaussures
en cuir • die
Lederschuhe
los zapatos de
piel • le scarpe
di cuoio

shirt	bathrobe	tracksuit	long
la chemise	le peignoir	le survêtement	long
das Hemd	der Bademantel	der Trainingsanzug	lang
la camisa	la bata	los pants	largo
la camicia	la vestaglia	la tuta da sport	lungo
cardigan	underwear	raincoat	short
le cardigan	les sous-vêtements	l'imperméable	court
die Strickjacke	die Unterwäsche	der Regenmantel	kurz
el cardigan	la ropa interior	el impermeable	corto
il cardigan	la biancheria intima	l'impermeabile	corto

Do you have this in a larger/smaller size?
Avez-vous ça en plus grand/petit?
Haben Sie das eine Nummer größer/kleiner?
¿Tiene una talla más grande/chica?
Ha una taglia più grande/più piccola?

May I try this on?
Je peux l'essayer?
Kann ich das anprobieren?
¿Me lo puedo probar?
Posso provarmelo?

blazer • le blazer • der Blazer
• el saco •il blazer

sport coat • la veste de sport
• das Sportjackett • el saco
sport • la giacca sportiva

vest • le gilet • die
Weste • el chaleco
• il gilet

v-neck
l'encolure en V
der V-Ausschnitt
el cuello en V
il collo a V

crew neck
le col rond
der runde Ausschnitt
el cuello redondo
il girocollo

t-shirt
le t-shirt
das T-Shirt
la camiseta
la maglietta

parka • l'anorak • der Anorak
• el chaquetón • il giaccone

sweatshirt • le sweat-shirt
• das Sweatshirt • la sudadera
• la felpa

windbreaker • le coupe-vent
• die Windjacke • la chamarra
• la giacca a vento

sweatpants
• le pantalon de
jogging • die
Trainingshose
• los pants
• i pantaloni di
felpa

sweater • le pullover
• der Pullover • el suéter
• il maglione

pajamas • le pyjama
• der Schlafanzug • la piyama
• il pigiama

undershirt • le tricot de corps
• das Unterhemd • la camiseta
de tirantes • la canottiera

sportswear • les vêtements
sport • die Freizeitkleidung
• la ropa casual • il casual

shorts • le short • die Shorts
• los shorts • i calzoncini

briefs • le slip • der Slip
• los calzoncillos • lo slip

boxer shorts • le caleçon
• die Boxershorts • los boxers
• i boxer

socks • les chaussettes
• die Socken • los calcetines
• i calzini

women's clothing • les vêtements pour femmes • die Damenkleidung • la ropa de dama • l'abbigliamento da donna

jacket
la veste
die Jacke
el saco
la giacca

neckline
l'encolure
der Ausschnitt
el escote
la scollatura

seam
la couture
die Naht
la costura
la cucitura

sleeve
la manche
der Ärmel
la manga
la manica

skirt
la jupe
der Rock
la falda
la gonna

hem
l'ourlet
der Saum
el dobladillo
l'orlo

knee-length
à genou
knielang
hasta la rodilla
al ginocchio

hose
les collants
die Strumpfhose
las pantimedias
il collant

shoes
les chaussures
die Schuhe
los zapatos
le scarpe

strapless
sans bretelles
trägerlos
sin tirantes
senza spalline

sleeveless
sans manches
ärmellos
sin mangas
senza maniche

ankle length
long
knöchellang
largo
alla caviglia

evening dress • la robe du soir • das Abendkleid • el traje de noche • l'abito da sera

dress • la robe • das Kleid • el vestido • il vestito

blouse
le chemisier
die Bluse
la blusa
la camicetta

pants
le pantalon
die Hose
los pantalones
i pantaloni

casual • décontracté • leger • casual • casual

lingerie • la lingerie • die Unterwäsche • la lencería • la biancheria intima

negligée • le négligé • das Negligé • el negligé • il négligé

slip • le caraco • der Unterrock • el fondo • la sottoveste

strap
la bretelle
der Träger
el tirante
la spallina

camisole • la camisole • das Mieder • la camisola • il corpetto

bustier • la guêpière • das Bustier • el corsé con liguero • la guêpière

garters
la jarretelle
der Strumpfhalter
las ligas
il reggicalze

stockings • les bas • die Strümpfe • las medias de liguero • le calze

panty hose • le collant • die Strumpfhose • las pantimedias • il collant

undershirt
la chemise
das Unterhemd
la camiseta de tirantes
la canottiera

bra • le soutien-gorge • der Büstenhalter • el brassiere • il reggiseno

underpants • le slip • der Slip • las pantaletas • lo slip

nightgown • la chemise de nuit • das Nachthemd • el camisón • la camicia da notte

wedding • le mariage • die Hochzeit • la boda • il matrimonio

lace
la dentelle
die Spitze
el encaje
il pizzo

veil
le voile
der Schleier
el velo
il velo

bouquet
le bouquet
das Bukett
el ramo de flores
il bouquet

train
la traîne
die Schleppe
la cola
lo strascico

wedding dress • la robe de mariée • das Hochzeitskleid • el vestido de novia • l'abito da sposa

corset	tailored
le corset	ajusté
das Korsett	gut geschnitten
el corsé	entallado
il busto	attilato
garter belt	halter neck
la jarretière	dos-nu
das Strumpfband	rückenfrei
la liga	con los hombros al aire
la giarrettiera	allacciato dietro il collo
shoulder pad	sports bra
l'épaulette	le soutien-gorge sport
das Schulterpolster	der Sport-BH
la hombrera	el brassiere deportivo
la spallina	il reggiseno sportivo
waistband	underwire
la ceinture	à armature
der Rockbund	mit Formbügeln
la cinturilla	con varillas
il girovita	con armatura

accessories • les accessoires • die Accessoires • los accesorios • gli accessori

cap • la casquette • die Mütze • la gorra • il berretto

hat • le chapeau • der Hut • el sombrero • il cappello

scarf • le foulard • das Halstuch • la mascada • il foulard

buckle
la boucle
die Gürtelschnalle
la hebilla
la fibbia

belt • la ceinture • der Gürtel • el cinturón • la cinta

handle
le manche
der Griff
el mango
il manico

handkerchief • le mouchoir • das Taschentuch • el pañuelo • il fazzoletto

bow tie • le nœud papillon • die Fliege • el moño • la farfalla

tiepin • l'épingle de cravate • die Krawattennadel • el alfiler de corbata • il fermacravatta

gloves • les gants • die Handschuhe • los guantes • i guanti

tip
la pointe
die Spitze
la punta
la punta

umbrella • le parapluie • der Regenschirm • el paraguas • l'ombrello

jewelry • les bijoux • der Schmuck • las joyas • i gioielli

pendant • le pendentif • der Anhänger • el colguije • il pendaglio

brooch • la broche • die Brosche • el prendedor • la spilla

cufflink • le bouton de manchette • der Manschettenknopf • las mancuernillas • il gemello

strand of pearls
le rang de perles
die Perlenkette
el collar de perlas
il filo di perle

link
le maillon
das Glied
el eslabón
la maglia

clasp
le fermoir
der Verschluss
el broche
il fermaglio

earring • la boucle d'oreille • der Ohrring • el arete • l'orecchino

ring
la bague
der Ring
el anillo
l'anello

stone
la pierre
der Edelstein
la piedra
la pietra

necklace
le collier
die Halskette
el collar
la collana

bracelet • le bracelet • das Armband • la pulsera • il bracciale

chain • la chaîne • die Kette • la cadena • la catena

watch • la montre • die Uhr • el reloj • l'orologio da polso

jewelry box • la boîte à bijoux • der Schmuckkasten • el joyero • il cofanetto portagioie

bags • les sacs • die Taschen • las bolsas • le borse

clasp
le fermoir
der Verschluss
el cierre
la cinghia

shoulder strap
la bretelle
der Schulterriemen
la correa
la bretella

handles
les poignées
die Griffe
las asas
i manici

wallet • le portefeuille • die Brieftasche • la cartera • il portafoglio

change purse • le porte-monnaie • das Portemonnaie • el monedero • il portamonete

shoulder bag • le sac à bandoulière • die Umhängetasche • la bolsa • la borsa a tracolla

duffle bag • le fourre-tout • die Reisetasche • la bolsa de viaje • la sacca da viaggio

briefcase • la serviette • die Aktentasche • el maletín • la valigetta

handbag • le sac à main • die Handtasche • la bolsa de mano • la borsetta

backpack • le sac à dos • der Rucksack • la mochila • lo zainetto

shoes • les chaussures • die Schuhe • los zapatos • le scarpe

eyelet
l'œillet
die Öse
el ojal
l'occhiello

lace
le lacet
der Schnürsenkel
la agujeta
il laccio

tongue • la languette • die Zunge • la lengüeta • la lingua

heel
le talon
der Absatz
el tacón
il tacco

sole
la semelle
die Sohle
la suela
la suola

lace-up • la chaussure lacée • der Schnürschuh • el zapato de agujetas • la scarpa con i lacci

walking boot • le pataugas • der Wanderschuh • la bota de trekking • la scarpa da trekking

sneaker • la basket • der Sportschuh • el tenis • la scarpa da ginnastica

leather shoe • la chaussure de cuir • der Lederschuh • el zapato de piel • la scarpa di cuoio

flip-flop • la tong • die Strandsandale • la chancla • la ciabatta

high heel shoe • la chaussure à talon • der Schuh mit hohem Absatz • el zapato de tacón • la scarpa con il tacco alto

platform shoe • la chaussure à semelle compensée • der Plateauschuh • el zapato de plataforma • lo zatterone

sandal • la sandale die Sandale • la sandalia • il sandalo

slip-on • le mocassin der Slipper • el mocasín • il mocassino

brogan • le richelieu der Herrenhalbschuh • el zapato de caballero • la scarpa da uomo

hair • les cheveux • das Haar • el cabello • i capelli

comb
le peigne
der Kamm
el peine
il pettine

comb (v) • peigner • kämmen
• peinar • pettinare

brush
la brosse
die Haarbürste
el cepillo
la spazzola

brush (v) • brosser • bürsten
• cepillar • spazzolare

rinse (v) • rincer • ausspülen
• enjuagar • sciacquare

hairdresser
la coiffeuse
die Friseurin
la estilista
la parrucchiera

sink
le lavabo
das Waschbecken
el lavabo
il lavandino

client
la cliente
die Kundin
la cliente
la cliente

wash (v) • laver • waschen • lavar • lavare

robe
le peignoir
der Frisierumhang
la bata
il grembiule

cut (v) • couper • schneiden
• cortar • tagliare

blowdry (v) • sécher • föhnen
• secar con la secadora
• asciugare con il phon

set (v) • faire une mise en
plis • legen • marcar
• mettere in piega

---

accessories • les accessoires • die Frisierartikel • los accesorios • gli accesori

blow-dryer • le
sèche-cheveux
• der Föhn
• la secadora
• l'asciugacapelli

shampoo • le shampoing
• das Shampoo • el
champú • lo shampoo

conditioner • le conditionneur
• die Haarspülung • el
acondicionador • il balsamo

gel • le gel • das
Haargel • el gel
• il gel

hairspray • la laque
• das Haarspray • la laca
• la lacca

curling iron
• le fer à friser
• der Lockenstab
• las tenazas •
l'arricciacapelli

scissors • les ciseaux
• die Schere • las
tijeras • le forbici

headband • le serre-tête
• der Haarreif • la diadema
• il cerchietto

curler • le bigoudi
• der Lockenwickler
• el rulo • i bigodini

bobby pin • la pince à
cheveux • die Haarklammer
• el pasador • la molletta

styles • les coiffures • die Frisuren • los estilos • le acconciature

ribbon
le ruban
das Band
el listón
il nastro

ponytail • la queue de
cheval • **der Pferdeschwanz**
• la cola de caballo
• la coda di cavallo

braid • la natte
• der Zopf • la trenza
• la treccia

French braid • le
rouleau • **die Hochfrisur**
• el chongo francés
• la piega alla francese

bun • le chignon
• der Haarknoten
• el chongo • la
crocchia

pigtails • les couettes
• die Schwänzchen • las
coletas • i codini

bob • au carré • der
Bubikopf • el príncipe
valiente • il caschetto

crop • la coupe courte •
der Kurzhaarschnitt • el pelo
corto • la sfumatura alta

curly • frisé • kraus
• rizado • ricci

perm • la permanente • die
Dauerwelle • la permanente
• la permanente

straight • raide
• glatt • lacio
• lisci

roots
les racines
die Wurzeln
las raíces
le radici

highlights • les reflets
• die Strähnen • las luces
• i colpi di sole

bald • chauve • kahl
• calvo • calvo

wig • la perruque
• die Perücke • la
peluca • la parrucca

hair band	greasy
la bande de cheveux	gras
das Haarband	fettig
la goma del pelo	graso
l'elastico	grassi
trim (v)	dry
rafraîchir	sec
nachschneiden	trocken
despuntar	seco
spuntare	secchi
barber	normal
le coiffeur	normal
der Herrenfriseur	normal
el peluquero	normal
il barbiere	normali
dandruff	scalp
les pellicules	le cuir chevelu
die Schuppen	die Kopfhaut
la caspa	el cuero cabelludo
la forfora	il cuoio capelluto
split ends	straighten (v)
les fourches	décrêper
die gespaltenen Haarspitzen	glätten
la orzuela	alaciar
le doppie punte	lisciare

colours • les couleurs • die Haarfarben • los colores • i colori

blonde • blond
• blond • güero
• biondo

brunette • châtain
• brünett • castaño
• bruno

auburn • auburn
• rotbraun • rojizo
• castano

red • roux
• rot • pelirrojo
• rosso

black • noir
• schwarz
• negro • nero

gray • gris
• grau • gris
• grigio

white • blanc
• weiß • blanco
• bianco

dyed • teint
• gefärbt • teñido
• tinto

beauty • la beauté • die Schönheit • la belleza • la bellezza

hair dye
la teinture de cheveux
das Haarfärbemittel
el tinte para el pelo
la tintura per capelli

eye shadow
le fard à paupières
der Lidschatten
la sombra de ojos
l'ombretto

mascara
le mascara
die Wimperntusche
el rímel
il mascara

eyeliner
l'eye-liner
der Eyeliner
el delineador
la matita per gli occhi

blusher
le fard à joues
das Puderrouge
el rubor
il fard

foundation
le fond de teint
die Grundierung
la base
il fondotinta

lipstick
le rouge à lèvres
der Lippenstift
el lápiz labial
il rossetto

makeup • le maquillage • das Make-up
• el maquillaje • il trucco

eyebrow pencil • le crayon à sourcils • der Augenbrauenstift
• el lápiz de cejas • la matita per le sopracciglia

eyebrow brush • la brosse à
sourcils • das Brauenbürstchen
• el cepillo para las cejas
• la spazzolina per le sopracciglia

tweezers • la pince à épiler
• die Pinzette • las pinzas
• le pinzette

lip gloss • le brillant à lèvres
• das Lipgloss • el brillo de
labios • lo smalto per
le labbra

lip brush • le pinceau à lèvres
• der Lippenpinsel • el pincel
de labios • il pennello per
le labbra

lip liner • le crayon à lèvres • der Lippenkonturenstift
• el lápiz de labios • il marcatore per le labbra

brush • le pinceau • der
Puderpinsel • la brocha
• il pennello

concealer • le correcteur
• der Korrekturstift • el lápiz
corrector • il correttore

mirror
le miroir
der Spiegel
el espejo
lo specchio

face powder
la poudre
der Gesichtspuder
el maquillaje
la cipria

powder puff
la houppette
die Puderquaste
la borla
il piumino

compact • le poudrier
• die Puderdose • la polvera • il porta cipria

beauty treatments • les soins de beauté • die Schönheitsbehandlungen • los tratamientos de belleza • i trattamenti di bellezza

face pack • le masque de beauté • die Gesichtsmaske • la mascarilla • la maschera di bellezza

sunbed • le lit U.V. • die Sonnenbank • la cama de rayos ultravioletas • il lettino solare

facial • le soin du visage • die Gesichtsbehandlung • la limpieza de cutis • il trattamento per il viso

exfoliate (v) • exfolier • die Haut schälen • exfoliar • esfoliare

wax • l'épilation • die Enthaarung • la depilación a la cera • la ceretta

pedicure • la pédicurie • die Pediküre • la pedicura • la pedicure

toiletries • les accessoires de toilette • die Toilettenartikel • los artículos de tocador • gli articoli da toeletta

cleanser • le démaquillant • der Reiniger • la crema limpiadora • il latte detergente

toner • le tonique • das Gesichtswasser • el tónico • la lozione tonificante

moisturizer • la crème hydratante • die Feuchtigkeitscreme • la crema hidratante • la crema idratante

self-tanning lotion • l'autobronzant • die Selbstbräunungscreme • la crema bronceadora • la crema autoabbronzante

perfume • le parfum • das Parfum • el perfume • il profumo

eau de toilette • l'eau de toilette • das Eau de Toilette • el agua de colonia • l'acqua di colonia

manicure • la manicure • die Maniküre • la manicura • la manicure

nail polish remover le dissolvant der Nagellackentferner el quitaesmalte l'acetone

nail file • la lime à ongles • die Nagelfeile • la lima de uñas • la limetta

nail polish • le vernis à ongles • der Nagellack • el esmalte de uñas • lo smalto per unghie

nail scissors les ciseaux à ongles die Nagelschere las tijeras de uñas le forbicine per le unghie

nail clippers le coupe-ongles der Nagelknipser el cortaúñas il tagliaunghie

complexion	oily	tan
le teint	gras	le bronzage
der Teint	fettig	die Sonnenbräune
el cutis	graso	el bronceado
la carnagione	grasso	l'abbronzatura
fair	sensitive	tattoo
clair	sensible	le tatouage
hell	empfindlich	die Tätowierung
claro	sensible	el tatuaje
chiaro	sensibile	il tatuaggio
dark	hypoallergenic	cotton balls
foncé	hypoallergénique	les boules de coton
dunkel	hypoallergen	die Wattebällchen
moreno	hipoalergénico	las bolas de algodón
scuro	ipoallergenico	i batuffoli di ovatta
dry	shade	antiwrinkle
sec	le ton	antirides
trocken	der Farbton	Antifalten-
seco	el tono	antiarrugas
secco	la tonalità	antirughe

health
la santé
die Gesundheit
la salud
la salute

illness • la maladie • die Krankheit • la enfermedad • la malattia

fever • la fièvre • das Fieber • la fiebre
• il febbre

headache • le mal de tête • die Kopfschmerzen • el dolor de cabeza • il mal di testa

nosebleed • le saignement de nez • das Nasenbluten • la hemorragia nasal • l'emorragia nasale

cough • la toux • der Husten • la tos • la tosse

sneeze • l'éternuement • das Niesen • el estornudo • lo starnuto

cold • le rhume • die Erkältung • el resfriado • il raffreddore

the flu • la grippe • die Grippe • la gripe • l'influenza

asthma • l'asthme • das Asthma • el asma • l'asma

inhaler l'inhalateur der Inhalationsapparat el inhalador l'inalatore

cramps • les crampes • die Krämpfe • los calambres • i crampi

nausea • la nausée • die Übelkeit • la náusea • la nausea

the chickenpox • la varicelle • die Windpocken • la varicela • la varicella

rash • l'éruption • der Hautausschlag • el sarpullido • lo sfogo

heart attack la crise cardiaque der Herzinfarkt el ataque cardiaco l'infarto	diabetes le diabète die Zuckerkrankheit la diabetes il diabete	eczema l'eczéma das Ekzem el eccema l'eczema	chill le refroidissement die Verkühlung el resfriado l'infreddatura	vomit (v) vomir sich übergeben vomitar vomitare	diarrhea la diarrhée der Durchfall la diarrea la diarrea
stroke l'attaque der Schlaganfall la aplopejía l'apoplessia	hay fever le rhume des foins der Heuschnupfen la fiebre del heno la febbre da fieno	infection l'infection die Infektion la infección l'infezione	stomach ache le mal d'estomac die Magenschmerzen el dolor de estómago il mal di stomaco	epilepsy l'épilepsie die Epilepsie la epilepsia l'epilessia	measles la rougeole die Masern el sarampión il morbillo
blood pressure la tension der Blutdruck la presión arterial la pressione del sangue	allergy l'allergie die Allergie la alergia l'allergia	virus le virus der Virus el virus il virus	faint (v) s'évanouir in Ohnmacht fallen desmayarse svenire	migraine la migraine die Migräne la migraña l'emicrania	mumps les oreillons der Mumps las paperas gli orecchioni

doctor • le médecin • der Arzt • el doctor • il medico

consultation • la consultation • die Konsultation • la consulta • la visita

doctor
le médecin
der Arzt
el doctor
il medico

x-ray viewer
la lampe de radio
der Röntgenbildbetrachter
el lector de rayos X
il negatoscopio

prescription
l'ordonnance
das Rezept
la receta
la ricetta

patient
la patiente
die Patientin
la paciente
la paziente

height bar
la toise
der Körpergrößenmesser
el metro
il misuratore di altezza

nurse
l'infirmière
die Krankenschwester
la enfermera
l'infermiera

scales
la balance
die Personenwaage
la báscula
la bilancia

blood pressure gauge • le sphygmotensiomètre • der Blutdruckmesser • el indicador para medir la presión • il misuratore di pressione

stethoscope • le stéthoscope • das Stethoskop • el estetoscopio • lo stetoscopio

cuff • le manchon • die Luftmanschette • el brazal • il manicotto

appointment	medical examination
le rendez-vous	l'examen médical
der Termin	die Untersuchung
la cita	el examen médico
l'appuntamento	la visita medica
doctor's office	inoculation
le cabinet	l'inoculation
das Sprechzimmer	die Impfung
la consulta	la inoculación
l'ambulatorio	l'inoculazione
waiting room	thermometer
la salle d'attente	le thermomètre
der Warteraum	das Thermometer
la sala de espera	el termómetro
la sala d'attesa	il termometro

I need to see a doctor.
J'ai besoin de voir un médecin.
Ich muss einen Arzt sprechen.
Necesito ver a un doctor.
Ho bisogno di vedere un medico.

It hurts here.
J'ai mal ici.
Es tut hier weh.
Me duele aquí.
Ho un dolore qui.

injury • la blessure • die Verletzung • la lesión • la ferita

sling
l'écharpe
die Schlinge
el cabestrillo
la fascia a tracolla

neck brace
la minerve
die Halskrawatte
el collarín
il collare

sprain • l'entorse • die Verstauchung • la torcedura • la slogatura

fracture • la fracture • die Fraktur • la fractura • la frattura

whiplash • le coup du lapin • das Schleudertrauma • el tirón en el cuello • il colpo di frusta

cut • la coupure • der Schnitt • la cortada • il taglio

graze • l'écorchure • die Abschürfung • la raspada • la sbucciatura

bruise • la contusion • die Prellung • el moretón • il livido

splinter • l'écharde • der Splitter • la astilla • la scheggia

sunburn • le coup de soleil • der Sonnenbrand • la ardida • la scottatura

burn • la brûlure • die Brandwunde • la quemadura • l'ustione

bite • la morsure • der Biss • el mordisco • il morso

sting • la piqûre • der Stich • la picadura • la puntura

accident	hemorrhage	concussion	Will he/she be all right?
l'accident	l'hémorragie	la commotion cérébrale	Est-ce qu'il/elle va se remettre?
der Unfall	die Blutung	die Gehirnerschütterung	Wird er/sie es gut überstehen?
el accidente	la hemorragia	la conmoción	¿Se pondrá bien?
l'incidente	l'emorragia	la commozione	Si rimetterà?
emergency	blister	head injury	Please call an ambulance.
l'urgence	l'ampoule	le traumatisme crânien	Appelez une ambulance s'il vous plaît.
der Notfall	die Blase	die Kopfverletzung	Rufen Sie bitte einen Krankenwagen.
la emergencia	la ampolla	la lesión en la cabeza	Por favor llame a una ambulancia.
l'emergenza	la vescica	la ferita alla testa	Chiami un'ambulanza, per favore.
wound	poisoning	electric shock	Where does it hurt?
la blessure	l'empoisonnement	le choc électrique	Où avez-vous mal?
die Wunde	die Vergiftung	der elektrische Schlag	Wo haben Sie Schmerzen?
la herida	el envenenamiento	el shock eléctrico	¿Dónde le duele?
la ferita	l'avvelenamento	la scossa elettrica	Dove le fa male?

first aid • les premiers secours • die erste Hilfe • los primeros auxilios • il pronto soccorso

ointment • la pommade • die Salbe • la pomada • la pomata

adhesive bandage • le pansement • das Pflaster • la tirita • il cerotto

safety pin
l'épingle de sûreté
die Sicherheitsnadel
el seguro
la spilla da balia

bandage
le bandage
die Bandage
la venda
la benda

painkillers
les analgésiques
die Schmerztabletten
los analgésicos
gli antidolarifici

antiseptic wipe
la serviette antiseptique
das Desinfektionstuch
la toallita antiséptica
la salvietta antisettica

tweezers
la pince fine
die Pinzette
las pinzas
le pinzette

scissors
les ciseaux
die Schere
las tijeras
le forbici

antiseptic
l'antiseptique
das Antiseptikum
el desinfectante
il disinfettante

first aid kit • la trousse de premiers secours • der Erste-Hilfe-Kasten • el botiquín • la cassetta di pronto soccorso

gauze • la gaze • die Gaze • la gasa • la garza

dressing • le pansement • der Verband • el vendaje • la bendatura

splint • l'attelle • die Schiene • la tablilla • la stecca

adhesive tape
• le sparadrap
• das Leukoplast
• la tela adhesiva
• il nastro adesivo

resuscitation • la réanimation • die Wiederbelebung • la re-animación • la rianimazione

shock	pulse	choke (v)	Can you help?
le choc	le pouls	étouffer	Est-ce que vous pouvez m'aider?
der Schock	der Puls	ersticken	Können Sie mir helfen?
el shock	el pulso	ahogarse	¿Me puede ayudar?
lo shock	le pulsazioni	soffocare	Può aiutarmi?
unconscious	breathing	sterile	Do you know first aid?
sans connaissance	la respiration	stérile	Pouvez-vous donner les soins d'urgence?
bewusstlos	die Atmung	steril	Beherrschen Sie die Erste Hilfe?
inconsciente	la respiración	estéril	¿Sabe primeros auxilios?
privo di sensi	la respirazione	sterile	Sa dare pronto soccorso?

hospital • l'hôpital • das Krankenhaus • el hospital • l'ospedale

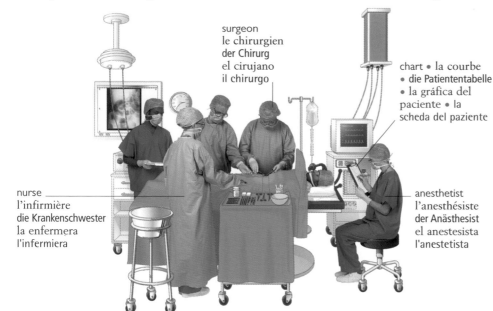

surgeon
le chirurgien
der Chirurg
el cirujano
il chirurgo

chart • la courbe
• die Patiententabelle
• la gráfica del
paciente • la
scheda del paziente

blood test • l'analyse de sang
• die Blutuntersuchung • el
análisis de sangre • l'analisi
del sangue

nurse
l'infirmière
die Krankenschwester
la enfermera
l'infermiera

anesthetist
l'anesthésiste
der Anästhesist
el anestesista
l'anestetista

injection • l'injection
• die Spritze • la inyección
• l'iniezione

operating room • la salle d'opération • der Operationssaal • el quirófano
• la sala operatoria

gurney • le chariot • die
fahrbare Liege • la camilla
• la lettiga

call button • le bouton d'appel
• der Rufknopf • el timbre • il
pulsante di chiamata

x-ray • la radio • die
Röntgenaufnahme • la
radiografia • la radiografia

emergency room • la salle
des urgences • die Notaufnahme
• la sala de urgencias • la sala
emergenze

ward • la salle • die
Krankenhausstation • la planta
• il reparto

wheelchair • la chaise
roulante • der Rollstuhl
• la silla de ruedas • la sedia
a rotelle

scan • la scanographie
• der CT-Scan • el ultrasonido
• l'ecografia

operation	discharged	visiting hours	maternity ward	intensive care unit
l'opération	renvoyé	les heures de visite	la maternité	le service de soins intensifs
die Operation	entlassen	die Besuchszeiten	die Entbindungsstation	die Intensivstation
la operación	dado de alta	las horas de visita	la sala de maternidad	la unidad de cuidados intensivos
l'operazione	dimesso	l'orario delle visite	il reparto maternità	il reparto di cura intensiva
admitted	clinic	children's ward	private room	outpatient
admis	la clinique	la pédiatrie	la chambre privée	le malade en consultation externe
aufgenommen	die Klinik	die Kinderstation	das Privatzimmer	der ambulante Patient
internado	la clínica	la sala de pediatría	la habitación privada	el paciente externo
ricoverato	la clinica	il reparto pediatrico	la camera privata	il paziente esterno

english • français • deutsch • español • italiano

departments • les services • die Abteilungen • los servicios • i reparti

Ear, Nose, and Throat
• l'O.R.L. • die HNO-Abteilung
• la otorrinonaringología
• l'otorinolaringologia

cardiology • la cardiologie
• die Kardiologie • la
cardiología • la cardiologia

orthopedics • l'orthopédie
• die Orthopädie • la
ortopedia • l'ortopedia

gynecology • la gynécologie
• die Gynäkologie • la
ginecología • la ginecologia

physiotherapy • la
kinésithérapie • die
Physiotherapie • la fisioterapia
• la fisioterapia

dermatology • la dermatologie
• die Dermatologie • la
dermatología • la dermatologia

pediatrics • la pédiatrie
• die Pädiatrie • la pediatría
• la pediatria

radiology • la radiologie
• die Radiologie • la radiología
• la radiologia

surgery • la chirurgie • die
Chirurgie • la cirugía • la
chirurgia

maternity • la maternité
• die Entbindungsstation • la
maternidad • la maternità

psychiatry • la psychiatrie
• die Psychiatrie • la
psiquiatría • la psichiatria

ophthalmology
• l'ophtalmologie
• die Ophthalmologie • la
oftalmología • l'oftalmologia

neurology	urology	plastic surgery	pathology	result
la neurologie	l'urologie	la chirurgie esthétique	la pathologie	le résultat
die Neurologie	die Urologie	die plastische Chirurgie	die Pathologie	das Ergebnis
la neurología	la urología	la cirugía plástica	la patología	el resultado
la neurologia	l'urologia	la chirurgia plastica	la patologia	il risultato
oncology	endocrinology	referral	test	consultant
l'oncologie	l'endocrinologie	l'orientation d'un patient	l'analyse	le spécialiste
die Onkologie	die Endokrinologie	die Überweisung	die Untersuchung	der Facharzt
la oncología	la endocrinología	la referencia	el análisis	el especialista
l'oncologia	l'endocrinologia	mandare da uno specialista	l'analisi	lo specialista

dentist • le dentiste • der Zahnarzt • el dentista • il dentista

tooth • la dent • der Zahn • el diente
• il dente

enamel
l'émail
der Zahnschmelz
el esmalte
lo smalto

gum
la gencive
das Zahnfleisch
la encía
la gengiva

nerve
le nerf
der Nerv
el nervio
il nervo

root
la racine
die Zahnwurzel
la raíz
la radice

premolar
la prémolaire
der vordere
 Backenzahn
el premolar
il premolare

incisor
l'incisive
der Schneidezahn
el incisivo
l'incisivo

molar
la molaire
der Backenzahn
la muela
il molare

canine
la canine
der Eckzahn
el colmillo
il canino

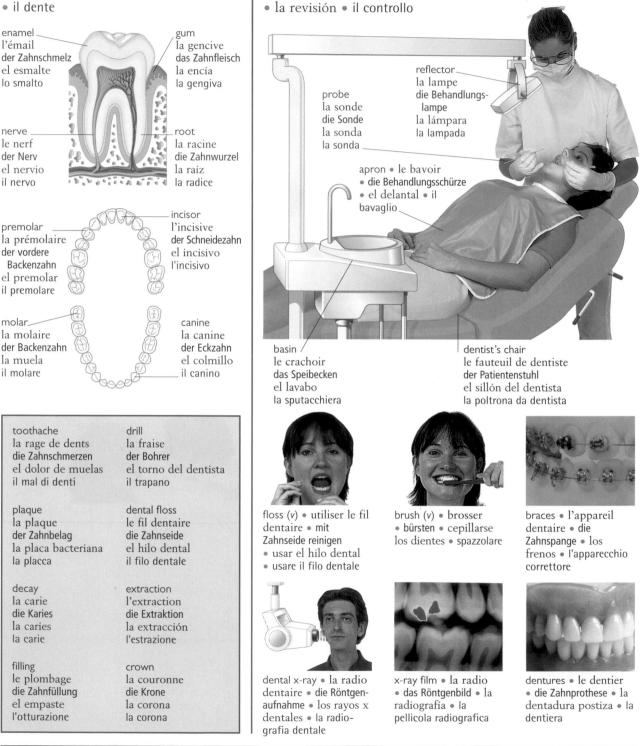

check-up • la visite de contrôle • der Check-up
• la revisión • il controllo

reflector
la lampe
die Behandlungs-
lampe
la lámpara
la lampada

probe
la sonde
die Sonde
la sonda
la sonda

apron • le bavoir
• die Behandlungsschürze
• el delantal • il
bavaglio

basin
le crachoir
das Speibecken
el lavabo
la sputacchiera

dentist's chair
le fauteuil de dentiste
der Patientenstuhl
el sillón del dentista
la poltrona da dentista

toothache	drill
la rage de dents	la fraise
die Zahnschmerzen	der Bohrer
el dolor de muelas	el torno del dentista
il mal di denti	il trapano
plaque	dental floss
la plaque	le fil dentaire
der Zahnbelag	die Zahnseide
la placa bacteriana	el hilo dental
la placca	il filo dentale
decay	extraction
la carie	l'extraction
die Karies	die Extraktion
la caries	la extracción
la carie	l'estrazione
filling	crown
le plombage	la couronne
die Zahnfüllung	die Krone
el empaste	la corona
l'otturazione	la corona

floss (v) • utiliser le fil
dentaire • mit
Zahnseide reinigen
• usar el hilo dental
• usare il filo dentale

brush (v) • brosser
• bürsten • cepillarse
los dientes • spazzolare

braces • l'appareil
dentaire • die
Zahnspange • los
frenos • l'apparecchio
correttore

dental x-ray • la radio
dentaire • die Röntgen-
aufnahme • los rayos x
dentales • la radio-
grafía dentale

x-ray film • la radio
• das Röntgenbild • la
radiografía • la
pellicola radiografica

dentures • le dentier
• die Zahnprothese • la
dentadura postiza • la
dentiera

optician • l'opticien • der Augenoptiker • el óptico • l'ottico

case
l'etui
das Futteral
el estuche
la custodia

lens
le verre
das Glas
el cristal
la lente

frame
la monture
das Brillengestell
la montura
la montatura

glasses • les lunettes • die Brille •
los lentes • gli occhiali

sunglasses • les lunettes de soleil
• die Sonnenbrille • los lentes
obscuros • gli occhiali da sole

cleaning fluid
la solution nettoyante
das Reinigungsmittel
el líquido limpiador
la soluzione per la pulizia

disinfectant solution
la solution désinfectante
das Desinfektionsmittel
la solución desinfectante
la soluzione disinfettante

lens case
l'étui à lentilles
der Kontaktlinsenbehälter
el estuche para los pupilentes
la custodia per le lenti

eye test • l'examen de la vue • der Sehtest • el
examen de ojos • l'esame della vista

contact lenses • les lentilles de contact • die Kontaktlinsen • los pupilentes
• le lenti a contatto

eye • l'œil • das Auge • el ojo • l'occhio

eyebrow
le sourcil
die Augenbraue
la ceja
il sopracciglio

pupil
la pupille
die Pupille
la pupila
la pupilla

eyelid
la paupière
das Lid
el párpado
la palpebra

eyelash
le cil
die Wimper
la pestaña
il ciglio

iris • l'iris • die Iris
• el iris • l'iride

lens
le cristallin
die Linse
el cristalino
la lente

retina
la rétine
die Netzhaut
la retina
la retina

cornea • la cornée
• die Hornhaut • la
córnea • la cornea

optic nerve
le nerf optique
der Sehnerv
el nervio óptico
il nervo ottico

vision	astigmatism
la vue	l'astigmatisme
die Sehkraft	der Astigmatismus
la vista	el astigmatismo
la vista	l'astigmatismo
diopter	farsighted
la dioptrie	la presbytie
die Dioptrie	die Weitsichtigkeit
la dioptría	la hipermetropía
la diottria	la presbiopia
tear	nearsighted
la larme	la myopie
die Träne	die Kurzsichtigkeit
la lágrima	la miopía
la lacrima	la miopia
cataract	bifocal
la cataracte	bifocal
der graue Star	Bifokal-
la catarata	bifocal
la cataratta	bifocale

pregnancy • la grossesse • die Schwangerschaft • el embarazo • la gravidanza

nurse
l'infirmière
die Krankenschwester
la enfermera
l'infermiera

pregnancy test • le test de grossesse • der Schwangerschaftstest • la prueba del embarazo • il test di gravidanza

scan
l'échographie
die Ultraschallaufnahme
el ultrasonido
l'ecografia

ultrasound • les ultrasons • der Ultraschall • el ultrasonido • l'ultrasuono

umbilical cord
le cordon ombilical
die Nabelschnur
el cordón umbilical
il cordone ombelicale

placenta
le placenta
die Plazenta
la placenta
la placenta

cervix
le col de l'utérus
der Gebärmutterhals
el cuello uterino
la cervice

uterus
l'utérus
die Gebärmutter
el útero
l'utero

fetus • le fœtus • der Fetus • el feto • il feto

ovulation	antenatal	amniotic fluid	dilation	stitches	breech
l'ovulation	prénatal	le liquide amniotique	la dilatation	les points de suture	par le siège
der Eisprung	vorgeburtlich	das Fruchtwasser	die Erweiterung	die Naht	Steiß-
la ovulación	prenatal	el líquido amniótico	la dilatación	las puntadas	de espaldas
l'ovulazione	prenatale	il liquido amniotico	la dilatazione	i punti	podalico
conception	trimester	amniocentesis	epidural	delivery	premature
la conception	le trimestre	l'amniocentèse	la péridurale	l'accouchement	prématuré
die Empfängnis	das Trimester	die Amniozentese	die Periduralanästhesie	die Entbindung	vorzeitig
la concepción	el trimestre	la amniocentesis	la epidural	el parto	prematuro
la concezione	il trimestre	l'amniocentesi	l'epidurale	il parto	prematuro
pregnant	embryo	contraction	cesarean section	birth	gynecologist
enceinte	l'embryon	la contraction	la césarienne	la naissance	le gynécologue
schwanger	der Embryo	die Wehe	der Kaiserschnitt	die Geburt	der Gynäkologe
embarazada	el embrión	la contracción	la cesárea	el nacimiento	el ginecólogo
incinta	l'embrione	la contrazione	il taglio cesareo	la nascita	il ginecologo
expectant	womb	break water (v)	episiotomy	miscarriage	obstetrician
enceinte	l'utérus	perdre les eaux	l'épisiotomie	la fausse couche	l'obstétricien
schwanger	die Gebärmutter	das Fruchtwasser geht ab	der Dammschnitt	die Fehlgeburt	der Geburtshelfer
embarazada	la matriz	romper aguas	la episiotomía	el aborto espontáneo	el obstetra
in stato interessante	il grembo	rompere le acque	l'episiotomia	l'aborto spontaneo	l'ostetrico

childbirth • la naissance • die Geburt • el parto • il parto

drip • la perfusion • die Tropfinfusion • el suero • il gocciolatore

midwife
la sage-femme
die Hebamme
la partera
l'ostetrica

monitor
le moniteur
der Monitor
el monitor
il monitor

catheter
le cathéter
der Katheter
el catéter
il catetere

induce labour (v) • déclencher l'accouchement • die Geburt einleiten • inducir el parto • il travaglio indotto

forceps • le forceps • die Geburtszange • los fórceps • il forcipe

suction cup • la ventouse • die Saugglocke • la ventosa • la ventosa

assisted delivery • l'accouchement assisté • die assistierte Entbindung • el parto asistido • il parto assistito

identity tag • le bracelet d'identité • das Erkennungsetikett • la pulsera de identificación • la targhetta d'identità

newborn baby • le nouveau-né • das Neugeborene • el recién nacido • il neonato

incubator • la couveuse • der Brutkasten • la incubadora • l'incubatrice

scales
le pèse-bébé
die Waage
la báscula
la bilancia

birth weight • le poids de naissance • das Geburtsgewicht • el peso al nacer • il peso alla nascita

nursing • l'allaitement • das Stillen • la lactancia • l'allattamento

breast pump • la pompe à lait • die Brustpumpe • el tiraleches • la pompa da seno

nursing bra • le soutien-gorge d'allaitement • der Stillbüstenhalter • el brassiere para la lactancia • il reggiseno da allattamento

breastfeed (v) • donner le sein • stillen • amamantar • allattare al seno

pads • les coussinets • die Einlagen • los discos protectores • le coppe

alternative therapy • les thérapies alternatives • die Alternativtherapien • las terapias alternativas • le terapie alternative

teacher
le maître
der Lehrer
el profesor
l'allenatore

massage • le massage
• die Massage • el masaje
• il massaggio

shiatsu • le shiatsu
• das Shiatsu • el shiatsu
• lo shiatsu

yoga • le yoga • das Yoga • el yoga • lo yoga

mat
le tapis
die Matte
la colchoneta
il tappetino

chiropractic • la chiropractie
• die Chiropraktik • la
quiropráctica • la chiropratica

osteopathy • l'ostéopathie
• die Osteopathie • la
osteopatía • l'osteopatia

reflexology • la réflexiologie
• die Reflexzonenmassage • la
reflexología • la riflessologia

meditation • la méditation
• die Meditation • la
meditación • la meditazione

counselor • le conseiller
• der Berater • el terapeuta
• l'assistente socio-psicologico

group therapy • la thérapie de groupe • die Gruppentherapie
• la terapia de grupo • la terapia di gruppo

reiki • le reiki • das Reiki
• el reiki • il reiki

acupuncture • l'acuponcture
• die Akupunktur • la
acupuntura • l'agopuntura

ayurveda • la médecine
ayurvédique • das Ayurveda
• la ayurveda • la medicina
aiurvedica

hypnotherapy
• l'hypnothérapie
• die Hypnotherapie • la
hipnoterapia • l'ipnositerapia

essential oils • les huiles
essentielles • die ätherischen
Öle • los aceites esenciales
• gli oli essenziali

herbalism • l'herboristerie
• die Kräuterheilkunde • el
herbolario • l'erbalismo

aromatherapy • l'aromathérapie
• die Aromatherapie • la
aromaterapia • l'aromaterapia

homeopathy • l'homéopathie
• die Homöopathie • la
homeopatía • l'omeopatia

acupressure • l'acupression
• die Akupressur • la
acupresión • l'agopressione

therapist • la thérapeute • die Therapeutin
• la terapeuta • la terapista

psychotherapy • la psychothérapie
• die Psychotherapie • la
psicoterapia • la psicoterapia

crystal healing	naturopathy	relaxation	herb
la guérison par cristaux	la naturopathie	la relaxation	l'herbe
die Kristalltherapie	die Naturheilkunde	die Entspannung	das Heilkraut
la cristaloterapia	la naturopatía	la relajación	la hierba
la cristalloterapia	la naturopatia	il rilassamento	l'erba
hydrotherapy	feng shui	stress	supplement
l'hydrothérapie	le feng shui	le stress	le supplément
die Wasserbehandlung	das Feng Shui	der Stress	die Ergänzung
la hidroterapia	el feng shui	el estrés	el suplemento
l'idroterapia	il feng shui	lo stress	l'integratore

home
la maison
das Haus
la casa
la casa

house • la maison • das Haus • la casa • la casa

roof
le toit
das Dach
el tejado
il tetto

chimney
la cheminée
der Schornstein
la chimenea
il camino

dormer window
le chien assis
das Mansardenfenster
la ventana de la buhardilla
l'abbaino

gutter
la gouttière
die Dachrinne
el canalón
la grondaia

tile
la tuile
der Dachziegel
la teja
la tegola

wall
le mur
die Mauer
la pared
il muro

eaves
l'avant-toit
der Dachvorsprung
el alero
la gronda

shutter
le volet
der Fensterladen
el postigo
la persiana

porch
le porche
das Vordach
el porche
il portico

window
la fenêtre
das Fenster
la ventana
la finestra

addition
l'agrandissement
der Anbau
la ampliación
l'annesso

path
l'allée
der Weg
el camino
il viottolo

front door
la porte d'entrée
die Haustür
la puerta principal
il portone

basement	row (house)	garage	floor	burglar alarm	rent (v)
le sous-sol	attenante	le garage	l'étage	l'alarme	louer
das Kellergeschoss	Reihen(haus)	die Garage	das Stockwerk	die Alarmanlage	mieten
el sótano	(condominio) horizontal	la cochera	el piso	la alarma antirrobo	rentar
il seminterrato	a schiera	il garage	il piano	l'allarme antifurto	affittare
single-family	townhouse	attic	courtyard	mailbox	rent
individuelle	la maison de deux étages	le grenier	la cour	la boîte aux lettres	le loyer
Einzel(haus)	das dreistöckige Haus	der Dachboden	der Hof	der Briefkasten	die Miete
solo	la casa de la ciudad	el ático	el patio	el buzón	la renta
unifamiliare	la casa di città	l'attico	il cortile	la cassetta per le lettere	l'affitto
duplex	bungalow	room	porch light	landlord	tenant
mitoyenne	la pavillon	la chambre	la lampe d'entrée	le propriétaire	le locataire
Doppel(haus)	der Bungalow	das Zimmer	die Haustürlampe	der Vermieter	der Mieter
dúplex	la vivienda de una planta	el cuarto	la luz del porche	el propietario	el inquilino
bifamiliare	il villino	la stanza	la luce del portico	il padrone di casa	l'inquilino

entrance • l'entrée • **der Eingang** • la entrada • l'ingresso

hand rail
la main courante
das Geländer
el pasamanos
la ringhiera

landing
le palier
der Treppenabsatz
el descanso
il pianerottolo

banister
la rampe
das Treppengeländer
el barandal
il corrimano

staircase
l'escalier
die Treppe
la escalera
le scale

hallway • le vestibule • **die Diele** • el vestíbulo • l'entrata

doorbell • la sonnette
• **die Türklingel** • el timbre
• il campanello

doormat • le paillasson
• **der Fußabtreter** • el tapete
• lo zerbino

door knocker • le marteau
de porte • **der Türklopfer**
• la aldaba • il battente

door chain • la chaîne de
sûreté • **die Türkette**
• la cadena • la catenella

key • la clef • **der Schlüssel**
• la llave • la chiave

lock • la serrure • **das
Schloss** • la cerradura
• la serratura

bolt • le verrou • **der Türriegel**
• el cerrojo • il chiavistello

apartment • l'appartement
• **die Wohnung** • el departa-
mento • l'appartamento

balcony • le balcon
• **der Balkon** • el balcón
• il balcone

apartment block • l'immeuble
• **der Wohnblock** • el edificio
• il caseggiato

intercom • l'interphone
• **die Sprechanlage** • el interfono
• il citofono

elevator • l'ascenseur
• **der Fahrstuhl** • el elevador
• l'ascensore

internal systems • les systèmes domestiques • die Hausanschlüsse • las instalaciones internas • i sistemi interni

radiator • le radiateur • der Heizkörper • el radiador • il calorifero

blade • l'aile • der Flügel • el aspa • la pala

fan • le ventilateur • der Ventilator • el ventilador • il ventilatore

space heater • l'appareil de chauffage • der Heizofen • el calentador • la stufa

portable heater • le convecteur • der Heizlüfter • el calentador de convección • la stufa a convezione

electricity • l'électricité • die Elektrizität • la electricidad • l'elettricità

filament
le filament
der Glühfaden
el filamento
il filamento

threads • le culot • die Fassung • el portalámparas • l'attacco

light bulb • l'ampoule • die Birne • el foco • la lampadina

ground • la mise à la terre • die Erdung • la toma de tierra • la messa a terra

prong • la broche • der Pol • la clavija • il piedino

plug • la prise • der Stecker • el enchufe • la spina

hot • sous tension • geladen • con corriente • in tensione

neutral • neutre • neutral • neutro • neutro

wires • les fils • die Leitung • los cables • i fili

voltage	fuse	socket	direct current	transformer
la tension	le fusible	la prise de courant	le courant continu	le transformateur
die Spannung	die Sicherung	die Steckdose	der Gleichstrom	der Transformator
el voltaje	el fusible	el enchufe	la corriente continua	el transformador
la tensione	il fusibile	la presa	la corrente continua	il trasformatore
amp	fuse box	switch	electric meter	household current
l'ampère	la boîte à fusibles	l'interrupteur	le compteur d'électricité	le réseau d'électricité
das Ampère	der Sicherungskasten	der Schalter	der Stromzähler	das Stromnetz
el amperio	la caja de los fusibles	el interruptor	el contador de la luz	el suministro de electricidad
l'ampere	la valvoliera	l'interruttore	il contatore di corrente	l'alimentazione di rete
power	generator	alternating current	power outage	
le courant	la génératrice	le courant alternatif	la coupure de courant	
der Strom	der Generator	der Wechselstrom	der Stromausfall	
la corriente eléctrica	el generador	la corriente alterna	el corte de luz	
l'elettricità	il generatore	la corrente alternata	l'interruzione di corrente	

plumbing • la plomberie • die Installation • la fontanería • l'impianto idraulico

inlet • l'arrivée • die Zuleitung • la toma • l'entrata

outlet • la sortie • der Auslass • la salida • l'uscita

pressure valve • la soupape de sûreté • das Sicherheitsventil • la válvula de la presión • la valvola della pressione

insulation l'isolation die Isolierung el aislamiento l'isolamento

overflow pipe • le trop-plein • der Überlauf • el tubo de desagüe • il tubo di troppopieno

tank le réservoir der Kessel el tanque il serbatoio

drain valve • le robinet de purge • der Ablasshahn • la llave del desagüe • il rubinetto di scarico

water chamber • la chambre d'eau • der Wasserraum • el tanque del agua • il serbatoio dell'acqua

thermostat le thermostat der Thermostat el termostato il termostato

burner • le brûleur à gaz • der Gasbrenner • el quemador • il ruciatore a gas

heating element la résistance das Heizelement la resistencia l'elemento riscaldante

boiler • la chaudière • der Boiler • la caldera • lo scaldaacqua

sink • l'évier • die Spüle • el fregador • l'acquaio

faucet • le robinet • der Hahn • el grifo • il rubinetto

lever • la manette • der Hebel • la palanca • la leva

gasket le joint die Dichtung la junta la guarnizione

supply pipe la conduite d'amenée die Zuleitung la toma del agua il tubo dell'acqua

shutoff valve • le robinet de sectionnement • der Absperrhahn • la llave de paso • il rubinetto di arresto

waste disposal unit • le broyeur d'ordures • der Müllschlucker • el triturador de basuras • il macinatore di rifiuti

drain • le tuyau d'écoulement • der Abfluss • el desagüe • lo scolo

toilet • les W.-C. • das WC • el retrete • il water

float ball • le flotteur • der Schwimmer • el flotador • il galleggiante

tank • la chasse-d'eau • der Spülkasten • el depósito • la cassetta

seat • le siège • der Toilettensitz • la tapa • il sedile

bowl la cuvette das Becken la taza la tazza

drain • le tuyau d'écoulement • das Abflussrohr • el desagüe • il tubo di scolo

waste disposal • l'enlèvement de déchets • die Abfallentsorgung • la eliminación de desechos • lo smaltimento dei rifiuti

bottle la bouteille die Flasche la botella la bottiglia

lid le couvercle der Deckel la tapa il coperchio

pedal la pédale der Trethebel el pedal il pedale

recycling bin • la boîte à déchets recyclables • der Recyclingbehälter • el cubo para reciclar • il secchio di riciclaggio

trash can • la poubelle • der Abfalleimer • el cubo de la basura • la pattumiera

sorting unit • la boîte de tri • die Abfallsortiereinheit • el armario para clasificar la basura • l'unità di smistamento

organic waste • les déchets bios • der Bio-Abfall • los desperdicios orgánicos • i rifiuti organici

living room • le salon • das Wohnzimmer • la sala • il salotto

painting
le tableau
das Gemälde
el cuadro
il quadro

frame
le cadre
der Bilderrahmen
el marco
la cornice

lamp
la lampe
die Lampe
la lámpara
la lampada

wall light
l'applique
die Wandlampe
el arbotante
l'applique

clock
la pendule
die Uhr
el reloj
l'orologio

ceiling
le plafond
die Decke
el techo
il soffitto

cabinet
la vitrine
die Vitrine
la vitrina
l'armadietto

sofa
le canapé
das Sofa
el sofá
il divano

pillow
le coussin
das Sofakissen
el cojín
il cuscino

coffee table
la table basse
der Couchtisch
la mesa de centro
il tavolino

floor
le sol
der Fußboden
el piso
il pavimento

mirror
le miroir
der Spiegel
el espejo
lo specchio

vase
le vase
die Vase
el jarrón
il vaso

mantelpiece
la tablette de cheminée
der Kaminsims
la repisa de la chimenea
la mensola del caminetto

fireplace
la cheminée
der Kamin
la chimenea
il caminetto

screen
le garde-feu
das Kamingitter
el biombo
il parafuoco

candle
la bougie
die Kerze
la vela
la candela

bookshelf
la bibliothèque
das Bücherregal
el librero
la libreria

sofabed
le canapé-lit
die Bettcouch
el sofá-cama
il divano letto

rug
le tapis
der Teppich
el tapete
il tappeto

curtain • le rideau • der Vorhang • la cortina • la tenda

net curtain • le brise-bise • die Gardine • el visillo • la tendina

venetian blind • le store vénitien • die Jalousie • la persiana • la veneziana

roller blind • le store • das Rollo • el estor • l'avvolgibile

molding • la moulure • der Stuck • la moldura • la cornice

armchair • le fauteuil • der Sessel • el sillón • la poltrona

study • le bureau • das Arbeitszimmer • el estudio • lo studio

dining room • la salle à manger • das Esszimmer • el comedor • la sala da pranzo

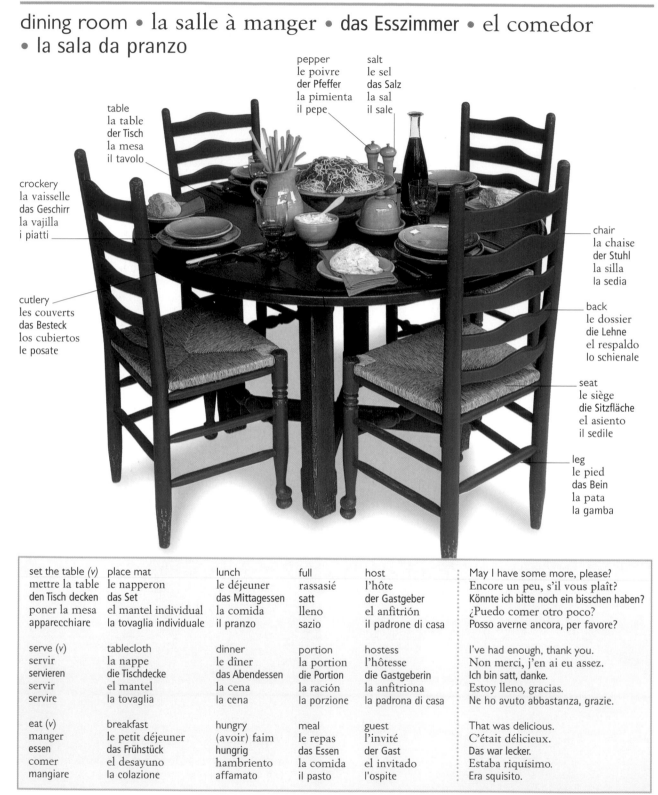

pepper
le poivre
der Pfeffer
la pimienta
il pepe

salt
le sel
das Salz
la sal
il sale

table
la table
der Tisch
la mesa
il tavolo

crockery
la vaisselle
das Geschirr
la vajilla
i piatti

cutlery
les couverts
das Besteck
los cubiertos
le posate

chair
la chaise
der Stuhl
la silla
la sedia

back
le dossier
die Lehne
el respaldo
lo schienale

seat
le siège
die Sitzfläche
el asiento
il sedile

leg
le pied
das Bein
la pata
la gamba

set the table (v)	place mat	lunch	full	host	May I have some more, please?
mettre la table	le napperon	le déjeuner	rassasié	l'hôte	Encore un peu, s'il vous plaît?
den Tisch decken	das Set	das Mittagessen	satt	der Gastgeber	Könnte ich bitte noch ein bisschen haben?
poner la mesa	el mantel individual	la comida	lleno	el anfitrión	¿Puedo comer otro poco?
apparecchiare	la tovaglia individuale	il pranzo	sazio	il padrone di casa	Posso averne ancora, per favore?
serve (v)	tablecloth	dinner	portion	hostess	I've had enough, thank you.
servir	la nappe	le dîner	la portion	l'hôtesse	Non merci, j'en ai eu assez.
servieren	die Tischdecke	das Abendessen	die Portion	die Gastgeberin	Ich bin satt, danke.
servir	el mantel	la cena	la ración	la anfitriona	Estoy lleno, gracias.
servire	la tovaglia	la cena	la porzione	la padrona di casa	Ne ho avuto abbastanza, grazie.
eat (v)	breakfast	hungry	meal	guest	That was delicious.
manger	le petit déjeuner	(avoir) faim	le repas	l'invité	C'était délicieux.
essen	das Frühstück	hungrig	das Essen	der Gast	Das war lecker.
comer	el desayuno	hambriento	la comida	el invitado	Estaba riquísimo.
mangiare	la colazione	affamato	il pasto	l'ospite	Era squisito.

crockery and cutlery • la vaisselle et les couverts • das Geschirr und das Besteck
• la vajilla y los cubiertos • le stoviglie e le posate

teaspoon • la cuiller à café
• der Teelöffel • la cucharilla
de café • il cucchiaino

mug • la grande tasse
• der Becher • la taza
• la tazza

coffee cup • la tasse à
café • die Kaffeetasse
• la taza de café
• la tazzina di caffé

teacup • la tasse à thé
• die Teetasse • la taza
de té • la tazza da té

plate • l'assiette
• der Teller • el plato
• il piatto

bowl • le bol • die
Schüssel • el plato
sopero • la ciotola

wine glass • le verre à vin
• das Weinglas • la copa de
vino • il calice da vino

tumbler
le verre
das Wasserglas
el vaso
il bicchiere

French press • la cafetière
• die Cafetière • la cafetera
de émbolo • la caffettiera

teapot • la théière
• die Teekanne • la
tetera • la teiera

pitcher • le pot
• das Kännchen • la
jarra • la brocca

egg cup • le coquetier
• der Eierbecher • la taza
para el huevo • il
portauovo

glassware • la verrerie
• die Glaswaren • la
cristalería • la cristalleria

napkin ring
le rond de serviette
der Serviettenring
el servilletero
il portatovagliolo

dessert plate
l'assiette à dessert
der Beilagenteller
el plato del pan
il piattino

dinner plate
l'assiette plate
der Essteller
el plato
il piatto piano

soup bowl
l'assiette à soupe
der Suppenteller
el plato sopero
la scodella

soup spoon • la cuiller à
soupe • der Suppenlöffel
• la cuchara sopera • il
cucchiaio da minestra

napkin
la serviette
die Serviette
la servilleta
il tovagliolo

fork • la fourchette
• die Gabel • el tenedor
• la forchetta

spoon
la cuiller
der Löffel
la cuchara
il cucchiaio

knife
le couteau
das Messer
el cuchillo
il coltello

place setting • le couvert • das Gedeck • el lugar en la mesa • il coperto

kitchen • la cuisine • die Küche • la cocina • la cucina

shelves
l'étagère
das Küchenregal
los estantes
le mensole

splashback
le revêtement
der Spritzschutz
el frente de la cocina
il pannello di protezione

faucet
le robinet
der Wasserhahn
el grifo
il rubinetto

sink
l'évier
das Spülbecken
el fregadero
il lavandino

drawer
le tiroir
die Schublade
el cajón
il cassetto

ventilation hood
la hotte
der Dunstabzug
el extractor
la cappa

ceramic stovetop
• la table de cuisson
céramique • **das
Glaskeramikkochfeld**
• la placa vitrocerámica
• il fornello di ceramica

countertop
le plan de travail
die Arbeitsfläche
la plancha
il piano di lavoro

oven
le four
der Backofen
el horno
il forno

cabinet
le placard
der Küchenschrank
la gaveta
l'armadietto

---

appliances • les appareils ménagers • **die Küchengeräte** • los electrodomésticos • gli elettrodomestici

microwave oven • le micro-ondes
• **die Mikrowelle** • el microondas • il
forno a microonde

tea kettle • la bouilloire
électrique • **der Elektro-
kessel** • la jarra para
hervir • il bollitore

toaster • le grille-
pain • **der Toaster**
• el tostador • il
tostapane

work bowl
le bol du mixeur
die Mixerschüssel
el recipiente
il recipiente

blade
la lame
das Messer
la cuchilla
la lama

food processor • le robot
ménager • **die
Küchenmaschine** • el multi-
mezclador • il miscelatore

lid
le couvercle
der Deckel
la tapa
il coperchio

blender • le mixeur
• **der Mixer** • la
licuadora • il frullatore

dishwasher • le lave-
vaisselle • **die Spülmaschine**
• la lavavajilla • la
lavastoviglie

english • français • **deutsch** • español • italiano

ice maker
• le freezer
• das Eisfach
• la máquina
de los hielos
• il fabbrica-
ghiaccio

freezer
le congélateur
das Gefrierfach
el congelador
il congelatore

refrigerator
le frigidaire
der Kühlschrank
el refrigerador
il frigorifero

shelf
la clayette
der Rost
la charola
la mensola

crisper • le bac
à légumes • das
Gemüsefach • el
cajón de las
verduras • il
cassetto per la
verdura

stove	freeze (v)
la table de cuisson	congeler
das Kochfeld	einfrieren
la hornilla	congelar
la piastra	congelare
draining board	defrost (v)
l'égouttoir	décongeler
das Abtropfbrett	auftauen
el escurridor	descongelar
il gocciolatoio	scongelare
burner	steam (v)
le brûleur	cuire à la vapeur
der Brenner	dämpfen
el quemador	cocer al vapor
il fornello	cuocere al vapore
garbage can	sauté (v)
la poubelle	sauter
der Mülleimer	anbraten
el bote de basura	saltear
la pattumiera	saltare in padella

refrigerator-freezer • le réfrigérateur-congélateur • der Gefrier-Kühlschrank
• el refrigerador congelador • il frigocongelatore

cooking • la cuisine • **das Kochen** • cocinar • cucinare

peel (v) • éplucher
• schälen • pelar
• sbucciare

slice (v) • couper
• schneiden • cortar
• affettare

grate (v) • râper
• reiben • rallar
• grattugiare

pour (v) • verser
• gießen • vaciar
• versare

mix (v) • mélanger
• verrühren • mezclar
• mescolare

whisk (v) • battre
• schlagen • batir
• sbattere

boil (v) • bouillir
• kochen • hervir
• bollire

fry (v) • frire
• braten • freír
• friggere

roll (v) • abaisser à rouleau
• ausrollen • amasar con el
rodillo • spianare

stir (v) • remuer
• rühren • remover
• rimestare

simmer (v) • mijoter
• köcheln lassen
• cocer a fuego lento
• cuocere a fuoco lento

poach (v) • pocher
• pochieren • escalfar
• affogare

bake (v) • cuire au
four • backen •
hornear • cuocere al
forno

roast (v) • rôtir
• braten • asar
• arrostire

grill (v) • griller
• grillen • asar a la
parrilla • cuocere
alla griglia

kitchenware • les ustensiles de cuisine • die Küchengeräte • los utensilios de cocina • gli utensili da cucina

cutting board
• la planche à hacher
• **das Hackbrett**
• la tabla para cortar
• il tagliere

bread knife • le couteau
à pain • **das Brotmesser**
• el cuchillo de sierra
• il coltello da pane

paring knife
• le couteau de cuisine
• **das Küchenmesser**
• el cuchillo de cocina
• il coltello da cucina

meat cleaver
• le fendoir • **das
Hackmesser** • el hacha
de cocina • la mannaia

knife sharpener
• l'aiguisoir • **der Messerschärfer** • el afilador
• l'affilacoltelli

meat tenderizer
• l'écrase-viande • **der
Fleischklopfer** • el mazo
de cocina • il martello

skewer • la broche • **der Spieß** • el pincho
• lo spiedino

pestle
le pilon
der Stößel
la mano de
mortero
il pestello

peeler • l'épluche-
légume • **der Schäler**
• el pelador • il
pelapatate

apple corer
• le vide-pomme
• **der Apfelstecher**
• el descorazonador
• il cavatorsoli

grater • la râpe
• **die Reibe** • el
rallador • la grattugia

mortar • le mortier
• **der Mörser** • el
mortero • il mortaio

masher • le presse-
purée • **der Kartoffel-
stampfer** • el
machacador • lo
schiacciapatate

can opener • l'ouvre-
boîte • **der Dosenöffner**
• el abrelatas
• l'apriscatole

bottle opener
• l'ouvre-bouteille
• **der Flaschenöffner**
• el destapador
• l'apribottiglie

garlic press • le presse-
ail • **die Knoblauchpresse**
• el exprimidor de
ajos • lo spremiaglio

serving spoon
• la cuiller à servir
• **der Servierlöffel** • la
cuchara de servir • il
cucchiaio da portata

fish spatula • la truelle
• **der Pfannenwender**
• la pala • la paletta
forata

colander • la passoire
• **das Sieb** • el
escurridor • lo
scolapasta

spatula • la spatule
• **der Spachtel** • la
espátula • la spatola

wooden spoon • la
cuiller en bois • **der
Holzlöffel** • la cuchara
de madera • il
cucchiaio di legno

mesh skimmer
• l'écumoire
• **der Schaumlöffel**
• la espumadera • il
cucchiaio perforato

ladle • la louche
• **der Schöpflöffel** • el
cucharón • il mestolo

carving fork • la fourchette à découper
• **die Tranchiergabel** • el trinche • il forchettone

ice-cream scoop • la cuiller
à glace • **der Portionierer**
• la cuchara para helado
• il cucchiaio dosatore

whisk • le fouet
• **der Schneebesen**
• el globo para batir
• la frusta

strainer • la passoire
• **das Sieb** • el colador
• il colino

lid • le couvercle • **der Deckel**
• la tapa • il coperchio

nonstick • anti-adhérent
• **kunststoffbeschichtet**
• antiadherente • antiaderente

frying pan • la poêle
• die Bratpfanne • la
sartén • la padella

saucepan • la casserole
• der Kochtopf • la
cacerola • la pentola

griddle • le gril • **das
Grillblech** • la parrilla
• la padella per grigliare

wok • le wok • **der
Wok** • el wok • il wok

earthenware dish • le fait-
tout • der Schmortopf
• la olla de barro • la
casseruola di terracotta

glass • en verre • Glas-
• de cristal • di vetro

ovenproof • allant au four
• **feuerfest** • resistente al
horno • pirofilo

mixing bowl • le grand
bol • die Rührschüssel
• la ensaladera • la
scodella

soufflé dish • le moule à
soufflé • die Souffléform
• el molde para suflé
• lo stampo per soufflé

gratin dish • le plat à
gratin • die Auflaufform
• la fuente para gratinar
• il piatto da gratin

ramekin • le ramequin
• das Auflaufförmchen
• el molde individual
• lo stampo

casserole dish • la
cocotte • die Kasserolle
• la cazuela
• la casseruola

baking cakes • la pâtisserie • **das Kuchenbacken** • la repostería • la cottura dei dolci

scales • la balance
• die Haushaltswaage
• la báscula de cocina
• la bilancia

measuring cup • le pot
gradué • **der
Messbecher** • la taza
medidora • il bricco
misuratore

cake pan • le moule à
gâteaux • die
Kuchenform • el molde
para pastel • lo
stampo per dolci

pie pan • la tourtière
• die Pastetenform
• el molde redondo
• lo stampo per torte

flan pan • le moule à
tarte • die Obstkuchen-
form • la flanera • lo
stampo per flan

pastry brush • le pinceau à pâtisserie
• der Backpinsel • la brocha de cocina
• il pennello da cucina

rolling pin • le rouleau pâtissier • das Nudelholz
• el rodillo de cocina • il mattarello

piping bag • la poche à douille • **der
Spritzbeutel** • la dulla • la tasca da
pasticciere

muffin pan • le moule à
muffins • die Törtchen-
form • el molde para
panqués • la teglia per
pasticcini

cookie sheet • la
plaque à gâteaux
• das Kuchenblech
• la charola de horno
• la placca da forno

cooling rack • la grille
de refroidissement
• das Abkühlgitter • la
rejilla • la gratella

oven mitt • le gant
isolant • der
Topfhandschuh • el
guante de cocina
• il guanto da forno

apron • le tablier
• die Schürze • el
delantal • il grembiule

bedroom • la chambre • das Schlafzimmer • la recámara • la camera da letto

wardrobe
l'armoire
der Kleiderschrank
el armario
l'armadio

bedside lamp
la lampe de chevet
die Nachttischlampe
la lámpara del buró
la lampadina

headboard
la tête de lit
das Kopfende
la cabecera
la testata

nightstand
la table de nuit
der Nachttisch
el buró
il comodino

chest of drawers
la commode
die Kommode
la cómoda
il cassettone

drawer
le tiroir
die Schublade
el cajón
il cassetto

bed
le lit
das Bett
la cama
il letto

mattress
le matelas
die Matratze
el colchón
il materasso

bedspread
le couvre-lit
die Tagesdecke
la colcha
il copriletto

pillow
l'oreiller
das Kopfkissen
la almohada
il guanciale

hot-water bottle
• la bouillotte • die
Wärmflasche • la bolsa
de agua caliente
• la borsa calda

clock radio • le radio-
réveil • der Radiowecker
• la radio despertador
• la radiosveglia

alarm clock • le réveil
• der Wecker • el reloj
despertador • la
sveglia

box of tissues • la boîte
de kleenex • die
Papiertaschentuchschachtel
• la caja de pañuelos
desechables • la
scatola di fazzolettini

coat hanger • le cintre
• der Kleiderbügel • el
gancho • la gruccia

bed linen • le linge de lit • die Bettwäsche
• la ropa de cama • la biancheria da letto

pillowcase
la taie d'oreiller
der Kissenbezug
la funda de la almohada
la federa

sheet
le drap
das Bettlaken
la sábana
il lenzuolo

valance
la frange de lit
der Volant
el cubrecanapé
il volant

mirror
le miroir
der Spiegel
el espejo
lo specchio

vanity table
la coiffeuse
der Frisiertisch
el tocador
la toeletta

comforter
la couette
die Bettdecke
el edredón
la coperta imbottita

quilt
l'édredon
die Steppdecke
la colcha
la trapunta

blanket
la couverture
die Decke
la cobija
la coperta

floor
le sol
der Fußboden
el suelo
il pavimento

single bed	footboard	insomnia	wake up (v)	set the alarm (v)
le lit simple	le pied de lit	l'insomnie	se réveiller	mettre le réveil
das Einzelbett	das Fußende	die Schlaflosigkeit	aufwachen	den Wecker stellen
la cama individual	el pie de la cama	el insomnio	despertarse	poner el despertador
il letto singolo	la pedana del letto	l'insonnia	svegliarsi	mettere la sveglia
double bed	box spring	go to bed (v)	get up (v)	snore (v)
le grand lit	le ressort	se coucher	se lever	ronfler
das Doppelbett	die Sprungfeder	ins Bett gehen	aufstehen	schnarchen
la cama matrimonial	el resorte	acostarse	levantarse	roncar
il letto matrimoniale	la molla	andare a letto	alzarsi	russare
electric blanket	carpet	go to sleep (v)	make the bed (v)	closet
la couverture chauffante	le tapis	s'endormir	faire le lit	l'armoire encastrée
die Heizdecke	der Teppich	einschlafen	das Bett machen	der Einbauschrank
la cobija eléctrica	el tapete	dormirse	hacer la cama	el armario empotrado
la termocoperta	il tappeto	addormentarsi	fare il letto	l'armadio a muro

bathroom • la salle de bain • das Badezimmer • el baño • la stanza da bagno

towel rack
le porte-serviettes
der Handtuchhalter
el toallero
il portasciugamani

shower door
la porte de douche
die Duschtür
la puerta de la regadera
la porta della doccia

cold faucet
le robinet d'eau froide
der Kaltwasserhahn
la llave de agua fría
il rubinetto dell'acqua fredda

hot faucet
le robinet d'eau chaude
der Heißwasserhahn
la llave de agua caliente
il rubinetto dell'acqua calda

shower head
le pommeau de douche
der Duschkopf
la piña de la regadera
il soffione della doccia

sink
le lavabo
das Waschbecken
el lavabo
il lavandino

shower
la douche
die Dusche
la regadera
la doccia

stopper
la bonde
der Stöpsel
el tapón
il tappo

drain
le tuyau d'écoulement
der Abfluss
el desagüe
lo scolo

toilet seat
le siège des toilettes
der Toilettensitz
la tapa del excusado
il sedile

toilet
les toilettes
die Toilette
el excusado
il water

bathtub • la baignoire
• die Badewanne • la tina
• la vasca

bidet • le bidet • das Bidet
• el bidé • il bidè

toilet brush
la brosse
die Toilettenbürste
la escobilla del excusado
la spazzola da water

---

medicine cabinet	bathmat
la pharmacie de ménage	le tapis de bain
die Hausapotheke	die Badematte
el botiquín	el tapete de baño
l'armadietto dei medicinali	lo scendibagno
toilet paper	shower curtain
le rouleau de papier hygiénique	le rideau de douche
die Rolle Toilettenpapier	der Duschvorhang
el rollo de papel higiénico	la cortina de la regadera
la carta igienica	la tenda da doccia
take a shower (v)	take a bath (v)
prendre une douche	prendre un bain
duschen	baden
bañarse	darse un baño
farsi la doccia	farsi il bagno

dental hygiene • l'hygiène dentaire • die Zahnpflege • la higiene dental • l'igiene dentale

toothbrush • la brosse à dents • die Zahnbürste • el cepillo de dientes • lo spazzolino da denti

dental floss
le fil dentaire
die Zahnseide
el hilo dental
il filo interdentale

toothpaste • le dentifrice • die Zahnpasta • la pasta de dientes • il dentifricio

mouthwash • l'eau dentifrice • das Mundwasser • el enjuague bucal • il colluttorio

loofah
le luffa
der Luffaschwamm
el zacate
la luffa

sponge • l'éponge • der
Schwamm • la esponja
• la spugna

pumice stone • la pierre
ponce • der Bimsstein • la
piedra pómez • la pomice

back brush • la brosse pour
le dos • die Rückenbürste
• el cepillo para la espalda
• la spazzola

deodorant • le déodorant
• das Deo • el desodorante
• il deodorante

soap dish
le porte-savon
die Seifenschale
la jabonera
il portasapone

shower gel
le gel douche
das Duschgel
el shampoo para el cuerpo
la docciaschiuma

soap • le savon • die Seife •
el jabón • il sapone

face cream • la crème pour
le visage • die Gesichtscreme •
la crema para la cara • la
crema per il viso

bubble bath • le bain
moussant • das Schaumbad
• el gel de baño •
il bagnoschiuma

hand towel
la serviette
das Handtuch
la toalla de mano
l'asciugamano piccolo

bath towel
la serviette de bain
das Badetuch
la toalla de baño
l'asciugamano grande

towels • les serviettes • die
Handtücher • las toallas • gli
asciugamani

body lotion • la lotion pour le corps
• die Körperlotion • la crema para el
cuerpo • la lozione per il corpo

talcum powder • le talc
• der Körperpuder • el
talco • il talco

bathrobe • le peignoir
• der Bademantel • la bata •
l'accappatoio

shaving • le rasage • das Rasieren • el afeitado • la rasatura

electric razor
le rasoir électrique
der Elektrorasierer
la rasuradora
il rasoio elettrico

razor blade
la lame de rasoir
die Rasierklinge
la hoja de afeitar
la lametta

shaving cream • la mousse à
raser • der Rasierschaum
• la espuma de afeitar
• la schiuma da barba

disposable razor • le rasoir
jetable • der Einwegrasierer
• la navaja de afeitar
desechable • il rasoio monouso

aftershave • l'after-shave
• das Rasierwasser • el
aftershave • il dopobarba

nursery • la chambre d'enfants • das Kinderzimmer • la habitación de los niños • la camera dei bambini

baby care • les soins de bébé • die Säuglingspflege • el cuidado del bebé • l'igiene del neonato

diaper rash cream • la crème pour l'érythème • die Wundsalbe • la crema para las rozaduras • la pomata antirossore

wet wipe • la serviette humide • das Erfrischungs-tuch • la toallita húmeda • la salviettina umidificata

sponge l'éponge der Schwamm la esponja la spugna

baby bath • la baignoire en plastique • die Babywanne • la tina de plástico • la vaschetta

potty • le pot • das Töpfchen • el orinal • il vasino

changing mat • le matelas à langer • die Wickelmatte • el cambiador • il materassino

---

sleeping • le coucher • das Schlafen • la hora de dormir • la dormita

mobile le mobile das Mobile el móvil il mobile

bars les barreaux die Gitterstäbe los barrotes le sbarre

bumper le protège-barreaux der Kopfschutz el protector il paracolpi

sheet le drap das Laken la sábana il lenzuolo

blanket • la couverture • die Decke • la cobija • la coperta

fleece • la couverture laineuse • die Flauschdecke • el vellón • la felpa

bedding • la literie • das Bettzeug • la ropa de cama • la biancheria da letto

mattress • le matelas • die Matratze • el colchón • il materasso

crib • le lit d'enfant • das Kinderbett • la cuna • il lettino

rattle • le hochet • die Rassel • la sonaja • il sonaglio

moses basket • le moïse • das Körbchen • el moisés • il portabebè

playing • le jeu • das Spielen • los juegos • il gioco

doll • la poupée • die Puppe • la muñeca • la bambola

stuffed toy • le jouet en peluche • das Kuscheltier • el muñeco de peluche • il giocattolo di pezza

dollhouse • la maison de poupée • das Puppenhaus • la casa de muñecas • la casa delle bambole

playhouse • la maison pliante • das Spielhaus • la casa de juguete • la casa da gioco

teddy bear • l'ours en peluche • der Teddy • el oso de peluche • l'orsacchiotto

toy
le jouet
das Spielzeug
el juguete
il giocattolo

ball
la balle
der Ball
la pelota
la palla

toy basket • le panier à jouets • der Spielzeugkorb • el cesto de los juguetes • il cesto dei giocattoli

playpen • le parc • der Laufstall • el corral • il box

safety • la sécurité • die Sicherheit • la seguridad • la sicurezza

child latches • la serrure de sécurité • die Kindersicherung • el cierre de seguridad • il fermo di sicurezza

baby monitor • le moniteur • die Babysprechanlage • el intercomunicador • la trasmittente

stair gate • la barrière d'escalier • das Treppengitter • la barrera de seguridad • lo sbarramento

eating • le manger • das Essen • la comida • il pasto

high chair • la chaise haute • der Kinderstuhl • la periquera • il seggiolone

nipple • la tétine • der Sauger • el chupón • la tettarella

drinking cup
la tasse
der Babybecher
la taza
la tazza per bere

bottle • le biberon • die Babyflasche • la mamila • il biberon

going out • la sortie • das Ausgehen • el paseo • la passeggiata

stroller • la poussette • der Sportwagen • la carriola • il passeggino

hood
la capote
das Verdeck
la capota
la capote

baby buggy • le landau • der Kinderwagen • la carriola • la carrozzina

bassinet • le couffin • das Tragebettchen • el bambineto • la culla portatile

diaper
la couche
die Windel
el pañal
il pannolino

diaper bag • le sac • die Babytasche • la pañalera • la borsa dei ricambi

front pack • le porte-bébé • die Babytrageschlinge • la cangurera • il marsupio

utility room • la buanderie • der Allzweckraum • la lavandería • la lavanderia

laundry • le linge • die Wäsche • la colada • il bucato

dirty laundry
le linge sale
die schmutzige Wäsche
la ropa sucia
i panni sporchi

clean clothes
le linge propre
die saubere Wäsche
la ropa limpia
i vestiti puliti

laundry basket • le panier à linge • der Wäschekorb • el cesto de la ropa sucia • il cesto della biacheria da lavare

washing machine • le lave-linge • die Waschmaschine • la lavadora • la lavatrice

washer-dryer • le lave-linge séchant • der Waschautomat mit Trockner • la lavadora secadora • il lavasciuga

tumble dryer • le sèche-linge • der Trockner • la secadora • l'asciugabiancheria

linen basket • le panier à linge • der Wäschekorb • el cesto de la ropa para planchar • il cesto della biancheria pulita

clothespin
la pince à linge
die Wäscheklammer
la pinza para la ropa
la molletta

clothesline
la corde à linge
die Wäscheleine
el tendedero
la corda per bucato

iron • le fer à repasser • das Bügeleisen • la plancha • il ferro da stiro

dry (v) • sécher • trocknen • secar • asciugare

ironing board • la planche à repasser • das Bügelbrett • el burro de la plancha • l'asse da stiro

load (v)	spin (v)	iron (v)	How do I operate the washing machine?
charger	essorer	repasser	Comment fonctionne le lave-linge?
füllen	schleudern	bügeln	Wie benutze ich die Waschmaschine?
cargar	centrifugar	planchar	¿Cómo funciona la lavadora?
caricare	centrifugare	stirare	Come funziona la lavatrice?
rinse (v)	spin dryer	fabric conditioner	What is the setting for colors/whites?
rincer	l'essoreuse	le produit assouplissant	Quel est le programme pour les couleurs/le blanc?
spülen	die Wäscheschleuder	der Weichspüler	Welches Programm nehme ich für farbige/weiße Wäsche?
aclarar	la centrífuga	el suavizante	¿Cuál es el programa para la ropa de color/blanca?
sciacquare	la centrifuga	l'ammorbidente	Qual è il programma per i tessuti colorati/bianchi?

cleaning equipment • l'équipement d'entretien • die Reinigungsartikel • el equipo de limpieza • gli accessori per la pulizia

suction hose • le tuyau flexible • der Saugschlauch • el tubo de la aspiradora • il tubo di aspirazione

brush
la balayette
der Handfeger
el cepillo
la spazzola

dustpan • la pelle • die Müllschaufel • el recogedor • la paletta

bleach • l'eau de Javel • das Reinigungsmittel • la lejía • la varechina

pail
le seau
der Eimer
el cubo
il secchio

powder
la poudre
das Pulver
en polvo
en polvere

liquid
le liquide
die Flüssigkeit
líquido
liquido

dust cloth • le chiffon • das Staubtuch • el sacudidor • lo spolverino

vacuum cleaner • l'aspirateur • der Staubsauger • la aspiradora • l'aspirapolvere

mop • le balai laveur • der Mopp • el trapeador • la scopa di spugna

detergent • le détergent • das Waschmittel • el detergente • il detergente

polish • la cire • die Politur • la cera • la cera

activities • les activités • die Tätigkeiten • las acciones • le attività

clean (v) • nettoyer • putzen • limpiar • pulire

wash (v) • laver • spülen • fregar • lavare

wipe (v) • essuyer • wischen • trapear • asciugare

scrub (v) • laver à la brosse • schrubben • restregar • fregare

scrape (v) • racler • kratzen • raspar • raschiare

broom
le balai
der Besen
la escoba
la scopa

sweep (v) • balayer • fegen • barrer • spazzare

dust (v) • épousseter • Staub wischen • sacudir • spolverare

polish (v) • cirer • polieren • pulir • lucidare

workshop • l'atelier • die Heimwerkstatt • el taller • il laboratorio

chuck
le mandrin
das Bohrfutter
el cabezal
il mandrino

drill bit
la mèche
der Bohrer
la broca
la punta

battery pack
la pile
die Batterie
la batería
la batteria

jigsaw • la scie sauteuse
• die Stichsäge • la sierra de
vaivén • la sega da traforo

rechargeable drill • la perceuse
rechargeable • der Bohrer mit
Batteriebetrieb • el taladro
inalámbrico • il trapano ricaricabile

electric drill • la perceuse
électrique • der Elektrobohrer
• el taladro eléctrico
• il trapano elettrico

glue gun • le pistolet à colle
• die Leimpistole • la pistola para
encolar • la pistola per colla

clamp • le serre-joint
• die Zwinge • la
abrazadera • il morsetto

blade • la lame
• das Blatt • la
cuchilla • la lama

vise • l'étau • der Schraubstock
• el tornillo de banco
• la morsa

sander • la ponceuse • die
Schleifmaschine • la lijadora
• la levigatrice

circular saw • la scie circulaire
• die Kreissäge • la sierra
circular • la sega circolare

workbench • l'établi • die
Werkbank • el banco de
trabajo • il banco da lavoro

wood glue
la colle à bois
der Holzleim
el pegamento de carpintero
la colla da legno

tool rack
• le porte-outils
• das Werkzeuggestell
• el organizador de
las herramientas
• la rastrelliera per
gli arnesi

router
la guimbarde
der Grundhobel
la guimbarda
la contornitrice

bit brace
le vilebrequin
die Bohrwinde
el taladro manual
il girabacchino

wood shavings
les copeaux
die Holzspäne
las virutas de madera
i trucioli

extension cord
le prolongateur
die Verlängerungsschnur
la extensión
la prolunga

english • français • deutsch • español • italiano

techniques • les techniques • die Fertigkeiten • las técnicas • le tecniche

cut (v) • découper • schneiden • cortar • tagliare

saw (v) • scier • sägen • serrar • segare

drill (v) • percer • bohren • taladrar • forare

hammer (v) • marteler • hämmern • clavar • martellare

plane (v) • raboter • hobeln • cepillar • piallare

turn (v) • tourner • drechseln • tornear • tornire

carve (v) • sculpter • schnitzen • tallar • incidere

solder
la soudure
der Lötzinn
la soldadura
la lega per saldatura

solder (v) • souder • löten • soldar • saldare

materials • les matériaux • die Materialien • los materiales • i materiali

plywood
le contreplaqué
das Sperrholz
el contrachapado
il compensato

medium-density fiberboard
le médium
die MDF-Platte
el tablero de densidad media
l'MDF

hardwood
le bois dur
das Hartholz
la madera noble
il legno duro

wire
le fil de fer
der Draht
el alambre
il fil di ferro

cable • le câble • das Kabel • el cable • il cavo

chipboard
l'aggloméré
das Spanholz
el aglomerado
il truciolato

varnish
le vernis
der Lack
el barniz
la lacca

stainless steel
l'inox
der rostfreie Stahl
el acero inoxidable
l'acciaio inossidabile

hardboard • l'isorel
• die Hartfaserplatte
• el cartón madera
• il cartone di
fibra compressa

woodstain • la
couleur pour
bois • die Beize
• el tinte para
madera • il
mordente per
legno

galvanized
galvanisé
galvanisiert
galvanizado
zincato

softwood • le
bois tendre •
das Weichholz • la
madera de pino
• il legno dolce

wood • le bois • das Holz • la madera • il legno

metal • le métal • das Metall • el metal • il metallo

toolbox • la boîte à outils • der Werkzeugkasten • la caja de las herramientas • la scatola degli attrezzi

wrench
la clef
der Schraubenschlüssel
la llave de boca
la chiave

adjustable wrench
• la clef à molette
• der verstellbare Schraubenschlüssel • la llave inglesa
• la chiave regolabile

hammer • le marteau
• der Hammer • el martillo
• il martello

needle-nose pliers • la pince plate
• die Flachzange • las pinzas de
alambre • le pinze ad ago

socket wrench • la clef à pipe • der Steckschlüssel
• la llave de tubo • la chiave a tubo

screwdriver bits
• les embouts de
tournevis • die
Schraubenziehereinsätze
• los cabezales de
destornillador • la
punte per cacciavite

level
le niveau
die Wasserwaage
el nivel
la livella

screwdriver
le tournevis
der Schraubenzieher
el destornillador
il cacciavite

washer
le joint
der Dichtungsring
la rondana
la rondella

nut
l'écrou
die Mutter
la tuerca
il dado

tape measure • le mètre • das
Metermaß • la cinta métrica
• il metro

utility knife
le couteau
der Schneider
el cúter
il coltello

bull-nose pliers • la pince universelle
• die Kombinationszange • los alicates
• le pinze tonde

socket • la douille • die Tülle
• el encaje • la bussola

Allen wrench • la clef • der
Schlüssel • la llave • la chiave

---

drill bits • les forets • die Bohrer • las brocas • le punte

metal bit • le foret à métaux
• der Metallbohrer • la broca para
metal • la punta per metalli

spade bit • le foret à bois plat
• der Flachholzbohrer • la broca para
madera • la punta piana per legno

Phillips screwdriver • le tournevis cruciforme
• der Kreuzschlitzschraubenzieher • el
destornillador de cruz • il cacciavite a croce

reamer
l'alésoir
die Reibahle
el escariador
l'alesatore

head • la tête •
der Nagelkopf • la
cabeza • la testa

security bit
le foret de sécurité
der Sicherheitsbohrer
la broca de seguridad
la punta di sicurezza

nail • le clou • der
Nagel • el clavo
• il chiodo

wood bits
• les forets de bois
• die Holzbohrer
• las brocas para
madera • le punte
da falegnameria

masonry bit
le foret de maçonnerie
der Mauerwerkbohrer
la broca de albañilería
la punta per muratura

screw • la vis • die
Schraub • el tornillo
• la vite

wire stripper • la pince à dénuder • die Entisolierzange • el pelacables • la pinza spelafilo

wire cutter • la pince coupante • der Drahtschneider • el cortaalambres • la pinza tagliafilo

electrical tape
le ruban isolant
das Isolierband
la cinta aislante
il nastro isolante

soldering iron
le fer à souder
der Lötkolben
el soldador
il saldatoio

hobby knife
le scalpel
das Skalpell
el escalpelo
il bisturi

fretsaw • la scie à chantourner • die Schweifsäge • la sierra de calar • la sega da traforo

solder
la soudure
der Lötzinn
la soldadura
le lega per saldatura

tenon saw • la scie à dosseret • die Profilsäge • el serrucho de costilla • la sega per tenoni

safety goggles • les lunettes de sécurité • die Schutzbrille • las gafas de seguridad • gli occhiali protettivi

plane • le rabot • der Hobel • el cepillo • la pialla

handsaw • la scie égoïne • der Fuchsschwanz • el serrucho • il seghetto

miter block • la boîte à onglets • die Gehrungslade • la caja para cortar en inglete • la cassetta guidalama per ugnature

hacksaw • la scie à métaux • die Metallsäge • la sierra para metales • il seghetto per metalli

hand drill • la perceuse manuelle • der Handbohrer • el taladro manual • il trapano manuale

steel wool • la paille de fer • die Stahlwolle • la lana de acero • la lana d'acciaio

pipe wrench • la clef serre-tube • die Rohrzange • las tenazas • la chiave inglese

chisel • le burin • der Meißel • el formón • lo scalpello

sandpaper • le papier de verre • das Schmirgelpapier • el papel de lija • la carta vetrata

plunger • la ventouse • der Sauger • el destapacaños • lo sturalavandini

file • la lime • die Feile • la lima • la lima

sharpening stone • la pierre à aiguiser • der Wetzstahl • la piedra afiladora • l'affilatore

pipe cutter • le coupe-tube • der Rohrab-schneider • el cortatuberías • il tagliatubi

decorating • la décoration • das Tapezieren • la decoración • la decorazione

scissors • les ciseaux • die Tapezierschere • las tijeras • le forbici

craft knife • le cutter • das Tapeziermesser • el cúter • il coltello da pacchi

plumb line • le fil à plomb • das Senkblei • la plomada • il filo a piombo

scraper • le grattoir • der Spachtel • la espátula • il raschietto

decorator
le tapissier décorateur
der Tapezierer
el pintor
il decoratore

wallpaper
le papier peint
die Tapete
el papel tapiz
la carta da parati

stepladder
l'escabeau
die Trittleiter
la escalera de mano
la scala a pioli

wallpaper brush
• la brosse à tapisser
• die Tapezierbürste
• la brocha de tapicero
• la spazzola

pasting table
la table à encoller
der Tapeziertisch
la mesa de encolar
il tavolo da lavoro

pasting brush
la brosse à encoller
die Kleisterbürste
la brocha de encolar
il pennello da colla

wallpaper paste • la colle à tapisser • der Tapetenkleister • el pegamento para tapizar • la colla da parati

bucket
le seau
der Eimer
la cubeta
il secchio

wallpaper (v) • tapisser • tapezieren • tapizar • tappezzare

strip (v) • décoller • abziehen • despegar • staccare

fill (v) • mastiquer • spachteln • rellenar • otturare

sand (v) • poncer • schmirgeln • lijar • scartavetrare

plaster (v) • plâtrer • verputzen • enyesar • intonacare

hang (v) • poser • anbringen • empapelar • incollare

tile (v) • carreler • kacheln • poner azulejos • piastrellare

roller
le rouleau
der Roller
el rodillo
il rullo

paint tray • le bac à peinture • die Wanne • la bandeja para la pintura • la vaschetta per la vernice

paint • la peinture • die Farbe • la pintura • la vernice

brush
la brosse
die Streichbürste
la brocha
il pennello

sponge • l'éponge • der Schwamm • la esponja • la spugna

masking tape • le papier cache • das Abdeckband • el masking tape • il nastro adesivo coprente

sandpaper • le papier de verre • das Schmirgelpapier • el papel de lija • la carta vetrata

paint can
le pot de peinture
der Farbtopf
la lata de pintura
il barattolo di vernice

coveralls
les bleus
der Overall
el overol
la tuta

oilcloth
la couverture de protection
das Abdecktuch
el protector
il telo di protezione

turpentine
la térébenthine
das Terpentin
la trementina
la trementina

filler • le mastic • die Spachtelmasse • el mastique • lo stucco

paint thinner • le white-spirit • das Verdünnungsmittel • el aguarrás • l'acquaragia

paint (v) • peindre • anstreichen • pintar • dipingere

plaster	gloss	embossed paper	base coat	sealant
le plâtre	brillant	le papier gaufré	la couche de fond	l'enduit
der Gips	Glanz-	das Reliefpapier	die Grundierung	das Versiegelungsmittel
el yeso	con brillo	el papel estampado en relieve	la primera mano	el sellador
l'intonaco	lucido	la carta a rilievo	la mano di fondo	il sigillante
varnish	matte	lining paper	top coat	solvent
le vernis	mat	le papier d'apprêt	la dernière couche	le solvant
der Lack	matt	das Einsatzpapier	der Deckanstrich	das Lösungsmittel
el barniz	mate	el papel de apresto	la última mano	el solvente
la vernice trasparente	opaco	la carta di fondo	la mano finale	il solvente
latex paint	stencil	primer	preservative	grout
la peinture mate	le pochoir	l'apprêt	l'agent de conservation	le mastic
die Emulsionsfarbe	die Schablone	die Grundfarbe	der Schutzanstrich	der Fugenkitt
la pintura al agua	la plantilla	la base	el conservante	el cemento blanco
la pittura	lo stampino	la vernice di base	il conservante	la malta

garden • le jardin • der Garten • el jardín • il giardino

garden styles • les styles de jardin • die Gartentypen • los estilos de jardín • i tipi di giardino

garden features • les ornements de jardin • die Gartenornamente • los adornos para el jardín • gli ornamenti oggetti per giardini

patio garden • le patio • der Patio • el patio con jardín • il giardino a patio

roof garden • le jardin sur le toit • der Dachgarten • el jardín en la azotea • il giardino pensile

hanging basket • le panier suspendu • die Blumenampel • la cesta colgante • il cesto sospeso

rock garden • la rocaille • der Steingarten • la rocalla • il giardino di pietra

formal garden • le jardin à la française • der architektonische Garten • el jardín clásico • il giardino all'italiana

trellis • le treillis • das Spalier • la enredadera • il graticcio

courtyard • la cour • der Hof • el patio • il cortile

English garden • le jardin paysan • der Bauerngarten • el jardín campestre • il giardino all'inglese

herb garden • le jardin d'herbes aromatiques • der Kräutergarten • el jardín de plantas herbáceas • il giardino di erbe

water garden • le jardin d'eau • der Wassergarten • el jardín acuático • il giardino acquatico

arbor • la pergola • die Pergola • la pérgola • la pergola

patio
le pavé
die Platten
la terraza
la pavimentazione

path
l'allée
der Weg
el camino
il sentiero

compost heap
le tas de compost
der Komposthaufen
la composta
la concimaia

gate
le portail
das Tor
el portón
il cancello

flowerbed
le parterre
das Blumenbeet
el parterre
l'aivola

soil • le sol • der
Boden • la tierra
• il terreno

topsoil • la terre • die
Erde • la capa superior
de la tierra • lo strato
superficiale

sand • le sable
• der Sand • la arena
• la sabbia

chalk • la chaux • der
Kalk • la creta • il gesso

silt • le vase • der
Schlick • el cieno
• il limo

clay • l'argile • der
Lehm • la arcilla
• l'argilla

shed
la cabane
der Schuppen
el cobertizo
il capanno

lawn
la pelouse
der Rasen
el césped
il prato

greenhouse
la serre
das Gewächshaus
el invernadero
la ghiaia

pond
le bassin
der Teich
el estanque
lo stagno

fence
la clôture
der Zaun
la valla
il recinto

hedge
la haie
die Hecke
el seto
la siepe

arch
l'arceau
der Bogen
el arco
l'arco

vegetable garden
le potager
der Gemüsegarten
el huerto
l'orto

herbaceous border
la bordure de plantes herbacées
die Staudenrabatte
el arriate de plantas herbáceas
il bordo erbaceo

deck • les planches • die
Planken • el entarimado
• il patio in legno

fountain • la fontaine • der Springbrunnen • la fuente • la fontana

garden plants • les plantes de jardin • die Gartenpflanzen • las plantas de jardín • le piante da giardino

types of plants • les genres de plantes • die Pflanzenarten • los tipos de plantas • i tipi di piante

annual • annuel • einjährig • anual • annuale

biennial • bisannuel • zweijährig • bienal • biennale

perennial • vivace • mehrjährig • perenne • perenne

bulb • le bulbe • die Zwiebel • el bulbo • il bulbo

fern • la fougère • der Farn • el helecho • la felce

cattail • le jonc • die Binse • el junco • il giunco

bamboo • le bambou • der Bambus • el bambú • il bambù

weeds • les mauvaises herbes • das Unkraut • las malas hierbas • le erbacce

herb • l'herbe • das Kraut • la hierba • le erbe aromatica

water plant • la plante aquatique • die Wasserpflanze • la planta acuática • la pianta acquatica

tree • l'arbre • der Baum • el árbol • l'albero

palm • le palmier • die Palme • la palmera • la palma

conifer • le conifère • der Nadelbaum • la conifera • la conifera

evergreen • à feuilles persistantes • immergrün • de hoja perenne • sempreverde

deciduous • à feuilles caduques • der Laubbaum • de hoja caduca • a foglie caduche

topiary • la topiaire
• der Formschnitt • las plantas
podadas con formas • l'arte
topiaria

alpine • la plante alpestre
• die Alpenpflanze • la planta
alpestre • le piante da roccia

succulent • la plante grasse
• die Fettpflanze • la planta
suculenta • la pianta grassa

cactus • le cactus • der Kaktus
• el cactus • il cactus

potted plant • la plante en pot
• die Topfpflanze • la planta de
maceta • la pianta da vaso

shade plant • la plante d'ombre
• die Schattenpflanze • la planta de
sombra • la pianta d'ombra

climber
la plante grimpante
die Kletterpflanze
la planta trepadora
la pianta rampicante

flowering shrub
l'arbuste à fleurs
der Zierstrauch
el arbusto de flor
la pianta da fiore

ground cover
la couverture du sol
der Bodendecker
la planta para cubrir
suelo
la pianta copriterreno

creeper
la plante rampante
die Kriechpflanze
la planta trepadora
la pianta rampicante

ornamental
ornemental
Zier-
ornamental
ornamentale

grass
l'herbe
das Gras
el pasto
l'erba

gardening tools • les outils de jardin • die Gartengeräte • las herramientas de jardinería • gli attrezzi da giardino

compost • le terreau • die Komposterde • la composta • il terriccio

lawn rake
le balai à gazon
der Laubrechen
el rastrillo para el pasto
la scopa di ferro

seeds • les graines • die Samen • las semillas • i semi

bone meal • la cendre d'os • die Knochenasche • la harina de huesos • la farina di ossa

shovel • la bêche • der Spaten • la pala • la vanga

fork • la fourche • die Gabel • el trinche • il forcone

long-handled shears • la grande cisaille • die Schere • la podadora de mango largo • le forbici tagliabordi

rake • le râteau • der Rechen • el rastrillo • il rastrello

hoe • la houe • die Hacke • el azadón • la zappa

gravel • le gravier • der Kies • la grava • la ghiaia

grass bag
le sac à herbe
der Grasfangsack
la bolsa para la hierba
il raccoglierba

motor
le moteur
der Motor
el motor
il motore

handle
le bras
der Griff
el asa
il manico

gardening basket • le panier de jardinier • der Gartenkorb • la cesta de jardinero • il cestello

shield
l'écran de protection
der Schutz
el protector
la protezione

stand
le support
der Ständer
el soporte
il sostegno

trimmer • la tondeuse • der Schneider • la cortadora • il tagliabordi

lawnmower • la tondeuse à gazon • der Rasenmäher • la podadora • il tosaerba

wheelbarrow • la brouette • der Schubkarren • la carretilla • la carriola hand fork • la petite fourche • **die Handgabel** • el trinche • il forcone

trowel • le déplantoir • **die Pflanzschaufel** • la pala pequeña • la paletta

blade
la lame
das Messer
la hoja
la lama

shears • la cisaille • **die Heckenschere** • las tijeras • le forbici da giardino

hand saw • la scie à main • **die Handsäge** • la sierra de mano • la sega

pruning shears • le sécateur • **die Rosenschere** • las podadoras • la cesoia

seed tray • le germoir • **der Setzkasten** • el semillero • il semenzaio

pesticide
le pesticide
das Pestizid
el pesticida
il pesticida

twine
la ficelle
der Zwirn
el hilo de bramante
il fil di ferro

canes
les cannes
die Gartenstöcke
las cañas
le canne

sieve
le tamis
das Sieb
la criba
il setaccio

gardening gloves
les gants de jardinage
die Gartenhandschuhe
los guantes de jardín
i guanti da giardinaggio

labels
les étiquettes
die Pflanzenschildchen
las etiquetas
le etichette

twist ties
les attaches
die Befestigungen
el alambre
le fettucce

ring ties
les anneaux
die Ringbefestigungen
las anillas
gli anelli

plant pot
le pot à fleurs
der Blumentopf
la maceta
il vaso da fiori

rubber boots • les bottes • **die Gummistiefel** • las botas de goma • le galosce

watering • l'arrosage • **das Gießen** • el riego • l'annaffiatura

spray gun • le vaporisateur • **die Gartenspritze** • el pulverizador • il diffusore

watering can
l'arrosoir
die Gießkanne
la regadera
l'annaffiatoio

rose • la pomme • **die Brause** • la piña • la rosa

sprinkler • l'arroseur • **der Rasensprenger** • el aspersor • l'irrigatore

hose
le tuyau d'arrosage
der Gartenschlauch
la manguera
la pompa da giardino

nozzle
le jet
die Düse
la boquilla
il becco

hose reel • le dévidoir de tuyau • **der Schlauchwagen** • el enrollador de manguera • l'avvolgitubo

gardening • le jardinage • die Gartenarbeit • la jardinería • il giardinaggio

lawn
la pelouse
der Rasen
el pasto
il prato

flowerbed
le parterre
das Blumenbeet
el parterre
l'aiuola

lawnmower
la tondeuse
der Rasenmäher
la podadora
il tosaerba

hedge
la haie
die Hecke
el seto
la siepe

stake
le tuteur
die Stange
la estaca
il bastoncino

mow (v) • tondre • mähen • cortar el césped • tagliare l'erba

turf (v) • gazonner • mit Rasen bedecken • poner césped • ricoprire di zolle erbose

spike (v) • piquer • stechen • hacer agujeros con el trinche • inforcare

rake (v) • ratisser • harken • rastrillar • rastrellare

trim (v) • tailler • stutzen • podar • spuntare

dig (v) • bêcher • graben • cavar • scavare

sow (v) • semer • säen • sembrar • seminare

top dress (v) • fumer en surface • mit Kopfdünger düngen • abonar en la superficie • concimare a spandimento

water (v) • arroser • gießen • regar • annaffiare

train (v) • palisser • ziehen
• guiar • far crescere

deadhead (v) • enlever les
fleurs fanées • köpfen • quitar
las flores muertas • togliere i
fiori appassiti

spray (v) • asperger • sprühen
• rociar • spruzzare

cane
la canne
der Stock
la caña
la canna

graft (v) • greffer • pfropfen
• injertar • innestare

cutting
la coupe
der Ableger
el esqueje
la talea

propagate (v) • propager
• vermehren • propagar
• propagare

prune (v) • élaguer
• beschneiden • podar
• potare

stake (v) • mettre un tuteur
• hochbinden • apuntalar
• legare a un bastoncino

transplant (v) • transplanter
• umpflanzen • transplantar
• trapiantare

weed (v) • désherber
• jäten • escardar • sradicare
le erbacce

mulch (v) • pailler • mulchen
• cubrir la tierra • concimare

harvest (v) • récolter • ernten
• cosechar • raccogliere

cultivate (v)	landscape (v)	fertilize (v)	sieve (v)	organic	seedling	subsoil
cultiver	dessiner	fertiliser	tamiser	biologique	le semis	le sous-sol
züchten	gestalten	düngen	sieben	biodynamisch	der Sämling	der Untergrund
cultivar	diseñar	abonar	cribar	orgánico	el plantón	el subsuelo
coltivare	architettare	concimare	setacciare	biologico	il semenzale	il sottosuolo
tend (v)	pot (v)	pick (v)	aerate (v)	drainage	fertilizer	weedkiller
soigner	mettre en pot	cueillir	retourner	le drainage	l'engrais	l'herbicide
hegen	eintopfen	pflücken	auflockern	die Entwässerung	der Dünger	der Unkrautvernichter
cuidar	plantar en tiesto	arrancar	airear	el drenaje	el abono	el herbicida
curare	invasare	cogliere	aerare	lo scolo	il concime	il diserbante

services
les services
die Dienstleistungen
los servicios
i servizi

emergency services • les services d'urgence • die Notdienste • los servicios de emergencia • i servizi di emergenza

ambulance • l'ambulance • der Krankenwagen • la ambulancia • l'ambulanza

stretcher
le brancard
die Tragbahre
la camilla
la barella

ambulance • l'ambulance • der Krankenwagen • la ambulancia
• l'ambulanza

paramedic • l'infirmier du SAMU • der
Rettungssanitäter • el paramédico • il paramedico

police • la police • die Polizei • la policía • la polizia

badge
le badge
die Kennmarke
la placa
il distintivo

uniform
l'uniforme
die Uniform
el uniforme
l'uniforme

siren
la sirène
die Sirene
la sirena
la sirena

lights
les feux
das Licht
las luces
le luci

nightstick
la matraque
der Gummiknüppel
la macana
il manganello

gun
le pistolet
die Pistole
la pistola
la pistola

handcuffs
les menottes
die Handschellen
las esposas
le manette

police officer • le policier • der Polizist • el policía
• l'agente

police car • la voiture de police
• das Polizeiauto • la patrulla
• l'auto della polizia

police station • le poste de
police • die Polizeiwache
• la estación de policía
• la stazione di polizia

captain l'inspecteur der Inspektor el inspector il commissario	burglary le cambriolage der Einbruchdiebstahl el robo il furto	complaint la plainte die Beschwerde la denuncia la denuncia	arrest l'arrestation die Festnahme el arresto l'arresto
detective l'officier de police der Kriminalbeamte el detective l'investigatore	assault l'agression die Körperverletzung la agresión l'aggressione	investigation l'enquête die Ermittlung la investigación l'indagine	lockup la cellule die Polizeizelle la celda la cella
crime le crime das Verbrechen el crimen il reato	fingerprint les empreintes der Fingerabdruck la huella digital l'impronta digitale	suspect le suspect der Verdächtige el sospechoso il sospetto	charge l'accusation die Anklage el cargo l'accusa

english • français • deutsch • español • italiano

fire department • les pompiers • die Feuerwehr • los bomberos • i vigili del fuoco

helmet • la casque
• der Schutzhelm • el
casco • il casco

smoke
la fumée
der Rauch
el humo
il fumo

hose
le tuyau
der Schlauch
la manguera
l'idrante

cherry picker
la nacelle
der Auslegerkorb
la cesta
la gabbia

water jet
le jet d'eau
der Wasserstrahl
el chorro de agua
il getto d'acqua

firefighters • les
sapeurs-pompiers • die
Feuerwehrleute • los
bomberos • i vigili del fuoco

boom
la flèche
der Ausleger
el brazo
il braccio

ladder
l'échelle
die Leiter
la escalera
la scala

cab
la cabine
die Fahrerkabine
la cabina
la cabina

fire • l'incendie • der Brand • el incendio • l'incendio

fire station • le poste
d'incendie • die Feuerwache
• la estación de bomberos
• la caserma dei vigili del fuoco

fire escape • l'escalier de
secours • die Feuertreppe
• la escalera de incendios
• la scala di sicurezza

fire engine • la voiture de pompiers • das Löschfahrzeug
• el carro de bomberos • l'autopompa

smoke alarm • le
détecteur de fumée
• der Rauchmelder
• el detector de humo
• l'allarme antifumo

fire alarm • l'avertisseur
d'incendie • der
Feuermelder • la alarma
contra incendios
• l'allarme antincendio

ax • la hache • das
Beil • el hacha • l'ascia

fire extinguisher
• l'extincteur • der
Feuerlöscher • el
extintor • l'estintore

hydrant • la borne
d'incendie • der
Hydrant • la bomba de
agua • l'idrante

I need the police/fire department/ambulance.	There's a fire at…	There's been an accident.	Call the police!
La police/les pompiers/une ambulance, s'il vous plaît.	Il y a un incendie à…	Il y a eu un accident.	Appelez la police!
Die Polizei/die Feuerwehr/einen Krankenwagen, bitte.	Es brennt in…	Es ist ein Unfall passiert.	Rufen Sie die Polizei!
Necesito la policía/los bomberos/una ambulancia.	Hay un incendio en…	Ha habido un accidente.	¡Llame a la policía!
Ho bisogno della polizia/dei vigili del fuoco/di un'ambulanza.	C'è un incendio a…	C'è stato un incidente.	Chiamate la polizia!

bank • la banque • die Bank • el banco • la banca

customer
le client
der Kunde
el cliente
il cliente

brochures
les dépliants
die Broschüren
los folletos
i dépliants

window
le guichet
der Schalter
la ventanilla
lo sportello

counter
le comptoir
der Schalter
el mostrador
il banco

teller
le caissier
der Kassierer
el cajero
il cassiere

deposit slips
les fiches de versement
die Einzahlungsscheine
las fichas de depósito
i moduli di versamento

debit card
la carte bancaire
die EC-Karte
la tarjeta de débito
la carta di debito

stub
le talon
der Abschnitt
la matriz
la matrice

account number
le numéro de compte
die Kontonummer
el número de cuenta
il numero di conto

signature
la signature
die Unterschrift
la firma
la firma

amount
le montant
der Betrag
la cantidad
l'importo

branch manager
• le directeur d'agence
• der Filialleiter • el gerente
del banco • il direttore

credit card • la carte de
crédit • die Kreditkarte
• la tarjeta de crédito
• la carta di credito

checkbook • le carnet de chèques
• das Scheckheft • el talonario de cheques
• il libretto degli assegni

check
le chèque
der Scheck
el cheque
l'assegno

savings	mortgage	payment	deposit (v)	checking account
l'épargne	l'hypothèque	le paiement	verser	le compte courant
die Spareinlagen	die Hypothek	die Zahlung	einzahlen	das Girokonto
los ahorros	la hipoteca	el pago	depositar	la cuenta corriente
i risparmi	l'ipoteca	il pagamento	versare	il conto corrente
tax	line of credit	automatic bill payment	direct deposit	savings account
l'impôt	le découvert	le prélèvement	le virement bancaire	le compte d'épargne
die Steuer	die Kontoüberziehung	der Einzugsauftrag	die Banküberweisung	das Sparkonto
los impuestos	el sobregiro	el débito directo	la transferencia bancaria	la cuenta de ahorros
l'imposta	lo scoperto	l'addebito diretto	il bonifico bancario	il conto di risparmio
loan	interest rate	withdrawal slip	service charge	pin number
le prêt	le taux d'intérêt	la fiche de retrait	les frais bancaire	le code secret
das Darlehen	der Zinssatz	das Abhebungsformular	die Bankgebühr	der PIN-Kode
el préstamo	la tasa de interés	la ficha de retiro	la comisión del banco	el pin
il prestito	il tasso d'interesse	il modulo di prelievo	la commissione bancaria	il pin

coin
la pièce
die Münze
la moneda
la moneta

bill
le billet
der Schein
el billete
la banconota

screen
l'écran
der Bildschirm
la pantalla
lo schermo

keypad
le clavier
das Tastenfeld
el teclado
la tastiera

card reader
la fente
der Kartenschlitz
la ranura de la tarjeta
la fessura per la carta

money • l'argent • das Geld • el dinero • il denaro

ATM • le distributeur • der Geldautomat • el cajero automático • la cassa automatica

foreign currency • les devises étrangères • die ausländische Währung • las divisas • la valuta estera

currency exchange • le bureau de change • die Wechselstube • la oficina de cambio • l'ufficio di cambio

traveler's check
• le traveller
• der Reisescheck
• el cheque de viajero
• il travel cheque

exchange rate
• le taux de change
• der Wechselkurs
• el tipo de cambio
• il tasso di cambio

finance • la finance • die Geldwirtschaft • las finanzas • la finanza

stock price
le prix des actions
der Aktienpreis
el valor de las acciones
il corso per azione

stockbroker
l'agent de la bourse
der Börsenmakler
el agente de bolsa
il broker

financial advisor • la conseillère financière • die Finanzberaterin • la asesora financiera • la consulente finanziaria

stock exchange • la bourse • die Börse • la bolsa de valores • la borsa valori

cash (v) encaisser einlösen cobrar incassare	stocks les actions die Aktien las acciones le azioni
denomination la valeur der Nennwert la denominación la denominazione	dividends les dividendes die Gewinnanteile los dividendos i dividendi
commission la commission die Provision la comisión la commissione	accountant le comptable der Wirtschaftsprüfer el contador il contabile
investment l'investissement die Kapitalanlage la inversión l'investimento	portfolio le portefeuille das Portefeuille la cartera il portafoglio
securities les titres die Wertpapiere las acciones i titoli	equity l'action die Stammaktie el patrimonio neto il capitale netto

Can I change this, please?
Est-ce que je peux changer ça, s'il vous plaît?
Könnte ich das bitte wechseln?
¿Podría cambiar esto por favor?
Posso cambiare questo?

What's today's exchange rate?
Quel est le taux de change aujourd'hui?
Wie ist der heutige Wechselkurs?
¿Cómo está el tipo de cambio hoy?
Qual è il tasso di cambio oggi?

communications • les communications • die Kommunikation • las comunicaciones • le comunicazioni

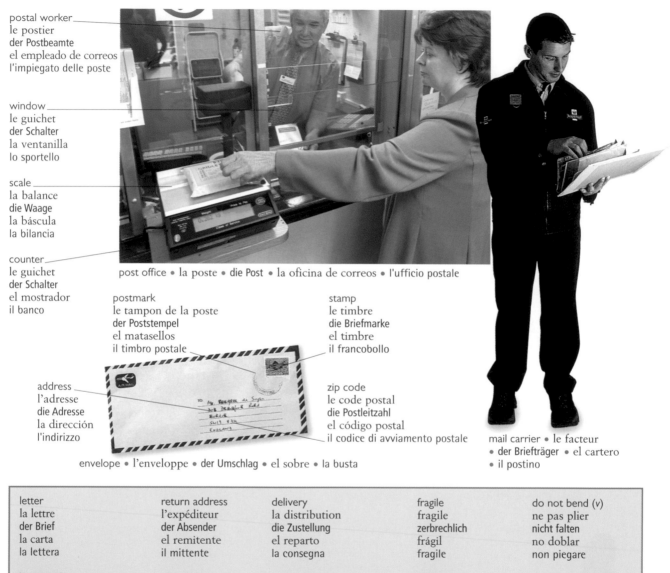

postal worker
le postier
der Postbeamte
el empleado de correos
l'impiegato delle poste

window
le guichet
der Schalter
la ventanilla
lo sportello

scale
la balance
die Waage
la báscula
la bilancia

counter
le guichet
der Schalter
el mostrador
il banco

post office • la poste • die Post • la oficina de correos • l'ufficio postale

postmark
le tampon de la poste
der Poststempel
el matasellos
il timbro postale

stamp
le timbre
die Briefmarke
el timbre
il francobollo

address
l'adresse
die Adresse
la dirección
l'indirizzo

zip code
le code postal
die Postleitzahl
el código postal
il codice di avviamento postale

envelope • l'enveloppe • der Umschlag • el sobre • la busta

mail carrier • le facteur
• der Briefträger • el cartero
• il postino

letter	return address	delivery	fragile	do not bend (v)
la lettre	l'expéditeur	la distribution	fragile	ne pas plier
der Brief	der Absender	die Zustellung	zerbrechlich	nicht falten
la carta	el remitente	el reparto	frágil	no doblar
la lettera	il mittente	la consegna	fragile	non piegare
by airmail	signature	postage	mailbag	this way up
par avion	la signature	le tarif d'affranchissement	le sac postal	dessus
per Luftpost	die Unterschrift	die Postgebühr	der Postsack	oben
por avión	la firma	el franqueo	la bolsa de correo	hacia arriba
posta aerea	la firma	l'affrancatura	il sacco postale	alto
registered mail	pickup	postal order	telegram	fax
l'envoi en recommandé	la levée	le mandat postal	le télégramme	le fax
das Einschreiben	die Leerung	die Postanweisung	das Telegramm	das Fax
el correo certificado	la recogida	el giro postal	el telegrama	el fax
la posta raccomandata	la raccolta	il vaglia postale	il telegramma	il fax

english • français • deutsch • español • italiano

mailbox • la boîte aux lettres
• der Briefkasten • el buzón
• la buca delle lettere

letter slot • la boîte aux lettres
• der Hausbriefkasten • el buzón
• la cassetta delle lettere

parcel • le colis • das Paket
• el paquete • il pacco

courier • le service de
messagerie • der Kurierdienst
• la mensajería • il corriere

telephone • le téléphone • das Telefon • el teléfono • il telefono

handset
le combiné
der Apparat
el auricular
il ricevitore

answering machine
le répondeur
der Anrufbeantworter
la contestadora
la segreteria telefonica

base station
la base
die Feststation
la base
la base

cordless phone • le téléphone sans fil • das schnurlose Telefon
• el teléfono inalámbrico • il telefono senza fili

video phone • le visiophone
• das Fernsehtelefon
• el videoteléfono
• il videotelefono

phone booth • la cabine
téléphonique • die Telefonzelle
• la cabina telefónica
• la cabina telefonica

keypad
le clavier
das Tastenfeld
el teclado
la tastiera

cellular phone • le portable
• das Handy • el celular • il
telefonino

receiver
le combiné
der Hörer
el auricular
il ricevitore

coin return
le rendu de monnaie
die Münzrückgabe
las monedas devueltas
le monete non utilizzate

pay phone • le téléphone
à pièces • der Münzfernsprecher
• el teléfono de monedas
• il telefono a monete

card phone • le téléphone
à carte • das Kartentelefon
• el teléfono de tarjeta
• il telefono a scheda

directory assistance
les renseignements
die Auskunft
la información telefónica
le informazioni telefoniche
	answer (v)
	répondre
	abheben
	contestar
	rispondere
		operator
		le téléphoniste
		die Vermittlung
		el operador
		l'operatore
			Can you give me the number for...?
			Pouvez-vous me donner le
			  numéro pour...?
			Können Sie mir die Nummer
			  für...geben?
			¿Me podría dar el número de...?
			Può darmi il numero per...?

collect call le P.C.V. das R-Gespräch la llamada a por cobrar la chiamata a carico del destinatario	text message le texto die SMS el mensaje de texto il messaggio di testo	busy occupé besetzt ocupado occupato	What is the area code for...? Quel est l'indicatif pour...? Was ist die Vorwahl für...? ¿Cuál es el prefijo de larga distancia para llamar a...?
dial (v) composer wählen marcar comporre	voice message le message vocal die Sprachmitteilung el mensaje de voz il messaggio vocale	disconnected coupé unterbrochen desconectado staccato	Qual è il prefisso per...?

hotel • l'hôtel • das Hotel • el hotel • l'albergo

lobby • le hall • die Empfangshalle • el lobby • l'ingresso

guest
le client
der Gast
el huésped
l'ospite

room key
la clef de la chambre
der Zimmerschlüssel
la llave de la habitación
la chiave della camera

messages
les messages
die Nachrichten
los mensajes
i messaggi

pigeonhole
le casier
das Fach
la casilla
la casella

receptionist
la réceptionniste
die Empfangsdame
la recepcionista
l'addetta alla ricezione

register
le registre
das Gästebuch
el registro
il registro

counter
le comptoir
der Schalter
el mostrador
il banco

reception • la réception • der Empfang • la recepción • la ricezione

luggage
les bagages
das Gepäck
el equipaje
il bagaglio

luggage rack
le diable
der Kofferkuli
el diablito
il carrello

porter • le porteur • der Hoteldiener
• el botones • il facchino

escalator • l'ascenseur • der Fahrstuhl
• el elevador • l'ascensore

room number • le numéro de
chambre • die Zimmernummer
• el número de la habitación
• il numero della camera

rooms • les chambres • die Zimmer • los habitaciones • le camere

single room • la chambre
simple • das Einzelzimmer
• la habitación sencilla
• la camera singola

double room • la chambre
double • das Doppelzimmer
• la habitación doble
• la camera doppia

twin room • la chambre à
deux lits • das Zweibettzimmer
• la habitación con dos
camas individuales
• la camera a due letti

private bathroom
• la salle de bain privée
• das Privatbadezimmer
• el baño privado
• il bagno privato

english • français • deutsch • español • italiano

services • les services • die Dienstleistungen • los servicios • i servizi

breakfast tray • le plateau à petit déjeuner • das Frühstückstablett • la charola del desayuno • il vassoio della colazione

maid service • le service de ménage • die Zimmerreinigung • el servicio de limpieza • il servizio di pulizia

laundry service • le service de blanchisserie • der Wäschedienst • el servicio de lavandería • il servizio di lavanderia

room service • le service d'étage • der Zimmerservice • el servicio de habitaciones • il servizio in camera

minibar • le minibar • die Minibar • el minibar • il minibar

restaurant • le restaurant • das Restaurant • el restaurante • il ristorante

gym • la salle de sport • der Fitnessraum • el gimnasio • la palestra

swimming pool • la piscine • das Schwimmbad • la piscina • la piscina

full board la pension complète die Vollpension la pensión completa la pensione completa	Do you have any vacancies? Avez-vous une chambre de libre? Haben Sie ein Zimmer frei? ¿Tiene alguna habitación libre? Avete una camera libera?	I'd like a room for three nights. Je voudrais une chambre pour trois nuits. Ich möchte ein Zimmer für drei Nächte. Quiero una habitación para tres días. Vorrei una camera per tre notti.
half board la demi-pension die Halbpension la media pensión la mezza pensione	I have a reservation. J'ai une réservation. Ich habe ein Zimmer reserviert. Tengo una reservación. Ho una prenotazione	What is the charge per night? C'est combien par nuit? Was kostet das Zimmer pro Nacht? ¿Cuánto cuesta la habitación por día? Quanto costa la camera a notte?
bed and breakfast la chambre avec le petit déjeuner die Übernachtung mit Frühstück la habitación con desayuno incluido la pensione con colazione	I'd like a single room. Je voudrais une chambre simple. Ich möchte ein Einzelzimmer. Quiero una habitación sencilla. Vorrei una camera singola	When do I have to vacate the room? Quand est-ce que je dois quitter la chambre? Wann muss ich das Zimmer räumen? ¿Cuándo tengo que dejar la habitación? Quando devo lasciare la stanza?

shopping
les courses
der Einkauf
las compras
gli acquisti

shopping mall • le centre commercial • das Einkaufszentrum • el centro comercial • il centro commerciale

atrium
l'atrium
das Atrium
el atrio
l'atrio

sign
l'enseigne
das Schild
el letrero
l'insegna

elevator
l'ascenseur
der Fahrstuhl
el elevador
l'ascensore

third floor
le deuxième étage
die zweite Etage
el segundo piso
il secondo piano

second floor
le premier étage
die erste Etage
el primer piso
il primo piano

escalator
l'escalier mécanique
die Rolltreppe
la escalera eléctrica
la scala mobile

ground floor
le rez-de-chaussée
das Erdgeschoss
la planta baja
il piano terra

customer
le client
der Kunde
el cliente
il cliente

children's department le rayon enfants die Kinderabteilung el departamento de niños il reparto bambini	store directory le guide die Anzeigetafel el directorio la guida al negozio	fitting rooms les cabines d'essayage die Anprobe los probadores i camerini	How much is this? C'est combien? Was kostet das? ¿Cuánto cuesta esto? Quanto costa questo?
luggage department le rayon bagages die Gepäckabteilung el departamento de equipajes il reparto bagagli	sales clerk le vendeur der Verkäufer el vendedor il commesso	baby changing room les soins de bébés der Wickelraum el cuarto para cambiar a los bebés la stanza di cambio pannolini	May I exchange this? Est-ce que je peux changer ça? Kann ich das umtauschen? ¿Puedo cambiar esto? Posso cambiare questo?
shoe department le rayon chaussures die Schuhabteilung el departamento de zapatería il reparto calzature	rest room les toilettes die Toiletten los baños le toilettes	customer services le service après-vente der Kundendienst el servicio al cliente l'assistenza ai clienti	

department store • le grand magasin • das Kaufhaus • las tiendas departamentales • il grande magazzino

menswear • les vêtements pour hommes • die Herrenbekleidung • la ropa de caballero • l'abbigliamento da uomo

womenswear • les vêtement pour femmes • die Damenoberbekleidung • la ropa de dama • l'abbigliamento da donna

lingerie • la lingerie • die Damenwäsche • la lencería • la biancheria intima

perfumes • la parfumerie • die Parfümerie • la perfumería • la profumeria

cosmetics • la beauté • die Schönheitspflege • los cosméticos • la bellezza

linens • le linge de maison • die Wäsche • los blancos • la biancheria

home furnishings • l'ameublement • die Möbel • el mobiliario para el hogar • l'arredamento per la casa

notions • la mercerie • die Kurzwaren • la mercería • la merceria

kitchenware • la vaisselle • die Küchengeräte • los artículos de cocina • gli articoli da cucina

china • la porcelaine • das Porzellan • las vajillas • la porcellana

electronics • l'électroménager • die Elektroartikel • los aparatos eléctricos • gli articoli elettronici

lighting • l'éclairage • die Lampen • la iluminación • l'illuminazione

sportswear • les articles de sport • die Sportartikel • los artículos deportivos • gli articoli sportivi

toys • les jouets • die Spielwaren • la juguetería • i giocattoli

stationery • la papeterie • die Scheibwaren • la papelería • la cancelleria

groceries • l'alimentation • die Lebensmittelabteilung • los abarrotes • il reparto alimentari

supermarket • le supermarché • der Supermarkt • el supermercado • il supermercato

aisle • l'allée • der
Gang • el pasillo
• il passaggio

shelf • l'étàgere
• das Warenregal • el
estante • lo scaffale

checkout counter
le tapis roulant
das Laufband
la banda transportadora
il nastro convogliatore

cashier
le caissier
der Kassierer
el cajero
il cassiere

offers
les promotions
die Angebote
las ofertas
le offerte

checkout • la caisse • die Kasse • la caja • la cassa

customer
le client
der Kunde
el cliente
il cliente

cash register
la caisse
die Kasse
la caja
la cassa

shopping bag
la sac à provisions
die Einkaufstasche
la bolsa
la busta della spesa

groceries
les provisions
die Lebensmittel
la compra
la spesa

handle
l'anse
der Henkel
el asa
il manico

grocery cart • le caddie • der Einkaufswagen
• el carrito • il carrello

basket • le panier • der Einkaufskorb
• la canasta • il cestino

780863 185779

bar code • le code barres
• der Strichkode • el código
de barras • il codice a barre

scanner • le lecteur optique • der
Scanner • el escáner • il lettore ottico

bakery • la boulangerie • die Backwaren • la panadería • il pane

dairy • la crémerie • die Milchprodukte • los lácteos • i latticini

breakfast cereals • les céréales • die Getreideflocken • los cereales • i cereali da colazione

canned goods • les conserves • die Konserven • las conservas • lo scatolame

candies • la confiserie • die Süßwaren • la dulcería • i dolci

vegetables • les légumes • das Gemüse • la verdura • le verdure

fruits • les fruits • das Obst • la fruta • la frutta

meat and poultry • la viande et la volaille • das Fleisch und das Geflügel • la carne y las aves • la carne e il pollame

fish • le poisson • der Fisch • el pescado • il pesce

deli • la charcuterie • die Feinkost • la charcutería • i salumi

frozen food • les produits surgelés • die Gefrierware • los congelados • i surgelati

prepared food • les plats cuisinés • die Fertiggerichte • los platos preparados • i cibi cotti

drinks • les boissons • die Getränke • las bebidas • le bibite

household products • les produits d'entretien • die Haushaltswaren • los productos de limpieza • i casalinghi

toiletries • les articles de toilette • die Toilettenartikel • los artículos de aseo • i prodotti per il bagno

baby products • les articles pour bébés • die Babyprodukte • los artículos para el bebé • i prodotti per bambini

electrical goods • l'électroménager • die Elektroartikel • los electrodomésticos • gli elettrodomestici

pet food • la nourriture pour animaux • das Tierfutter • la comida para animales • il cibo per animali

magazines • les magazines • die Zeitschriften • las revistas • le riviste

english • français • deutsch • español • italiano

chemist • la pharmacie • die Apotheke • la farmacia • la farmacia

dental care
le soin dentaire
die Zahnpflege
el cuidado dental
i prodotti per i denti

feminine hygiene
l'hygiène féminine
die Monatshygiene
la higiene femenina
l'igiene femminile

deodorants
les déodorants
die Deos
los desodorantes
i deodoranti

vitamins
les cachets de vitamines
die Vitamintabletten
las vitaminas
le vitamine

pharmacy
l'officine
die Apotheke
el dispensario
il dispensario

pharmacist
le pharmacien
der Apotheker
el farmacéutico
il farmacista

cough medicine
le médicament pour la toux
das Hustenmedikament
el jarabe para la tos
la medicina per la tosse

herbal remedies
l'herboristerie
Kräuterheilmittel
los remedios naturistas
i rimedi alle erbe

skin care
les soins de la peau
die Hautpflege
el cuidado de la piel
i prodotti per la pelle

aftersun care
• l'après-soleil
• die After-Sun-Lotion
• la crema para
  después del sol
• il doposole

sunscreen • l'écran solaire
• die Sonnenschutzcreme • la
crema protectora • la crema
schermo

sun block • l'écran total
• der Sonnenblock • la
crema protectora total
• la crema schermo totale

insect repellent • le produit anti-
insecte • das Insektenschutzmittel
• el repelente de insectos
• l'insettifugo

wet wipe • la serviette humide
• das Reinigungstuch • la toallita
húmeda • la salviettina
umidificata

tissue • le kleenex • das
Papiertaschentuch • el pañuelo
desechable • il fazzolettino

sanitary napkin • la serviette
hygiénique • die Damenbinde
• las toallas femeninas
• l'assorbente

tampon • le tampon • der
Tampon • el tampón • il
tampone

panty liner • le protège-slip
• die Slipeinlage • el
pantiprotector • i salvaslip

measuring spoon
la cuiller pour mesurer
der Messlöffel
la cuchara medidora
il cucchiaio misuratore

instructions
le mode d'emploi
die Gebrauchsanweisung
el modo de empleo
le istruzioni

capsule • la capsule
• die Kapsel • la cápsula
• la pasticca

pill • la pilule • die Pille
• la píldora • la pillola

syrup • le sirop • der Saft
• el jarabe • lo sciroppo

inhaler • l'inhalateur • der
Inhalierstift • el inhalador
• l'inalatore

cream • la crème • die Creme
• la crema • la crema

ointment • la pommade • die
Salbe • la pomada • l'unguento

gel • le gel • das Gel • el gel
• il gel

suppository • le suppositoire
• das Zäpfchen • el
supositorio • la supposta

eye dropper
le compte-gouttes
der Tropfer
el gotero
il contagocce

needle
l'aiguille
die Nadel
la aguja
l'ago

eye drops • les gouttes • die
Tropfen • las gotas • le gocce

syringe • la seringue
• die Spritze • la jeringa
• la siringa

spray • le spray • der Spray
• el spray • lo spray

powder • la poudre
• der Puder • los polvos
• la polvere

iron	multivitamins	disposable	medicine	painkiller
le fer	le médicament multivitamine	jetable	le médicament	l'analgésique
das Eisen	das Multivitaminmittel	Wegwerf-	das Medikament	das Schmerzmittel
el hierro	el complejo vitamínico	desechable	el medicamento	el analgésico
il ferro	la multivitamina	monouso	la medicina	l'antidolorifico
calcium	side-effects	soluble	laxative	sedative
le calcium	les effets secondaires	soluble	le laxatif	le sédatif
das Kalzium	die Nebenwirkungen	löslich	das Abführmittel	das Beruhigungsmittel
el calcio	los efectos secundarios	soluble	el laxante	el calmante
il calcio	gli effetti collaterali	solubile	il lassativo	il sedativo
magnesium	expiration date	dosage	diarrhea	sleeping pill
le magnésium	la date d'expiration	la posologie	la diarrhée	le somnifère
das Magnesium	das Verfallsdatum	die Dosierung	der Durchfall	die Schlaftablette
el magnesio	la fecha de caducidad	la dosis	la diarrea	el somnífero
il magnesio	la data di scadenza	il dosaggio	la diarrea	il sonnifero
insulin	travel sickness pills	medication	throat lozenge	anti-inflammatory
l'insuline	les cachets antinaupathiques	la médication	la pastille pour la gorge	l'anti-inflammatoire
das Insulin	die Reisekrankheitstabletten	die Verordnung	die Halspastille	der Entzündungshemmer
la insulina	las píldoras para el mareo	la medicación	la pastilla para la garganta	el antiinflamatorio
l'insulina	le pasticche per il mal d'auto	il medicamento	la pasticca per la gola	l'antinfiammatorio

english • français • deutsch • español • italiano

florist • le fleuriste • das Blumengeschäft • la florería • il fioraio

flowers
les fleurs
die Blumen
las flores
i fiori

lily
le lis
die Lilie
la azucena
il giglio

acacia
l'acacia
die Akazie
la acacia
l'acacia

carnation
l'œillet
die Nelke
el clavel
il garofano

potted plant
la plante en pot
die Topfpflanze
la maceta
la pianta da vaso

gladiolus
le glaïeul
die Gladiole
la gladiola
il gladiolo

iris
l'iris
die Iris
el iris
l'iris

daisy
la marguerite
die Margerite
la margarita
la margherita

chrysanthemum
le chrysanthème
die Chrysantheme
el crisantemo
il crisantemo

gypsophila
la gypsophile
das Schleierkraut
la nube
la gipsofila

stocks • la giroflée
• die Levkoje • el alhelí
• la violacciocca

gerbera • le gerbera
• die Gerbera • la
gerbera • la gerbera

foliage • le feuillage
• die Blätter • el follaje
• il fogliame

rose • la rose • die
Rose • la rosa • la rosa

freesia • le freesia
• die Freesie • la fresia
• la fresia

vase • le vase • die Blumenvase • el florero • il vaso

arrangements • les compositions florales • die Blumenarrangements • los arreglos • gli arrangiamenti

ribbon
le ruban
das Band
la cinta
il nastro

orchid • l'orchidée • die Orchidee • la orquídea • l'orchidea

peony • la pivoine • die Pfingstrose • la peonía • la peonia

bouquet • le bouquet • das Bukett • el ramo • il mazzo di fiori

dried flowers • les fleurs séchées • die Trockenblumen • las flores secas • i fiori secchi

bunch
la botte
der Strauß
el ramo
il mazzetto

stem
la tige
der Stengel
el tallo
lo stelo

daffodil • la jonquille • die Osterglocke • el narciso • il narciso

pot-pourri • le pot-pourri • das Duftsträußchen • el popurrí • il pot-pourri

wreath • la couronne • der Kranz • la corona • la corona

garland • la guirlande de fleurs • die Blumengirlande • la guirnalda • la ghirlanda

bud
le bourgeon
die Knospe
el capullo
il bocciolo

wrapping
l'emballage
das Einwickelpapier
la envoltura
l'incarto

tulip • la tulipe • die Tulpe • el tulipán • il tulipano

May I have a bunch of… please.
Je voudrais un bouquet de…, SVP.
Ich möchte einen Strauß…, bitte.
¿Me da un ramo de… por favor?
Mi dà un mazzo di… per favore?

How long will these last?
Elles tiennent combien de temps?
Wie lange halten sie?
¿Cuánto tiempo durarán éstos?
Quanto dureranno?

May I have them wrapped?
Pouvez-vous les emballer?
Können Sie die Blumen bitte einwickeln?
¿Me los puede envolver?
Me li può incartare?

Are they fragrant?
Est-ce qu'elles sentent bon?
Duften sie?
¿Huelen?
Sono profumati?

May I attach a message?
Je peux y attacher un message?
Kann ich eine Nachricht mitschicken?
¿Puedo poner un mensaje?
Posso allegare un messaggio?

Would you send them to….?
Pouvez-vous les envoyer à…?
Können Sie die Blumen an… schicken?
¿Los puede enviar a…?
Li può mandare a…?

newsstand • le marchand de journaux • der Zeitungshändler • los tabacos y las revistas • l'edicola

cigarettes
les cigarettes
die Zigaretten
los cigarros
le sigarette

pack of cigarettes
le paquet de cigarettes
das Päckchen Zigaretten
la cajetilla de cigarros
il pacchetto di sigarette

matches
les allumettes
die Streichhölzer
los cerillos
i fiammiferi

lottery tickets
les billets de loterie
die Lottoscheine
los billetes de lotería
i biglietti della lotteria

stamps
les timbres
die Briefmarken
los timbres
i francobolli

postcard • la carte postale • die Postkarte • la tarjeta postal • la cartolina

comic • la bande dessinée • das Comicheft • la historieta • il giornalino a fumetti

magazine • le magazine • die Zeitschrift • la revista • la rivista

newspaper • le journal • die Zeitung • el periódico • il giornale

---

smoking • fumer • das Rauchen • fumar • fumare

tobacco • le tabac • der Tabak • el tabaco • il tabacco

lighter • le briquet • das Feuerzeug • el encendedor • l'accendino

bowl
le fourneau
der Kopf
la cazoleta
il fornello

stem
le tuyau
der Stiel
el tubo
la cannuccia

pipe • la pipe • die Pfeife • la pipa • la pipa

cigar • le cigare • die Zigarre • el puro • il sigaro

candy store • le confiseur • der Konditor • la dulcería • il confettiere

box of chocolates
la boîte de chocolats
die Schachtel Pralinen
la caja de chocolates
la scatola di cioccolatini

snack bar
la friandise
die Nascherei
la barrita
la tavoletta spuntino

potato chips
les chips
die Chips
las papas fritas
le patatine

milk chocolate
le chocolat au lait
die Milchschokolade
el chocolate de leche
il cioccolato al latte

caramel
le caramel
der Karamell
el caramelo
il caramello

dark chocolate
le chocolat noir
die bittere Schokolade
el chocolate negro
il cioccolato amaro

truffle
la truffe
der Trüffel
la trufa
il tartufo

white chocolate
le chocolat blanc
die weiße Schokolade
el chocolate blanco
il cioccolato bianco

cookie
le biscuit
der Keks
la galleta
il biscotto

pick and mix
les bonbons assortis
die bunte Mischung
los dulces a granel
la caramelle assortite

hard candy
les bonbons
die Bonbons
los caramelos duros
le caramelle

candy store • la confiserie • das Süßwarengeschäft • la dulcería • il negozio di dolciumi

---

confectionery • la confiserie • die Süßwaren • los dulces • i dolciumi

chocolate • le chocolat • die Praline • el chocolate • il cioccolatino

chocolate bar • la tablette de chocolat • die Tafel Schokolade • la tablilla de chocolate • la tavoletta di cioccolata

hard candy • les bonbons • die Bonbons • los caramelos duros • le caramelle

lollipop • la sucette • der Lutscher • la paleta • la lecca lecca

toffee • le caramel • das Toffee • el toffee • la caramella mou

nougat • le nougat • der Nugat • el turrón • il torrone

marshmallow • la guimauve • das Marshmallow • el malvarisco • la caramella gommosa

mint • le bonbon à la menthe • das Pfefferminz • la pastilla de menta • la mentina

chewing gum • le chewing-gum • der Kaugummi • el chicle • la gomma da masticare

jellybean • la dragée à la gelée • der Geleebonbon • el caramelo blando • la caramella di gelatina

gumdrop • le bonbon au fruit • der Fruchtgummi • la gomita • la caramella alla frutta

licorice • le réglisse • die Lakritze • el regaliz • la liquirizia

other stores • les autres magasins • andere Geschäfte • las otras tiendas • gli altri negozi

bakery • la boulangerie
• die Bäckerei • la panadería
• il panificio

cake shop • la pâtisserie
• die Konditorei • la confitería
• la pasticceria

butcher shop • la boucherie
• die Metzgerei • la carnicería
• la macelleria

fish counter • la poissonnerie
• das Fischgeschäft • la
pescadería • la pescheria

produce stand • le marchand
de légumes • der Gemüseladen
• la verdulería • il
fruttivendolo

grocery store • l'épicerie
• das Lebensmittelgeschäft • los
abarrotes • la drogheria

shoe store • le magasin de
chaussures • das Schuhgeschäft
• la zapatería • il negozio di
calzature

hardware store • la
quincaillerie • die Eisenwaren-
handlung • la ferretería • il
negozio di ferramenta

antique store • le magasin
d'antiquités • der
Antiquitätenladen • la tienda
de antigüedades • il negozio
di antiquariato

gift store • la boutique de
cadeaux • der Geschenkartikel-
laden • la tienda de regalos
• il negozio di articoli da regalo

travel agency • l'agence de
voyage • das Reisebüro
• la agencia de viajes
• l'agenzia di viaggi

jewelry store • la bijouterie
• das Juweliergeschäft
• la joyería • la gioielleria

bookstore • la librairie
• der Buchladen • la librería
• la libreria

record store • le magasin de
disques • das Plattengeschäft
• la tienda de discos
• il negozio di dischi

liquor store • le magasin de
vins et spiritueux • die
Weinhandlung • la tienda de
licores • il negozio di liquori

pet store • l'animalerie
• die Tierhandlung • la tienda
de mascotas • il negozio
di animali

furniture store • le magasin
de meubles • das
Möbelgeschäft • la mueblería
• il negozio di mobili

boutique • la boutique
• die Boutique • la boutique
• la boutique

realty office
l'agent immobilier
der Immobilienmakler
la agencia inmobiliaria
l'agenzia immobiliare

camera store
le magasin d'appareils photos
das Fotogeschäft
la tienda de fotografía
il negozio di articoli fotografici

garden center
la pépinière
das Gartencenter
el vivero
il vivaio

second-hand store
le marchand d'occasion
der Gebrauchtwarenhändler
la tienda de artículos usados
il negozio dell'usato

dry cleaner
le pressing
die Reinigung
la tintorería
il lavasecco

health food store
le magasin bio
das Reformhaus
la tienda naturista
il negozio di alimenti biologici

laundromat
la laverie automatique
der Waschsalon
la lavandería
la lavanderia

art store
la boutique d'art
die Kunsthandlung
la galería de arte
il negozio di articoli per l'arte

tailor shop • le tailleur • die
Schneiderei • la sastrería
• la sartoria

hair salon • le salon de
coiffure • der Frisiersalon • la
estética • il parrucchiere

market • le marché • der Markt • el mercado • il mercato

food
la nourriture
die Nahrungsmittel
los alimentos
il cibo

meat • la viande • das Fleisch • la carne • la carne

lamb
l'agneau
das Lamm
el cordero
l'agnello

butcher
le boucher
der Metzger
el carnicero
il macellaio

meat hook
l'allonge
der Fleischerhaken
el gancho
il gancio

scales
la balance
die Waage
la báscula
la bilancia

knife sharpener
le fusil
der Messerschärfer
el afilador
l'affilacoltelli

bacon • le bacon • der Speck
• el tocino • la pancetta

sausages • les saucisses • die
Würstchen • las salchichas • le salsicce

liver • le foie • die Leber
• el hígado • il fegato

pork	venison	offal	free range	red meat
le porc	la venaison	les abats	de ferme	la viande rouge
das Schweinefleisch	das Wild	die Innereien	aus Freilandhaltung	das rote Fleisch
el cerdo	el venado	las asaduras	de granja	la carne roja
il maiale	il cervo	le frattaglie	ruspante	la carne rossa
beef	rabbit	cured	organic	lean meat
le bœuf	le lapin	salé	naturel	la viande maigre
das Rindfleisch	das Kaninchen	gepökelt	biologisch kontrolliert	das magere Fleisch
la vaca	el conejo	curado	orgánico	la carne magra
il manzo	il coniglio	trattato	biologico	la carne magra
veal	tongue	smoked	white meat	cooked meat
le veau	la langue de bœuf	fumé	la viande blanche	la viande cuite
das Kalbfleisch	die Zunge	geräuchert	das weiße Fleisch	das gekochte Fleisch
la ternera	la lengua	ahumado	la carne blanca	el fiambre
il vitello	la lingua	affumicato	la carne bianca	la carne cotta

cuts • les morceaux de viande • die Fleischsorten • los cortes • i tagli

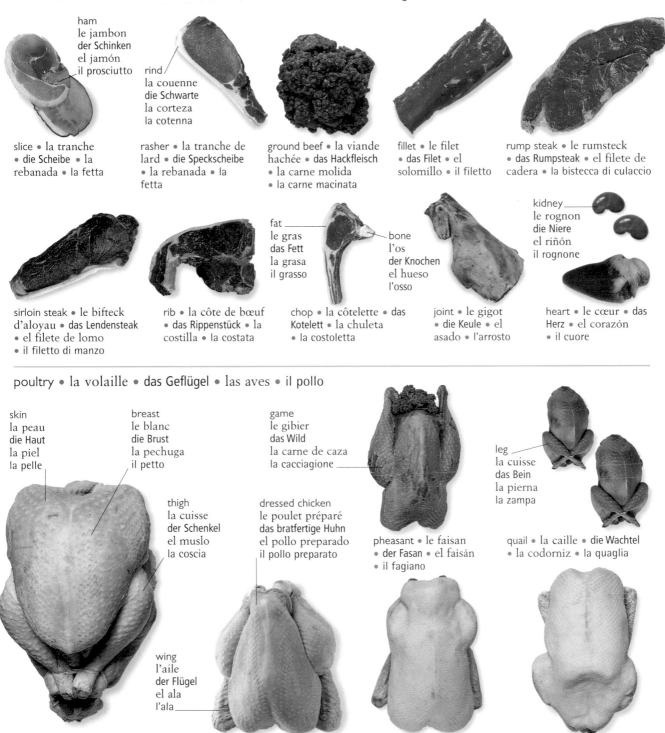

ham
le jambon
der Schinken
el jamón
il prosciutto

rind
la couenne
die Schwarte
la corteza
la cotenna

slice • la tranche
• die Scheibe • la
rebanada • la fetta

rasher • la tranche de
lard • die Speckscheibe
• la rebanada • la
fetta

ground beef • la viande
hachée • das Hackfleisch
• la carne molida
• la carne macinata

fillet • le filet
• das Filet • el
solomillo • il filetto

rump steak • le rumsteck
• das Rumpsteak • el filete de
cadera • la bistecca di culaccio

fat
le gras
das Fett
la grasa
il grasso

bone
l'os
der Knochen
el hueso
l'osso

kidney
le rognon
die Niere
el riñón
il rognone

sirloin steak • le bifteck
d'aloyau • das Lendensteak
• el filete de lomo
• il filetto di manzo

rib • la côte de bœuf
• das Rippenstück • la
costilla • la costata

chop • la côtelette • das
Kotelett • la chuleta
• la costoletta

joint • le gigot
• die Keule • el
asado • l'arrosto

heart • le cœur • das
Herz • el corazón
• il cuore

poultry • la volaille • das Geflügel • las aves • il pollo

skin
la peau
die Haut
la piel
la pelle

breast
le blanc
die Brust
la pechuga
il petto

game
le gibier
das Wild
la carne de caza
la cacciagione

leg
la cuisse
das Bein
la pierna
la zampa

thigh
la cuisse
der Schenkel
el muslo
la coscia

dressed chicken
le poulet préparé
das bratfertige Huhn
el pollo preparado
il pollo preparato

pheasant • le faisan
• der Fasan • el faisán
• il fagiano

quail • la caille • die Wachtel
• la codorniz • la quaglia

wing
l'aile
der Flügel
el ala
l'ala

turkey • la dinde • die Pute
• el pavo • il tacchino

chicken • le poulet • das
Hähnchen • el pollo • il pollo

duck • le canard • die
Ente • el pato • l'anatra

goose • l'oie • die Gans
• el ganso • l'oca

fish • le poisson • der Fisch • el pescado • il pesce

peeled shrimp
les crevettes décortiquées
die geschälten Garnelen
los camarones pelados
i gamberi sgusciati

red mullet
le rouget barbet
die rote Meeräsche
el salmonete
la triglia

halibut fillets
les filets de flétan
die Heilbuttfilets
los filetes de mero
i filetti di ippoglosso

rainbow trout
la truite arc-en-ciel
die Regenbogenforelle
la trucha arco iris
la trota

ice
la glace
das Eis
el hielo
il ghiaccio

skate wings
les ailes de raie
die Rochenflügel
las aletas de raya
le pinne di razza

fish seller • la poissonnerie • das Fischgeschäft • la pescadería • la pescheria

monkfish • la lotte
• die Quappe • el rape
• la rana pescatrice

mackerel • le maquereau
• die Makrele • la caballa
• lo sgombro

trout • la truite • die
Forelle • la trucha
• la trota

swordfish • l'espadon • der Schwertfisch
• el pez espada • il pesce spada

Dover sole • la sole
• die Seezunge • el
lenguado • la sogliola

lemon sole • la limande-
sole • die Rotzunge
• la platija • la sogliola
limanda

haddock • l'aiglefin
• der Schellfisch • el
abadejo • l'eglefino

sardine • la sardine
• die Sardine • la
sardina • la sardina

skate • la raie • der
Rochen • la raya
• la razza

silver hake • le merlan •
der Weißfisch • la pescadilla
• il merlango

sea bass • le bar • der Seebarsch
• la lubina • la spigola

salmon • le saumon • der Lachs • el salmón
• il salmone

cod • la morue • der Kabeljau • el bacalao
• il merluzzo

sea bream • la daurade
• der Seebrassen • el
besugo • l'abramide

tuna • le thon • der Tunfisch • el atún • il tonno

english • français • deutsch • español • italiano

seafood • les fruits de mer • die Meeresfrüchte • el marisco • i frutti di mare

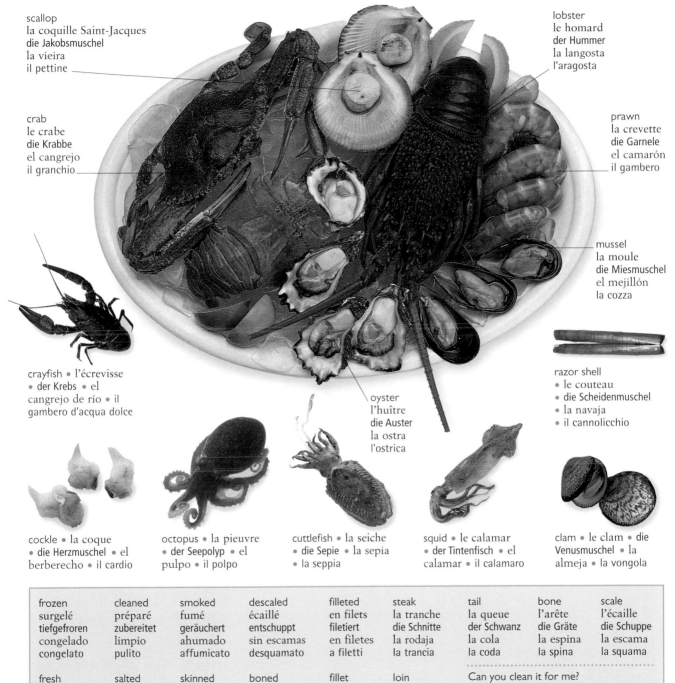

scallop
la coquille Saint-Jacques
die Jakobsmuschel
la vieira
il pettine

crab
le crabe
die Krabbe
el cangrejo
il granchio

lobster
le homard
der Hummer
la langosta
l'aragosta

prawn
la crevette
die Garnele
el camarón
il gambero

mussel
la moule
die Miesmuschel
el mejillón
la cozza

crayfish • l'écrevisse
• der Krebs • el
cangrejo de río • il
gambero d'acqua dolce

oyster
l'huître
die Auster
la ostra
l'ostrica

razor shell
• le couteau
• die Scheidenmuschel
• la navaja
• il cannolicchio

cockle • la coque
• die Herzmuschel • el
berberecho • il cardio

octopus • la pieuvre
• der Seepolyp • el
pulpo • il polpo

cuttlefish • la seiche
• die Sepie • la sepia
• la seppia

squid • le calamar
• der Tintenfisch • el
calamar • il calamaro

clam • le clam • die
Venusmuschel • la
almeja • la vongola

frozen	cleaned	smoked	descaled	filleted	steak	tail	bone	scale
surgelé	préparé	fumé	écaillé	en filets	la tranche	la queue	l'arête	l'écaille
tiefgefroren	zubereitet	geräuchert	entschuppt	filetiert	die Schnitte	der Schwanz	die Gräte	die Schuppe
congelado	limpio	ahumado	sin escamas	en filetes	la rodaja	la cola	la espina	la escama
congelato	pulito	affumicato	desquamato	a filetti	la trancia	la coda	la spina	la squama
fresh	salted	skinned	boned	fillet	loin	Can you clean it for me?		
frais	salé	sans peau	sans arêtes	le filet	la longe	Pouvez-vous le préparer pour moi?		
frisch	gesalzen	enthäutet	entgrätet	das Filet	die Lende	Können Sie ihn mir fertig zubereiten?		
fresco	salado	sin piel	sin espinas	el filete	el lomo	¿Me lo puede limpiar?		
fresco	salato	spellato	spinato	il filetto	il lombo	Me lo pulisce?		

vegetables 1 • les légumes 1 • das Gemüse 1 • las verduras 1 • la verdura 1

seed
la graine
der Samen
la semilla
il seme

fava bean • la fève
• die dicke Bohne
• la haba • la fava

runner bean
• le haricot grimpant
• die Stangenbohne
• el ejote
• il fagiolino

green bean • le
haricot vert • die
grüne Bohne • el ejote
• il fagiolino

pea • le petit pois • die
grüne Erbse • el chícharo
• il pisello

pod
la gousse
die Schote
la vaina
il baccello

bean sprout • le germe
de soja • die
Sojabohnensprosse
• el germinado de soja
• il germoglio di soia

bamboo • le bambou
• der Bambus • el
bambú • il bambù

okra • l'okra • die
Okra • el quingombó
• l'okra

corn • le maïs
• der Mais • el maíz
dulce • il granturco

chicory • l'endive
• der Chicorée • la
endibia • la cicoria

fennel • le fenouil
• der Fenchel • el
hinojo • il finocchio

palm hearts • les cœurs
de palmier • die
Palmherzen • los palmitos
• i cuori di palma

celery • le céleri
• der Stangensellerie
• el apio • il sedano

leaf	floret	tip	organic	Do you sell organic vegetables?
la feuille	la fleurette	la pointe	biologique	Est-ce que vous vendez des légumes bios?
das Blatt	das Röschen	die Spitze	biodynamisch	Verkaufen Sie Biogemüse?
la hoja	la cabezuela	la punta	biológico	¿Vende verduras orgánicas?
la foglia	il germoglio	la punta	biologico	Vendete verdure biologiche?
stalk	kernel	heart	plastic bag	Are these grown locally?
le trognon	le grain	le cœur	le sac en plastique	Est-ce qu'ils sont cultivés dans la région?
der Strunk	der Kern	das Herz	die Plastiktüte	Werden sie in dieser Gegend angebaut?
el tallo	la almendra	el corazón	la bolsa de plástico	¿Son productos locales?
lo stelo	il nocciolo	il cuore	la busta di plastica	Queste sono della zona?

arugula • la roquette • die Rauke • la roqueta • la rucola

watercress • le cresson • die Brunnenkresse • el berro • il crescione

radicchio • le radicchio • der Radicchio • el radicchio • il radicchio

Brussels sprout • le chou de Bruxelles • der Rosenkohl • la col de bruselas • il cavolino di Bruxelles

swiss chard • la bette • der Mangold • la acelga • la bietola

kale • le chou frisé • der Grünkohl • la col rizada • il cavolo verde

sorrel • l'oseille • der Garten-Sauerampfer • la acedera • l'acetosa

endive • la chicorée • die Endivie • la escarola • l'indivia

dandelion • le pissenlit • der Löwenzahn • el diente de león • il dente di leone

spinach • les épinards • der Spinat • la espinaca • gli spinaci

kohlrabi • le chou-rave • der Kohlrabi • el colinabo • il cavolo rapa

bok choy • le chou chinois • der Chinakohl • la acelga china • la bieta

lettuce • la laitue • der Salat • la lechuga • la lattuga

broccoli • le brocoli • der Brokkoli • el brócoli • il broccolo

cabbage • le chou • der Kohl • la col • il cavolo

young cabbage • le chou précoce • der Frühkohl • la berza • la verza

vegetables 2 • les légumes 2 • das Gemüse 2 • las verduras 2 • le verdure 2

artichoke
l'artichaut
die Artischocke
la alcachofa
il carciofo

radish
le radis
das Radieschen
el rábano
il ravanello

cauliflower
le chou-fleur
der Blumenkohl
la coliflor
il cavolfiore

turnip
le navet
die Rübe
el nabo
la rapa

potato
la pomme
 de terre
die Kartoffel
la papa
la patata

onion
l'oignon
die Zwiebel
la cebolla
la cipolla

pepper
le poivron
die Paprika
el pimiento
il peperone

chili • le piment • die Peperoni
• la chilaca • il peperoncino

squash
la courge
der Gartenkürbis
la calabacita gigante
la zucca

cherry tomato	celeriac	frozen	bitter	May I have one kilo of potatoes please?
la tomate cerise	le céleri	surgelé	amer	Puis-je avoir un kilo de pommes de
die Kirschtomate	der Sellerie	tiefgefroren	bitter	terre s'il vous plaît?
el jitomate cherry	el apio-nabo	congelado	amargo	Könnte ich bitte ein Kilo Kartoffeln
il pomodorino	il sedano rapa	congelato	amaro	haben?
				¿Me da un kilo de papas, por favor?
carrot	taro root	raw	firm	Mi dà un chilo di patate per favore?
la carotte	le taro	cru	ferme	
die Karotte	die Tarowurzel	roh	fest	What's the price per kilo?
la zanahoria	la raíz del taro	crudo	firme	C'est combien le kilo?
la carota	la radice di taro	crudo	sodo	Was kostet ein Kilo?
				¿Cuánto vale el kilo?
breadfruit	water chestnut	hot (spicy)	pulp	Quanto costa al chilo?
le fruit de l'arbre à pain	la châtaigne d'eau	épicé	la pulpe	
die Brotfrucht	die Wasserkastanie	scharf	das Fleisch	What are those called?
el fruto del pan	la castaña de agua	picante	la pulpa	Ils s'appellent comment?
il frutto dell'albero del pane	la castagna d'acqua	piccante	la polpa	Wie heißen diese?
				¿Cómo se llaman?
new potato	cassava	sweet	root	Quelli come si chiamano?
la pomme de terre nouvelle	le manioc	sucré	la racine	
die neue Kartoffel	der Maniok	süß	die Wurzel	
la papa nueva	la mandioca	dulce	la raíz	
la patata novella	la cassava	dolce	la radice	

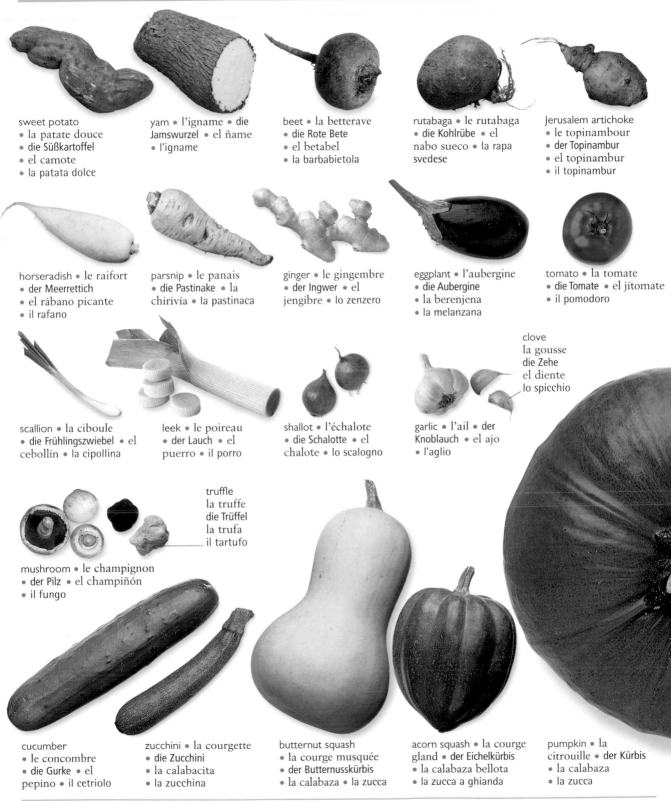

sweet potato
• la patate douce
• die Süßkartoffel
• el camote
• la patata dolce

yam • l'igname • die
Jamswurzel • el ñame
• l'igname

beet • la betterave
• die Rote Bete
• el betabel
• la barbabietola

rutabaga • le rutabaga
• die Kohlrübe • el
nabo sueco • la rapa
svedese

Jerusalem artichoke
• le topinambour
• der Topinambur
• el topinambur
• il topinambur

horseradish • le raifort
• der Meerrettich
• el rábano picante
• il rafano

parsnip • le panais
• die Pastinake • la
chirivía • la pastinaca

ginger • le gingembre
• der Ingwer • el
jengibre • lo zenzero

eggplant • l'aubergine
• die Aubergine
• la berenjena
• la melanzana

tomato • la tomate
• die Tomate • el jitomate
• il pomodoro

scallion • la ciboule
• die Frühlingszwiebel • el
cebollín • la cipollina

leek • le poireau
• der Lauch • el
puerro • il porro

shallot • l'échalote
• die Schalotte • el
chalote • lo scalogno

garlic • l'ail • der
Knoblauch • el ajo
• l'aglio

clove
la gousse
die Zehe
el diente
lo spicchio

truffle
la truffe
die Trüffel
la trufa
il tartufo

mushroom • le champignon
• der Pilz • el champiñón
• il fungo

cucumber
• le concombre
• die Gurke • el
pepino • il cetriolo

zucchini • la courgette
• die Zucchini
• la calabacita
• la zucchina

butternut squash
• la courge musquée
• der Butternusskürbis
• la calabaza • la zucca

acorn squash • la courge
gland • der Eichelkürbis
• la calabaza bellota
• la zucca a ghianda

pumpkin • la
citrouille • der Kürbis
• la calabaza
• la zucca

fruit 1 • le fruit 1 • das Obst 1 • la fruta 1 • la frutta 1

citrus fruit • les agrumes • die Zitrusfrüchte
• los cítricos • gli agrumi

stone fruit • les fruits à noyau • das Steinobst
• la fruta con hueso • la frutta con nocciolo

orange • l'orange
• die Orange • la naranja
• l'arancio

clementine • la clémentine
• die Klementine • la mandarina
clementina • la clementina

peach • la pêche • der Pfirsich
• el durazno • la pesca

nectarine • la nectarine
• die Nektarine • la nectarina
• la pesca noce

pulp
la peau
blanche
die weiße
Haut
la piel
la scorza
interna

tangelo • le tangelo • die
Tangelo • el ugli • il mapo

grapefruit • le pamplemousse
• die Grapefruit • la toronja
• il pompelmo

apricot • l'abricot
• die Aprikose •
el chabacano
• l'albicocca

plum • la prune
• die Pflaume •
la ciruela
• la prugna

cherry • la cerise
• die Kirsche • la
cereza • la ciliegia

segment
le quartier
die Rippe
el gajo
lo spicchio

satsuma • la satsuma
• die Satsuma • la mandarina
satsuma • il satsuma

tangerine • la mandarine
• die Mandarine • la mandarina
il mandarino

apple • la pomme • der Apfel
• la manzana • la mela

pear • la poire • die Birne
• la pera • la pera

zest
le zeste
die Schale
la cáscara
la buccia

lime • le citron vert
• die Limone • la lima •
la limetta

lemon • le citron • die Zitrone
• el limón • il limone

kumquat • le kumquat
• die Kumquat • la naranja
china • l'arancino cinese

basket of fruit • la corbeille de fruits • der Obstkorb
• el frutero • il cestino di frutta

berries and melons • les fruits rouges et les melons • das Beerenobst und die Melonen • las bayas y los melones • i frutti di bosco e i meloni

strawberry • la fraise
• die Erdbeere • la fresa
• la fragola

raspberry • la framboise
• die Himbeere • la frambuesa
• il lampone

melon • le melon
• die Melone • el melón
• il melone

grapes • les raisins
• die Weintrauben • la uva
• l'uva

blackberry • la mûre
• die Brombeere • la zarzamora • la mora

redcurrant • la groseille
• die Johannisbeere • la grosella • il ribes rosso

cranberry • la canneberge
• die Preiselbeere • el arándano rojo • l'ossicocco

blackcurrant • le cassis
• die schwarze Johannisbeere
• la grosella negra
• il ribes nero

blueberry • la myrtille
• die Heidelbeere •
el arándano • il mirtillo

white currant • la groseille blanche • die weiße Johannisbeere • la grosella blanca • il ribes bianco

rind
l'écorce
die Schale
la cáscara
la buccia

seed
le pépin
der Kern
la semilla
il seme

flesh
la pulpe
das Fruchtfleisch
la pulpa
la polpa

watermelon • la pastèque • die Wassermelone • la sandía
• l'anguria

loganberry • la loganberry
• die Loganbeere • la frambuesa Logan • la mora-lampone

gooseberry • la groseille à maquereau • die Stachelbeere
• el capulín • l'uva spina

rhubarb	sour	crisp	seedless	Are they ripe?
la rhubarbe	aigre	croquant	sans pépins	Est-ce qu'ils sont mûrs?
der Rhabarber	sauer	knackig	kernlos	Sind sie reif?
el ruibarbo	amargo	fresco	sin semillas	¿Están maduros?
il rabarbaro	amaro	croccante	senza semi	Sono maturi?
fiber	fresh	rotten	juice	May I try one?
la fibre	frais	pourri	le jus	Je peux goûter?
die Faser	frisch	faul	der Saft	Könnte ich eine probieren?
la fibra	fresco	podrido	el jugo	¿Puedo probar uno?
la fibra	fresco	marcio	il succo	Posso assaggiarne uno?
sweet	juicy	pulp	core	How long will they keep?
sucré	juteux	la pulpe	le trognon	Ils se gardent combien de temps?
süß	saftig	das Fruchtmark	das Kerngehäuse	Wie lange halten sie sich?
dulce	jugoso	la pulpa	el corazón	¿Hasta cuándo durarán?
dolce	sugoso	la polpa	il torsolo	Per quanto tempo si mantengono?

fruit 2 • les fruits 2 • das Obst 2 • la fruta 2 • la frutta 2

mango
la mangue
die Mango
el mango
il mango

pineapple
l'ananas
die Ananas
la piña
l'ananas

avocado
l'avocat
die Avocado
el aguacate
l'avocado

papaya
la papaye
die Papaya
la papaya
la papaia

peach
la pêche
der Pfirsich
el melocotón
la pesca

lychee
le litchi
die Litschi
el lichi
il litchi

pit
le pépin
der Kern
la semilla
il seme

kiwifruit
le kiwi
die Kiwi
el kiwi
il kiwi

Cape gooseberry
le physalis
die Kapstachelbeere
el capulín
l'alchechengi

peel
la peau
die Schale
la piel
la buccia

quince • le coing • die Quitte • el membrillo • la mela cotogna

passion fruit • le fruit de la passion • die Passionsfrucht • el maracuyá • il frutto della passione

banana • la banane • die Banane • el plátano • la banana

guava • la goyave • die Guave • la guayaba • la guaiava

pomegranate • la grenade • der Granatapfel • la granada • il melograno

persimmon • le kaki • die Persimone • el caqui • il cachi

feijoa • le feijoa • die Feijoa • la feijoa • il feijoa

prickly pear • la figue de Barbarie • die Kaktusfeige • la tuna • il fico d'india

star fruit • la carambole • die Sternfrucht • la carambola • la carambola

mangosteen • le mangoustan • die Mangostane • el mangostán • la mangostina

nuts and dried fruit • les noix et les fruits secs • die Nüsse und das Dörrobst • los frutos secos • le noci e la frutta secca

pine nut • le pignon
• die Piniennuss
• el piñón • il pinolo

pistachio • la pistache
• die Pistazie • el
pistache • il pistacchio

cashew nut • la noix de
cajou • die Cashewnuss
• la nuez de la India
• l'anacardio

peanut • la cacahouète
• die Erdnuss • el
cacahuete • l'arachide

hazelnut • la noisette
• die Haselnuss
• la avellana
• la nocciola

Brazil nut • la noix du
Brésil • die Paranuss
• la nuez de Brasil
• la mandorla brasiliana

pecan • la noix
pacane • die Pecannuss
• la nuez • il pecan

almond • l'amande
• die Mandel • la
almendra • la mandorla

walnut • la noix • die
Walnuss • la nuez de
Castilla • la noce

chestnut • le marron
• die Esskastanie • la
castaña • la castagna

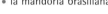

macadamia
• le macadamia
• die Macadamianuss
• la macadamia
• caramellato per intero

fig • la figue • die Feige
• el higo • il fico

date • la datte
• die Dattel • el dátil
• il dattero

prune • le pruneau
• die Backpflaume
• la ciruela pasa
• la prugna secca

shell
la coquille
die Schale
la cáscara
il guscio

flesh
la chair
das Fruchtfleisch
la pulpa
la polpa —

sultana • le raisin de
Smyrne • die Sultanine
• la pasa sultana
• l'uva sultanina

raisin • le raisin sec
• die Rosine • la pasa
• l'uvetta

currant • le raisin de
Corinthe • die Korinthe
• la pasa de Corinto
• l'uva passa

coconut • la noix de
coco • die Kokosnuss
• el coco • la noce di
cocco

green	hard	kernel	salted	roasted	tropical fruit	shelled
vert	dur	l'amande	salé	grillé	les fruits tropicaux	décortiqué
grün	hart	der Kern	gesalzen	geröstet	die Südfrüchte	geschält
verde	duro	la almendra	salado	tostado	las frutas tropicales	pelado
verde	duro	il nocciolo	salato	arrostito	la frutta tropicale	sgusciato
ripe	soft	dried	raw	seasonal	candied fruit	whole
mûr	mou	séché	cru	de saison	le fruit confit	complet
reif	weich	getrocknet	roh	Saison-	die kandierten Früchte	ganz
maduro	blando	desecado	crudo	de temporada	la fruta escarchada	entero
maturo	morbido	essiccato	crudo	stagionale	la frutta candita	intero

grains and pulses • les céréales et les légumes secs • die Getreidearten und die Hülsenfrüchte • los granos y las legumbres • le granaglie e i legumi secchi

grains • les céréales • das Getreide • los granos • le granaglie

wheat • le blé • der Weizen • el trigo • il grano

oats • l'avoine • der Hafer • la avena • l'avena

barley • l'orge • die Gerste • la cebada • l'orzo

millet • le millet • die Hirse • el mijo • il miglio

corn • le maïs • der Mais • el maíz • il mais

quinoa • le quinoa • die Reismelde • la quinoa • la quinoa

seed	fresh	easy-to-cook
la graine	frais	facile à cuisiner
der Samen	frisch	leicht zu kochen
la semilla	fresco	de fácil cocción
il seme	fresco	cottura facile
husk	fragranced	whole-grain
la balle	parfumé	complet
die Hülse	aromatisch	Vollkorn-
la cáscara	perfumado	integral
la pula	profumato	integrale
kernel	cereal	long-grain
le grain	la céréale	à grains longs
der Kern	die Getreideflocken	Langkorn-
el grano	los cereales	largo
il seme	il cereale	a chicco lungo
dry	soak (v)	short-grain
sec	laisser tremper	à grains ronds
trocken	einweichen	Rundkorn-
seco	poner a remojo	corto
secco	mettere a bagno	a chicco corto

rice • le riz • der Reis • el arroz • il riso

white rice • le riz blanc • der weiße Reis • el arroz largo • il riso bianco

brown rice • le riz complet • der Naturreis • el arroz integral • il riso integrale

wild rice • le riz sauvage • der Wasserreis • el arroz salvaje • il riso selvatico

dessert rice • le riz rond • der Milchreis • el arroz bomba • il riso da budino

processed grains • les céréales traitées • die verarbeiteten Getreidearten • los granos procesados • i cereali trattati

couscous • le couscous • der Kuskus • el cuscús • il cuscus

cracked wheat • le blé écrasé • der Weizenschrot • el trigo partido • il grano spezzato

semolina • la semoule • der Grieß • la sémola • la semola

bran • le son • die Kleie • el salvado • la crusca

beans and peas • les haricots et les pois • die Bohnen und die Erbsen • los frijoles y los chícharos • i fagioli e i piselli

lima beans • les gros haricots blancs • die Mondbohnen • el frijol blanco • i fagioli cannellini

navy beans • les haricots blancs • die weißen Bohnen • el frijol blanco chico • i fagioli bianchi

kidney beans • les haricots rouges • die roten Bohnen • el frijol rojo • i fagioli di Spagna

aduki beans • les adzukis • die Adzuki-bohnen • el frijol morado • i fagioli aduki

fava beans • les fèves • die Saubohnen • las habas • le fave

soybeans • les graines de soja • die Sojabohnen • la semilla de soja • i semi di soia

black-eyed peas • les haricots à œil noir • die Teparybohnen • el frijol de ojo negro • i fagioli dall'occhio nero

pinto beans • les haricots pinto • die Pintobohnen • el frijol pinto • i fagioli borlotti

mung beans • les haricots mung • die Mungbohnen • el frijol mung • i fagioli mung

flageolet beans • les flageolets • die französischen Bohnen • el frijol flageolet • i fagioli nani

brown lentils • les lentilles • die braunen Linsen • la lenteja castellana • le lenticchie marroni

red lentils • les lentilles rouges • die roten Linsen • la lenteja roja • le lenticchie rosse

peas • les petits pois • die grünen Erbsen • los chícharos • i piselli

chick peas • les pois chiches • die Kichererbsen • los garbanzos • i ceci

split peas • les pois cassés • die getrockneten Erbsen • los chícharos secos • i piselli spaccati

seeds • les graines • die Körner • las semillas • i semi

pumpkin seed • la graine de potiron • der Kürbiskern • la pepita de calabaza • il seme di zucca

mustard seed • le grain de moutarde • das Senfkorn • la semilla de mostaza • il seme di mostarda

caraway • la graine de carvi • der Kümmel • el carvi • il seme di carvi

sesame seed • la graine de sésame • das Sesamkorn • la semilla de sésamo • il seme di sesamo

sunflower seed • la graine de tournesol • der Sonnenblumenkern • la semilla de girasol • il seme di girasole

herbs and spices • les herbes et les épices • die Kräuter und Gewürze • las hierbas y las especias • le erbe aromatiche e le spezie

spices • les épices • die Gewürze • las especias • le spezie

vanilla • la vanille
• die Vanille • la
vainilla • la vaniglia

nutmeg • la noix
de muscade • die
Muskatnuss • la nuez
moscada • la noce
moscata

mace • le macis • die
Muskatblüte • la macis
• il macis

turmeric • le curcuma
• die Kurkuma • la
cúrcuma • la curcuma

cumin • le cumin • der
Kreuzkümmel • el
comino • il cumino

bouquet garni
• le bouquet garni
• die Kräutermischung
• el ramillete
aromático • il
mazzetto odoroso

allspice • le poivre de
la Jamaïque • der
Piment • la pimienta
de Jamaica • il pepe
della Giamaica

peppercorn • le grain
de poivre • das Pfeffer-
korn • la pimienta en
grano • il grano di pepe

fenugreek • le fenugrec
• der Bockshornklee
• el heno griego • il
fieno greco

chili • le piment • der
Chili • el chile piquín
• il peperoncino rosso

whole
en morceaux
ganz
entero
intero

crushed
écrasé
zerstoßen
machacado
tritato

saffron • le safran
• der Safran • el
azafrán • lo zafferano

cardamom • la
cardamome • der
Kardamom • el
cardamono • il
cardamomo

curry powder • la
poudre de curry • das
Currypulver • el curry
en polvo • la polvere
di curry

paprika • le paprika
• der Paprika • el
pimentón • la paprica

ground
en poudre
gemahlen
molido
macinato

flakes
en flocons
geraspelt
a hojuelas
a scaglie

garlic • l'ail • der
Knoblauch • el ajo
• l'aglio

english • français • deutsch • español • italiano

herbs • les herbes • die Kräuter • las hierbas • le erbe aromatiche

sticks
les bâtons
die Stangen
las rajas
i bastoncini

cinnamon • la cannelle • **der Zimt** • la canela • la cannella

lemon grass • la citronnelle • **das Zitronengras** • la citronela • la citronella

cloves • le clou de girofle • **die Gewürznelke** • los clavos • i chiodi di garofano

star anise • l'anis étoilé • **der Sternarnis** • el anís estrellado • l'anice stellato

ginger • le gingembre • **der Ingwer** • el jengibre • lo zenzero

fennel • le fenouil • **der Fenchel** • el hinojo • il finocchio

fennel seeds
les graines de fenouil
die Fenchelsamen
las semillas de hinojo
i semi di finocchio

bay leaf • la feuille de laurier • **das Lorbeerblatt** • el laurel • l'alloro

parsley • le persil • **die Petersilie** • el perejil • il prezzemolo

chives • la ciboulette • **der Schnittlauch** • los cebollinos • l'erba cipollina

mint • la menthe • **die Minze** • la menta • la menta

thyme • le thym • **der Thymian** • el tomillo • il timo

sage • la sauge • **der Salbei** • la salvia • la salvia

tarragon • l'estragon • **der Estragon** • el estragón • il dragoncello

marjoram • la marjolaine • **der Majoran** • la mejorana • la maggiorana

basil • le basilic • **das Basilikum** • la albahaca • il basilico

oregano • l'origan • **der Oregano** • el orégano • l'origano

coriander • la coriandre • **der Koriander** • el cilantro • il coriandolo

dill • l'aneth • **der Dill** • el eneldo • l'aneto

rosemary • le romarin • **der Rosmarin** • el romero • il rosmarino

bottled foods • les aliments en bouteilles • die Nahrungsmittel in Flaschen • los alimentos embotellados • i cibi imbottigliati

walnut oil • l'huile de noix • das Walnussöl • el aceite de nueces • l'olio di noce

grapeseed oil • l'huile de raisin • das Traubenkernöl • el aceite de semillas de uva • l'olio di semi d'uva

cork
le bouchon
der Korken
el corcho
il tappo

sunflower oil • l'huile de tournesol • das Sonnenblumenöl • el aceite de girasol • l'olio di semi di girasole

almond oil • l'huile d'amande • das Mandelöl • el aceite de almendras • l'olio di mandorla

sesame seed oil • l'huile de sésame • das Sesamöl • el aceite de sésamo • l'olio di sesamo

hazelnut oil • l'huile de noisette • das Haselnussöl • el aceite de avellanas • l'olio di noccioline

olive oil • l'huile d'olive • das Olivenöl • el aceite de oliva • l'olio d'oliva

herbs • les herbes • die Kräuter • las hierbas • le erbe aromatiche

flavored oil • l'huile parfumée • das aromatische Öl • el aceite aromatizado • l'olio aromatizzato

oils • les huiles • die Öle • los aceites • gli oli

sweet spreads • les produits à tartiner • der süße Aufstrich • las conservas dulces • le confetture

jar • le pot • das Glas • el tarro • il barattolo

honeycomb • le gâteau de miel • die Honigwabe • el panal • il favo

set honey
le miel solide
der feste Honig
la miel cristalizada
il miele condensato

lemon curd • la pâte à tartiner au citron • der Zitronenaufstrich • la crema de limón • la crema al limone

raspberry jam • la confiture de framboises • die Himbeerkonfitüre • la mermelada de frambuesa • la marmellata di lamponi

marmalade • la confiture d'oranges • die Orangenmarmelade • la mermelada de naranja • la marmellata di agrumi

clear honey • le miel liquide • der flüssige Honig • la miel líquida • il miele sciolto

maple syrup • le sirop d'érable • der Ahornsirup • la miel de maple • lo sciroppo d'acero

condiments and spreads • les condiments • die Würzen • los condimentos • condimenti e cibi da spalmare

bottle
la bouteille
die Flasche
la botella
la bottiglia

cider vinegar
le vinaigre de cidre
der Apfelweinessig
el vinagre de sidra
l'aceto di sidro

balsamic vinegar
le vinaigre balsamique
der Gewürzessig
el vinagre balsámico
l'aceto balsamico

English mustard
• la moutarde anglaise
• der englische Senf
• la mostaza inglesa
• la senape

mayonnaise • la mayonnaise
• die Majonäse • la mayonesa
• la maionese

ketchup • le ketchup
• der Ketchup • la
catsup • il ketchup

French mustard • la
moutarde française
• der französische Senf
• la mostaza francesa
• la mostarda

malt vinegar
• le vinaigre de malt
• der Malzessig • el
vinagre de malta
• l'aceto di malto

wine vinegar
• le vinaigre de vin
• der Weinessig
• el vinagre de vino
• l'aceto di vino

sauce • la sauce
• die Soße
• la salsa
• la salsa

wholegrain mustard
• la moutarde en
grains • der grobe Senf
• la mostaza en grano
• la mostarda con semi

chutney • le chutney
• das Chutney
• el chutney
• il chutney

vinegar • le vinaigre • der Essig • el vinagre • l'aceto

---

sealed jar • le bocal
scellé • das Einmachglas
• el tarro hermético
• il barattolo a chiusura
ermetica

vegetable oil	canola oil
l'huile végétale	l'huile de colza
das Pflanzenöl	das Rapsöl
el aceite vegetal	el aceite de colza
l'olio vegetale	l'olio di colza
corn oil	cold-pressed oil
l'huile de maïs	l'huile pressée à froid
das Maiskeimöl	das kaltgepresste Öl
el aceite de maíz	el aceite de presión
l'olio di mais	en frío
	l'olio spremuto a
peanut oil	freddo
l'huile d'arachide	
das Erdnussöl	
el aceite de	
cacahuete	
l'olio di arachide	

peanut butter • le beurre
de cacahouètes • die
Erdnussbutter • la crema
de cacahuete • il burro
di arachidi

chocolate spread • la pâte
à tartiner au chocolat
• der Schokoladenaufstrich
• el chocolate para untar
• la cioccolata spalmabile

preserved fruit
les fruits en bocaux
das eingemachte Obst
la fruta en conserva
la conserva di frutta

dairy products • les produits laitiers • die Milchprodukte • los productos lácteos • i latticini

cheese • le fromage • der Käse • el queso • il formaggio

grated cheese
le fromage râpé
der geriebene Käse
el queso rallado
il formaggio grattugiato

rind
la croûte
die Rinde
la corteza
la crosta

semihard cheese
le fromage à pâte pressée non cuite
der mittelharte Käse
el queso semicurado
il formaggio semiduro

hard cheese • le fromage à pâte pressée cuite • der Hartkäse • el queso curado • il formaggio duro

cream cheese • le fromage à la crème • der Rahmkäse • el queso cremoso • il formaggio cremoso

cottage cheese • le cottage • der Hüttenkäse • el requesón • il formaggio molle fresco

semisoft cheese • le fromage à pâte semi-molle • der halbfeste Käse • el queso cremoso semicurado • il formaggio semimorbido

blue cheese • le bleu • der Blauschimmelkäse • el queso azul • il formaggio tipo gorgonzola

soft cheese • le fromage à pâte molle • der Weichkäse • el queso cremoso • il formaggio morbido

fresh cheese • le fromage frais • der Frischkäse • el queso fresco • il formaggio fresco

---

milk • le lait • die Milch • la leche • il latte

whole milk
le lait entier
die Vollmilch
la leche entera
il latte intero

reduced-fat milk
le lait demi-écrémé
die Halbfettmilch
la leche semidescremada
il latte parzialmente scremato

fat-free milk
le lait écrémé
die Magermilch
la leche descremada
il latte scremato

milk carton
le carton de lait
die Milchtüte
el cartón de leche
il cartone di latte

goat's milk • le lait de chèvre • die Ziegenmilch • la leche de cabra • il latte di capra

condensed milk
le lait condensé
die Kondensmilch
la leche condensada
il latte condensato

cow's milk • le lait de vache • die Kuhmilch • la leche de vaca • il latte di mucca

english • français • deutsch • español • italiano

butter • le beurre • die Butter
• la mantequilla • il burro

margarine • la margarine
• die Margarine • la margarina
• la margarina

cream • la crème • die Sahne
• la crema • la panna

half-and-half cream • la crème
allégée • die fettarme Sahne • la
crema líquida • la panna liquida

whipping cream
• la crème épaisse
• die Schlagsahne
• la crema para batir
• la panna densa

whipped cream
• la crème fouettée
• die Schlagsahne
• la crema batida
• la panna montata

sour cream • la crème
fraîche • die saure
Sahne • la crema ácida
• la panna acida

yogurt • le yaourt
• der Joghurt • el
yogurt • lo yogurt

ice cream • la glace
• das Eis • el helado
• il gelato

eggs • les œufs • die Eier • los huevos • le uova

yolk
le jaune d'œuf
das Eigelb
la yema
il tuorlo

egg white
le blanc d'œuf
das Eiweiß
la clara
la chiara

shell
la coquille
die Eierschale
la cáscara
il guscio

eggcup
le coquetier
der Eierbecher
la huevera
il porta uovo

hen's egg • l'œuf de
poule • das Hühnerei
• el huevo de
gallina • l'uovo
di gallina

duck egg • l'œuf de
cane • das Entenei
• el huevo de pato
• l'uovo di anatra

goose egg • l'œuf
d'oie • das Gänseei
• el huevo de ganso
• l'uovo d'oca

quail egg • l'œuf de caille
• das Wachtelei • el huevo de
codorniz • l'uovo di quaglia

soft-boiled egg • l'œuf à la coque • das gekochte Ei
• el huevo tibio • l'uovo alla coque

pasteurized	fat-free	salted	sheep's milk	lactose	milkshake
pasteurisé	sans matières grasses	salé	le lait de brebis	le lactose	le milk-shake
pasteurisiert	fettfrei	gesalzen	die Schafmilch	die Laktose	der Milchshake
pasteurizado	sin grasa	salado	la lech`e de oveja	la lactosa	la malteada
pastorizzato	senza grassi	salato	il latte di pecora	il lattosio	il frullato
unpasteurized	powdered milk	unsalted	buttermilk	homogenized	frozen yogurt
non pasteurisé	le lait en poudre	non salé	le babeurre	homogénéisé	le yaourt surgelé
unpasteurisiert	das Milchpulver	ungesalzen	die Buttermilch	homogenisiert	der gefrorene Joghurt
sin pasteurizar	la leche en polvo	sin sal	el suero de la leche	homogeneizado	el yogurt helado
non pastorizzato	il latte in polvere	senza sale	il siero di latte	omogeneizzato	lo yogurt gelato

breads and flours • les pains et la farine • das Brot und das Mehl • el pan y las harinas • il pane e le farine

sliced bread
le pain tranché
das Scheibenbrot
el pan de caja
il pane affettato

poppy seeds
les graines de pavot
der Mohn
las semillas de amapola
i semi di papavero

rye bread
le pain de seigle
das Roggenbrot
el pan de centeno
il pane di segale

French bread
la baguette
das Baguette
la baguette
il filone

bakery • la boulangerie • die Bäckerei • la panadería • il panificio

making bread • faire du pain • Brot backen • haciendo pan • fare il pane

white flour • la farine blanche • das Weizenmehl • la harina blanca • la farina bianca

whole-wheat flour • la farine complète • das Roggenmehl • la harina morena • la farina integrale

stone-ground flour • la farine brute • das Vollkornmehl • la harina integral • la farina integrale

yeast • la levure • die Hefe • la levadura • il lievito

dough
la pâte
der Teig
la masa
la pasta

sift (v) • tamiser • sieben • cernir • setacciare

mix (v) • mélanger • verrühren • mezclar • mescolare

knead (v) • pétrir • kneten • amasar • impastare

bake (v) • faire cuir au four • backen • hornear • cuocere al forno

crust
la croûte
die Kruste
la corteza
la crosta

white bread • le pain blanc
• das Weißbrot • el pan
blanco • il pane bianco

loaf
le pain
der Laib
la hogaza
il filone

brown bread • le pain bis
• das Graubrot • el pan negro
• il pane nero

slice
la tranche
die Scheibe
la rebanada
la fetta

whole-wheat bread • le pain
de son • das Vollkornbrot • el
pan integral • il pane integrale

multigrain bread • le pain
complet • das Mehrkornbrot
• el pan con grano • il pane
di granaio

corn bread • le pain de maïs
• das Maisbrot • el pan de
maíz • il pane di mais

soda bread • le pain à la
bicarbonate de soude
• das Sodabrot • el pan al
bicarbonato sódico • il pane
lievitato con bicarbonato di sodio

sourdough bread • le pain au
levain • das Sauerteigbrot
• el pan fermentado
• il pane aspro

flat bread • le pain plat
• das Fladenbrot • el pan sin
levadura • la schiacciata

bagel • le petit pain américain
• das Hefebrötchen • la dona
• la ciambella

bun • le petit pain rond • das
weiche Brötchen • el bollo
• il panino

roll • le petit pain • das
Brötchen • el panecillo
• il filoncino

fruit bread • le pain aux
raisins secs • das Rosinenbrot
• el pan de frutas • il pane
alla frutta

seeded bread • le pain aux
graines • das Körnerbrot • el pan
con semillas • il pane con semi

naan bread • le naan
• der Naan • el naan
• il naan

pita bread • le pita
• das Pitabrot • la pita
• la pita

crispbread • le biscuit
scandinave • das Knäckebrot
• el pan danés • i crackers

self-rising flour la farine avec la levure das Mehl mit Backpulver la harina con levadura la farina autolievitante	all-purpose flour la farine sans levure das Mehl ohne Backpulver la harina blanca la farina semplice	prove (v) lever gehen lassen levar lievitare	breadcrumbs la chapelure das Paniermehl el pan molido le briciole	slicer la machine à couper der Brotschneider el rebanador l'affettatrice
bread flour la farine traitée das angereicherte Mehl la harina para pan la farina per il pane	rise (v) se lever aufgehen subir crescere	glaze (v) glacer glasieren glasear glassare	flute la flûte die Flöte la barra il filoncino	baker le boulanger der Bäcker el panadero il panettiere

cakes and desserts • les gâteaux et les desserts • Kuchen und Nachspeisen • la repostería • i dolci e i dessert

éclair
l'éclair
das Eclair
el profiterol
il bigné

cream
la crème
die Sahne
la crema
la panna

filling
la garniture
die Füllung
el relleno
il ripieno

profiterole pastry
la pâte à choux
der Brandteig
la masa de profiteroles
il bignè

puff pastry
la pâte feuilletée
der Blätterteig
el hojaldre
la pasta sfoglia

filo dough
la pâte de filo
der Blätterteig
la masa brisa
la pasta filo

fruit cake
le cake
der englische Kuchen
el plum-cake
il dolce alla frutta

fruit pie
la tarte aux fruits
das Obsttortelett
la tartaleta de fruta
la crostatina

meringue
la meringue
das Baiser
el merengue
la meringa

chocolate coated
enrobé de chocolat
mit Schokolade überzogen
cubierto de chocolate
ricoperto di cioccolato

muffin
le muffin
der Muffin
el muffin
il muffin

sponge cake
la madeleine
das Biskuittörtchen
la magdalena
il pan di Spagna

cakes • les gâteaux • das Gebäck • los pasteles • i dolci

pastry cream	bun	pastry	rice pudding	May I have a slice please?
la crème pâtissière	le petit gâteau	la pâte	le riz au lait	Est-ce que je peux avoir une
die Konditorcreme	das Teilchen	der Teig	der Milchreis	tranche s'il vous plaît?
la crema pastelera	el bollo	la masa	el arroz con leche	Könnte ich bitte ein Stück haben?
la crema pasticcera	la focaccina	la pasta	il budino di riso	¿Puedo tomar una rebanada?
				Posso avere una fetta?
chocolate cake	custard	slice	celebration	
le gâteau au chocolat	la crème anglaise	la tranche	la fête	
die Schokoladentorte	der Vanillepudding	das Stück	die Feier	
el pastel de chocolate	las natillas	la rebanada	la celebración	
la torta al cioccolato	la crema	la fetta	la festa	

chocolate chip • les pépites de chocolat • das Schokoladenstückchen • los chips de chocolate • il biscotto con scaglie di cioccolato

lady fingers les boudoirs die Löffelbiskuits las soletillas i savoiardi

florentine • le florentine • der Florentiner • la florentina • il biscotto alle noci

trifle • le diplomate • das Trifle • el postre de soletillas, gelatina de frutas y crema • la zuppa inglese

cookies • les biscuits • die Kekse • las galletas • i biscotti

mousse • la mousse • die Mousse • el mousse • il mousse

sorbet • le sorbet • das Sorbett • el sorbete • il sorbetto

custard pie • la tarte à la crème • die Sahnetorte • el pastel de crema • la torta alla crema

crème caramel • la crème caramel • der Karamellpudding • el flan • il crème caramel

special occasion cakes • les gâteaux de fête • die festlichen Kuchen • los pasteles para celebraciones • le torte per celebrazioni

top tier l'étage supérieur der obere Kuchenteil el último piso il piano superiore

bottom tier l'étage inférieur der untere Kuchenteil el primer piso il piano inferiore

marzipan la pâte d'amandes das Marzipan el mazapán il marzapane

ribbon le ruban das Band el listón il nastro

icing le glaçage der Zuckerguss la alcorza la glassa

wedding cake • le gâteau de mariage • die Hochzeitstorte • el pastel de bodas • la torta nuziale

decoration la décoration die Dekoration la decoración la decorazione

birthday candles les bougies d'anniversaire die Geburtstagskerzen las velas de cumpleaños le candeline

blow out (v) souffler ausblasen apagar soffiare

birthday cake • le gâteau d'anniversaire • der Geburtstagskuchen • el pastel de cumpleaños • la torta di compleanno

delicatessen • la charcuterie • die Feinkost • la charcutería • la salumeria

spicy sausage
le saucisson piquant
die pikante Wurst
el fiambre
la salsiccia piccante

quiche • la quiche • die
Quiche • la quiche
• lo sformato

vinegar
le vinaigre
der Essig
el vinagre
l'aceto

oil
l'huile
das Öl
el aceite
l'olio

uncooked meat •
la viande non cuite •
das frische Fleisch
• la carne fresca
• la carne cruda

counter • le comptoir
• die Theke
• el mostrador
• il banco

salami • le salami
• die Salami
• el salami
• il salame

pepperoni • le pepperoni
• die Pepperoniwurst
• el salchichón
• il salame piccante

pâté • le pâté
• die Pastete
• el paté
• il pâté

mozzarella • la mozzarella
• der Mozzarella • la
mozzarella • la mozzarella

Brie • le brie • der Brie
• el brie • il brie

goat's cheese • le fromage de
chèvre • der Ziegenkäse • el
queso de cabra • il formaggio
di capra

Cheddar • le cheddar • der
Cheddar • el cheddar • il
cheddar

Parmesan • le parmesan
• der Parmesan • el
parmesano • il parmigiano

Camembert • le camembert
• der Camembert • el
camembert • il camembert

rind
la croûte
die Rinde
la corteza
la scorza

Edam • l'édam • der Edamer
• el queso de bola • l'edam

Manchego • le manchego
• der Manchego • el
manchego • il manchego

meat pies • les pâtés en croûte • die Pasteten • los pasteles de carne • i pasticci di carne

black olive
l'olive noire
die schwarze Olive
la aceituna negra
l'oliva nera

chili
le piment
die Peperoni
el chile piquín
il peperoncino

sauce
la sauce
die Soße
la salsa
la salsa

roll
le petit pain
das Brötchen
el panecillo
il panino

cooked meat
• la viande cuite
• das gekochte Fleisch
• el fiambre
• la carne cotta

green olive
l'olive verte
die grüne Olive
la aceituna verde
l'oliva verde

sandwich counter • le comptoir sandwichs • die Sandwichtheke
• el mostrador de bocadillos • la paninoteca

ham • le jambon
• der Schinken
• el jamón
• il prosciutto

smoked fish • le poisson fumé • der Räucherfisch
• el pescado ahumado
• il pesce affumicato

capers • les câpres • die Kapern • las alcaparras
• i capperi

chorizo • le chorizo
• die Chorizo • el chorizo
• il chorizo

in oil • à l'huile • in Öl • en aceite • sott'olio

in brine • en saumure • in Lake • en salmuera • in salamoia

marinated • mariné • mariniert • marinado • marinato

salted • salé • gepökelt • salado • salato

smoked • fumé • geräuchert • ahumado • affumicato

cured • séché • getrocknet • curado • trattato

Take a number, please.
Prenez un numéro, s'il vous plaît.
Nehmen Sie bitte eine Nummer.
Tome un número, por favor.
Prenda un numero, per favore.

Can I try some of that, please?
Est-ce que je peut goûter un peu de ça, s'il vous plaît?
Kann ich bitte etwas davon probieren?
¿Puedo probar un poco de eso?
Posso assaggiare un po' di quello, per favore?

May I have six slices of that, please?
Je voudrais six tranches, s'il vous plaît.
Ich hätte gerne sechs Scheiben davon, bitte.
¿Me pone seis rebanadas de aquél?
Mi dà sei fette di quello, per favore?

prosciutto • le prosciutto
• der Prosciutto • el jamón
serrano • il prosciutto crudo

stuffed olive • l'olive fourrée
• die gefüllte Olive • la aceituna
rellena • le olive ripiene

drinks • les boissons • die Getränke • las bebidas • le bevande

water • l' eau • das Wasser • el agua • l'acqua

bottled water
l'eau en bouteille
das Flaschenwasser
el agua embotellada
l'acqua in bottiglia

sparkling
gazeux
mit Kohlensäure
con gas
frizzante

tap water • l'eau du robinet •
das Leitungswasser • el agua de
la llave • l'acqua dal rubinetto

noncarbonated
non gazeux
ohne Kohlensäure
sin gas
liscia

tonic water • le tonic
• das Tonicwater
la tónica • l'acqua
tonica

soda water • le soda
• das Sodawasser • la
soda • la soda

mineral water • l'eau minérale • das Mineralwasser
• el agua mineral • l'acqua minerale

hot drinks • les boissons chaudes • die heißen Getränke • las bebidas calientes • le bevande calde

teabag • le sachet de thé
• der Teebeutel • la bolsita
de té • la bustina di tè

loose leaf tea
• les feuilles de
thé • die Teeblätter
• el té en hoja
• il tè sciolto

tea • le thé • der Tee • el té • il tè

beans • les grains •
die Bohnen • los
granos • i chicchi

ground coffee
le café moulu
der gemahlene Kaffee
el café molido
il caffè macinato

coffee • le café • der Kaffee • el café • il caffè

hot chocolate • le
chocolat chaud • die
heiße Schokolade • el
chocolate caliente
• il cioccolato caldo

malted drink • la
boisson maltée • das
Malzgetränk • la bebida
malteada • la bevanda
al malto

soft drinks • les boissons non alcoolisées • die alkoholfreien Getränke • los refrescos • le bibite

straw • la paille
• der Strohhalm • el
popote • la cannuccia

tomato juice • le jus de
tomate • der Tomatensaft
• el jugo de tomate
• il succo di pomodoro

grape juice • le jus de
raisin • der Traubensaft
• el jugo de uva
• il succo d'uva

lemonade • la limonade
• die Limonade • la
limonada • la limonata

orangeade • l'orangeade
• die Orangeade • la
naranjada • la spremuta
d'arancia

cola • le coca
• die Cola • la cola
• la coca

alcoholic drinks • les boissons alcoolisées • die alkoholischen Getränke • las bebidas alcohólicas • le bevande alcoliche

can
la boîte
die Dose
la lata
la lattina

beer • la bière • das Bier • la cerveza • la birra

hard cider • le cidre • der Apfelwein • la sidra • il sidro

bitter • la bière anglaise • das halbdunkle Bier • la cerveza amarga • la birra amara

stout • la bière brune • der Stout • la cerveza negra • la birra scura

gin • le gin • der Gin • la ginebra • il gin

vodka • la vodka • der Wodka • el vodka • la vodka

whiskey • le whisky • der Whisky • el whisky • il whisky

rum • le rhum • der Rum • el ron • il rum

brandy • le brandy • der Weinbrand • el brandy • il brandy

dry • sec • trocken • seco • secco

rosé
rosé
rosé
rosado
rosé

white
blanc
weiß
blanco
bianco

red
rouge
rot
tinto
rosso

port • le porto • der Portwein • el oporto • il porto

sherry • le sherry • der Sherry • el vino de jerez • lo sherry

campari • le campari • der Campari • el campari • il campari

liqueur • la liqueur • der Likör • el licor • il liquore

tequila • la téquila • der Tequila • el tequila • la tequila

champagne • le champagne • der Champagner • el champán • lo champagne

wine • le vin • der Wein • el vino • il vino

eating out
sortir manger
auswärts essen
comer fuera
mangiare fuori

café • le café • das Café • la cafetería • il caffè

umbrella
le parasol
der Sonnenschirm
la sombrilla
l'ombrellone

awning
le store
die Markise
el toldo
la tenda

menu
le menu
die Speisekarte
la carta
il menù

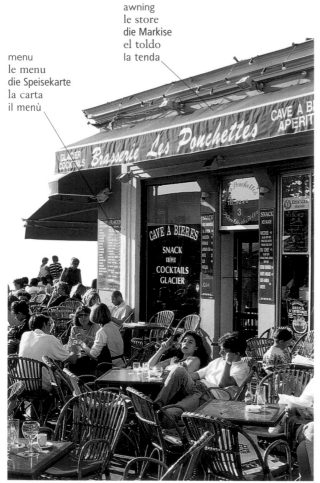

terrace café • la terrasse de café • das Terrassencafé
• la terraza • il bar con terrazza

server	coffee machine	table
le serveur	le percolateur	la table
der Kellner	die Kaffeemaschine	der Tisch
el mesero	la máquina del café	la mesa
il cameriere	la macchina del caffè	il tavolo

sidewalk café • la terrasse de café • das Straßencafé
• la cafetería con mesas fuera • il bar all'aperto

snack bar • le snack • die Snackbar • el bar • lo snack bar

---

coffee • le café • der Kaffee • el café • il caffè

coffee with cream
le crème
der Kaffee mit Milch
el café con leche
il caffè macchiato

black coffee
le noir
der schwarze Kaffee
el café solo
il caffè nero

cocoa powder
le chocolat en poudre
das Kakaopulver
la cocoa
la polvere di cacao

froth
la mousse
der Schaum
la espuma
la schiuma

filter coffee • le café filtre • der
Filterkaffee • el café de cafetera
eléctrica • il caffè filtrato

espresso • l'expresso
• der Espresso • el
expreso • l'espresso

cappuccino • le cappuccino
• der Cappuccino • el
cappuccino • il cappuccino

iced coffee • le café glacé
• der Eiskaffee • el café con
hielo • il caffè freddo

tea • le thé • der Tee • el té • il tè

herbal tea
la tisane
der Kräutertee
el té de hierbas
il tè alle erbe

camomile tea • la camomille • der Kamillentee • la manzanilla • la camomilla

green tea • le thé vert • der grüne Tee • el té verde • il tè verde

tea with milk • le thé au lait • der Tee mit Milch • el té con leche • il tè con latte

black tea • le thé nature • der schwarze Tee • el té sólo • il tè nero

tea with lemon • le thé au citron • der Tee mit Zitrone • el té con limón • il tè al limone

mint tea • l'infusion de menthe • der Pfefferminztee • la menta poleo • il tè alla menta

iced tea • le thé glacé • der Eistee • el té con hielo • il tè freddo

juices and milkshakes • les jus et milk-shakes • die Säfte und Milchshakes • los jugos y las malteadas • le spremute e i frappé

chocolate milkshake
le milk-shake au chocolat
der Schokoladenmilchshake
la malteada de chocolate
il frappé al cioccolato

strawberry milkshake
le milk-shake à la fraise
der Erdbeermilchshake
la malteada de fresa
il frappé alle fragole

coffee milkshake
le milk-shake au café
der Kaffeemilchshake
la malteada de café
il frappé al caffè

orange juice • le jus d'orange • der Orangensaft • el jugo de naranja • il succo d'arancia

apple juice • le jus de pomme • der Apfelsaft • el jugo de manzana • il succo di mela

pineapple juice • le jus d'ananas • der Ananassaft • el jugo de piña • il succo d'ananas

tomato juice • le jus de tomate • der Tomatensaft • el jugo de tomate • il succo di pomodoro

food • la nourriture • das Essen • la comida • il cibo

brown bread
le pain bis
das Graubrot
el pan integral
il pane integrale

scoop
la boule
die Kugel
la bola
la pallina

toasted sandwich • le sandwich grillé • der getoastete Sandwich • el sandwich tostado • il tramezzino tostato

salad • la salade • der Salat • la ensalada • l'insalata

ice cream • la glace • das Eis • el helado • il gelato

pastry • la pâtisserie • das Gebäck • el pan dulce • la pasta

bar • le bar • die Bar • el bar • il bar

glasses
les verres
die Gläser
las copas
i bicchieri

dispenser
la mesure
das Maß
el medidor óptico
il misurino

cash register
la caisse
die Kasse
la caja
la cassa

bartender
le barman
der Barkeeper
el barman
il barista

beer tap
la pompe à biere
der Zapfhahn
la llave de cerveza
lo spillatore di birra

coffee machine
le percolateur
die Kaffeemaschine
la cafetera
la macchina da caffè

ice bucket
le seau à glace
der Eiskübel
la champanera
il portaghiaccio

bar stool
le tabouret de bar
der Barhocker
la silla
lo sgabello

ashtray
le cendrier
der Aschbecher
el cenicero
il posacenere

coaster
le dessous de verre
der Untersetzer
el posavasos
il sottobicchiere

bar
le comptoir
die Theke
la barra
il banco

bottle opener
l'ouvre-bouteille
der Flaschenöffner
el destapador
l'apribottiglie

lever
le levier
der Hebel
la palanca
la leva

tongs
les pinces
die Eiszange
las pinzas
le pinze

stirrer
l'agitateur
der Cocktailrührer
el agitador
il miscelatore

measure
le verre gradué
der Messbecher
el medidor
il misurino

corkscrew • le tire-bouchon • der Korkenzieher
• el sacacorchos • il cavatappi

cocktail shaker • le shaker à cocktails • der Cocktailshaker
• la coctelera • lo shaker

pitcher
le pichet
der Krug
la jarra
la brocca

ice cube
le glaçon
der Eiswürfel
el cubito de hielo
il cubetto di ghiaccio

gin and tonic • le gin tonic
• der Gin Tonic • el gin tonic
• il gin tonic

scotch and water • le scotch
à l'eau • der Scotch mit Wasser
• el whiskey escocés con
agua • il whisky con acqua

rum and coke • le rhum coca
• der Rum mit Cola • la cuba
libre • il rum con coca cola

vodka and orange • la vodka
à l'orange • der Wodka mit
Orangensaft • el desarmador
• la vodka all'arancia

martini • le martini
• der Martini • el martini
• il martini

cocktail • le cocktail
• der Cocktail • el cóctel
• il cocktail

wine • le vin • der Wein
• el vino • il vino

beer • la bière • das Bier
• la cerveza • la birra

single
simple
einfach
sencillo
singolo

double
double
doppelt
doble
doppio

ice and lemon
citron et glaçons
Eis und Zitrone
con hielo y limón
con ghiaccio e limone

a shot • un coup • ein Schuss
• un trago • un bicchiere

measure • la mesure • das
Maß • la medida • la misura

without ice • sans glaçons
• ohne Eis • sin hielo • liscio

with ice • avec des glaçons
• mit Eis • con hielo • con
ghiaccio

bar snacks • les amuse-gueule • die Knabbereien • la botana • gli stuzzichini

almonds
les amandes
die Mandeln
las almendras
le mandorle

cashews
les noix de cajou
die Cashewnüsse
las nueces de la India
gli anacardi

peanuts
les cacahouètes
die Erdnüsse
los cacahuetes
le noccioline americane

potato chips • les chips • die Kartoffelchips
• las papas fritas • le patatine

nuts • les noix • die Nüsse • los frutos secos
• le noccioline

olives • les olives • die Oliven
• las aceitunas • le olive

restaurant • le restaurant • das Restaurant • el restaurante • il ristorante

nonsmoking section
• la partie non-
fumeurs • der Nicht-
raucherbereich • el área
de no fumar • la zona
non fumatori

napkin
la serviette
die Serviette
la servilleta
il tovagliolo

assistant chef
le commis
der Hilfskoch
el ayudante del chef
l'aiuto cuoco

place setting
le couvert
das Gedeck
el cubierto
il coperto

chef
le chef de cuisine
der Küchenchef
el chef
il cuoco

glass
le verre
das Glas
la copa
il bicchiere

tray
le plateau
das Tablett
la charola
il vassoio

kitchen • la cuisine • die Küche • la cocina
• la cucina

server • le garçon • der Kellner
• el mesero • il cameriere

lunch menu	specials	price	smoking section	tip	customer
le menu du déjeuner	les spécialités	le prix	la partie fumeurs	le pourboire	le client
das Mittagsmenü	die Spezialitäten	der Preis	der Raucherbereich	das Trinkgeld	der Kunde
el menú de la comida	los platillos del día	el precio	el área de fumar	la propina	el cliente
il menù del pranzo	i piatti del giorno	il prezzo	la zona fumatori	la mancia	il cliente
dinner menu	à la carte	check	service charge included	buffet	salt
le menu du soir	à la carte	l'addition	service compris	le buffet	le sel
das Abendmenü	à la carte	die Rechnung	Bedienung inbegriffen	das Buffet	das Salz
el menú de la cena	a la carta	la cuenta	servicio incluido	el buffet	la sal
il menù della cena	a la carte	il conto	servizio compreso	il buffet	il sale
wine list	dessert cart	receipt	service charge not included	bar	pepper
la carte des vins	le plateau à desserts	le reçu	service non compris	le bar	le poivre
die Weinkarte	der Dessertwagen	die Quittung	ohne Bedienung	die Bar	der Pfeffer
la lista de vinos	el carrito de los postres	el recibo	servicio no incluido	el bar	la pimienta
la lista dei vini	il carrello dei dolci	la ricevuta	servizio non compreso	il bar	il pepe

english • français • deutsch • español • italiano

menu • la carte • die Speisekarte
• la carta • il menù

child's meal • le menu
d'enfant • die Kinderportion
• el menú para niños
• il menù per bambini

order (v) • commander • bestellen
• ordenar • ordinare

pay (v) • payer • bezahlen • pagar • pagare

courses • les plats • die Gänge • los platos • le portate

apéritif • l'apéritif • der
Aperitif • el aperitivo
• l'aperitivo

appetizer • l'entrée
• die Vorspeise • la
entrada • l'antipasto

soup • la soupe
• die Suppe • la sopa
• la minestra

main course • le plat principal
• das Hauptgericht • el plato principal
• il piatto principale

side order • l'accompagnement
• die Beilage • el acompañamiento
• il contorno

fork
la fourchette
die Gabel
el tenedor
la forchetta

coffee spoon
la cuiller à café
der Kaffeelöffel
la cucharilla de café
il cucchiaino da caffè

dessert • le dessert • der Nachtisch
• el postre • il dessert

coffee • le café • der Kaffee
• el café • il caffè

A table for two, please.
Une table pour deux, s'il vous plaît.
Einen Tisch für zwei Personen, bitte.
Una mesa para dos, por favor.
Un tavolo per due, per favore.

Can I see the menu/wine list, please?
La carte/la carte des vins, s'il vous plaît.
Die Speisekarte/Weinkarte, bitte.
¿Podría ver la carta/lista de vinos, por favor?
Posso vedere il menù\la lista dei vini, per favore?

Is there a prix fixe menu?
Avez-vous un menu à prix fixe?
Haben Sie ein Tagesmenü?
¿Hay menú del día?
C'è un menù a prezzo fisso ?

Do you have any vegetarian dishes?
Avez vous des plats végétariens?
Haben Sie vegetarische Gerichte?
¿Tiene platos vegetarianos?
Avete dei piatti vegetariani ?

Could I have the check/a receipt, please?
L'addition/un reçu, s'il vous plaît.
Könnte ich bitte die Rechnung/eine Quittung haben?
¿Me podría traer la cuenta/un recibo?
Posso avere il conto\una ricevuta per favore?

Can we pay separately?
Pouvons-nous payer chacun notre part?
Können wir getrennt zahlen?
¿Podemos pagar por separado?
Possiamo pagare separatamente?

Where are the rest rooms, please?
Où sont les toilettes, s'il vous plaît?
Wo sind die Toiletten, bitte?
¿Dónde están los baños, por favor?
Dove sono i bagni per favore?

fast food • la restauration rapide • der Schnellimbiss • la comida rápida • il fast food

burger
le hamburger
der Hamburger
la hamburguesa
l'hamburger

straw
la paille
der Strohhalm
el popote
la cannuccia

soft drink
la boisson non-alcoolisée
das alkoholfreie Getränk
el refresco
la bibita

French fries
les frites
die Pommes frites
las papas fritas
le patate fritte

paper napkin
la serviette en papier
die Papierserviette
la servilleta de papel
il tovagliolo di carta

tray
le plateau
das Tablett
la charola
il vassoio

burger meal • le hamburger avec des frites • der Hamburger mit Pommes frites • la hamburguesa con papas fritas • il pasto con hamburger

pizza • la pizza • die Pizza • la pizza • la pizza

price list • le tarif • die Preisliste • la lista de precios • il listino

canned drink
la boisson en boîte
das Dosengetränk
el refresco en lata
la bibita in lattina

pizzeria
la pizzeria
die Pizzeria
la pizzería
la pizzeria

fast food restaurant
le restaurant rapide
die Imbissstube
el restaurant de hamburguesas
il fastfood

menu
la carte
die Speisekarte
el menú
il menù

eat in
manger sur place
hier essen
para comer en el local
mangiare sul posto

carry out
à emporter
zum Mitnehmen
para llevar
da portar via

reheat (v)
réchauffer
aufwärmen
recalentar
riscaldare

ketchup
le ketchup
der Tomatenketchup
la catsup
la salsa di pomodoro

Can I have that to go, please?
À emporter, s'il vous plaît.
Ich möchte das mitnehmen.
¿Me lo pone para llevar?
Me lo dà da portar via?

Do you deliver?
Est-ce que vous livrez à domicile?
Liefern Sie ins Haus?
¿Entregan a domicilio?
Consegnate a domocilio?

delivery • la livraison à domicile • die Lieferung ins Haus • la entrega a domicilio • la consegna a domicilio

hot-dog stand • le marchand de hot-dogs • der Imbissstand • el puesto • il venditore ambulante

bun
le petit pan
das Brötchen
el bollo
il panino

mustard
la moutarde
der Senf
la mostaza
la senape

sausage
la saucisse
die Wurst
la salchicha
il wurstel

hamburger • le hamburger • der Hamburger • la hamburguesa • l'hamburger

chicken burger • le hamburger au poulet • der Chickenburger • la hamburguesa de pollo • l'hamburger di pollo

veggie burger • le hamburger végétarien • der vegetarische Hamburger • la hamburguesa vegetariana • l'hamburger vegetariano

hot dog • le hot-dog • das Hot Dog • el hot dog • l'hot dog

filling
la garniture
die Füllung
el relleno
il ripieno

sub • le sandwich • der Sandwich • el bocadillo • il tramezzino

club sandwich • le sandwich mixte • der Klubsandwich • el club sandwich • il tramezzino a strati

open-face sandwich • le canapé • das belegte Brot • el sandwich abierto • il tramezzino aperto

wrap • le taco • das gefüllte Fladenbrot • el taco • la piadina

sauce
la sauce
die Soße
la salsa
la salsa

savory
salé
salzig
salado
salato

sweet
sucré
süß
dulce
dolce

topping
la garniture
der Pizzabelag
los ingredientes
il condimento

kabob • le kébab • der Kebab • el alambre • il kebab

chicken nuggets • les beignets de poulet • die Hähnchenstückchen • los nuggets de pollo • i bocconcini di pollo

crepes • les crêpes • die Crêpes • la crêpe • la crêpe

fish and chips • le poisson avec des frites • der Bratfisch mit Pommes frites • el pescado con papas fritas • il pesce con patatine

ribs • les côtes • die Rippen • las costillas • le costolette

fried chicken • le poulet frit • das gebratene Hähnchen • el pollo frito • il pollo fritto

pizza • la pizza • die Pizza • la pizza • la pizza

breakfast • le petit déjeuner • das Frühstück • el desayuno • la colazione

milk
le lait
die Milch
la leche
il latte

cereal
les céréales
die Getreideflocken
los cereales
il cereale

jam
la confiture
die Konfitüre
la mermelada
la marmellata

dried fruit
les fruit secs
das Dörrobst
la fruta seca
la frutta secca

ham
le jambon
der Schinken
el jamón
il prosciutto

cheese
le fromage
der Käse
el queso
il formaggio

crispbread
le biscuit scandinave
das Knäckebrot
la galleta de centeno
il pane biscottato

breakfast buffet • le buffet du petit déjeuner • das Frühstücks-
buffet • el buffet de desayuno • il buffet della colazione

marmalade
la confiture d'oranges
die Orangenmarmelade
la mermelada de naranja
la marmellata di agrumi

pâté
le pâté
die Pastete
el paté
il pâté

butter
le beurre
die Butter
la mantequilla
il burro

fruit juice
le jus de fruit
der Obstsaft
el jugo de frutas
il succo di frutta

coffee
le café
der Kaffee
el café
il caffè

croissant
le croissant
das Croissant
el croissant
il cornetto

hot chocolate
le chocolat chaud
die Schokolade
el chocolate caliente
la cioccolata calda

tea
le thé
der Tee
el té
il tè

breakfast table • la table du petit déjeuner • der Frühstückstisch •
la mesa del desayuno • il tavolo della colazione

drinks • les boissons • die Getränke • las bebidas
• le bevande

brioche • la brioche • **die Brioche** • el pan dulce • la brioche

bread • le pain • **das Brot** • el pan • il pane

toast
le toast
der Toast
el pan tostado
il pane tostato

tomato
la tomate
die Tomate
el jitomate
il pomodoro

blood sausage
le boudin
die Blutwurst
la morcilla
il sanguinaccio

sausage
la saucisse
das Würstchen
la salchicha
la salsiccia

fried egg
l'œuf sur le plat
das Spiegelei
el huevo estrellado
l'uovo fritto

bacon
le bacon
der Frühstücksspeck
el tocino
la pancetta

English breakfast • le petit déjeuner anglais • **das englische Frühstück** • el desayuno inglés • la colazione all'inglese

smoked herring • les kippers • **die Räucherheringe** • los arenques ahumados • le aringhe affumicate

French toast • le pain perdu • **das in Ei gebratene Brot** • el pan francés • il pane fritto all'uovo

yolk
le jaune d'œuf
das Eigelb
la yema
il tuorlo

soft-boiled egg • l'œuf à la coque • **das gekochte Ei** • el huevo tibio • l'uovo alla coque

scrambled eggs • les œufs brouillés • **das Rührei** • los huevos revueltos • le uova strapazzate

whipped cream
la crème
die Sahne
la crema
la panna

fruit yogurt
le yaourt aux fruits
der Früchtejoghurt
el yogurt de frutas
lo yogurt alla frutta

crepes • les crêpes • **die Pfannkuchen** • las crepas • le crêpes

waffles • les gaufres • **die Waffeln** • los waffles • i waffle

oatmeal • le porridge • **der Porridge** • la avena • il porridge

fresh fruit • les fruits • **das Obst** • la fruta fresca • la frutta fresca

dinner • le repas • die Hauptmahlzeit • la comida principal • la cena

soup • le potage • die Suppe
• la sopa • la minestra

broth • le bouillon • die
Brühe • el caldo • la zuppa

stew • le ragoût • der Eintopf
• el guiso • lo stufato

curried lamb • le curry • das
Curry • el curry • il curry

roast • le rôti • der Braten
• el asado • l'arrosto

pie • la tourte • die Pastete
• la empanada • il pasticcio

soufflé • le soufflé • das
Soufflé • el soufflé • il soufflé

kabob • le chiche-kébab
• der Schaschlik • la brocheta
• lo spiedino

meatballs • les boulettes de
viande • die Fleischklöße
• las albóndigas • le polpette

omelette • l'omelette
• das Omelett • la omelette
• la frittata

noodles • les nouilles
• die Nudeln • los
fideos • i taglierini

stir fry • le sauté • das
Schnellbratgericht • el
revuelto • la frittura

pasta • les pâtes • die Nudeln
• la pasta • la pasta

rice • le riz • der Reis
• el arroz • il riso

tossed salad • la salade composée
• der gemischte Salat • la ensalada
mixta • l'insalata mista

green salad • la salade verte
• der grüne Salat • la ensalada
verde • l'insalata verde

dressing • la vinaigrette
• die Salatsoße • el aderezo
• il condimento

techniques • la préparation • die Zubereitung • las técnicas • i metodi

stuffed • farci • gefüllt
• relleno • imbottito

in sauce • en sauce • in Soße
• en salsa • al sugo

grilled • grillé • gegrillt • a la
plancha • alla griglia

marinated • mariné
• mariniert • adobado
• marinato

poached • poché
• pochiert • escalfado
• affogato

mashed • en purée • püriert
• hecho puré • schiacciato

baked • cuit • gebacken
• al horno • cotto al forno

pan fried • sauté • kurzgebraten
• frito con poco aceite
• fritto in padella

fried • frit • gebraten • frito
• fritto

pickled • macéré • eingelegt
• en vinagre • sottaceto

smoked • fumé • geräuchert
• ahumado • affumicato

deep fried • frit • frittiert
• frito con mucho aceite
• fritto in olio abbondante

in syrup • au sirop • in Saft
• en almíbar • allo sciroppo

dressed • assaisonné
• angemacht • sazonado
• condito

steamed • cuit à la vapeur
• gedämpft • al vapor
• al vapore

cured • séché • getrocknet
• curado • seccato

study
l'étude
das Lernen
el estudio
lo studio

school • l'école • die Schule • la escuela • la scuola

teacher
l'institutrice
die Lehrerin
la maestra
l'insegnante

chalkboard
le tableau
die Tafel
el pizarrón
la lavagna

schoolboy • l'écolier • der Schuljunge • el colegial • lo scolaro

pupil
l'élève
der Schüler
el alumno
l'alunno

school uniform
l'uniforme
die Schuluniform
el uniforme
la divisa scolastica

desk
le pupitre
das Pult
el pupitre
il banco

book bag
le cartable
die Schultasche
la mochila
la cartella

chalk
la craie
die Kreide
el gis
il gesso

classroom • la salle de classe • das Klassenzimmer • el salón • l'aula

schoolgirl • l'écolière • das Schulmädchen • la colegiala • la scolara

history	art	physics
l'histoire	l'art	la physique
die Geschichte	die Kunst	die Physik
la historia	el arte	la física
la storia	l'arte	la fisica
geography	music	chemistry
la géographie	la musique	la chimie
die Erdkunde	die Musik	die Chemie
la geografía	la música	la química
la geografia	la musica	la chimica
literature	math	biology
la littérature	les mathématiques	la biologie
die Literatur	die Mathematik	die Biologie
la literatura	las matemáticas	la biología
la letteratura	la matematica	la biologia
languages	science	physical education
les langues	les sciences	l'éducation physique
die Sprachen	die Naturwissenschaft	der Sport
los idiomas	la ciencia	la educación física
le lingue	la scienza	l'educazione fisica

activities • les activités • die Aktivitäten • las actividades • le attività

read (v) • lire • lesen • leer • leggere

write (v) • écrire • schreiben • escribir • scrivere

spell (v) • épeler • buchstabieren • deletrear • scandire

draw (v) • dessiner • zeichnen • dibujar • disegnare

english • français • deutsch • español • italiano

colored pencil
le crayon de couleur
der Buntstift
el color
la matita colorata

pencil sharpener
le taille-crayon
der Spitzer
el sacapuntas
il temperamatite

overhead projector • le rétro-projecteur • der Overhead-projektor • el proyector de acetatos • la lavagna luminosa

pen • le stylo • der Füller • la pluma • la penna

pencil • le crayon • der Bleistift • el lápiz • la matita

notebook • le cahier • das Heft • el cuaderno • il quaderno

eraser • la gomme • der Radiergummi • la goma • la gomma

textbook • le livre • das Schulbuch • el libro de texto • il libro di testo

pencil case • la trousse • das Federmäppchen • el estuche • l'astuccio

ruler • la règle • das Lineal • la regla • il righello

question (v) • questionner • fragen • preguntar • domandare

answer (v) • répondre • antworten • contestar • rispondere

discuss (v) • discuter • diskutieren • discutir • discutere

learn (v) • apprendre • lernen • aprender • imparare

principal	answer	grade
le directeur	la réponse	la note
der Schulleiter	die Antwort	die Note
el director	la respuesta	la calificación
il preside	la risposta	il livello
class	homework	year
la leçon	les devoirs	la classe
die Stunde	die Hausaufgabe	die Klasse
la lección	la tarea	el año
la lezione	i compiti	la classe
take notes (v)	essay	dictionary
prendre des notes	la rédaction	le dictionnaire
Notizen machen	der Aufsatz	das Wörterbuch
tomar apuntes	la redacción	el diccionario
prendere appunti	il tema	il dizionario
question	examination	encyclopedia
la question	l'examen	l'encyclopédie
die Frage	die Prüfung	das Lexikon
la pregunta	el examen	la enciclopedia
la domanda	l'esame	l'enciclopedia

english • français • deutsch • español • italiano

math • les mathématiques • die Mathematik • las matemáticas • la matematica

shapes • les formes • die Formen • las formas • le forme

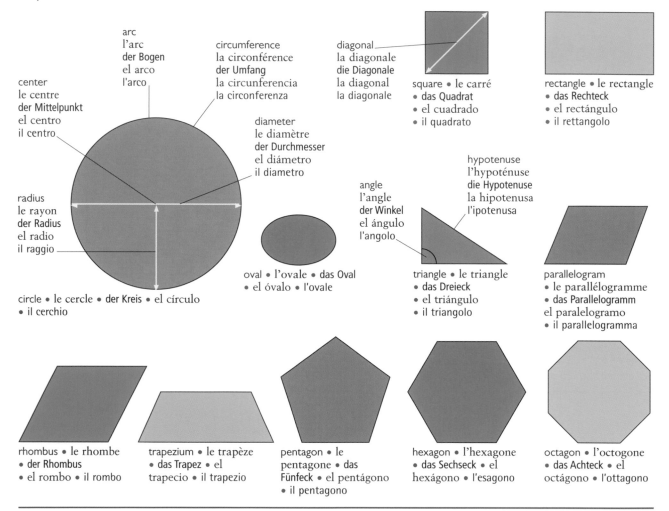

arc
l'arc
der Bogen
el arco
l'arco

circumference
la circonférence
der Umfang
la circunferencia
la circonferenza

diameter
le diamètre
der Durchmesser
el diámetro
il diametro

diagonal
la diagonale
die Diagonale
la diagonal
la diagonale

square • le carré
• das Quadrat
• el cuadrado
• il quadrato

rectangle • le rectangle
• das Rechteck
• el rectángulo
• il rettangolo

center
le centre
der Mittelpunkt
el centro
il centro

radius
le rayon
der Radius
el radio
il raggio

circle • le cercle • der Kreis • el círculo
• il cerchio

oval • l'ovale • das Oval
• el óvalo • l'ovale

angle
l'angle
der Winkel
el ángulo
l'angolo

hypotenuse
l'hypoténuse
die Hypotenuse
la hipotenusa
l'ipotenusa

triangle • le triangle
• das Dreieck
• el triángulo
• il triangolo

parallelogram
• le parallélogramme
• das Parallelogramm
el paralelogramo
• il parallelogramma

rhombus • le rhombe
• der Rhombus
• el rombo • il rombo

trapezium • le trapèze
• das Trapez • el
trapecio • il trapezio

pentagon • le
pentagone • das
Fünfeck • el pentágono
• il pentagono

hexagon • l'hexagone
• das Sechseck • el
hexágono • l'esagono

octagon • l'octogone
• das Achteck • el
octágono • l'ottagono

solids • les solides • die Körper • los cuerpos geométricos • i solidi

base
la base
die Grundfläche
la base
la base

side
le côté
die Seite
el lado
il lato

apex
le sommet
die Spitze
el ápice
l'apice

cone • le cône
• der Kegel • el cono
• il cono

cylinder • le cylindre
• der Zylinder • el
cilindro • il cilindro

cube • le cube
• der Würfel • el cubo
• il cubo

pyramid • la pyramide
• die Pyramide • la
pirámide • la piramide

sphere • la sphère
• die Kugel • la esfera
• la sfera

lines • les lignes • die Linien • las líneas • le linee

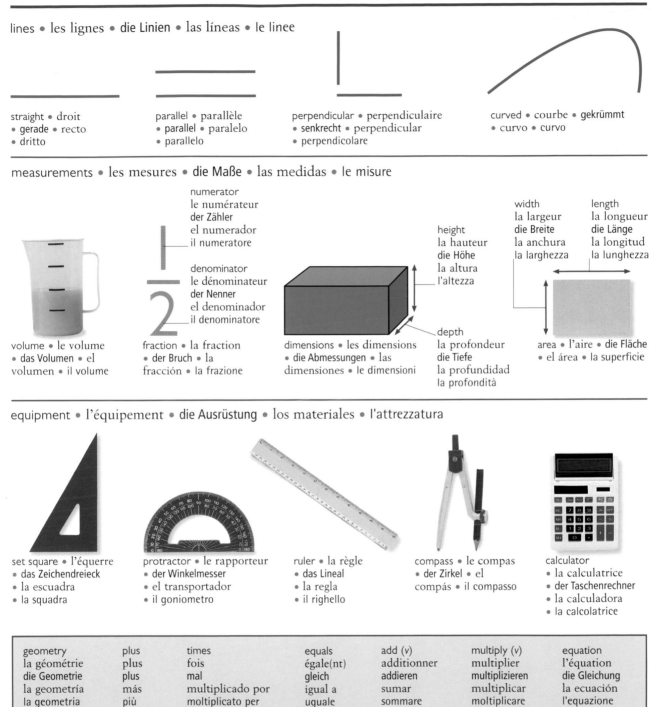

straight • droit • gerade • recto • dritto

parallel • parallèle • parallel • paralelo • parallelo

perpendicular • perpendiculaire • senkrecht • perpendicular • perpendicolare

curved • courbe • gekrümmt • curvo • curvo

measurements • les mesures • die Maße • las medidas • le misure

volume • le volume • das Volumen • el volumen • il volume

numerator
le numérateur
der Zähler
el numerador
il numeratore

denominator
le dénominateur
der Nenner
el denominador
il denominatore

fraction • la fraction • der Bruch • la fracción • la frazione

dimensions • les dimensions • die Abmessungen • las dimensiones • le dimensioni

height
la hauteur
die Höhe
la altura
l'altezza

depth
la profondeur
die Tiefe
la profundidad
la profondità

width
la largeur
die Breite
la anchura
la larghezza

length
la longueur
die Länge
la longitud
la lunghezza

area • l'aire • die Fläche • el área • la superficie

equipment • l'équipement • die Ausrüstung • los materiales • l'attrezzatura

set square • l'équerre • das Zeichendreieck • la escuadra • la squadra

protractor • le rapporteur • der Winkelmesser • el transportador • il goniometro

ruler • la règle • das Lineal • la regla • il righello

compass • le compas • der Zirkel • el compás • il compasso

calculator • la calculatrice • der Taschenrechner • la calculadora • la calcolatrice

geometry	plus	times	equals	add (v)	multiply (v)	equation
la géométrie	plus	fois	égale(nt)	additionner	multiplier	l'équation
die Geometrie	plus	mal	gleich	addieren	multiplizieren	die Gleichung
la geometría	más	multiplicado por	igual a	sumar	multiplicar	la ecuación
la geometria	più	moltiplicato per	uguale	sommare	moltiplicare	l'equazione
arithmetic	minus	divided by	count (v)	subtract (v)	divide (v)	percentage
l'arithmétique	moins	divisé par	compter	soustraire	diviser	le pourcentage
die Arithmetik	minus	geteilt durch	zählen	subtrahieren	dividieren	der Prozentsatz
la aritmética	menos	dividido entre	contar	restar	dividir	el porcentaje
l'aritmetica	meno	diviso per	contare	sottrarre	dividere	la percentuale

science • la science • die Wissenschaft • las ciencias • la scienza

crucible • le creuset
• der Tiegel • el crisol
• il crogiolo

weight
le poids
das Gewicht
la pesa
il peso

bunsen burner
le bec Bunsen
der Bunsenbrenner
el mechero Bunsen
il becco Bunsen

laboratory • le laboratoire
• das Labor • el laboratorio
• il laboratorio

scales • la balance • die
Laborwaage • la báscula
• la bilancia

spring balance • la balance
à ressort • die Federwaage
• la balanza de muelle
• la bilancia a molla

tripod • le trépied
• der Dreifuß • el trípode
• il treppiede

test tube
l'éprouvette
das Reagenzglas
el tubo de ensayo
la provetta

glass bottle
la bouteille
die Glasflasche
el frasco de cristal
la bottiglia di vetro

clamp stand • le statif
• das Stativ • el poste
• il sostegno del morsetto

rack • le support • das Gestell
• el portatubos • la rastrelliera

clamp
la pince
die Klammer
el brazo
il morsetto

stopper
le bouchon
der Stöpsel
el tapón
il tappo

timer • le chronomètre • der
Zeitmesser • el cronómetro
• il cronometro

funnel
l'entonnoir
der Trichter
el embudo
l'imbuto

beaker
la fiole
der Kolben
el matraz
l'ampolla

petri dish • la boîte de Pétri
• die Petrischale • la cápsula
de Petri • la capsula di Petri

experiment • l'expérience • der Versuch • el experimento • l'esperimento thermometer • le thermomètre • das Thermometer • el termómetro • il termometro

syringe • la seringue • die Spritze • la jeringa • la siringa

tweezers • la pince fine • die Pinzette • las pinzas • le pinzette

scalpel • le scalpel • das Skalpell • el bisturí • il bisturi

dropper • le compte-gouttes • der Tropfer • el gotero • il contagocce

forceps • le forceps • die Zange • los fórceps • il forcipe

tongs • la pince • die Greifzange • las tenazas • le tenaglie

spatula • la spatule • der Spatel • la espátula • la spatola

pestle • le pilon • die Keule • la mano de mortero • il pestello

mortar • le mortier • der Mörser • el mortero • il mortaio

filter paper • le papier filtre • das Filterpapier • el filtro de papel • il filtro di carta

safety goggles • les lunettes de protection • die Schutzbrille • las gafas protectoras • gli occhiali protettivi

eyepiece • l'oculaire das Okular • el ocular l'oculare

focusing knob • le bouton de mise au point • der Einstellknopf • la perilla de ajuste • la manopola di messa a fuoco

objective lens la lentille de l'objectif die Objektivlinse la lente del objectivo l'obiettivo

glass rod la tige de verre das Glasstäbchen la varilla de cristal la bacchetta di vetro

stage la platine der Tisch la platina il ripiano

pipette • la pipette • die Pipette • la pipeta • la pipetta

beaker • le bécher • das Becherglas • el vaso de precipitados • il becher

magnet • l'aimant • der Magnet • el imán • la calamita

alligator clip • la pince crocodile • die Krokodilklemme • la pinza • il morsetto

slide le porte-objet der Objektträger el portaobjetos la lastrina

negative electrode • l'électrode négative • die negative Elektrode • el electrodo negativo • l'elettrodo negativo

positive electrode • l'électrode positive • die positive Elektrode • el electrodo positivo • l'elettrodo positivo

mirror le miroir der Spiegel el espejo lo specchio

microscope • le microscope • das Mikroskop • el microscopio • il microscopio

battery • la pile • die Batterie • la pila • la batteria

college • l'enseignement supérieur • die Hochschule • la enseñanza superior • l'università

admissions office
le secrétariat
das Sekretariat
la secretaría
l'ufficio iscrizioni

playing field
• le terrain
de sport • der
Sportplatz
• el campo
deportivo • il
campo sportivo

dining room
le restaurant
universitaire
die Mensa
el comedor
il refettorio

residence hall
• la résidence
universitaire •
das Studentenheim
• la residencia
estudiantil
• la casa dello
studente

health center
le service de santé
die Gesundheitsfürsorge
el centro de salud
l'ambulatorio

card catalogue
le catalogue
der Katalog
el catálogo
il catalogo

campus • le campus • der Campus • el campus • il campus

library card	inquiries	renew (v)
la carte de lecteur	les renseignements	renouveler
der Leserausweis	die Auskunft	verlängern
la credencial	la información	renovar
il tesserino	il banco informazioni	rinnovare
reading room	borrow (v)	book
la salle de lecture	emprunter	le livre
der Lesesaal	ausleihen	das Buch
la sala de lecturas	coger prestado	el libro
la sala di lettura	prendere in prestito	il libro
reading list	reserve (v)	title
les ouvrages recommandés	réserver	le titre
die Literaturliste	vorbestellen	der Titel
la lista de lecturas	reservar	el título
la lista dei libri	prenotare	il titolo
due date	loan	aisle
la date de retour	le prêt	le couloir
das Rückgabedatum	die Ausleihe	der Gang
la fecha de devolución	el préstamo	el pasillo
la data di restituzione	il prestito	la corsia

checkout desk • le
service de prêt
• die Ausleihe
• el mostrador de
préstamos • il
banco prestiti

librarian
la bibliothécaire
die Bibliothekarin
la bibliotecaria
la bibliotecaria

bookshelf
les rayons
das Bücherregal
el librero
lo scaffale

periodical
le périodique
das Periodikum
el periódico
il periodico

journal
la revue
die Zeitschrift
la revista
la rivista

library • la bibliothèque • die Bibliothek
• la biblioteca • la biblioteca

undergraduate • l'étudiant • der Student • el estudiante • lo studente universitario

professor • l'assistant • der Dozent • el profesor • il docente

graduate • la licenciée • die Graduierte • la licenciada • la laureata

gown • la robe • die Robe • la toga • la toga

lecture hall • la salle de cours • der Hörsaal • el auditorio • l'aula

graduation ceremony • la cérémonie de la remise des diplômes • die Graduierungsfeier • la ceremonia de graduación • la consegna delle lauree

schools • les écoles • die Fachhochschulen • las escuelas • le scuole

model
le modèle
das Modell
la modelo
la modella

art school • l'école des beaux arts • die Kunsthochschule • la escuela de Bellas Artes • la scuola d'arte

music school • le Conservatoire • die Musikhochschule • el conservatorio • il conservatorio

dance school • l'école de danse • die Tanzakademie • la academia de danza • l'accademia di danza

scholarship la bourse das Stipendium la beca la borsa di studio	research la recherche die Forschung la investigación la ricerca	dissertation la dissertation die Examensarbeit la tesina la dissertazione	medicine la medecine die Medizin la medicina la medicina	economics les sciences économiques die Wirtschaftswissenschaft las ciencias económicas l'economia
diploma le diplôme das Diplom el diploma il diploma	master's degree la maîtrise der Magister la mestría il master	department l'U.F.R. der Fachbereich el departamento il dipartimento	zoology la zoologie die Zoologie la zoología la zoologia	political science les sciences politiques die Politologie la política la politica
degree la licence der akademische Grad la carrera la laurea	doctorate le doctorat die Promotion el doctorado il dottorato	law le droit die Rechtswissenschaft el derecho il diritto	physics la physique die Physik la fisica la fisica	literature la littérature die Literatur la literatura la letteratura
postgraduate de troisième cycle postgradual posgrado di perfezionamento	thesis la thèse die Dissertation la tesis la tesi	engineering les études d'ingénieur der Maschinenbau la ingeniería l'ingegneria	philosophy la philosophie die Philosophie la filosofía la filosofia	art history l'histoire d'art die Kunstgeschichte la historia del arte la storia dell'arte

work
le travail
die Arbeit
el trabajo
il lavoro

office 1 • le bureau 1 • das Büro 1 • la oficina 1 • l'ufficio 1

office • le bureau • das Büro • la oficina • l'ufficio

computer
l'ordinateur
der Computer
la computadora
il computer

monitor
le moniteur
der Bildschirm
la pantalla
il monitor

desktop organizer
le porte-crayons
der Stifthalter
el portaplumas
il portapenne

file
le classeur
der Ordner
la carpeta
la cartellina

in-tray
la corbeille arrivée
die Ablage für Eingänge
la bandeja de entrada
il vassoio in arrivo

out-tray
la corbeille départ
die Ablage für Ausgänge
la bandeja de salida
il vassoio in partenza

keyboard
le clavier
die Tastatur
el teclado
la tastiera

notebook
le carnet
das Notizbuch
el cuaderno
il blocco

telephone
le téléphone
das Telefon
el teléfono
il telefono

label
l'étiquette
das Schild
la etiqueta
l'etichetta

desk
le bureau
der Schreibtisch
el escritorio
la scrivania

wastebasket
la corbeille à papier
der Papierkorb
el bote de basura
il cestino

swivel chair
le chaise tournante
der Drehstuhl
la silla giratoria
la sedia girevole

drawer unit
le meuble à tiroirs
das Schreibtischschränkchen
la cajonera
la cassettiera

drawer
le tiroir
die Schublade
el cajón
il cassetto

filing cabinet
le meuble-classeur
der Aktenschrank
el archivero
lo schedario

---

office equipment • l'équipement de bureau • die Büroausstattung
• el equipo de oficina • l'apparecchiature da ufficio

paper tray
le magasin à papier
der Papierbehälter
la bandeja para el papel
la contenitore per la carta

paper guide
le guide
die Papierführung
la guía
la guida

fax
le fax
das Fax
el fax
il fax

printer • l'imprimante • der Drucker
• la impresora • la stampante

fax machine • le fax • das Faxgerät
• el fax • il fax

print (v)	enlarge (v)
imprimer	agrandir
drucken	vergrößern
imprimir	ampliar
stampare	ingrandire
copy (v)	reduce (v)
photocopier	réduire
kopieren	verkleinern
fotocopiar	reducir
copiare	ridurre

I need to make some copies.
J'ai besoin de faire des photocopies.
Ich möchte fotokopieren.
Necesito sacar unas copias.
Devo fare delle copie.

office supplies • les fournitures de bureau • der Bürobedarf • la papelería • gli articoli di cancelleria

compliments slip
la fiche compliments
der Empfehlungszettel
la tarjeta membretada
il foglietto di omaggio

box file
le dossier-classeur
der Aktenordner
la caja archivador
la scatola d'archivio

letterhead • l'en-tête
• der Geschäftsbogen
• el membrete
• la carta intestata

envelope • l'enveloppe
• der Briefumschlag
• el sobre • la busta

divider
la fiche intercalaire
der Teiler
el divisor
il divisore

tab • l'étiquette • der
Kartenreiter • el rótulo
• l'etichetta

clipboard • le
clipboard • das
Klemmbrett • la tabla
con portapapeles
• il portablocco con
fermaglio

notepad • le bloc-notes
• der Notizblock
• la libreta • il blocco
per appunti

hanging file • le
dossier suspendu
• der Hängeordner • el
colgante • la cartella
sospesa

accordion file • le porte-
dossiers • der
Fächerordner • la carpeta
de acordeón • il
portacarte a fisarmonica

binder file
• le classeur à levier
• der Leitz-Ordner
• la carpeta de argollas
• il raccoglitore a leva

staples
les agrafes
die Klammern
las grapas
i punti

adhesive tape • le scotch
• der Tesafilm • la cinta
scotch • il nastro
adesivo

ink pad
le tampon encreur
das Stempelkissen
el cojín de la tinta
il tampone di inchiostro

personal organizer
• l'agenda • der
Terminkalender • la
agenda • l'agenda

stapler • l'agrafeuse
• der Hefter
• la engrapadora
• la cucitrice

tape dispenser • le
dévidoir de scotch
• der Tesafilmhalter
• el portacinta
• il dispenser

hole punch • le
perforateur • der Locher
• la perforadora
• il perforatore

rubber stamp • le
cachet • der Stempel
• el sello • il timbro
umido

rubber band
• l'élastique • das
Gummiband • la liga
• l'elastico

bulldog clip • la
pince à dessin • die
Papierklammer • la
pinza • la molletta

paper clip • le
trombone • die Büro-
klammer • el clip
• la grappetta

thumbtack
la punaise
der Reißnagel
la chinche
la puntina

bulletin board • le panneau d'affichage • die
Pinnward • el corcho • il tabellone

office 2 • le bureau 2 • das Büro 2 • la oficina 2 • l'ufficio 2

flipchart
le tableau à feuilles mobiles
das Flipchart
el pizarrón
il poster scorrevole

minutes
le compte rendu
das Protokoll
la minuta
il verbale

easel
le chevalet
das Gestell
el caballete
il cavalletto

report
le rapport
der Bericht
el reporte
la relazione

manager
le directeur
der Manager
el gerente
il direttore

proposal
la proposition
das Angebot
la propuesta
la proposta

executive
le cadre
der leitende Angestellte
el ejecutivo
il dirigente

meeting • le réunion • die Sitzung • la junta • la riunione

meeting room	attend (v)
la salle de conférence	assister à
der Sitzungsraum	teilnehmen
la sala de juntas	asistir
la sala da riunione	partecipare
agenda	chair (v)
l'ordre du jour	présider
die Tagesordnung	den Vorsitz führen
el orden del día	presidir
l'ordine del giorno	presiedere

What time is the meeting?
La conférence est à quelle heure?
Um wie viel Uhr ist die Sitzung?
¿A qué hora es la junta?
A che ora è la riunione?

What are your office hours?
Quelles sont vos heures de bureau?
Was sind Ihre Geschäftszeiten?
¿Cuál es su horario de oficina?
Qual è il vostro orario di lavoro?

projector
le projecteur
der Projektor
el proyector
la lavagna luminosa

speaker
le conférencier
der Sprecher
el orador
il relatore

presentation • la présentation • die Präsentation
• la presentación • la presentazione

business • les affaires • das Geschäft • los negocios • gli affari

laptop
le portable
der Laptop
el laptop
il laptop

notes
les notes
die Notizen
las notas
gli apunti

businessman
l'homme d'affaires
der Geschäftsmann
el hombre de negocios
l'uomo di affari

businesswoman
la femme d'affaires
die Geschäftsfrau
la mujer de negocios
la donna di affari

business lunch • le déjeuner d'affaires • das Arbeitsessen
• la comida de negocios • il pranzo di affari

business trip • le voyage d'affaires • die Geschäftsreise • el viaje
de negocios • il viaggio di affari

appointment
le rendez-vous
der Termin
la cita
l'appuntamento

palmtop computer
l'ordinateur de poche
der Palmtop
la palmtop
il palmtop

date book • l'agenda • der Terminkalender • la agenda • l'agenda

client • le client
• der Kunde • el
cliente • il cliente

managing director
• le directeur
général • der
Generaldirektor
• el director general
• l'amministratore
delegato

business deal • le contrat • das Geschäftsabkommen • el trato
• l'accordo di affari

company	staff	accounting department	legal department
la société	le personnel	la comptabilité	le service du contentieux
die Firma	das Personal	die Buchhaltung	die Rechtsabteilung
la empresa	el personal	el departamento de contabilidad	el departamento legal
la società	il personale	l'ufficio contabilità	l'ufficio legale
head office	payroll	marketing department	customer service department
le siège social	le livre de paie	le service marketing	le service après-vente
die Zentrale	die Lohnliste	die Marketingabteilung	die Kundendienstabteilung
la oficina central	la nómina	el departamento de márketing	el departamento de atención al cliente
la sede	il libro paga	l'ufficio marketing	l'ufficio di assistenza al cliente
branch	salary	sales department	human resources department
la succursale	le salaire	le service des ventes	le service de ressources humaines
die Zweigstelle	das Gehalt	die Verkaufsabteilung	die Personalabteilung
la sucursal	el sueldo	el departamento de ventas	el departamento de recursos humanos
la succursale	lo stipendio	l'ufficio vendite	l'ufficio del personale

computer • l'ordinateur • der Computer • la computadora • il computer

printer
l'imprimante
der Drucker
la impresora
la stampante

monitor
le moniteur
der Monitor
el monitor
il monitor

screen
l'écran
der Bildschirm
la pantalla
lo schermo

CPU • l'unité
centrale • die
Zentraleinheit
• la CPU • il CPU

scanner
le scanneur
der Scanner
el escáner
lo scanner

speaker • le
haut-parleur • der
Lautsprecher • la
bocina • l'altoparlante

key
la touche
die Taste
la tecla
il tasto

keyboard • le
clavier • die Tastatur
• el teclado • la
tastiera

mouse • la souris
• die Maus • el ratón
• il mouse

hardware • le matériel • die Hardware • el hardware • l'hardware

memory	software	server
la mémoire	le logiciel	le serveur
der Speicher	die Software	der Server
la memoria	el software	el servidor
la memoria	il software	il server
RAM	application	port
la RAM	l'application	le port
das RAM	die Anwendung	der Port
el RAM	la aplicación	el puerto
la RAM	l'applicazione	la porta
bytes	program	power cable
les bytes	le programme	le câble électrique
die Bytes	das Programm	das Stromkabel
los bytes	el programa	el cable de alimentación
i byte	il programma	il cavo di alimentazione
system	network	processor
le système	le réseau	le processeur
das System	das Netzwerk	der Prozessor
el sistema	la red	el precesador
il sistema	la rete	il processare

disk • le disque • die Diskette
• el disquete • il dischetto

laptop • le portable • der
Laptop • el laptop • il
computer portatile

hard drive • le disque dur
• das Festplattenlaufwerk
• el disco duro • l'hard drive

modem
le modem
das Modem
el módem
il modem

desktop • le bureau • **das Desktop** • el escritorio • il desktop

menubar
la barre de menus
der Menübalken
la barra del menú
la barra del menu

font • la police • die Schriftart
• la fuente • il carattere

icon • l'icône • **das
Symbol** • el icono
• l'icona

file • le fichier • die
Datei • el archivo
• il file

toolbar • la barre
d'outils • **die
Werkzeugleiste**
• la barra de herra-
mientas • la barra
degli strumenti

scrollbar • la barre de
défilement • **der
Scrollbalken** • la barra
de desplazamiento
• la barra di scorrimento

folder • le dossier
• **der Ordner** • la
carpeta • la cartella

window • la fenêtre
• **das Fenster** • la
ventana • la finestra

wallpaper • le
papier peint • **die
Tapete** • el fondo
• lo sfondo

trash • la poubelle
• **der Papierkorb** • el
basurero • il cestino

Internet • l'internet • **das Internet** • el internet
• **Internet**

email • le courrier électronique • **die E-Mail**
• el correo electrónico • la posta elettronica

browser
le navigateur
der Browser
el navegador
il browser

inbox • la boîte
de réception • **die
Inbox** • la bandeja
de entrada • la
posta in arrivo

website
le site web
die Web-Site
el sitio web
il sito web

email address • l'adresse de courrier électronique
• **die E-Mail-Adresse** • la dirección de correo
electrónico • l'indirizzo di posta elettronica

browse (v) • naviguer • **browsen** • navegar • la navigazione

---

connect (v)	service provider	log on (v)	download (v)	send (v)	save (v)
connecter	le fournisseur d'accès	entrer	télécharger	envoyer	sauvegarder
verbinden	der Serviceprovider	einloggen	herunterladen	senden	sichern
conectar	el proveedor de servicios	entrar en el sistema	bajar	enviar	guardar
collegare	il fornitore di servizi	collegarsi	scaricare	spedire	salvare
install (v)	email account	online	attachment	receive (v)	search (v)
installer	le compte de courrier électronique	en ligne	le document attaché	recevoir	chercher
installieren	das E-Mail-Konto	online	der Anhang	erhalten	suchen
instalar	la cuenta de correo	en línea	el documento adjunto	recibir	buscar
installare	l'account di posta elettronica	in rete	l"allegato	ricevere	cercare

---

media • les médias • die Medien • los medios de comunicación • i mass media

television studio • le studio de télévision • das Fernsehstudio • el estudio de televisión • lo studio televisivo

host	light	set
le présentateur	l'éclairage	le plateau
der Moderator	die Beleuchtung	die Studioeinrichtung
el presentador	el reflector	el plató
il presentatore	la lampada	il set

camera	camera crane	cameraman
la caméra	la grue de caméra	le cameraman
die Kamera	der Kamerakran	der Kameramann
la cámara	la grúa de la cámara	el camarógrafo
la telecamera	il carrello della telecamera	il cameraman

channel	documentary	press	soap	cartoon	live
la chaîne	le documentaire	la presse	le feuilleton	le dessin animé	en direct
der Kanal	der Dokumentarfilm	die Presse	die Seifenoper	der Zeichentrickfilm	live
el canal	el documental	la prensa	la telenovela	las caricaturas	en directo
il canale	il documentario	la stampa	la telenovela	il cartone animato	in diretta

programming	news	television series	game show	prerecorded	broadcast (v)
la programmation	les nouvelles	la série télévisée	le jeu télévisé	en différé	émettre
die Programmgestaltung	die Nachrichten	die Fernsehserie	die Spielshow	vorher aufgezeichnet	senden
la programación	el noticiario	la serie televisiva	el concurso	pregrabado	transmitir
la programmazione	il telegiornale	le serie televisiva	il gioco a premi	in differita	trasmettere

interviewer • l'interviewer • der Interviewer • el entrevistador • l'intervistatore

reporter • la reporter • die Reporterin • la reportera • la cronista

teleprompter • le télésouffleur • der Teleprompter • el teleprompter • il gobbo

anchor • la présentatrice • die Nachrichtensprecherin • la presentadora de las noticias • la presentatrice

actors • les acteurs • die Schauspieler • los actores • gli attori

sound boom • la perche • der Mikrophongalgen • el micrófono de aire • la giraffa

clapper board • la claquette • die Klappe • la pizarra • il ciac

film set • le décor de cinéma • das Set • el plató de rodaje • il set

radio • la radio • das Radio • la radio • la radio

mixing desk
le pupitre de mixage
das Mischpult
la consola
il piano di mixaggio

microphone
le microphone
das Mikrophon
el micrófono
il microfono

sound technician
l'ingénieur du son
der Tonmeister
el técnico de sonido
il tecnico del suono

recording studio • le studio d'enregistrement • das Tonstudio • el estudio de grabación • lo studio di registrazione

radio station	short wave
la station de radio	les ondes courtes
die Rundfunkstation	die Kurzwelle
la estación de radio	la onda corta
il canale radiofonico	l'onda corta
DJ	medium wave
le D.J.	les ondes moyennes
der DJ	die Mittelwelle
el DJ	la onda media
il DJ	l'onda media
broadcast	frequency
l'émission	la fréquence
die Sendung	die Frequenz
la transmisión	la frecuencia
la trasmissione	la frequenza
wavelength	volume
la longueur d'ondes	le volume
die Wellenlänge	die Lautstärke
la longitud de onda	el volumen
la lunghezza d'onda	il volume
long wave	tune (v)
les grandes ondes	régler
die Langwelle	einstellen
la onda larga	sintonizar
l'onda lunga	sintonizzare

law • le droit • das Recht • el derecho • la legge

bailiff
l'huissier de tribunal
der Gerichtsdiener
el guardia
la guardia

witness
le témoin
der Zeuge
el testigo
il testimone

judge • le juge • der Richter
• el juez • il giudice

lawyer
l'avocat
der Rechtsanwalt
el abogado
l'avvocato

jury
le jury
die Geschworenen
el jurado
la giuria

jury box
le banc des jurés
die Geschworenenbank
la tribuna del jurado
il banco della giuria

courtroom • la salle de tribunal • der Gerichtssaal
• la sala del tribunal • l'aula del tribunale

prosecution • l'accusation
• die Staatsanwaltschaft • la
acusación • il pubblico ministero

court official • le greffier
• der Protokollführer • el
auditor • il cancelliere

lawyer's office	summons	writ	court case
le cabinet	l'assignation	l'acte judiciaire	la cause
das Anwaltsbüro	die Vorladung	die Verfügung	der Rechtsfall
el bufete	la citación	la orden judicial	el juicio
lo studio dell'avvocato	la citazione	l'ordine	il procedimento
legal advice	statement	court date	charge
le conseil juridique	la déposition	la date du procès	l'accusation
die Rechtsberatung	die Aussage	der Gerichtstermin	die Anklage
la asesoría jurídica	la declaración	la fecha del juicio	el cargo
la consulenza legale	la dichiarazione	la data di comparizione	l'imputazione
client	warrant	plea	accused
le client	le mandat	le plaidoyer	l'accusé
der Klient	der Haftbefehl	das Plädoyer	der Angeklagte
el cliente	la orden judicial	cómo se declara el acusado	el acusado
il cliente	il mandato	la petizione	l'accusato

english • français • deutsch • español • italiano

court reporter
le sténographe
der Gerichtsstenograf
la taquígrafa
lo stenografo

suspect
le suspect
der Verdächtige
el sospechoso
la persona suspetta

criminal
le criminel
der Straftäter
el criminal
il criminale

defense • la défense
• die Verteidigung • la
defensa • la difesa

defendant • l'accusé
• der Angeklagte • el
acusado • l'imputato

facial composite • le portrait-robot • das Phantombild
• el retrato hablado • il fotofit

criminal record • le casier judiciare • das Strafregister • los antecedentes • la fedina penale

prison guard • le gardien de prison
• der Gefängniswärter • el celador
• la guardia carceraria

cell • la cellule • die Gefängniszelle • la celda
• la cella

prison • la prison • das Gefängnis
• la cárcel • il carcere

evidence	guilty	bail	I want to see a lawyer.
la preuve	coupable	la caution	Je voudrais voir un avocat.
das Beweismittel	schuldig	die Kaution	Ich möchte mit einem Anwalt sprechen.
la evidencia	culpable	la fianza	Quiero ver a un abogado.
la prova	colpevole	la cauzione	Voglio vedere un avvocato.
verdict	acquitted	appeal	Where is the courthouse?
le verdict	acquitté	l'appel	Où est le palais de justice?
das Urteil	freigesprochen	die Berufung	Wo ist das Gericht?
el veredicto	absuelto	la apelación	¿Dónde está el juzgado?
il verdetto	assolto	il ricorso	Dov'è il palazzo di giustizia?
innocent	sentence	parole	Can I post bail?
innocent	la condamnation	la liberté conditionnelle	Est-ce que je peux verser la caution?
unschuldig	das Strafmaß	die Haftentlassung auf Bewährung	Kann ich die Kaution leisten?
inocente	la sentencia	la libertad condicional	¿Puedo pagar la fianza?
innocente	la sentenza	la libertà per buona condotta	Posso versare una cauzione?

farm I • la ferme 1 • der Bauernhof 1 • la granja 1 • la fattoria 1

farmland
les terres cultivées
das Ackerland
las tierras de labranza
il terreno agricolo

farmyard
la cour de ferme
der Hof
el corral
l'aia

outbuilding
la dépendence
das Nebengebäude
el cobertizo
il capanno

farmhouse
la maison d'habitation
das Bauernhaus
la casa de labranza
il casolare

field
le champ
das Feld
el campo
il campo

barn
la grange
die Scheune
el granero
il granaio

farmer
• le fermier
• der Bauer
• el granjero
• l'agricoltore

vegetable garden
le potager
der Gemüsegarten
el huerto
l'orto

hedge
la haie
die Hecke
el seto
la siepe

gate
la barrière
das Tor
la puerta
il cancello

fence
la clôture
der Zaun
la cerca
il recinto

pasture
le pré
die Weide
el pasto
il pascolo

livestock
les bestiaux
das Vieh
el ganado
il bestiame

cultivator
le cultivateur
der Kultivator
el cultivador
l'aratro

tractor • le tracteur • der Traktor • el tractor • il trattore

combine • la moissonneuse-batteuse
• der Mähdrescher • la cosechadora • la mietitrebbia

types of farms • les exploitations agricoles • die landwirtschaftlichen Betriebe • los tipos de granja • i tipi di fattoria

crop • la culture • die Feldfrucht • la cosecha • il raccolto

flock • le troupeau • die Herde • el rebaño • il gregge

crop farm • la ferme de culture • der Ackerbaubetrieb • la granja de tierras cultivables • l'azienda agricola

dairy farm • la ferme laitière • der Betrieb für Milchproduktion • la vaquería • il caseificio

sheep farm • la ferme d'élevage de moutons • die Schaffarm • la granja de ganado ovino • l'allevamento di pecore

poultry farm • la ferme d'aviculture • die Hühnerfarm • la granja avícola • l'azienda avicola

vine • la vigne • der Weinstock • la viña • la vigna

pig farm • la ferme d'élevage porcin • die Schweinefarm • la granja de ganado porcino • l'allevamento di maiali

fish farm • le centre de pisciculture • die Fischzucht • el criadero de peces • il vivaio ittico

fruit farm • l'exploitation fruitière • der Obstanbau • la granja de frutales • l'azienda ortofrutticola

vineyard • la vigne • der Weinberg • el viñedo • il vigneto

actions • les activités • die Tätigkeiten • las actividades • le attività

furrow
le sillon
die Furche
el surco
il solco

plow (v) • labourer • pflügen • arar • arare

sow (v) • semer • säen • sembrar • seminare

milk (v) • traire • melken • ordeñar • mungere

feed (v) • donner à manger • füttern • alimentar • dar da mangiare

water (v) • arroser • bewässern • regar • irrigare

harvest (v) • récolter • ernten • recolectar • raccogliere

herbicide	herd	trough
l'herbicide	le troupeau	l'auge
das Herbizid	die Herde	der Trog
el herbicida	la manada	el comedero
l'erbicida	la mandria	la mangiatoia
pesticide	silo	plant (v)
le pesticide	le silo	planter
das Pestizid	der Silo	pflanzen
el pesticida	el silo	plantar
il pesticida	il silos	piantare

farm 2 • la ferme 2 • der Bauernhof 2 • la granja 2 • la fattoria 2

crops • les cultures • die Feldfrüchte • los cultivos • le colture

wheat • le blé • der Weizen
• el trigo • il grano

corn • le maïs • der Mais
• el maíz • il granturco

barley • l'orge • die Gerste
• la cebada • l'orzo

rapeseed • le colza • der Raps
• la colza • la colza

sunflower • le tournesol
• die Sonnenblume • el girasol
• il girasole

bale • la balle
• der Ballen • la
paca • la balla

hay • le foin • das Heu
• el heno • il fieno

alfalfa • la luzerne
• die Luzerne • la alfalfa
• l'alfalfa

tobacco • le tabac • der
Tabak • el tabaco • il tabacco

rice • le riz • der Reis
• el arroz • il riso

tea • le thé • der Tee • el té
• il tè

coffee • le café • der Kaffee
• el café • il caffè

flax • le lin • der Flachs
• el lino • il lino

sugarcane • la canne à sucre
• das Zuckerrohr • la caña de
azúcar • la canna da zucchero

cotton • le coton • die
Baumwolle • el algodón
• il cotone

scarecrow • l'épouvantail
• die Vogelscheuche
• el espantapájaros
• lo spaventapasseri

livestock • le bétail • das Vieh • el ganado • il bestiame

piglet • le porcelet
• das Ferkel • el chanchito
• il maialino

calf
le veau
das Kalb
el ternero
il vitello

pig • le cochon • das Schwein
• el puerco • il maiale

cow • la vache • die Kuh
• la vaca • la mucca

bull • le taureau • der Stier
• el toro • il toro

sheep • le mouton • das
Schaf • la oveja • la pecora

kid
le chevreau
das Zicklein
el cabrito
il capretto

foal
le poulain
das Fohlen
el potro
il puledro

lamb • l'agneau • das
Lamm • el cordero • l'agnello

goat • la chèvre • die
Ziege • la cabra • la capra

horse • le cheval • das
Pferd • el caballo • il cavallo

donkey • l'âne • der Esel
• el burro • l'asino

chick • le poussin
• das Küken • el
pollito • il pulcino

duckling
le caneton
das Entenküken
el patito
l'anatroccolo

chicken • le poulet • das Huhn
• la gallina • la gallina

rooster • le coq • der
Hahn • el gallo • il gallo

turkey • le dindon
• der Truthahn • el guajolote
• il tacchino

duck • le canard • die Ente
• el pato • l'anatra

stable • l'écurie • der Stall
• el establo • la stalla

pen • l'enclos • der Pferch
• el redil • il recinto

chicken coop • le poulailler
• der Hühnerstall • el gallinero
• il pollaio

pigsty • la porcherie
• der Schweinestall • el
chiquero • il porcile

construction • la construction • der Bau • la construcción • l'edilizia

scaffolding • l'échafaudage
das Gerüst • el andamio
• l'impalcatura

pallet
la palette
die Palette
la tarima
il pallet

ladder
l'échelle
die Leiter
la escalera
la scala

window
la fenêtre
das Fenster
la ventana
la finestra

rafter • le chevron
• der Dachsparren • la viga
del tejado • la trave

construction site • le chantier • die Baustelle • la obra • il cantiere

forklift
le chariot de levage
der Gabelstapler
el montacargas
il carrello elevatore

toolbelt • la ceinture à outils
• der Werkzeuggürtel • el cinturón
de las herramientas • la cintura
per gli attrezzi

beam
la poutre
der Balken
la viga de madera
la trave

lintel
le linteau
der Sturz
el dintel
l'architrave

wall
le mur
die Mauer
la pared
il muro

girder
la poutre
der Träger
la viga de acero
la trave

hard hat • le casque
de sécurité • der
Schutzhelm • el casco
• il casco

cement
le ciment
der Zement
el cemento
il cemento

build (v) • construire • bauen • construir
• costruire

construction worker • le maçon
• der Bauarbeiter • el albañil
• il muratore

cement mixer • la bétonnière • die
Betonmischmaschine • la mezcladora de
cemento • la betoniera

materials • les matériaux • das Material • los materiales • i materiali

brick • la brique • der Ziegelstein • el ladrillo • il mattone

timber • le bois • das Bauholz • la madera • il legno

roof tile • la tuile • der Dachziegel • la teja • la tegola

cinder block • le bloc de béton • der Betonblock • el bloque de hormigón • il blocco di calcestruzzo

tools • les outils • die Werkzeuge • las herramientas • gli attrezzi

mortar • le mortier • der Mörtel • la argamasa • la malta

trowel • la truelle • die Kelle • la paleta • la cazzuola

spirit level • le niveau à bulle • die Wasserwaage • el nivel • la livella

handle
le manche
der Stiel
el mango
il manico

sledgehammer • le marteau de forgeron • der Vorschlaghammer • el mazo • la mazza

pickax • la pioche • die Spitzhacke • el zapapico • il piccone

shovel • la pelle • die Schaufel • la pala • la pala

machinery • les machines • die Maschinen • la maquinaria • i macchinari

steam roller • le rouleau compresseur • die Walze • la aplanadora • il rullo compressore

dump truck • le tombereau • der Kipper • el camión de volteo • il camion con cassone ribaltabile

support • le support • die Stütze • el soporte • il supporto

hook
le crochet
der Haken
el gancho
il gancio

crane • la grue • der Kran • la grúa • la gru

roadwork • les travaux • die Straßenarbeiten • las obras viales • i lavori stradali

tarmac
le macadam goudronné
der Asphalt
el asfalto
il catrame

cone
le cône
der Leitkegel
el cono
il birillo

pneumatic drill • le marteau-piqueur • der Pressluftbohrer • el martillo neumático • il martello pneumatico

resurfacing
le revêtement
der Neubelag
el revestimiento
la riasfaltatura

mechanical digger • la pelle mécanique • der Bagger • la pala mecánica • l'escavatrice meccanica

occupations 1 • les professions 1 • die Berufe 1 • los profesiones 1 • i mestieri 1

carpenter • le menuisier • der Schreiner • el carpintero • il falegname

electrician • l'électricien • der Elektriker • el electricista • l'elettricista

plumber • le plombier • der Klempner • el plomero • l'idraulico

construction worker • le maçon • der Bauhandwerker • el albañil • il muratore

gardener • le jardinier • der Gärtner • el jardinero • il giardiniere

vacuum cleaner l'aspirateur der Staubsauger la aspiradora l'aspirapolvere

cleaner • le nettoyeur • der Gebäudereiniger • el empleado de la limpieza • l'addetto alle pulizie

mechanic • le mécanicien • der Mechaniker • el mecánico • il meccanico

butcher • le boucher • der Metzger • el carnicero • il macellaio

scissors les ciseaux die Schere las tijeras le forbici

fishmonger • la marchande de poissons • die Fischhändlerin • la pescadera • la pescivendola

greengrocer • le marchand de légumes • der Gemüsehändler • el frutero • il fruttivendolo

florist • la fleuriste • die Floristin • la florista • la fioraia

hairdresser • le coiffeur • der Friseur • el estilista • il parrucchiere

barber • le coiffeur • der Friseur • el peluquero • il barbiere

jeweler • le bijoutier • der Juwelier • el joyero • il gioielliere

sales assistant • l'employée de magasin • die Verkäuferin • la vendedora • la commessa estate agent • l'agent immobilier • die Immobilienmaklerin • la agente inmobiliario • l'agente immobiliare

optician • l'opticien • der Optiker • el optometrista • l'ottico

dentist • la dentiste • die Zahnärztin • la dentista • la dentista

mask
la masque
die Maske
la mascarilla
la mascherina

doctor • le docteur • der Arzt • el médico • il medico

pharmacist • la pharmacienne • die Apothekerin • la farmacéutica • la farmacista

nurse • l'infirmière • die Krankenschwester • la enfermera • l'infermiera

vet • la vétérinaire • die Tierärztin • la veterinaria • la veterinaria

farmer • le fermier • der Bauer • el agricultor • l'agricoltore

fisherman • le pêcheur • der Fischer • el pescador • il pescatore

machine gun
• la mitrailleuse
• das Maschinen-
gewehr • la
metralleta
• la mitragliatrice

soldier • le soldat • der Soldat • el soldado • il soldato

uniform
l'uniforme
die Uniform
el uniforme
la divisa

policeman • le policier • der Polizist • el policía • il poliziotto

identity card
• le badge
• das Abzeichen
• la placa de
identificación
• il distintivo

security guard • le garde • der Wächter • el guardia de seguridad • la guardia di sicurezza

sailor • le marin • der Seemann • el marino • il marinaio

fireman • le pompier • der Feuerwehrmann • el bombero • il vigile del fuoco

occupations 2 • les professions 2 • die Berufe 2 • las profesiones 2 • i mestieri 2

model
la maquette
das Modell
la maqueta
il modello

lawyer • l'avocat • der Rechtsanwalt • el abogado • l'avvocato

accountant • le comptable • der Wirtschaftsprüfer • el contador • il commercialista

architect • l'architecte • der Architekt • el arquitecto • l'architetto

scientist • le scientifique • der Wissenschaftler • el científico • lo scienziato

teacher • l'institutrice • die Lehrerin • la maestra • l'insegnante

librarian • le bibliothécaire • der Bibliothekar • el bibliotecario • il bibliotecario

receptionist • la réceptionniste • die Empfangsdame • la recepcionista • l'addetta alla ricezione

mailbag
le sac postal
die Posttasche
la cartera
la borsa

mail carrier • le facteur • der Briefträger • el cartero • il postino

bus driver • le conducteur de bus • der Busfahrer • el chófer • l'autista

truck driver • le camionneur • der Lastwagenfahrer • el chófer • il camionista

taxi driver • le chauffeur de taxi • der Taxifahrer • el taxista • il tassista

pilot • le pilote • der Pilot • el piloto • il pilota

flight attendant • l'hôtesse de l'air • die Flugbegleiterin • la sobrecargo • l'assistente di volo

travel agent • l'agent de voyages • die Reisebürokauffrau • la agente de viajes • l'agente di viaggio

chef's hat
• la toque
• die Kochmütze
• el gorro
de cocinero
• il cappello

chef • le chef • der Koch • el chef • il cuoco

tutu
le tutu
das Ballettröckchen
el tutú
il tutù

musician • le musicien
• der Musiker • el músico
• il musicista

dancer • la danseuse
• die Tänzerin • la bailarina
• la ballerina

actor • le comédien
• der Schauspieler • el actor
• l'attore

singer • la chanteuse
• die Sängerin • la cantante
• la cantante

waitress • la serveuse
• die Kellnerin • la mesera
• la cameriera

barman • le barman
• der Barkeeper • el barman
• il barista

sportsman • le sportif
• der Sportler • el deportista
• l'atleta

sculptor • le sculpteur
• der Bildhauer • el escultor
• lo scultore

notes
les notes
die Notizen
las notas
gli appunti

painter • la peintre
• die Malerin • la pintora
• la pittrice

photographer • le
photographe • der Fotograf
• el fotógrafo • il fotografo

anchor • le présentateur
• der Nachrichtensprecher • el
presentador • l'annunciatore

journalist • le journaliste
• der Journalist • el periodista
• il giornalista

editor • la rédactrice
• die Redakteurin • la
redactora • la redattrice

designer • la dessinatrice
• die Designerin • la diseñadora
• la disegnatrice

seamstress • la couturière
• die Damenschneiderin
• la modista • la costumista

tailor • le couturier • der
Schneider • el sastre • il sarto

transportation
le transport
der Verkehr
el transporte
i trasporti

roads • les routes • die Straßen • las carreteras • le strade

highway
l'autoroute
die Autobahn
la autopista
l'autostrada

toll booth
le poste de péage
die Mautstelle
la caseta de cobro
il casello

road markings
les signalisations
die Straßenmarkierungen
las señales de piso
la segnaletica orizzontale

entrance ramp
la bretelle d'accès
die Zufahrtsstraße
la entrada
la rampa di accesso

one-way
à sens unique
Einbahn-
de sentido único
a senso unico

divider
l'îlot directionnel
die Verkehrsinsel
la línea divisoria
la linea divisoria

junction
le carrefour
die Kreuzung
el crucero
lo svincolo

traffic light
les feux
die Verkehrsampel
el semáforo
il semaforo

inside lane • la file
de droite • **die rechte
Spur** • el carril de
baja • la corsia
interna

middle lane
la voie centrale
die mittlere Spur
el carril central
la corsia centrale

outside lane
la voie de
dépassement
die Überholspur
el carril
izquierdo
la corsia esterna

exit ramp
la bretelle de sortie
die Ausfahrts
la rampa de salida
la rampa di uscita

traffic
la circulation
der Verkehr
el tránsito
il traffico

overpass
l'autopont
die Überführung
el puente
il cavalcavia

hard shoulder
l'accotement stabilisé
der Seitenstreifen
el acotamiento
la corsia d'emergenza

underpass
le passage inférieur
die Unterführung
el paso a desnivel
il sottopassaggio

truck
le camion
der Lastwagen
el camión
il camion

median strip
le terre-plein
der Mittelstreifen
el muro de división
la banchina spartitraffico

crosswalk • le passage clouté • der Fußgängerüberweg • el paso de peatones • il passaggio pedonale

emergency phone • le téléphone de secours • die Notrufsäule • el teléfono de emergencia • il telefono per emergenze

disabled parking place • le parking réservé aux personnes handicapées • der Behindertenparkplatz • el estacionamiento para minusválidos • il parcheggio per disabili

traffic jam • l'embouteillage • der Verkehrsstau • el tráfico • l'ingorgo

map
la carte
die Landkarte
el mapa
la mappa

parking meter • le parc-mètre • die Parkuhr • el parquímetro • il parchimetro

traffic policeman • l'agent de la circulation • der Verkehrspolizist • el policía de tránsito • il vigile urbano

rotary	reverse (v)	tow away (v)
le rond-point	faire marche arrière	remorquer
der Kreisverkehr	rückwärts fahren	abschleppen
la glorieta	meter reversa	remolcar
la rotatoria	fare marcia indietro	rimorchiare
detour	drive (v)	divided highway
la déviation	conduire	la route à quatre voies
die Umleitung	fahren	die Schnellstraße
la desviación	manejar	la autovía
la deviazione	guidare	la carreggiata doppia
park (v)	roadworks	Is this the road to...?
garer	les travaux	C'est la route pour...?
parken	die Straßenbaustelle	Ist dies die Straße nach…?
estacionar	las obras	¿Es ésta la carretera hacia...?
parcheggiare	i lavori stradali	È questa la strada per …?
pass (v)	guardrail	Where can I park?
doubler	la glissière de sécurité	Où peut-on se garer?
überholen	die Leitplanke	Wo kann ich parken?
rebasar	el muro de contención	¿Dónde me puedo estacionar?
sorpassare	il guardrail	Dove posso parcheggiare?

road signs • les panneaux routiers • die Verkehrsschilder • las señales de tráqnsito • i cartelli stradali

no entry • sens interdit • keine Einfahrt • prohibido el paso • ingresso vietato

speed limit • la limitation de vitesse • die Geschwindig-keitsbegrenzung • el límite de velocidad • il limite di velocità

hazard • danger • Gefahr • peligro • pericolo

no stopping • arrêt interdit • Halten verboten • prohibido parar • sosta vietata

no right turn • interdit de tourner à droite • rechts abbiegen verboten • no dar vuelta a la derecha • svolta a destra vietata

bus • le bus • der Bus • el autobús • l'autobus

driver's seat
le siège du conducteur
der Fahrersitz
el asiento del conductor
il sedile dell'autista

handrail
la poignée
der Haltegriff
la barandilla
la maniglia

automatic door
la porte automatique
die Automatiktür
la puerta automática
la porta a soffietto

front wheel
la roue avant
das Vorderrad
la rueda delantera
la ruota anteriore

luggage hold
le compartiment à bagages
das Gepäckfach
el portaequipaje
il bagagliaio

door • la porte • die Tür • la puerta
• la porta

bus • le car • der Reisebus • el autocar • il pullman

types of buses • les types de bus • die Bustypen • los tipos de autobuses • i tipi di autobus

route number
le numéro de bus
die Liniennummer
el número de ruta
il numero del percorso

driver
le conducteur
der Fahrer
el chófer
l'autista

double-decker bus • le bus
à deux étages • der Doppeldecker
• el autobús de dos pisos
• l'autobus a due piani

tram • le tramway
• die Straßenbahn
• el tranvía
• il tram

streetcar • le trolleybus • der Obus • el trolebús
• il filobus

school bus • le bus scolaire • der Schulbus
• el autobús escolar • lo scuolabus

english • français • deutsch • español • italiano

rear wheel
la roue arrière
das Hinterrad
la rueda trasera
la ruota posteriore

window
la fenêtre
das Fenster
la ventanilla
il finestrino

stop button • le bouton
d'arrêt • der Halteknopf
• el botón de parada
• il pulsante di chiamata

bus ticket • le ticket
• der Fahrschein
• el boleto de autobús
• il biglietto

bell • la sonnette
• die Klingel
• el timbre
• il campanello

bus station • la gare routière
• der Busbahnhof • la estación de autobuses
• l'autostazione

bus stop • l'arrêt de
bus • die Bushaltestelle
• la parada de
autobús • la fermata
dell'autobus

fare	wheelchair access
le prix du ticket	l'accès aux handicapés
der Fahrpreis	der Rollstuhlzugang
la tarifa	la rampa para sillas de ruedas
la tariffa	l'accesso per sedie a rotelle
timetable	bus shelter
l'horaire	l'abribus
der Fahrplan	das Wartehäuschen
el horario	la marquesina
l'orario	la pensilina
Do you stop at…?	Which bus goes to…?
Vous stoppez à…?	C'est quel bus pour aller à…?
Halten Sie am…?	Welcher Bus fährt nach…?
¿Para usted en…?	¿Qué autobús va a…?
Ferma a…?	Qual è l'autobus per…?

minibus • le minibus • der Kleinbus
• el microbús • il pulmino

tourist bus • le bus de touristes • der Touristenbus • el autobús turístico
• il pullman

shuttle bus • la navette • der Zubringer
• el autobús directo • la navetta

car | • la voiture 1 • das Auto 1 • el carro 1 • l'automobile 1

exterior • l'extérieur • das Äußere • el exterior • l'esterno

mirror
le rétroviseur
der Seitenspiegel
el espejo lateral
lo specchietto laterale

windshield
le pare-brise
die Windschutzscheibe
el parabrisas
il parabrezza

rearview mirror
le rétroviseur
der Rückspiegel
el espejo retrovisor
lo specchietto retrovisore

windscreen wiper
l'essuie-glace
der Scheibenwischer
el limpiaparabrisas
il tergicristallo

door
la porte
die Autotür
la puerta
lo sportello

hood
le capot
die Motorhaube
el cofre
il cofano

trunk
le coffre
der Kofferraum
la cajuela
il bagagliaio

turn signal
le clignotant
der Blinker
la direccional
la freccia

license plate
la plaque d'immatriculation
das Nummernschild
la matrícula
la targa

bumper
le pare-chocs
die Stoßstange
la defensa
il paraurti

headlight
le phare
der Scheinwerfer
el faro
i fari anabbaglianti

wheel
la roue
das Rad
la rueda
la ruota

tire
le pneu
der Reifen
la llanta
il pneumatico

luggage
les bagages
das Gepäck
el equipaje
i bagagli

roof rack • la galerie • der Dachgepäckträger • la baca • il portabagagli

tailgate • le hayon • die Hecktür • la puerta abatible • il portellone

seat belt • la ceinture de sécurité • der Sicherheitsgurt • el cinturón de seguridad • la cintura di sicurezza

child seat • le siège d'enfant • der Kindersitz • la silla para niños • il seggiolino per bambino

english • français • deutsch • español • italiano

types • les modèles • die Wagentypen • los modelos • i tipi

subcompact • la petite
voiture • der Kleinwagen
• el compacto • l'auto piccola

hatchback • la berline à
hayon • die Fließhecklimousine
• el carro de cinco puertas
• l'auto a cinque porte

sedan • la berline • die
Limousine • el carro familiar
• la berlina

station wagon • le break
• der Kombiwagen • la
camioneta • l'auto familiare

convertible • la décapotable
• das Kabriolett • el
convertible • l'auto
decappottabile

sports car • le cabriolet sport
• das Sportkabriolett • el carro
deportivo • l'auto sportiva

minivan • la voiture à six
places • die Großraumlimousine
• la minivan
• la monovolume

four-wheel drive • la quatre-
quatre • der Geländewagen
• la doble tracción
• il fuoristrada

vintage • la voiture d'époque • das Vorkriegsmodell
• el auto de época • l'auto d'epoca

limousine • la limousine • die verlängerte Limousine • la limousine
• la limousine

gas station • la station-service • die Tankstelle • la gasolinera • la stazione di servizio

gas pump
la pompe
die Zapfsäule
la bomba
la pompa di benzina

price
le tarif
der Benzinpreis
el precio
il prezzo

forecourt
l'aire de stationnement
der Tankstellenplatz
la zona de abastecimiento
l'area di stazionamento

air hose
le compresseur
das Druckluftgerät
la bomba del aire
il distributore di aria compressa

oil	leaded	car wash
l'huile	avec plomb	le lave-auto
das Öl	verbleit	die Autowaschanlage
el aceite	con plomo	el auto-lavado
l'olio	piombata	l'autolavaggio
gasoline	diesel	antifreeze
l'essence	le diesel	l'antigel
das Benzin	der Diesel	das Frostschutzmittel
la gasolina	el diesel	el anticongelante
la benzina	il diesel	l'antigelo
unleaded	garage	windshield wiper fluid
sans plomb	le garage	le lave-glace
bleifrei	die Werkstatt	die Scheibenwaschanlage
sin plomo	el taller	el líquido limpiaparabrisas
senza piombo	il garage	il detergente per vetri

Fill it up, please.
Le plein, s'il vous plaît.
Voll tanken, bitte.
Llénelo por favor.
Il pieno per favore.

car 2 • la voiture 2 • das Auto 2 • el carro 2 • l'automobile 2

interior • l'intérieur • die Innenausstattung • el interior • l'interno

backseat	armrest	headrest	door lock	handle
le siège arrière	l'accoudoir	le repose-tête	le verrouillage	la poignée
der Rücksitz	die Armstütze	die Kopfstütze	die Türverriegelung	der Türgriff
el asiento trasero	el reposabrazos	el reposacabezas	el seguro	la manija
il sedile posteriore	il bracciolo	il poggiatesta	la sicura	la maniglia

two-door	four-door	automatic	brake	accelerator
à deux portes	à quatre portes	automatique	le frein	l'accélérateur
zweitürig	viertürig	mit Automatik	die Bremse	das Gaspedal
dos puertas	de cuatro puertas	automático	el freno	el acelerador
a due porte	a quattro porte	automatico	il freno	l'acceleratore
three-door	manual	ignition	clutch	air-conditioning
à trois portes	manuel	l'allumage	l'embrayage	la climatisation
dreitürig	mit Handschaltung	die Zündung	die Kupplung	die Klimaanlage
de tres puertas	manual	el encendido	el embrague	el aire acondicionado
a tre porte	manuale	l'accensione	la frizione	l'aria condizionata

Can you tell me the way to…?	Where is the parking lot?	Can I park here?
Pouvez-vous m'indiquer la route pour…?	Où est le parking?	On peut se garer ici?
Wie komme ich nach…?	Wo ist hier ein Parkplatz?	Kann ich hier parken?
¿Me puede decir cómo se va a…?	¿Dónde hay un estacionamiento?	¿Se puede estacionar aquí?
Può indicarmi la strada per…?	Dov'è il parcheggio?	Posso parcheggiare qui?

controls • les commandes • die Armaturen • los controles • i comandi

steering wheel
le volant
das Lenkrad
el volante
il volante

horn
le klaxon
die Hupe
el claxon
il clacson

dashboard
le tableau de bord
das Armaturenbrett
el tablero
il cruscotto

hazard lights
les feux de détresse
die Warnlichter
las luces de emergencia
le luci intermittenti

satellite navigation
le navigateur par satellite
das GPS-System
la navegación por satélite
la navigazione via satellite

left-hand drive • la conduite à gauche • die Linkssteuerung • el volante a la izquierda • la guida a sinistra

temperature gauge
le thermomètre
die Temperaturanzeige
el indicador de temperatura
la spia della temperatura

tachometer
le compte-tours
der Drehzahlmesser
el tacómetro
il contagiri

speedometer
le compteur
der Tachometer
el velocímetro
il contachilometri

fuel gauge
la jauge d'essence
die Kraftstoffanzeige
el indicador de la gasolina
la spia del carburante

car stereo
la stéréo
die Autostereoanlage
la radio del coche
l'autoradio

light switch
l'interrupteur feux
der Lichtschalter
la palanca de luces
l'interruttore per le luci

heater controls
la manette de chauffage
der Heizungsregler
la calefacción
i comandi per il riscaldamento

odometer
l'odomètre
der Kilometerzähler
el odómetro
l'odometro

gearshift
le levier de vitesses
der Schalthebel
la palanca de velocidades
la leva del cambio

air bag
l'airbag
der Airbag
la bolsa de aire
l'airbag

right-hand drive • la conduite à droite • die Rechtssteuerung
• el volante a la derecha • la guida a destra

car 3 • la voiture 3 • das Auto 3 • el carro 3 • l'automobile 3

mechanics • la mécanique • die Mechanik • la mecánica • la meccanica

washer fluid reservoir
le réservoir de lave-glace
der Scheibenputzmittelbehälter
el depósito del limpiaparabrisas
il serbatoio del liquido lavavetri

dipstick
la jauge d'huile
der Ölmessstab
la varilla del nivel del aceite
l'indicatore di livello dell'olio

air filter
le filtre à air
der Luftfilter
el filtro del aire
il filtro dell'aria

brake fluid reservoir
le réservoir de liquide de frein
der Bremsflüssigkeitsbehälter
el depósito del líquido de frenos
il serbatoio del liquido per i freni

battery
la batterie
die Batterie
la batería
la batteria

bodywork
la carrosserie
die Karosserie
la chapa
la carrozzeria

coolant reservoir • le réservoir
de liquide de refroidissement
• der Kühlmittelbehälter
• el depósito del líquido
refrigerante • il serbatoio per il
liquido refrigerante

cylinder head
la culasse
der Zylinderkopf
la culata
la testa del cilindro

pipe
le tuyau
das Rohr
el tubo
il tubo

sunroof
le toit ouvrant
das Schiebedach
el quemacocos
il tettuccio

radiator
le radiateur
der Kühler
el radiador
il radiatore

fan
le ventilateur
der Ventilator
el ventilador
il ventilatore

engine
le moteur
der Motor
el motor
il motore

hubcap
l'enjoliveur
die Radkappe
el tapón
il coprimozzo

gearbox
la boîte de vitesses
das Getriebe
la caja de cambios
la scatola del cambio

transmission
la transmission
die Transmission
la transmisión
la trasmissione

drive shaft
l'arbre de transmission
die Kardanwelle
el eje de la transmisión
l'albero di transmissione

flat tire • la crevaison • die Reifenpanne • la ponchadura • la foratura

spare tire
la roue de secours
das Ersatzrad
la llanta de refacción
la ruota di scorta

tire iron
la manivelle
der Radschlüssel
la llave
la chiave

wheel lugs
les écrous de roue
die Radmuttern
los birlos
i bulloni della ruota

jack
le cric
der Wagenheber
el gato
il cric

change a tire (v) • changer une roue • ein Rad wechseln • cambiar una llanta • cambiare una ruota

roof
le toit
das Dach
el techo
il tetto

suspension
la suspension
die Aufhängung
la suspensión
la sospensione

muffler
le silencieux
der Auspufftopf
el silenciador
il silenziatore

exhaust pipe
le pot d'échappement
der Auspuff
el tubo de escape
il tubo di scappamento

car accident
l'accident de voiture
der Autounfall
el accidente de carro
l'incidente stradale

breakdown
la panne
die Panne
la avería
la panne

insurance
l'assurance
die Versicherung
el seguro
l'assicurazione

tow truck
la dépanneuse
der Abschleppwagen
la grúa
il carro attrezzi

mechanic
le mécanicien
der Mechaniker
el mecánico
il meccanico

tire pressure
la pression des pneus
der Reifendruck
la presión del neumático
la pressione dei pneumatici

fuse box
le porte-fusibles
der Sicherungskasten
la caja de fusibles
la scatola dei fusibili

spark plug
la bougie
die Zündkerze
la bujía
la candela

fan belt
la courroie de ventilateur
der Keilriemen
la banda del ventilador
la cinghia della ventola

gas tank
le réservoir d'essence
der Benzintank
el tanque de la gasolina
il serbatoio della benzina

cam belt
la courroie de cames
der Nockenriemen
la banda del disco
la cinghia della camma

turbocharger
le turbocompresseur
der Turbolader
el turbo
il tubocompressore

distributor
le distributeur
der Verteiler
el distribuidor
il distributore

timing
le réglage de l'allumage
die Einstellung
el ralentí
la messa in fase

chassis
le châssis
das Chassis
el chasis
il telaio

parking brake
le frein à main
die Handbremse
el freno de mano
il freno a mano

alternator
l'alternateur
die Lichtmaschine
el alternador
l'alternatore

My car has broken down.
Ma voiture est en panne.
Ich habe eine Panne.
Se descompuso el carro.
Sono in panne.

My car won't start.
Ma voiture ne démarre pas.
Mein Auto springt nicht an.
El carro no arranca.
La mia macchina non parte.

motorcycle • la moto • das Motorrad • la motocicleta • la motocicletta

helmet
le casque
der Motorradhelm
el casco
il casco

speedometer • le compteur
• der Tachometer • el velocímetro
• il contachilometri

turn signal
le clignotant
der Blinker
la direccional
la freccia

brake
le frein
die Bremse
el freno
il freno

horn
le klaxon
die Hupe
el claxon
il clacson

clutch
l'embrayage
die Kupplung
el embrague
la frizione

throttle
l'accélérateur
der Gashebel
el acelerador
l'acceleratore

carrier • le porte-bagages
• der Gepäckträger • el
portaequipaje • il portapacchi

controls • les commandes • die Steuerung • los controles • i comandi

reflector
le réflecteur
das Katzenauge
el reflector
il riflettore

passenger seat
le siège arrière
der Soziussitz
el asiento trasero
il sellino posteriore

seat
la selle
der Sitz
el asiento
il sedile

engine
le moteur
der Motor
el motor
il motore

fuel tank
le réservoir d'essence
der Kraftstofftank
el tanque de la gasolina
il serbatoio

taillight
le feu arrière
das Bremslicht
la luz trasera
il fanale posteriore

exhaust pipe
le pot d'échappement
das Auspuffrohr
el tubo de escape
il tubo di scappamento

muffler
le silencieux
der Auspufftopf
el silenciador
il silenziatore

oil tank
le réservoir d'huile
der Ölsumpf
el depósito del aceite
il serbatoio dell'olio

gearbox
la boîte de vitesses
das Getriebe
la caja de velocidades
la scatola del cambio

air filter
le filtre d'air
der Luftfilter
el filtro del aire
il filtro dell'aria

visor
la visière
das Visier
la visera
la visiera

leathers
le vêtement en cuir
der Lederanzug
el traje de cuero
la tuta di pelle

reflector strap
la bande fluorescente
der Leuchtstreifen
la cinta reflectante
la fascia rifrangente

kneepad
la genouillère
der Knieschützer
la rodillera
il paraginocchio

clothing • les vêtements • die Kleidung • el equipo • l'abbigliamento

headlight
le phare
der Scheinwerfer
el faro
il proiettore

suspension
la suspension
die Aufhängung
la suspensión
l'ammortizzatore

mudguard
le garde-boue
das Schutzblech
la salpicadera
il parafango

brake pedal
la pédale de frein
das Bremspedal
el pedal de los frenos
il pedale del freno

axle
l'essieu
die Achse
el eje
l'asse

tire
le pneu
der Reifen
la llanta
il pneumatico

types • les types • die Typen • los tipos
• i tipi

racing bike • la moto de course • die Rennmaschine
• la moto de carreras • la moto da corsa

windshield • le pare-brise
• die Windschutzscheibe • el
parabrisas • il parabrezza

tourer • la moto routière • der Tourer • la moto
de carretera • la moto da turismo

dirt bike • la moto tout-terrain • das Geländemotorrad
• la motocross • la moto da cross

stand • la béquille • der
Motorradständer • el soporte
• il cavalletto

scooter • le scooter • der Roller • la vespa • la vespa

bicycle • la bicyclette • das Fahrrad • la bicicleta • la bicicletta

tandem • le tandem • das Tandem
• el tándem • il tandem

racing bike • le vélo de
course • das Rennrad
• la bicicleta de carreras
• la bicicletta da corsa

mountain bike • le vélo tout-
terrain • das Mountainbike
• la bicicleta de montaña
• la mountain bike

touring bike • le vélo de
randonnée • das Tourenfahrrad
• la bicicleta de paseo
• la bicicletta da turismo

road bike • le vélo de ville
• das Straßenrad • la bicicleta
de pista • la bicicletta
da strada

saddle
la selle
der Sattel
el asiento
il sellino

seat post
le tube porte-selle
die Sattelstütze
el poste del asiento
il tubo reggisella

water bottle
la bouteille d'eau
die Wasserflasche
la botella del agua
la borraccia

frame
le cadre
der Rahmen
el cuadro
il telaio

brake
le frein
die Felgenbremse
el freno
il freno

hub
le moyeu
die Nabe
el eje
il mozzo

gears
les vitesses
die Gänge
los cambios
le marce

rim
la jante
die Felge
el rin
il cerchione

tire
le pneu
der Reifen
la llanta
il pneumatico

chain
la chaîne
die Fahrradkette
la cadena
la catena

cog
la roue dentée
das Zahnrad
la estrella
la ruota dentata

pedal
la pédale
das Pedal
el pedal
il pedale

helmet
le casque
der Fahrradhelm
el casco
il casco

cycle lane • la piste cyclable • der Fahrradweg
• el carril de bicicletas • la pista ciclabile

crossbar
la barre
die Stange
el tubo superior
la canna

handlebar
le guidon
die Lenkstange
el manubrio
il manubrio

gear lever
le levier de vitesse
der Schalthebel
la palanca de cambio
la leva del cambio

brake lever
le levier de frein
der Bremsgriff
los frenos
la leva del freno

fork
la fourche
die Gabel
las tijeras
la forcella

spoke
le rayon
die Speiche
el rayo
il raggio

wheel
la roue
das Rad
la llanta
la ruota

valve
la valve
das Ventil
el pivote
la valvola

tread
la bande de roulement
das Reifenprofil
la banda de rodadura
il battistrada

tire lever • le
démonte-pneu
• der Reifenschlüssel
• la palanca de la
llanta • la leva
per il pneumatico

patch
la rustine
der Flicken
el parche
la toppa

repair kit • la boîte d'outils • der Reparaturkasten
• el kit de reparaciones • il kit per riparazioni

key
la clef
der Schlüssel
la llave
la chiave

pump • la pompe • die
Luftpumpe • la bomba
• la pompa

lock • l'antivol • das
Fahrradschloss • el candado
• il lucchetto

inner tube • la chambre à air
• der Schlauch • la cámara
• la camera d'aria

child seat • le siège d'enfant
• der Kindersitz • la silla para
el niño • il seggiolino
per bambino

light le phare die Fahrradlampe el faro il fanale	kickstand la béquille der Fahrradständer la patilla de apoyo il cavalletto	brake block le patin de frein die Bremsbacke la goma del freno il blocca freni	basket le panier der Korb la canastilla il cestello	toe clip le cale-pied der Rennbügel el calzapié il fermapiedi	change gear (v) changer de vitesse schalten cambiar de velocidad cambiare marcia
rear light le feu arrière das Rücklicht el faro trasero il fanale posteriore	stabilizers les roues d'entraînement die Stützräder las ruedas de apoyo le rotelle	cable le câble das Kabel el cable il cavo	dynamo la dynamo der Dynamo la dinamo la dinamo	toe strap la lanière der Riemen la banda del calzapié il cinghietto	brake (v) freiner bremsen frenar frenare
reflector le cataphote der Rückstrahler el reflector il catarifrangente	bike rack la galerie à vélo der Fahrradständer el rack para bicicletas il posteggio per bici	sprocket le pignon das Kettenzahnrad el engrane il dente	flat tire la crevaison die Reifenpanne la ponchadura la foratura	pedal (v) pédaler treten pedalear pedalare	cycle (v) faire du vélo Rad fahren andar en bicicleta andare in bici

train • le train • der Zug • el tren • il treno

carriage
la voiture
der Wagen
el vagón
il vagone

platform
le quai
der Bahnsteig
el andén
il binario

cart
le caddie
der Kofferkuli
el carrito
il carrello

platform number
le numéro de voie
die Gleisnummer
el número de andén
il numero del binario

commuter
le voyageur
der Pendler
el viajero de cercanías
il pendolare

train station • la gare • der Bahnhof • la estación de tren • la stazione ferroviaria

types of train • les types de trains • die Zugtypen • los tipos de tren • i tipi di treno

steam train • le train à vapeur
• die Dampflokomotive • el tren de vapor
• il treno a vapore

engine
la locomotive
die Lokomotive
la locomotora
la locomotiva

conducter's cabin
la cabine du conducteur
der Führerstand
la cabina del conductor
la cabina del conducente

rail
le rail
die Schiene
el riel
la rotaia

diesel train • le train diesel • die Diesellokomotive • el tren diesel • il treno diesel

electric train • le train électrique
• die Elektrolokomotive • el tren eléctrico
• il treno elettrico

high-speed train • le train à grande vitesse
• der Hochgeschwindigkeitszug • el tren de
alta velocidad • il treno ad alta velocità

monorail • le monorail • die
Einschienenbahn • el monorriel
• la monorotaia

underground train • le métro
• die U-Bahn • el metro • la metropolitana

streetcar • le tram • die Straßenbahn
• el tranvía • il tram

freight train • le train de marchandises
• der Güterzug • el tren de carga
• il treno merci

luggage rack • le porte-bagages • die Gepäckablage • el portaequipajes • il portabagagli

window
la fenêtre
das Zugfenster
la ventanilla
il finestrino

door
la porte
die Tür
la puerta
la porta

seat
le siège
der Sitz
el asiento
il sedile

track
la voie ferrée
das Gleis
la vía
il binario

ticket barrier • le portillon • die Eingangssperre • la barrera • la barriera

compartment • le compartiment • das Abteil • el compartimento • lo scompartimento

public address system
le haut-parleur
der Lautsprecher
el altavoz
il sistema di altoparlanti

timetable
l'horaire
der Fahrplan
el horario
l'orario

41213
KUPONG 7.00 kr

ticket • le billet • die Fahrkarte • el boleto • il biglietto

dining car • la voiture-restaurant • der Speisewagen • el vagón restaurante • il vagone ristorante

concourse • le hall de gare • die Bahnhofshalle • el vestíbulo • l'atrio

sleeping compartment • le compartiment-couchettes • das Schlafabteil • el cochecama • lo scompartimento a cuccette

railroad network	underground map	ticket office	live rail
le réseau ferroviaire	le plan de métro	le guichet	le rail conducteur
das Bahnnetz	der U-Bahnplan	der Fahrkartenschalter	die stromführende Schiene
la red ferroviaria	el plano del metro	la taquilla	el riel electrificado
la rete ferroviaria	la mappa della metropolitana	la biglietteria	il binario elettrificato
inter-city train	delay	ticket inspector	signal
le rapide	le retard	le contrôleur	le signal
der Intercity	die Verspätung	der Schaffner	das Signal
el tren intercity	el retraso	el checador	la señal
il treno intercity	il ritardo	il controllore	il segnale
rush hour	fare	change (v)	emergency lever
l'heure de pointe	le prix	changer	la manette de secours
die Stoßzeit	der Fahrpreis	umsteigen	der Nothebel
la hora pico	el precio	cambiar	la palanca de emergencia
l'ora di punta	la tariffa	cambiare	la leva di emergenza

aircraft • l'avion • das Flugzeug • el avión • l'aeroplano

airliner • l'avion de ligne • das Verkehrsflugzeug • el avión de pasajeros • l'aereo di linea

nose
le nez
der Bug
la nariz
il muso

cockpit
le cockpit
das Cockpit
la cabina de pilotaje
la cabina di pilotaggio

engine
le réacteur
das Triebwerk
el motor
il motore

fuselage
le fuselage
der Rumpf
el fuselaje
la fusoliera

wing
l'aile
die Tragfläche
el ala
l'ala

tail
la queue
das Heck
la cola
la coda

rudder
la gouverne
das Seitenruder
el timón
il timone

nosewheel
la roue de nez
das Bugfahrwerk
el tren delantero
la ruota anteriore

exit
la sortie
der Ausgang
la salida
l'uscita

landing gear
le train d'atterrissage
das Hauptfahrwerk
el tren de aterrizaje
il carrello d'atterraggio

aileron
l'aileron
das Querruder
el alerón
l'alettone

fin
la dérive
das Seitenleitwerk
la aleta
l'aletta

tailplane
l'empennage
das Höhenleitwerk
el estabilizador
lo stabilizzatore

cabin • la cabine • die Kabine • la cabina • la cabina

emergency exit
la sortie de secours
der Notausgang
la salida de emergencia
l'uscita di emergenza

flight attendant
l'hôtesse de l'air
die Flugbegleiterin
la sobrecargo
l'assistente di volo

overhead bin
le casier à bagages
das Gepäckfach
el compartimento portaequipajes
il compartimento portabagagli

air vent
le ventilateur
die Luftdüse
el ventilador
la ventola per l'aria

window
le hublot
das Fenster
la ventanilla
il finestrino

reading light
la liseuse
die Leselampe
la luz de lectura
la luce di lettura

seat
le siège
der Sitz
el asiento
il sedile

row
la rangée
die Reihe
la fila
la fila

armrest
l'accoudoir
die Armlehne
el descansabrazos
il bracciolo

aisle
le couloir
der Gang
el pasillo
il corridoio

tray-table
la tablette
der Klapptisch
la mesa plegable
il vassoio

seat back
le dossier
die Rückenlehne
el respaldo
lo schienale

ultralight • l'U.L.M. • das Ultraleichtflugzeug • el ultraligero • l'aereo biposto

glider • le planeur • das Segelflugzeug • el planeador • l'aliante

biplane • le biplan • der Doppeldecker • el biplano • il biplano

propeller
l'hélice
der Propeller
la hélice
l'elica

light aircraft • l'avion léger • das Leichtflugzeug • la avioneta • l'aereo da diporto

seaplane • l'hydravion • das Wasserflugzeug • el hidroavión • l'idrovolante

hot-air balloon • la montgolfière • der Heißluftballon • el globo aerostático • la mongolfiera

private jet • le jet privé • der Privatjet • el jet privado • l'aereo privato

supersonic jet • l'avion supersonique • das Überschallflugzeug • el avión supersónico • l'aereo supersonico

rotor blade
la pale de rotor
das Rotorblatt
el aspa
la lama rotante

missile
le missile
die Rakete
el misil
il missile

helicopter • l'hélicoptère • der Hubschrauber • el helicóptero • l'elicottero

bomber • le bombardier • das Bombenflugzeug • el avión de bombardeo • il bombardiere

fighter plane • le chasseur • das Jagdflugzeug • el caza • l'aereo da caccia

pilot	take off (v)	land (v)	economy class	carry-on luggage
le pilote	décoller	atterrir	la classe économique	les bagages à main
der Pilot	starten	landen	die Economyclass	das Handgepäck
el piloto	despegar	aterrizar	la clase turista	el equipaje de mano
il pilota	decollare	atterrare	la classe economica	il bagaglio a mano
copilot	fly (v)	altitude	business class	seatbelt
le copilote	voler	l'altitude	la classe affaires	la ceinture de sécurité
der Kopilot	fliegen	die Höhe	die Businessclass	der Sicherheitsgurt
el copiloto	volar	la altitud	la clase preferente	el cinturón de seguridad
il copilota	volare	la quota	la business class	la cintura di sicurezza

airport • l'aéroport • der Flughafen • el aeropuerto • l'aeroporto

apron
l'aire de stationnement
das Vorfeld
la pista de estacionamiento
l'area di stazionamento

baggage trailer
le porte-bagages
der Gepäckanhänger
el remolque del equipaje
il carrello portabagagli

terminal
le terminal
der Terminal
la terminal
il terminale

service vehicle
le véhicule de service
das Versorgungsfahrzeug
el vehículo de servicio
il veicolo di servizio

jetway
la passerelle
die Fluggastbrücke
la pasarela
il passaggio pedonale

airliner • l'avion de ligne • das Verkehrsflugzeug • el avión de línea • l'aereo di linea

runway	flight number	baggage carousel	vacation
la piste	le numéro de vol	le tapis roulant	les vacances
die Start- und Landebahn	die Flugnummer	das Gepäckband	der Urlaub
la pista	el número de vuelo	la banda transportadora	las vacaciones
la pista	il numero del volo	il nastro trasportatore	la vacanza
international flight	immigration	security	make a flight reservation (v)
le vol international	l'immigration	la sécurité	faire une réservation de vol
der Auslandsflug	die Passkontrolle	die Sicherheitsvorkehrungen	einen Flug buchen
el vuelo internacional	migración	la seguridad	reservar un vuelo
il volo internazionale	il controllo passaporti	la sicurezza	prenotare un volo
domestic flight	customs	X-ray machine	check in (v)
le vol domestique	la douane	la machine de rayons x	enregistrer
der Inlandsflug	der Zoll	die Gepäckröntgenmaschine	einchecken
el vuelo nacional	la aduana	la máquina de rayos x	hacer check-in
il volo nazionale	la dogana	l'apparecchio a raggi x	fare il check-in
connection	excess baggage	travel brochure	control tower
la correspondance	l'excédent de bagages	la brochure de vacances	la tour de contrôle
die Flugverbindung	das Übergepäck	der Urlaubsprospekt	der Kontrollturm
la conexión	el exceso de equipaje	el folleto de viajes	la torre de control
la coincidenza	il bagaglio in eccedenza	l'opuscolo vacanze	la torre di controllo

english • français • deutsch • español • italiano

carry-on luggage
les bagages à main
das Handgepäck
el equipaje de mano
il bagaglio a mano

luggage
les bagages
das Gepäck
el equipaje
il bagaglio

cart
le chariot
der Kofferkuli
el carrito
il carrello

check-in desk • l'enregistrement des bagages • der Abfertigungsschalter • el mostrador de check-in • il banco accettazione

visa
le visa
das Visum
la visa
il visto

passport • le passeport • der Pass • el pasaporte • il passaporto

passport control • le contrôle de passeports • die Passkontrolle • el control de pasaportes • il controllo passaporti

boarding pass • la carte d'embarquement • die Bordkarte • la tarjeta de embarque • la carta d'imbarco

ticket • le billet • das Flugticket • el boleto • il biglietto

gate number • le numéro de la porte d'embarquement • die Gatenummer • el número de puerta de embarque • il numero dell'uscita

departures
les départs
der Abflug
las salidas
le partenze

departure lounge • la salle de départ • die Abflughalle • la sala de embarque • la sala delle partenze

destination
la destination
das Reiseziel
el destino
la destinazione

arrivals
les arrivées
die Ankunft
las llegadas
gli arrivi

information screen • l'écran d'information • die Fluginformationsanzeige • la pantalla informativa • il pannello degli orari

duty-free store • la boutique hors taxes • der Duty-free-Shop • el duty-free • il negozio duty free

baggage claim • le retrait des bagages • die Gepäckausgabe • la recogida de equipajes • il ricupero bagagli

taxi stand • la station de taxis • der Taxistand • el sitio de taxis • il posteggio dei taxi

car rental • la location de voitures • der Autoverleih • la renta de carros • l'autonoleggio

ship • le navire • das Schiff • el barco • la nave

radar
le radar
der Radar
el radar
il radar

radio antenna
l'antenne radio
die Funkantenne
la antena de radio
l'antenna della radio

deck
le pont
das Deck
la cubierta
il ponte

funnel
la cheminée
der Schornstein
la chimenea
il fumaiolo

quarterdeck
le pont arrière
das Achterdeck
el alcázar
il casseretto

prow
la proue
der Bug
la proa
la prua

Plimsoll mark
la marque de flottaison
die Höchstlademarke
la línea de flotación
la marca di bordo libero

porthole
le hublot
das Bullauge
el ojo de buey
l'oblò

hull
la coque
der Rumpf
el casco
lo scafo

lifeboat
le canot de sauvetage
das Rettungsboot
el bote salvavidas
la lancia di salvataggio

keel
la quille
der Kiel
la quilla
la chiglia

propeller
l'hélice
die Schiffsschraube
la hélice
l'elica

ocean liner • le paquebot • der Ozeandampfer • el transatlántico • la nave da crociera

bridge • la passerelle de commandement • die Kommandobrücke • el puente • il ponte di comando

engine room • la salle des moteurs • der Maschinenraum • la sala de máquinas • la sala macchine

cabin • la cabine • die Kabine • el camarote • la cabina

galley • la cuisine • die Kombüse • la cocina • la cucina di bordo

dock le dock das Dock el muelle il bacino	windlass le guindeau die Ankerwinde el cabrestante il mulinello
port le port der Hafen el puerto il porto	captain le capitaine der Kapitän el capitán il capitano
gangway la passerelle die Landungsbrücke la pasarela la passerella	speedboat le runabout das Rennboot la lancha de motor il motoscafo
anchor l'ancre der Anker el ancla l'ancora	rowboat la barque das Ruderboot la barca de remos la barca a remi
bollard le bollard der Poller el noray la colonna d'ormeggio	canoe le canoë das Kanu la piragua la canoa

other ships • autres bateaux • andere Schiffe • otras embarcaciones • altre imbarcazioni

ferryboat • le ferry • die Fähre • el ferry • il traghetto

outboard motor
le hors-bord
der Außenbordmotor
el motor fueraborda
il motore fuoribordo

inflatable dinghy • le dinghy pneumatique • das Schlauchboot • la zodiac • il gommone

hydrofoil • l'hydroptère • das Tragflügelboot • el hidrodeslizador • l'aliscafo

yacht • le yacht • die Jacht • el yate • lo yacht

catamaran • le catamaran • der Katamaran • el catamarán • il catamarano

tugboat • le remorqueur • der Schleppdampfer • el remolcador • il rimorchiatore

hovercraft • l'aéroglisseur • das Luftkissenboot • el aerodeslizador • l'hovercraft

container ship • le navire porte-conteneurs • das Containerschiff • el barco carguero • la nave porta container

rigging
le gréement
die Takelung
las jarcias
il sartiame

sailboat • le voilier • das Segelboot • el barco de vela • la barca a vela

hold
la cale
der Frachtraum
la bodega
la stiva

freighter • le cargo • das Frachtschiff • el buque de carga • la nave da trasporto

oil tanker • le pétrolier • der Öltanker • el buque tanque • la petroliera

aircraft carrier • le porte-avions • der Flugzeugträger • el portaaviones • la portaerei

battleship • le navire de guerre • das Kriegsschiff • el barco de guerra • la nave da guerra

conning tower • le kiosque • der Kommandoturm • la falsa torre • la torretta di comando

submarine • le sous-marin • das U-Boot • el submarino • il sottomarino

port • le port • der Hafen • el puerto • il porto

warehouse
l'entrepôt
das Warenlager
la bodega
il magazzino

crane
la grue
der Kran
la grúa
la gru

forklift
le chariot élévateur
der Gabelstapler
la carretilla elevadora
il carrello elevatore

access road
la route d'accès
die Zufahrtsstraße
la vía de acceso
la strada di accesso

customs house
le bureau des douanes
das Zollamt
las aduanas del puerto
l'ufficio della dogana

container
le conteneur
der Container
el contenedor
il container

dock
le dock
das Dock
la dársena
il bacino

quay
le quai
der Kai
el muelle
la banchina

cargo
la cargaison
die Fracht
la carga
il carico

ferry terminal
le terminal de ferrys
der Fährterminal
la terminal del ferry
il terminale dei traghetti

ferryboat
le ferry
die Fähre
el ferry
il traghetto

ticket office
le guichet
der Fahrkartenschalter
la ventanilla de boletos
la biglietteria

passenger
le passager
der Passagier
el pasajero
il passeggero

containerport • le port de conteneurs • der Containerhafen • el muelle comercial • il porto per container

passenger port • le port de passagers • der Passagier-hafen • el muelle de pasajeros • il porto per passeggeri

english • français • deutsch • español • italiano

net
le filet
das Netz
la red
la rete

fishing boat
le bateau de pêche
das Fischerboot
el barco pesquero
la barca da pesca

mooring
les amarres
die Verankerung
el punto de amarre
l'ormeggio

marina • la marina • die Marina • el puerto
deportivo • il porto turistico

fishing port • le port de pêche • der Fischereihafen • el puerto pesquero
• il porto da pesca

harbor • le port • der Hafen • el puerto • il porto

pier • l'embarcadère • der Pier
• el embarcadero • il pontile

jetty • la jetée • der Landungssteg
• el espigón • il molo

shipyard • le chantier naval • die Werft
• el astillero • il cantiere navale

lantern
le feu
die Laterne
la lámpara
la luce

lighthouse • le phare
• der Leuchtturm • el
faro • il faro

buoy • la bouée • die
Boje • la boya • la boa

coast guard	dry dock	board (v)
le garde-côte	la cale sèche	embarquer
die Küstenwache	**das Trockendock**	**an Bord gehen**
el guardacostas	el dique seco	embarcar
il guardacoste	il bacino di carenaggio	imbarcare
harbormaster	moor (v)	disembark (v)
le capitaine de port	mouiller	débarquer
der Hafenmeister	**festmachen**	**von Bord gehen**
el capitán del puerto	amarrar	desembarcar
il capitano di porto	ormeggiare	sbarcare
drop anchor (v)	dock (v)	set sail (v)
jeter l'ancre	se mettre à quai	prendre la mer
den Anker werfen	**anlegen**	**auslaufen**
anclar	atracar	zarpar
mollare l'ancora	entrare in bacino	salpare

sports
les sports
der Sport
los deportes
gli sport

football • le football américain • der Football • el fútbol americano • il football americano

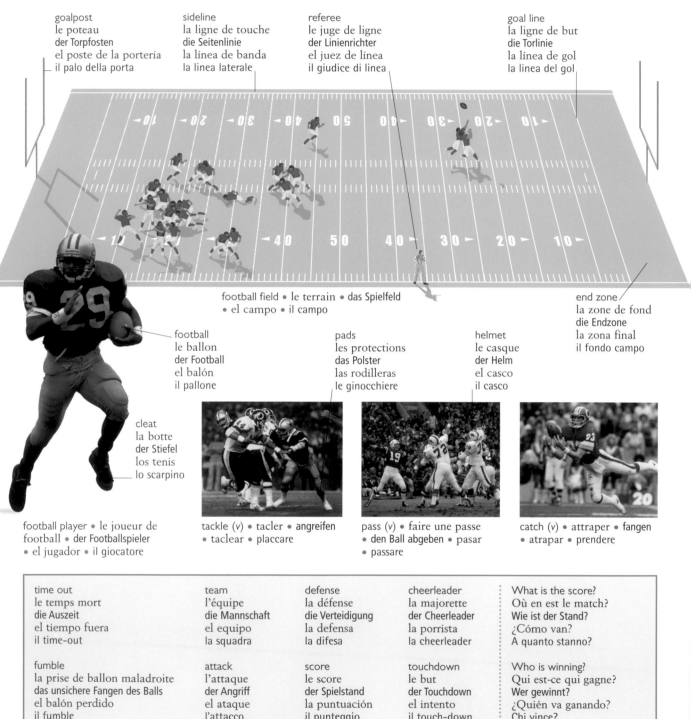

goalpost
le poteau
der Torpfosten
el poste de la portería
il palo della porta

sideline
la ligne de touche
die Seitenlinie
la línea de banda
la linea laterale

referee
le juge de ligne
der Linienrichter
el juez de línea
il giudice di linea

goal line
la ligne de but
die Torlinie
la línea de gol
la linea del gol

football field • le terrain • das Spielfeld • el campo • il campo

end zone
la zone de fond
die Endzone
la zona final
il fondo campo

football
le ballon
der Football
el balón
il pallone

pads
les protections
das Polster
las rodilleras
le ginocchiere

helmet
le casque
der Helm
el casco
il casco

cleat
la botte
der Stiefel
los tenis
lo scarpino

football player • le joueur de football • der Footballspieler • el jugador • il giocatore

tackle (v) • tacler • angreifen • taclear • placcare

pass (v) • faire une passe • den Ball abgeben • pasar • passare

catch (v) • attraper • fangen • atrapar • prendere

time out le temps mort die Auszeit el tiempo fuera il time-out	team l'équipe die Mannschaft el equipo la squadra	defense la défense die Verteidigung la defensa la difesa	cheerleader la majorette der Cheerleader la porrista la cheerleader	What is the score? Où en est le match? Wie ist der Stand? ¿Cómo van? A quanto stanno?
fumble la prise de ballon maladroite das unsichere Fangen des Balls el balón perdido il fumble	attack l'attaque der Angriff el ataque l'attacco	score le score der Spielstand la puntuación il punteggio	touchdown le but der Touchdown el intento il touch-down	Who is winning? Qui est-ce qui gagne? Wer gewinnt? ¿Quién va ganando? Chi vince?

rugby • le rugby • das Rugby • el rugby • il rugby

goal
le but
das Tor
la portería
la porta

in-goal area
la surface de but
der Torraum
la zona de marca
l'area della porta

touch line
la ligne de touche
die Seitenlinie
la línea de banda
la linea di touch

flag
le drapeau
die Fahne
la bandera
la bandierina

dead ball line
la ligne de ballon mort
die Feldauslinie
la linea de fondo
la linea di palla morta

rugby field • le terrain de rugby • das Spielfeld • el campo de rugby • il campo

ball
le ballon
der Rugbyball
el balón
il pallone

rugby uniform
le maillot de rugby
das Rugbytrikot
el uniforme de rugby
la camicetta da rugby

player
le joueur
der Rugbyspieler
el jugador
il giocatore

throw (v) • lancer • werfen
• lanzar • tirare

kick (v) • botter • kicken
• patear • calciare

pass (v) • faire une passe
• den Ball abgeben • pasar
• passare

tackle (v) • tacler • angreifen
• taclear • placcare

try • l'essai • der Versuch
• el intento • la meta

ruck • la mêlée ouverte • das offene Gedränge • la abierta • il ruck

scrum • la mêlée • das Gedränge • la cerrada • la mischia

soccer • le football • der Fußball • el fútbol • il calcio

soccer ball
le ballon
der Fußball
el balón
il pallone

forward
l'avant
der Mittelstürmer
el delantero
l'attaccante

referee
l'arbitre
der Schiedsrichter
el árbitro
l'arbitro

center circle
le cercle central
der Mittelkreis
el círculo central
il centro campo

goalkeeper
le gardien de but
der Torwart
el portero
il portiere

soccer uniform
la tenue
der Dress
el uniforme
la divisa

soccer player • le joueur de foot • der Fußballspieler • el futbolista • il calciatore

soccer field • le terrain • das Fußballfeld • el campo de fútbol • il campo di calcio

goalpost
le poteau
der Torpfosten
el poste
il palo

net
le filet
das Tornetz
la red
la rete

crossbar
la barre transversale
die Querlatte
el larguero
la traversa

dribble (v) • dribbler • dribbeln
• regatear • palleggiare

head (v) • faire une tête
• köpfen • cabecear
• colpire di testa

goal • le but • das Tor • el gol • il gol

wall
le mur
die Mauer
la barrera
il muro

free kick • le coup franc • der Freistoß • el tiro libre • il calcio di punizione

english • français • deutsch • español • italiano

penalty area
la surface de réparation
der Strafraum
el área de penalty
l'area di rigore

goal line
la ligne de but
die Torlinie
la línea de meta
la linea di fondo

goal area
la surface de but
der Torraum
el área de meta
l'area di porta

goal
le but
das Tor
la portería
la porta

defender
le défenseur
der Verteidiger
el defensa
il difensore

linesman
le juge de ligne
der Linienrichter
el juez de línea
il guardialinee

corner flag
le drapeau de coin
die Eckfahne
la bandera de esquina
la bandierina

throw-in • la rentrée en touche • der Einwurf • el saque de banda • la rimessa in gioco

kick (v) • botter • kicken • patear • calciare

pass (v) • faire une passe • den Ball abgeben • mandar un pase • passare

cleat
la botte
der Fußballschuh
los tacos
lo scarpino

shoot (v) • shooter • schießen • tirar • tirare

save (v) • sauver • halten • parar • parare

tackle (v) • tacler • angreifen • hacer una entrada • contrastare

stadium	foul	yellow card	league	extra time
le stade	la faute	le carton jaune	le championnat	la prolongation
das Stadion	das Foul	die gelbe Karte	die Liga	die Verlängerung
el estadio	la falta	la tarjeta amarilla	la liga	el tiempo extra
lo stadio	il fallo	il cartellino giallo	il campionato	il tempo supplementare
score a goal (v)	corner	offside	draw	substitute
marquer un but	le corner	l'hors-jeu	l'egalité	le remplaçant
ein Tor schießen	der Eckball	das Abseits	das Unentschieden	der Ersatzspieler
marcar un gol	el tiro de esquina	el fuera de juego	el empate	el reserva
segnare	il calcio d'angolo	il fuorigioco	il pareggio	il sostituto
penalty	red card	send off	halftime	substitution
le penalty	le carton rouge	l'expulsion	la mi-temps	le remplacement
der Elfmeter	die rote Karte	der Platzverweis	die Halbzeit	die Auswechslung
el penalty	la tarjeta roja	la expulsión	el descanso	el cambio
il rigore	il cartellino rosso	l'espulsione	l'intervallo	la sostituzione

hockey • le hockey • das Hockey • el hockey • l'hockey

ice hockey • le hockey sur glace • das Eishockey • el hockey sobre hielo • l'hockey su ghiaccio

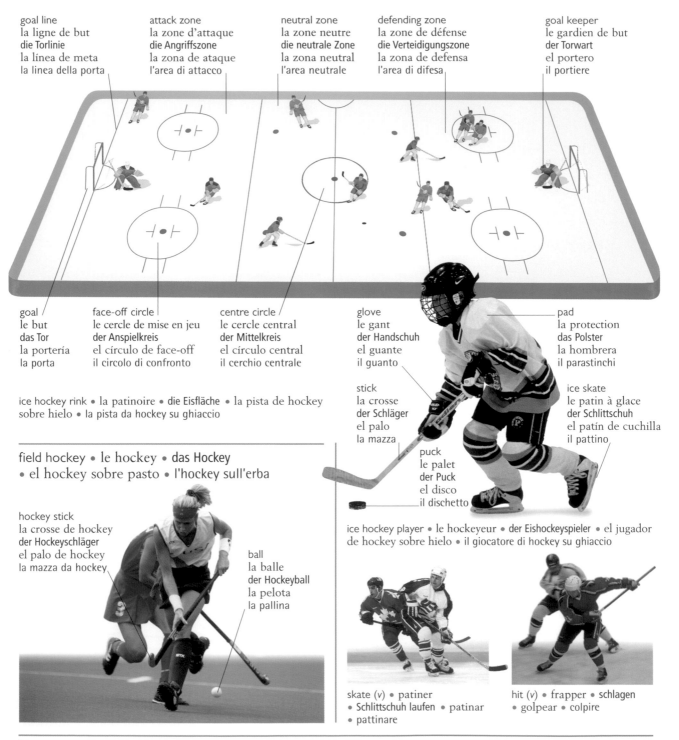

goal line
la ligne de but
die Torlinie
la línea de meta
la linea della porta

attack zone
la zone d'attaque
die Angriffszone
la zona de ataque
l'area di attacco

neutral zone
la zone neutre
die neutrale Zone
la zona neutral
l'area neutrale

defending zone
la zone de défense
die Verteidigungszone
la zona de defensa
l'area di difesa

goal keeper
le gardien de but
der Torwart
el portero
il portiere

goal
le but
das Tor
la portería
la porta

face-off circle
le cercle de mise en jeu
der Anspielkreis
el círculo de face-off
il circolo di confronto

centre circle
le cercle central
der Mittelkreis
el círculo central
il cerchio centrale

glove
le gant
der Handschuh
el guante
il guanto

pad
la protection
das Polster
la hombrera
il parastinchi

stick
la crosse
der Schläger
el palo
la mazza

ice skate
le patin à glace
der Schlittschuh
el patín de cuchilla
il pattino

ice hockey rink • la patinoire • die Eisfläche • la pista de hockey sobre hielo • la pista da hockey su ghiaccio

puck
le palet
der Puck
el disco
il dischetto

field hockey • le hockey • das Hockey • el hockey sobre pasto • l'hockey sull'erba

hockey stick
la crosse de hockey
der Hockeyschläger
el palo de hockey
la mazza da hockey

ball
la balle
der Hockeyball
la pelota
la pallina

ice hockey player • le hockeyeur • der Eishockeyspieler • el jugador de hockey sobre hielo • il giocatore di hockey su ghiaccio

skate (v) • patiner • Schlittschuh laufen • patinar • pattinare

hit (v) • frapper • schlagen • golpear • colpire

cricket • le cricket • das Kricket • el críquet • il cricket

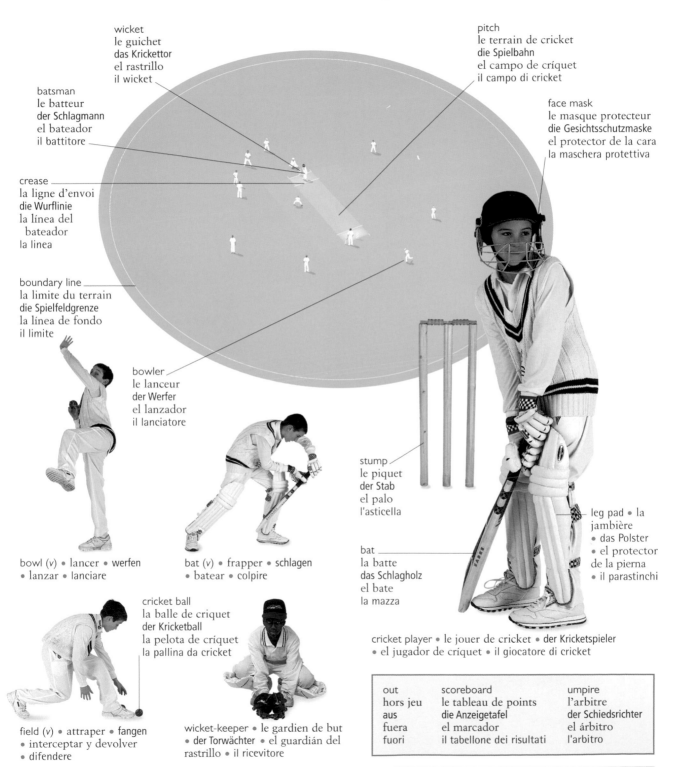

wicket
le guichet
das Krickettor
el rastrillo
il wicket

pitch
le terrain de cricket
die Spielbahn
el campo de críquet
il campo di cricket

batsman
le batteur
der Schlagmann
el bateador
il battitore

face mask
le masque protecteur
die Gesichtsschutzmaske
el protector de la cara
la maschera protettiva

crease
la ligne d'envoi
die Wurflinie
la línea del
bateador
la linea

boundary line
la limite du terrain
die Spielfeldgrenze
la línea de fondo
il limite

bowler
le lanceur
der Werfer
el lanzador
il lanciatore

stump
le piquet
der Stab
el palo
l'asticella

leg pad • la
jambière
• das Polster
• el protector
de la pierna
• il parastinchi

bowl (v) • lancer • werfen
• lanzar • lanciare

bat (v) • frapper • schlagen
• batear • colpire

bat
la batte
das Schlagholz
el bate
la mazza

cricket ball
la balle de criquet
der Kricketball
la pelota de críquet
la pallina da cricket

cricket player • le jouer de cricket • der Kricketspieler
• el jugador de críquet • il giocatore di cricket

field (v) • attraper • fangen
• interceptar y devolver
• difendere

wicket-keeper • le gardien de but
• der Torwächter • el guardián del
rastrillo • il ricevitore

out	scoreboard	umpire
hors jeu	le tableau de points	l'arbitre
aus	die Anzeigetafel	der Schiedsrichter
fuera	el marcador	el árbitro
fuori	il tabellone dei risultati	l'arbitro

basketball • le basket • der Basketball • el baloncesto • la pallacanestro

sideline
la ligne de touche
die Seitenlinie
la línea de banda
la linea laterale

referee
l'arbitre
der Schiedsrichter
el árbitro
l'arbitro

center circle
le cercle central
der Mittelkreis
el círculo central
il dischetto

free-throw line
la ligne de lancer franc
die Freiwurflinie
la línea de tiro libre
la linea di tiro libero

endline
la ligne de bout
die Endlinie
la línea de fondo
la linea di fondo

court • le terrain • das Spielfeld
• la cancha • il campo

centerline
la ligne de centre
die Mittellinie
la línea central
la linea di centro

three-point line
la ligne de trois points
die Dreipunktlinie
la línea de tres puntos
la linea dei tre punti

backboard
le panneau
das Korbbrett
el tablero
il tabellone

number
le numéro
die Spielernummer
el número
il numero

hoop
l'anneau
der Korbring
el aro
l'anello

ball
le ballon
der Basketball
el balón
il pallone

net
le filet
das Netz
la red
la rete

basketball player • le joueur de basket • der Basketballspieler
• el jugador de baloncesto • il giocatore di pallacanestro

basket • le panier
• der Korb • la canasta
• il canestro

pass	throw-in
la passe	la rentrée
der Pass	der Einwurf
el pase	el saque de banda
il passaggio	la rimessa
foul	jump ball
la faute	l'entre-deux
das Foul	der Schiedsrichterball
la falta	el salto entre dos
il fallo	il tiro in sospensione
rebound	out of bounds
le rebond	hors jeu
der Rebound	aus
el rebote	fuera de banda
il rimbalzo	fuori campo

actions • les actions • die Aktionen • las acciones • le azioni

throw (v) • lancer • **werfen**
• lanzar • tirare

catch (v) • attraper
• **fangen** • cachar
• acchiappare

shoot (v) • tirer
• **schießen** • tirar
• tirare

jump (v) • sauter
• **springen** • saltar
• saltare

cover (v) • marquer • **decken**
• marcar • marcare

block (v) • bloquer
• **blocken** • bloquear
• bloccare

dribble (v) • faire
rebondir • **springen lassen**
• botar • rimbalzare

dunk (v) • faire un dunk
• **einen Dunk spielen**
• marcar • segnare

volleyball • le volley • der Volleyball • el vóleibol • la pallavolo

block (v))
bloquer
blocken
bloquear
contrastare

net
le filet
das Netz
la red
la rete

dig (v))
faire une
manchette
baggern
recibir
difendere

referee
l'arbitre
der Schiedsrichter
el árbitro
l'arbitro

knee support
la genouillère
der Knieschützer
la rodillera
la ginocchiera

court • le terrain • **das Spielfeld** • la cancha • il campo

baseball • le baseball • der Baseball • el béisbol • il baseball

field • le terrain • das Spielfeld • el campo • il campo

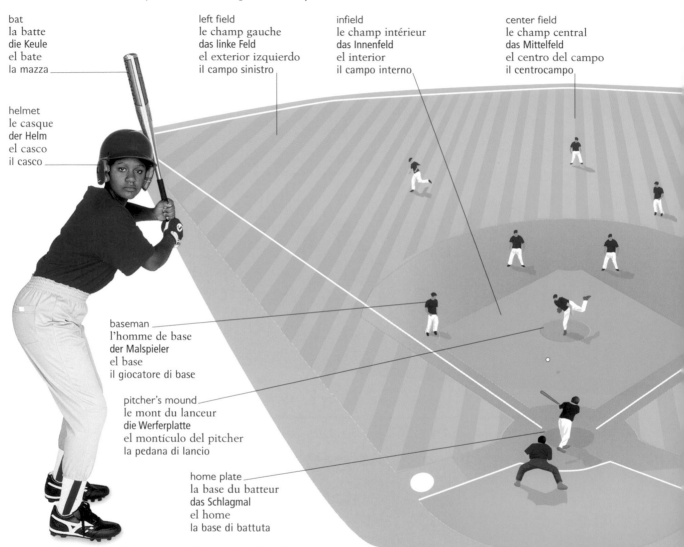

bat
la batte
die Keule
el bate
la mazza

left field
le champ gauche
das linke Feld
el exterior izquierdo
il campo sinistro

infield
le champ intérieur
das Innenfeld
el interior
il campo interno

center field
le champ central
das Mittelfeld
el centro del campo
il centrocampo

helmet
le casque
der Helm
el casco
il casco

baseman
l'homme de base
der Malspieler
el base
il giocatore di base

pitcher's mound
le mont du lanceur
die Werferplatte
el montículo del pitcher
la pedana di lancio

home plate
la base du batteur
das Schlagmal
el home
la base di battuta

batter • le batteur • der Schlagmann • el bateador • il battitore

inning	safe	strike
le tour de batte	sauf	le coup manqué
das Inning	in Sicherheit	der Schlagfehler
el turno	safe	el strike
il turno di battuta	salvo	lo strike
run	out	foul ball
le point	hors jeu	la fausse balle
der Lauf	aus	der ungültige Schlag
la carrera	fuera	el foul
il giro	fuori	il fallo

ball
la balle
der Baseball
la bola
la palla

glove • le gant • der Handschuh
• la manopla • il guantone

mask • le masque • die
Schutzmaske • la careta
• la maschera

english • français • deutsch • español • italiano

actions • les actions • **die Aktionen** • las acciones • le azioni

outfield
le champ extérieur
das Außenfeld
el exterior
il campo esterno

right field
le champ droit
das rechte Feld
el exterior derecho
il campo destro

foul line
la ligne de pénalité
die Foullinie
la línea de falta
la linea di fallo

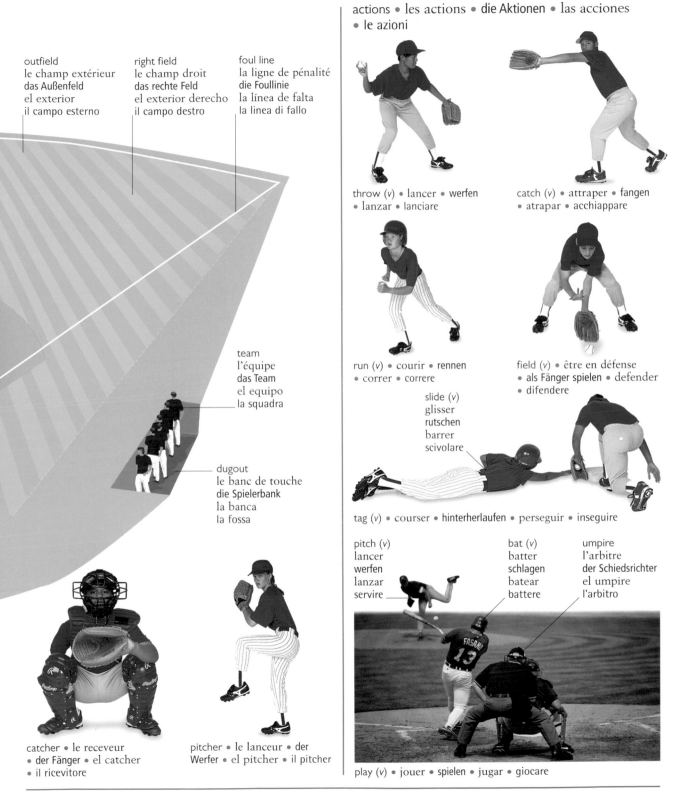

throw (*v*) • lancer • **werfen** • lanzar • lanciare

catch (*v*) • attraper • **fangen** • atrapar • acchiappare

run (*v*) • courir • **rennen** • correr • correre

field (*v*) • être en défense • als Fänger spielen • defender • difendere

team
l'équipe
das Team
el equipo
la squadra

dugout
le banc de touche
die Spielerbank
la banca
la fossa

slide (*v*)
glisser
rutschen
barrer
scivolare

tag (*v*) • courser • hinterherlaufen • perseguir • inseguire

pitch (*v*)
lancer
werfen
lanzar
servire

bat (*v*)
batter
schlagen
batear
battere

umpire
l'arbitre
der Schiedsrichter
el umpire
l'arbitro

catcher • le receveur • der Fänger • el catcher • il ricevitore

pitcher • le lanceur • der Werfer • el pitcher • il pitcher

play (*v*) • jouer • **spielen** • jugar • giocare

tennis • le tennis • das Tennis • el tenis • il tennis

handle
le manche
der Griff
el mango
l'impugnatura

head
la tête
der Kopf
la cabeza
la testa

string
la corde
die Saite
la cuerda
la corda

umpire
l'arbitre
der Schiedsrichter
el juez de silla
l'arbitro

baseline • la ligne de fond
• die Grundlinie • la línea de
fondo • la linea di fondo

racquet
• la raquette
• der Tennisschläger
• la raqueta • la racchetta

service line
la ligne de service
die Aufschlaglinie
la línea de servicio
la linea di servizio

sideline
la ligne de côté
die Seitenlinie
la línea de banda
la linea laterale

ball
la balle
der Tennisball
la bola
la palla

wristband • le poignet
• das Schweißband • la
muñequera • il polsino

tennis court • le court de tennis • der Tennisplatz • la pista de tenis • il campo

singles	set	deuce	fault	slice	spin
le simple	le set	l'égalité	la faute	le slice	l'effet
das Einzel	der Satz	der Einstand	der Fehler	der Slice	der Spin
el singles	el set	cuarenta iguales	la falta	el tiro con efecto	el efecto
il singolare	il set	il deuce	il fallo	il taglio	l'avvitamento
doubles	match	advantage	ace	rally	linesman
le double	le match	l'avantage	l'as	l'échange	le juge de ligne
das Doppel	das Match	der Vorteil	das Ass	der Ballwechsel	der Linienrichter
los dobles	el partido	la ventaja	el as	el peloteo	el juez de línea
il doppio	la partita	il vantaggio	l'asso	il palleggio	il giudice di linea
game	tiebreaker	love	dropshot	let!	championship
le jeu	le tiebreak	zéro	l'amorti	net!	le championnat
das Spiel	der Tiebreak	null	der Stoppball	Netz!	die Meisterschaft
el juego	el tiebreak	nada	la dejada	¡red!	el campeonato
il gioco	il tiebreak	a zero	la smorzata	colpo nullo!	il campionato

strokes • les coups • die Schläge • los golpes • i colpi

net
le filet
das Netz
la red
la rete

ballboy
le ramasseur de balles
der Balljunge
el recogebolas
il raccattapalle

serve (v)
servir
aufschlagen
sacar
battere il servizio

smash
le smash
der Schmetterball
el remate
la schiacciata

tennis shoes
• les tennis
• die Tennisschuhe
• los tenis • le
scarpe da tennis

player • le joueur • der Tennisspieler • el jugador • il giocatore

serve • le service • der
Aufschlag • el servicio
• il servizio

volley • la vollée • der Volley
• la volea • il palleggio

return • le retour • der Return
• el resto • il ritorno

lob • le lob • der Lob
• el globo • la schiacciata

forehand • le coup droit
• die Vorhand • el derecho
• il dritto

backhand • le revers
• die Rückhand • el revés
• il rovescio

racquet games • les jeux de raquette • die Schlägerspiele • los juegos de raqueta • i giochi con la racchetta

shuttlecock
le volant
der Federball
el gallo
il volano

bat • la raquette •
der Tischtennisschläger
• la raqueta
• la racchetta

badminton • le badminton
• das Badminton • el
bádminton • il badminton

table tennis • le tennis de
table • das Tischtennis • el
ping-pong • il ping pong

squash • le squash • das
Squash • el squash • lo
squash

racquetball • le racquetball
• der Racquetball • el
racketball • il racquetball

golf • le golf • das Golf • el golf • il golf

hole
le trou
das Loch
el hoyo
la buca

teeing ground
le départ
der Abschlag
la salida
il teeing-ground

green
le green
das Grün
el green
il green

bunker
le bunker
der Bunker
la trampa de arena
il bunker

flag
le drapeau
die Flagge
la banderola
la bandierina

swing (v)
exécuter un swing
schwingen
hacer un swing
fare lo swing

fairway
le fairway
das Fairway
la calle
il fairway

rough
le rough
das Rough
el rough
il rough

water hazard
l'obstacle d'eau
das Wasserhindernis
el estanque
lo stagno

golf course • le parcours de golf • der Golfplatz
• el campo de golf • il campo di golf

stance
la position
die Haltung
la postura
la posizione

buggy
le buggy
der Buggy
el carrito
il buggy

golfer • le joueur de golf • der Golfspieler • el golfista • il golfista

clubhouse • le pavillon • das Klubhaus • la casa
club • la sede del circolo

english • français • deutsch • español • italiano

equipment • l'équipement • die Ausrüstung • el equipo • le attrezzature

golf ball
la balle de golf
der Golfball
la bola de golf
la pallina da golf

tee • le tee • der
Aufsatz • el tee • il tee

glove • le gant • der
Handschuh • el guante
• il guanto

bag cart • le caddie • der Caddie
• el carrito de golf • il carrellino

umbrella
le parapluie
der Schirm
el paraguas
l'ombrello

golf bag
le sac de golf
die Golftasche
la bolsa de golf
la sacca da golf

spikes
les pointes
die Spikes
los spikes
i chiodi

golf shoe • la chaussure de
golf • der Golfschuh • el zapato
de golf • la scarpa da golf

golf clubs • les clubs de golf • die Golfschläger • los palos de golf • le mazze da golf

wood • le bois • das Holz
• la madera
• la mazza di legno

putter • le putter
• der Putter • el putter
• il putter

iron • le fer • das Eisen
• el fierro • la mazza di
ferro

wedge • la cale
• das Wedge • el wedge
• la mazza ricurva

actions • les actions • die Aktionen • las acciones • le azioni

tee-off (v) • partir du
tee • vom Abschlag
spielen • salir •
cominciare la partita

drive (v) • driver
• driven • hacer un
drive • colpire a
distanza

putt (v) • putter
• einlochen • tirar al
hoyo con un putter
• colpire leggermente

chip (v) • cocher
• chippen • hacer
un chip • colpire da
vicino

par	over par	handicap	caddy	stroke	backswing
le par	le over par	le handicap	le caddie	le coup	le swing en arrière
das Par	das Überpar	das Golfhandicap	der Caddie	der Schlag	der Durchschwung
el par	el sobre par	el handicap	el caddy	el golpe	el backswing
il par	l'overpar	l'handicap	il caddy	il colpo	il back-swing
under par	hole in one	tournament	spectators	practice swing	line of play
le under par	le trou en un	le tournoi	les spectateurs	le swing d'essai	la ligne de jeu
das Unterpar	das Hole-in-One	das Golfturnier	die Zuschauer	der Übungsschwung	die Spielbahn
el bajo par	el hoyo en uno	el torneo	los espectadores	el swing de práctica	la línea de juego
l'underpar	la buca in uno	il torneo	gli spettatori	lo swing di pratica	la linea di gioco

track and field • l'athlétisme • die Leichtathletik • el atletismo • l'atletica

lane
le couloir
die Bahn
el carril
la corsia

track
la piste
die Rennbahn
la pista
la pista

finish line
la ligne d'arrivée
die Ziellinie
la línea de meta
il traguardo

starting line
la ligne de départ
die Startlinie
la línea de salida
la linea di partenza

field • le terrain • das Feld • el campo • il campo

starting blocks
le bloc de départ
der Startblock
el cajón de salida
la pedana di partenza

athlete
l'athlète
die Leichtathletin
la atleta
l'atleta

sprinter • le sprinter
• der Sprinter • el esprinter
• il velocista

discus • le disque
• das Diskuswerfen
• el lanzamiento de disco
• il lancio del disco

shotput • le lancement du
poids • das Kugelstoßen
• el lanzamiento de bala
• il lancio del peso

javelin • le javelot • das
Speerwerfen • el lanzamiento
de jabalina • il lancio del
giavellotto

race	record	photo finish	pole vault
la course	le record	le photo-finish	le saut à la perche
das Rennen	der Rekord	das Fotofinish	der Stabhochsprung
la carrera	el récord	la foto final	el salto con pértiga
la gara	il primato	il fotofinish	il salto con l'asta
time	break a record (v)	marathon	personal best
le temps	battre un record	le marathon	le record personnel
die Zeit	einen Rekord brechen	der Marathon	die persönliche Bestleistung
el tiempo	batir un récord	la maratón	la marca personal
il tempo	battere un primato	la maratona	il primato personale

stopwatch • le chronomètre
• die Stoppuhr • el
cronómetro • il cronometro

baton • le bâton
• der Stab • el relevo
• il testimone

relay race • le relais • der Staffellauf • la carrera de relevos • la staffetta

bar • la barre
• die Latte • la barra
• la sbarra

high jump • le saut en hauteur • der Hochsprung • el salto de altura • il salto in alto

long jump • le saut en longueur • der Weitsprung • el salto de longitud • il salto in lungo

hurdles • les haies • der Hürdenlauf • la carrera de vallas • la corsa a ostacoli

gymnastics • la gymnastique • das Turnen • la gimnasia • la ginnastica

springboard
le tremplin
das Sprungbrett
el trampolín
la pedana elastica

gymnast
la gymnaste
die Turnerin
la gimnasta
la ginnasta

horse
le cheval
das Pferd
el caballo
il cavallo

somersault • le salto
• der Salto • el salto mortal
• la capriola

beam • la poutre • der Schwebebalken • la viga de equilibrio • la trave

ribbon • le drapeau
• das Gymnastikband
• el listón • il nastro

mat • le tapis • die Matte
• el tapete • la pedana

vault • le saut • der Sprung
• el salto • il salto

floor exercises • les exercises au sol • das Bodenturnen • los ejercicios de piso • la ginnastica a corpo libero

cartwheel • la cabriole • die Bodenakrobatik • la voltereta • la ruota

rhythmic gymnastics • la gymnastique rythmique • die rhythmische Gymnastik • la gimnasia rítmica • la ginnastica ritmica

horizontal bar	asymmetric bars	rings	medals	silver
la barre fixe	les barres asymétriques	les anneaux	les médailles	l'argent
das Reck	der Stufenbarren	die Ringe	die Medaillen	das Silber
la barra fija	las barras asimétricas	las argollas	las medallas	la plata
la sbarra	le sbarre asimmetriche	gli anelli	le medaglie	l'argento
parallel bars	pommel horse	podium	gold	bronze
les barres parallèles	le cheval d'arçons	le podium	l'or	le bronze
der Barren	das Seitpferd	das Siegerpodium	das Gold	die Bronze
las barras paralelas	el caballo con arcos	el podio	el oro	el bronce
le parallele	il cavallo	il podio	l'oro	il bronzo

combat sports • les sports de combat • der Kampfsport • los deportes de combate • gli sport da combattimento

opponent
l'adversaire
der Gegner
el adversario
l'avversario

glove
le gant
der Handschuh
el guante
il guanto

guard
le protège-tête
der Kopfschutz
el protector
il casco

belt
la ceinture
der Gürtel
el cinturón
la cintura

karate • le karaté • das Karate • el karate • il karate

tae kwon do • le taekwondo • das Taekwondo • el taekwondo • il tae kwondo

judo • le judo • das Judo • el judo • il judo

mask
le masque
die Maske
la careta
la maschera

sword
le sabre
der Säbel
la espada
la sciabola

aikido • l'aïkido • das Aikido • el aikido • l'aikido

kendo • le kendo • das Kendo • el kendo • il kendo

kung fu • le kung-fu • das Kung-Fu • el kung fu • il kung fu

kickboxing • la boxe thaïlandaise • das Kickboxen • el full contact • il kickboxing

wrestling • la lutte • das Ringen • la lucha libre • la lotta greco-romana

boxing • la boxe • das Boxen • el boxeo • il pugilato

actions • les actions • die Techniken • los movimientos • le mosse

fall • la chute • das Fallen
• la caída • la scivolata

hold • la prise • der Griff
• el agarre • la presa

throw • la projection • der Wurf
• el derribo • la proiezione

pin • l'immobilisation • das Fesseln
• la inmovilización • la caduta

kick • le coup de pied
• der Seitfußstoß • la patada
• il calcio

punch • le coup de poing
• der Stoß • el puñetazo
• il pugno

strike • le coup • der Angriff
• el golpe • il colpo

jump • le saut • der Sprung
• el salto • il salto

block • le blocage • der Block
• el bloqueo • la parata

chop • le coup • der Hieb
• el golpe • il colpo di taglio

boxing ring le ring der Boxring el ring il ring	round le round die Runde el round il round	fist le poing die Faust el puño il pugno	black belt la ceinture noire der schwarze Gürtel el cinturón negro la cintura nera	capoeira la capoeira das Capoeira la capoeira la capoeira
boxing gloves les gants de boxe die Boxhandschuhe los guantes de boxeo i guanti	bout le combat der Kampf el combate l'incontro	knockout le knock-out der Knockout el K.O. il k.o	self-defense l'autodéfense die Selbstverteidigung la defensa personal l'autodifesa	sumo wrestling le sumo das Sumo el sumo il sumo
mouth guard le protège-dents der Mundschutz el protegedientes il paradenti	sparring l'entraînement das Sparren el entrenamiento l'allenamento	punching bag le punching-bag der Sandsack el saco de arena il sacco	martial arts les arts martiaux die Kampfsportarten las artes marciales le arti marziali	tai-chi le taï chi das Tai Chi el tai-chi il tai-chi

swimming • la natation • der Schwimmsport • la natación • il nuoto

equipment • l'équipement • die Ausrüstung • el equipo • l'attrezzatura

swim band • la brassière
• der Schwimmflügel
• el flotador de brazo
• il bracciolo

goggles • les lunettes protectrices
• die Schwimmbrille • los goggles
• gli occhialetti

nose clip
la pince pour le nez
die Nasenklemme
la pinza para la nariz
la molletta per il naso

kickboard • la planche
• das Schwimmfloß
• la tabla • la tavoletta

swimsuit • le maillot de bain
• der Badeanzug • el traje de
baño • il costume da bagno

lane
le couloir
die Bahn
el carril
la corsia

water
l'eau
das Wasser
el agua
l'acqua

starting block
le plot de départ
der Startblock
el cajón de salida
il podio di partenza

swimming cap
• le bonnet de
natation • die
Badekappe
• la gorra
• la cuffia

trunks
le slip de bain
die Badehose
el traje de baño
il costume da
bagno

swimming pool • la piscine • das Schwimmbecken • la alberca • la piscina

diving board
le tremplin
das Sprungbrett
el trampolín
il trampolino

diver
le plongeur
der Springer
el clavadista
il tuffatore

swimmer • le nageur • der Schwimmer
• el nadador • il nuotatore

dive (v) • plonger • springen
• tirarse un clavado • tuffarsi

swim (v) • nager • schwimmen • nadar
• nuotare

turn • le tour • die Kehre • el giro
• la giravolta

english • français • deutsch • español • italiano

styles • les styles • **die Schwimmstile** • los estilos • gli stili

front crawl • le crawl • **das Kraulen** • el crol • lo stile libero

breaststroke • la brasse • **das Brustschwimmen** • el pecho • la rana

stroke
la nage
der Zug
la brazada
la bracciata

kick
le coup de pied
der Stoß
la patada
la gambata

backstroke • la nage sur le dos • **das Rückenschwimmen**
• el dorso • il dorso

butterfly • le papillon • **der Butterfly** • la mariposa
• la farfalla

scuba diving • la plongée • **das Tauchen** • el buceo • il nuoto subacqueo

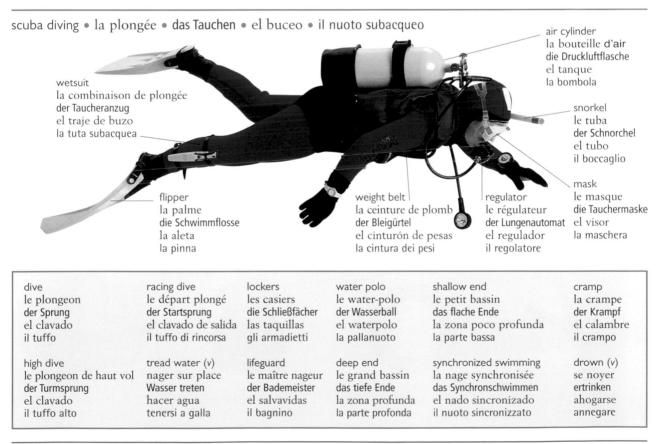

air cylinder
la bouteille **d'air**
die Druckluftflasche
el tanque
la bombola

wetsuit
la combinaison de plongée
der Taucheranzug
el traje de buzo
la tuta subacquea

snorkel
le tuba
der Schnorchel
el tubo
il boccaglio

flipper
la palme
die Schwimmflosse
la aleta
la pinna

weight belt
la ceinture de plomb
der Bleigürtel
el cinturón de pesas
la cintura dei pesi

regulator
le régulateur
der Lungenautomat
el regulador
il regolatore

mask
le masque
die Tauchermaske
el visor
la maschera

dive	racing dive	lockers	water polo	shallow end	cramp
le plongeon	le départ plongé	les casiers	le water-polo	le petit bassin	la crampe
der Sprung	**der Startsprung**	**die Schließfächer**	**der Wasserball**	**das flache Ende**	**der Krampf**
el clavado	el clavado de salida	las taquillas	el waterpolo	la zona poco profunda	el calambre
il tuffo	il tuffo di rincorsa	gli armadietti	la pallanuoto	la parte bassa	il crampo
high dive	tread water (v)	lifeguard	deep end	synchronized swimming	drown (v)
le plongeon de haut vol	nager sur place	le maître nageur	le grand bassin	la nage synchronisée	se noyer
der Turmsprung	**Wasser treten**	**der Bademeister**	**das tiefe Ende**	**das Synchronschwimmen**	**ertrinken**
el clavado	hacer agua	el salvavidas	la zona profunda	el nado sincronizado	ahogarse
il tuffo alto	tenersi a galla	il bagnino	la parte profonda	il nuoto sincronizzato	annegare

sailing • la voile • der Segelsport • la vela • la vela

compass • le compas
• der Kompass • la brújula
• la bussola

anchor • l'ancre • der
Anker • el ancla • l'ancora

mast
le mât
der Mast
el mástil
l'albero

rigging
le gréement
die Takelung
las jarcias
il sartiame

mainsail
la grand-voile
das Großsegel
la vela mayor
la vela di maestra

boom
la bôme
der Baum
la botavara
il boma

stern
l'arrière
das Heck
la popa
la poppa

cleat
le taquet
die Klampe
la escotera
la galloccia

sidedeck
le pont de côté
das Seitendeck
la cubierta
il ponte laterale

headsail
la voile d'avant
die Fock
el foque
la vela di prua

bow
l'avant
der Bug
la proa
la prua

tiller
la barre
die Pinne
la caña del
timón
la barra

hull
la coque
der Rumpf
el casco
lo scafo

navigate (v) • naviguer • navigieren • navegar
• navigare

yacht • le yacht • die Segeljacht • el yate • lo yacht

safety • la sécurité • die Sicherheit • la seguridad • la sicurezza

flare • la fusée éclairante
• die Leuchtrakete • la bengala
• il razzo illuminante

life preserver • la bouée de
sauvetage • der Rettungsring
• el salvavidas • il salvagente

life jacket • le gilet de
sauvetage • die Schwimmweste
• el chaleco salvavidas • il
giubbotto di salvataggio

life raft • le radeau de
sauvetage • das Rettungsboot
• la balsa salvavidas • la
zattera di salvataggio

watersports • les sports aquatiques • der Wassersport • los deportes acuáticos • gli sport acquatici

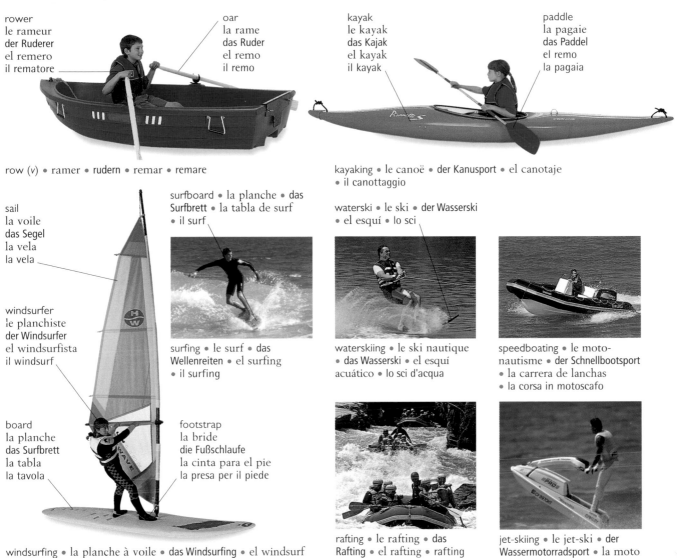

rower
le rameur
der Ruderer
el remero
il rematore

oar
la rame
das Ruder
el remo
il remo

kayak
le kayak
das Kajak
el kayak
il kayak

paddle
la pagaie
das Paddel
el remo
la pagaia

row (v) • ramer • rudern • remar • remare

kayaking • le canoë • der Kanusport • el canotaje
• il canottaggio

sail
la voile
das Segel
la vela
la vela

surfboard • la planche • das
Surfbrett • la tabla de surf
• il surf

waterski • le ski • der Wasserski
• el esquí • lo sci

windsurfer
le planchiste
der Windsurfer
el windsurfista
il windsurf

surfing • le surf • das
Wellenreiten • el surfing
• il surfing

waterskiing • le ski nautique
• das Wasserski • el esquí
acuático • lo sci d'acqua

speedboating • le moto-
nautisme • der Schnellbootsport
• la carrera de lanchas
• la corsa in motoscafo

board
la planche
das Surfbrett
la tabla
la tavola

footstrap
la bride
die Fußschlaufe
la cinta para el pie
la presa per il piede

rafting • le rafting • das
Rafting • el rafting • rafting

jet-skiing • le jet-ski • der
Wassermotorradsport • la moto
acuática • l'acquascooter

windsurfing • la planche à voile • das Windsurfing • el windsurf
• il windsurfing

waterskier	crew	wind	surf	sheet	centerboard
le skieur nautique	l'équipage	le vent	l'écume	l'écoute	la dérive
der Wasserskifahrer	die Crew	der Wind	die Brandung	die Schot	das Schwert
el esquiador acuático	la tripulación	el viento	la rompiente	la escota	la orza
lo sciatore d'acqua	l'equipaggio	il vento	la cresta dell'onda	la scotta	il centro della tavola
surfer	tack (v)	wave	rapids	rudder	capsize (v)
le surfeur	louvoyer	la vague	les rapides	le gouvernail	chavirer
der Surfer	aufkreuzen	die Welle	das Wildwasser	das Ruder	kentern
el surfista	virar	la ola	los rápidos	el timón	volcar
il surfista	bordeggiare	l'onda	le rapide	il timone	capovolgersi

horseback riding • l'équitation • der Reitsport • la equitación • l'equitazione

riding cap
la bombe
der Reithelm
la gorra de montar
il cappello da
equitazione

mane
la crinière
die Mähne
la crin
la criniera

rider
le cavalier
der Reiter
el jinete
il fantino

reins
les rênes
die Zügel
las riendas
le redini

saddle
la selle
der Sattel
la silla de montar
la sella

horse
le cheval
das Pferd
el caballo
il cavallo

jodhpurs
le jodhpur
die Reithose
el pantalón de montar
i pantaloni da equitazione

tail
la queue
der Schweif
la cola
la coda

cinch
la sangle
der Sattelgurt
la cincha
la cinghia

riding boot
la botte
der Reitstiefel
la bota de montar
lo stivale da
equitazione

stirrup
l'étrier
der Steigbügel
el estribo
la staffa

hoof
le sabot
der Huf
el casco
lo zoccolo

pommel
le pommeau
der Vorderzwiesel
el borrén
il pomo

browband
le frontail
der Stirnriemen
la frontalera
la cinghia frontale

noseband
la muserolle
der Nasenriemen
la muserola
la cinghia nasale

bit
le mors
die Kandare
el freno
il morso

seat
le siège
der Sitz
la silla
il sedile

bridle • la bride • das Zaumzeug • la brida • la briglia

horseshoe • le fer à cheval
• das Hufeisen • la herradura
• il ferro da cavallo

sidesaddle • la selle de femme
• der Damensattel • la silla de
montar de escaramuza
• la sella da signora

riding crop • la cravache • die Reitgerte • la fusta • il frustino events • les courses • die Veranstaltungen • las modalidades • le corse

racehorse • le cheval de course
• das Rennpferd • el caballo de
carreras • il cavallo da corsa

fence • l'obstacle • das Hindernis
• la valla • l'ostacolo

horse race • la course de chevaux • das
Pferderennen • la carrera de caballos
• la corsa di cavalli

steeplechase • le steeple • das Jagdrennen
• la carrera de obstáculos • la corsa a
ostacoli

harness race • la course de trot
• das Trabrennen • la carrera al trote
• la corsa di calessi

rodeo • le rodéo • das Rodeo • el rodeo
• il rodeo

show jumping • le jumping • das
Springreiten • el concurso de saltos
• il concorso di salto a ostacoli

carriage race • la course attelée
• das Zweispännerrennen • la carrera de
carrozas • la corsa di carrozze

trekking • la randonnée • das Trekking
• el paseo • l'escursione a cavallo

dressage • le dressage • das Dressurreiten
• la doma y monta • il dressage

polo • le polo • das Polo • el polo
• il polo

walk	canter	jump	halter	paddock	flat race
le pas	le petit galop	le saut	le licou	l'enclos	la course de plat
der Schritt	der Kanter	der Sprung	das Halfter	die Koppel	das Flachrennen
el paso	el medio galope	el salto	el cabestro	el cercado	la carrera sin obstáculos
il passo	il piccolo galoppo	il salto	la cavezza	il recinto	la corsa in piano
trot	gallop	groom	stable	arena	racecourse
le trot	le galop	le valet d'écurie	l'écurie	l'arène	le champs de courses
der Trab	der Galopp	der Stallbursche	der Pferdestall	der Turnierplatz	die Rennbahn
el trote	el galope	el mozo de cuadra	la cuadra	el ruedo	el hipódromo
il trotto	il galoppo	il palafreniere	la stalla	l'arena	l'ippodromo

fishing • la pêche • der Angelsport • la pesca • la pesca

sinker • le plomb • das Gewicht • el plomo • il peso

float • le flotteur • die Pose • el flotador • il galleggiante

barb
le barbillon
der Widerhaken
la punta
l'uncino

eye
l'œillet
das Öhr
el ojo
l'occhiello

fishhook • l'hameçon • der Angelhaken • el anzuelo • l'amo

lure • l'appât • der Köderhaken • el señuelo • l'esca

bait • l'amorce • der Köder • el cebo • l'esca

fly • la mouche • die Fliege • la mosca • la mosca

landing net • l'épuisette • der Kescher • la red para recoger • la retina

keep net • la bourriche • der Setzkescher • la red para las capturas • la rete da pesca

tackle box • la boîte d'équipement • der Spinnerkasten • la caja de aparejos • la scatola degli attrezzi

line
la ligne
die Schnur
el sedal
la lenza

fishing rod
la canne à pêche
die Angelrute
la caña de pescar
la canna da pesca

reel
le moulinet
die Rolle
el carrete
il mulinello

waders
les bottes de pêche
die Watstiefel
las botas altas de goma
gli stivaloni di gomma

fisherman • le pêcheur • der Angler • el pescador de caña • il pescatore

types of fishing • les genres de pêche • die Fischfangarten • los tipos de pesca • i tipi di pesca

freshwater fishing • la pêche en eau douce • das Süßwasserangeln • la pesca en agua dulce • la pesca in acqua dolce

fly fishing • la pêche à la mouche • das Fliegenangeln • la pesca con mosca • la pesca con la mosca

sport fishing • la pêche sportive • das Sportangeln • la pesca deportiva • la pesca sportiva

deep sea fishing • la pêche hauturière • die Hochseefischerei • la pesca de altura • la pesca il alto mare

surfcasting • la pêche au lancer en mer • das Brandungsangeln • la pesca en la orilla • la pesca dalla riva

activities • les activités • die Aktivitäten • las acciones • le attività

cast (v) • lancer • auswerfen • lanzar • lanciare

catch (v) • attraper • fangen • atrapar • prendere

reel in (v) • ramener • einholen • recoger • tirare con il mulinello

net (v) • prendre au filet • mit dem Netz fangen • atrapar con la red • pescare con la rete

release (v) • lâcher • loslassen • soltar • rilasciare

bait (v)	tackle	rain clothes	fishing license	creel
amorcer	le matériel de pêche	l'imperméable	le permis de pêche	le panier de pêche
ködern	die Angelgeräte	die Regenhaut	der Angelschein	der Fischkorb
cebar	los aparejos	la ropa impermeable	la licencia de pesca	la nasa
fornire di esca	l'attrezzatura	l'impermeabile	la licenza di pesca	la nassa
bite (v)	spool	pole	marine fishing	spearfishing
mordre	le tambour	la perche	la pêche maritime	la pêche sous-marine
anbeißen	die Rolle	die Stake	die Seefischerei	das Speerfischen
picar	el carrete	la pértiga	la pesca en alta mar	la pesca con arpón
abboccare	la bobina	il palo	la pesca in mare	la pesca con la fiocina

skiing • le ski • der Skisport • el esquí • lo sci

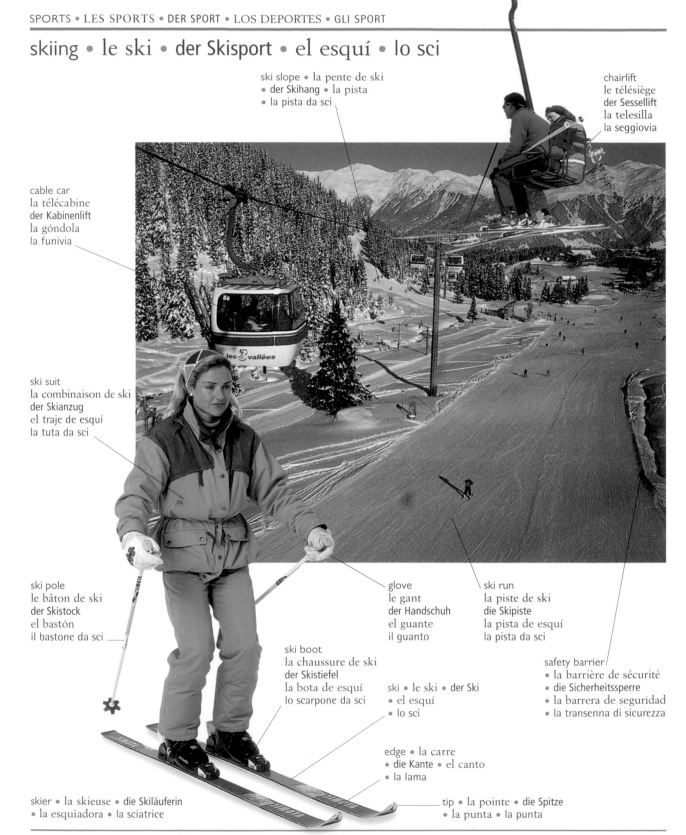

ski slope • la pente de ski
• der Skihang • la pista
• la pista da sci

chairlift
le télésiège
der Sessellift
la telesilla
la seggiovia

cable car
la télécabine
der Kabinenlift
la góndola
la funivia

ski suit
la combinaison de ski
der Skianzug
el traje de esquí
la tuta da sci

ski pole
le bâton de ski
der Skistock
el bastón
il bastone da sci

glove
le gant
der Handschuh
el guante
il guanto

ski run
la piste de ski
die Skipiste
la pista de esquí
la pista da sci

ski boot
la chaussure de ski
der Skistiefel
la bota de esquí
lo scarpone da sci

ski • le ski • der Ski
• el esquí
• lo sci

safety barrier
• la barrière de sécurité
• die Sicherheitssperre
• la barrera de seguridad
• la transenna di sicurezza

edge • la carre
• die Kante • el canto
• la lama

skier • la skieuse • die Skiläuferin
• la esquiadora • la sciatrice

tip • la pointe • die Spitze
• la punta • la punta

events • les épreuves • die Disziplinen • las modalidades • le gare

downhill skiing • la descente
• **der Abfahrtslauf**
• el descenso • la discesa

gate • la porte
• **das Tor** • el poste
• la porta

slalom • le slalom
• **der Slalom** • el slálom
• lo slalom

ski jump • le saut
• **der Skisprung** • el salto
• il salto

cross-country skiing • le ski de randonnée • **der Langlauf** • el esquí de fondo • lo sci di fondo

winter sports • les sports d'hiver • der Wintersport • los deportes de invierno • gli sport invernali

ice climbing • l'escalade en glace • **das Eisklettern** • la escalada en hielo • l'arrampicata su ghiaccio

ice skating • le patinage • **das Eislaufen** • el patinaje sobre hielo • il pattinaggio su ghiaccio

goggles • les lunettes de ski • **die Skibrille** • los goggles • gli occhiali

skate
le patin à glace
der Schlittschuh
el patín
il pattino

figure skating • le patinage artistique • **der Eiskunstlauf** • el patinaje artístico • il pattinaggio artistico

snowboarding • le surf des neiges • **das Snowboarding** • el snowboarding • lo snowboard

bobsled • le bobsleigh • **der Bobsport** • el bobsleigh • il bob

luge • la luge • **das Rennrodeln** • el luge • lo slittino

alpine skiing	dogsledding
le ski alpin	le traîneau à chiens
die alpine Kombination	**das Hundeschlittenfahren**
el esquí alpino	el trineo con perros
lo sci alpino	la corsa su slitta trainata da cani
giant slalom	speed skating
le slalom géant	le patinage de vitesse
der Riesenslalom	**das Eisschnelllauf**
el slálom gigante	el patinaje de velocidad
lo slalom gigante	il pattinaggio di velocità
off-piste	biathlon
hors piste	le biathlon
abseits der Piste	**das Biathlon**
fuera de pista	el biatlón
fuoripista	il biathlon
curling	avalanche
le curling	l'avalanche
das Curling	**die Lawine**
el curling	la avalancha
il curling	la valanga

snowmobile • l'autoneige • **das Schneemobil** • la moto de nieve • la motoslitta

sledding • la luge • **das Schlittenfahren** • tirarse en trineo • la corsa su slitta

other sports • les autres sports • die anderen Sportarten • los otros deportes • gli altri sport

glider
le planeur
das Segelflugzeug
el planeador
l'aliante

hang-glider
le deltaplane
der Drachen
el ala delta
il deltaplane

gliding • le vol plané • das Segelfliegen • el vuelo sin motor • il volo senza motore

parachute
le parachute
der Fallschirm
el paracaídas
il paracadute

hang-gliding • le deltaplane • das Drachenfliegen • el vuelo con ala delta • il volo in deltaplano

rope
la corde
das Seil
la cuerda
la corda

rock climbing • l'escalade • das Klettern • la escalada • l'alpinismo in parete

parachuting • le parachutisme • das Fallschirmspringen • el paracaidismo • il paracadutismo

parasailing • le parapente • das Gleitschirmfliegen • el parapente • il parapendio

skydiving • le saut en chute libre • das Fallschirmspringen • el paracaidismo en caída libre • il paracadutismo libero

rappeling • le rappel • das Abseilen • el rappel • la cordata

bungee jumping • le saut à l'élastique • das Bungeejumping • el salto bungee • il bungee jumping

race-car driver
le coureur automobile
der Rennfahrer
el piloto de carreras
il pilota da corsa

rally driving • le rallye • das Rallyefahren • el rally • il rally

auto racing • la course automobile • der Rennsport • el automovilismo • l'automobilismo

motocross • le motocross • das Motocross • el motocross • il motocross

motorbike racing • la course de moto • das Motorradrennen • el motociclismo • il motociclismo

skateboard
la planche à roulettes
das Skateboard
la patineta
la tavola da skateboard

rollerskate
le patin à roulettes
der Rollschuh
el patín de ruedas
il pattino a rotelle

stick
la crosse
der Lacrosseschläger
el palo
la mazza

mask
le masque
die Maske
la máscara
la maschera

foil
le fleuret
das Florett
el florete
il fioretto

skateboarding • la planche à roulettes • das Skateboard-fahren • andar en patineta • lo skate board

roller-skating • le patinage à roulettes • das Rollschuhfahren • el patinaje • il pattinaggio a rotelle

lacrosse • le lacrosse • das Lacrosse • el lacrosse • il lacrosse

fencing • l'escrime • das Fechten • la esgrima • la scherma

pin • la quille • der Kegel • el pino • il birillo

arrow
la flèche
der Pfeil
la flecha
la freccia

quiver
le carquois
der Köcher
el carcaj
la faretra

bow • l'arc • der Bogen • el arco • l'arco

target • la cible • die Zielscheibe • la diana • il bersaglio

bowling ball
la boule de bowling
die Bowlingkugel
la bola de boliche
la palla da bowling

archery • le tir à l'arc • das Bogenschießen • el tiro con arco • il tiro con l'arco

target shooting • le tir à cible • das Scheibenschießen • el tiro • il tiro al bersaglio

bowling • le bowling • das Bowling • el boliche • il bowling

pool • le billard américain • das Poolbillard • el pool • il biliardo

snooker • le billard • das Snooker • el billar • lo snooker

fitness • le conditionnement physique • die Fitness • la forma física • il fitness

gym machine • l'appareil de gym • das Fitnessgerät • la máquina de ejercicios • la macchina per esercizi

bench • le banc • die Bank • el banco • la panca

exercise bike • le vélo d'entraînement • das Trainingsrad • la bicicleta • la cyclette

free weights les poids die Gewichte las pesas i manubri

bar la barre die Stange la barra la sbarra

gym • le gymnase • das Fitnesscenter • el gimasio • la palestra

rowing machine • la machine à ramer • die Rudermaschine • la máquina de remos • il vogatore

treadmill • la tapis roulant • das Laufband • la banda caminadora • il treadmill

elliptical trainer • la machine de randonnée • die Langlauf-maschine • la máquina de cross • il cross trainer

personal trainer • l'entraîneuse individuelle • die private Fitness-trainerin • la entrenadora personal • l'istruttore individuale

step machine • l'escalier d'entraînement • die Tretmaschine • la máquina de step • la macchina per step

swimming pool • la piscine • das Schwimmbecken • la alberca • la piscina

sauna • le sauna • die Sauna • el sauna • la sauna

exercises • les exercices • die Übungen • los ejercicios • gli esercizi

stretch • l'étirement • das Strecken • el estiramiento • lo stretching

lunge • la fente en avant • der Ausfall • la flexión con estiramiento • lo stiramento

tights
le collant
die Strumpfhose
los leotardos
il collant

push-up • la traction • der Liegestütz • la flexión • le flessioni

squat • la flexion de jambes • die Kniebeuge • ponerse en cuclillas • lo squat

sit-up • le redressement assis • das Rumpfheben • el abdominal • gli addominali

dumbbell
l'haltère
die Hantel
la pesa
il manubrio

bicep curl • l'exercise pour les biceps • die Bizepsübung • el ejercicio de bíceps • le alzate con il manubrio

leg press • la traction pour les jambes • der Beinstütz • los ejercicios de piernas • la pressa per le gambe

chest press • l'exercice pour la poitrine • die Brustübung • los ejercicios pectorales • la pressa per pettorali

running shoes
• les baskets
• die Trainings-
schuhe • las
zapatillas
• gli scarponcini

weight bar
la barre à poids
die Gewichthantel
la barra de pesas
il bilanciere

vest
le maillot
das Hemd
la camiseta
la maglietta

weight training • l'entraînement poids et haltères • das Kraft-training • el levantamiento de pesas • l'addestramento ai pesi

jogging • le jogging • das Jogging • el jogging • il footing

aerobics • l'aérobic • das Aerobic • los aerobics • la ginnastica aerobica

train (v)	jog in place (v)	extend (v)	Pilates	circuit training
s'entraîner	jogger sur place	étendre	les exercices Pilates	l'entraînement en circuit
trainieren	auf der Stelle joggen	ausstrecken	die Pilates-Übungen	das Zirkeltraining
entrenar	correr en parada	estirar	el pilates	la tabla de gimnasia
allenarsi	correre sul posto	stendere	il pilates	l'allemamento in circuito
warm up (v)	flex (v)	pull up (v)	boxercise	jumping rope
s'échauffer	fléchir	tirer	l'aéroboxe	le saut à la corde
sich aufwärmen	beugen	hochziehen	die Boxgymnastik	das Seilspringen
calentar	flexionar	levantar	la gimnasia prepugilística	saltar a la comba
riscaldarsi	flettere	sollevare	la ginnastica prepugilistica	saltare con la corda

leisure
le temps libre
die Freizeit
el ocio
il tempo libero

theater • le théâtre • das Theater • el teatro • il teatro

curtain
le rideau
der Vorhang
el telón
il sipario

wings
les coulisses
die Kulisse
los bastidores
le quinte

set
le décor
das Bühnenbild
la escenografía
la scenografia

audience
le public
das Publikum
el público
il pubblico

orchestra
l'orchestre
das Orchester
la orquesta
l'orchestra

stage • la scène • die Bühne • el escenario • il palcoscenico

seat
le fauteuil
der Sitzplatz
la butaca
la poltrona

upper balcony
la deuxième galerie
der zweite Rang
la platea alta
la seconda galleria

row
la rangée
die Reihe
la fila
la fila

box
la loge
die Loge
el palco
il palco

mezzanine
la corbeille
der erste Rang
la platea
la galleria

balcony
le balcon
der Balkon
la galería
la balconata

orchestra
seats
l'orchestre
das Parkett
las butacas
generales
le poltrone
di platea

aisle
l'allée
der Gang
el pasillo
il corridoio

seating • les places • die Bestuhlung • las butacas
• le poltrone

play	director	opening night
la pièce de théâtre	le metteur en scène	la première
das Theaterstück	der Regisseur	die Premiere
la obra	el director	el estreno
l'opera teatrale	il regista	la prima
cast	producer	intermissionl
la distribution	le metteur en scène	l'entracte
die Besetzung	der Regisseur	die Pause
el reparto	el productor	el entreacto
il cast	il produttore	l'intervallo
actor	script	program
l'acteur	le texte	le programme
der Schauspieler	das Rollenheft	das Programm
el actor	el guión	el programa
l'attore	il copione	il programma
actress	backdrop	orchestra pit
l'actrice	la toile de fond	la fosse d'orchestre
die Schauspielerin	der Prospekt	der Orchestergraben
la actriz	el telón de fondo	el foso de la orquesta
l'attrice	il fondale	il golfo mistico

concert • le concert • **das Konzert** • el concierto • il concerto

musical • la comédie musicale • **das Musical** • el musical • il musical

costume
le costume
das Theaterkostüm
el vestuario
il costume

usher	soundtrack
le placeur	la bande sonore
der Platzanweiser	die Tonspur
el acomodador	la banda sonora
la maschera	la colonna sonora
classical music	applaud (v)
la musique classique	applaudir
die klassische Musik	applaudieren
la música clásica	aplaudir
la musica classica	applaudire
musical score	encore
la partition	le bis
die Noten	die Zugabe
la partitura	el bis
la partitura musicale	il bis

I'd like two tickets for tonight's performance.
Je voudrais deux billets pour la représentation de ce soir.
Ich möchte zwei Karten für die Aufführung heute Abend.
Quisiera dos entradas para la sesión de esta noche.
Vorrei due biglietti per lo spettacolo di stasera.

What time does it start?
Ça commence à quelle heure?
Um wie viel Uhr beginnt die Aufführung?
¿A qué hora empieza?
A che ora inizia?

ballet • le ballet • **das Ballett** • el ballet • il balletto

opera • l'opéra • **die Oper** • la ópera • l'opera

---

movies • le cinéma • **das Kino** • el cine • il cinema

popcorn
le pop-corn
das Popcorn
las palomitas
il popcorn

box office
la caisse
die Kasse
la taquilla
la biglietteria

lobby
le foyer
das Foyer
el vestíbulo
l'atrio

poster
l'affiche
das Plakat
el póster
il poster

movie theater • la salle de cinéma • **der Kinosaal** • el cine • il cinema

screen • l'écran • **die Leinwand** • la pantalla • lo schermo

comedy	romance
la comédie	la comédie romantique
die Komödie	der Liebesfilm
la comedia	la película romántica
la commedia	il film d'amore
thriller	science fiction movie
le thriller	le film de science-fiction
der Thriller	der Science-Fiction-Film
la película de suspenso	la película de ciencia ficción
il thriller	il film di fantascienza
horror movie	adventure
le film d'horreur	le film d'aventures
der Horrorfilm	der Abenteuerfilm
la película de miedo	la película de aventuras
il film di orrore	il film di avventura
Western	animated movie
le western	le film d'animation
der Western	der Zeichentrickfilm
la película de vaqueros	la película de dibujos animados
il western	il film di animazione

orchestra • l'orchestre • das Orchester • la orquesta • l'orchestra

strings • les cordes • die Saiteninstrumente • la cuerda • le corde

harp
la harpe
die Harfe
el arpa
l'arpa

conductor
le chef d'orchestre
der Dirigent
el director de orquesta
il direttore di orchestra

double bass
le contrebasse
der Kontrabass
el contrabajo
il contrabbasso

violin
le violon
die Geige
el violín
il violino

podium
le podium
das Podium
el podio
il podio

viola
l'alto
die Bratsche
la viola
la viola

cello
le violoncelle
das Cello
el violoncelo
il violoncello

score
la partition
die Noten
la partitura
lo spartito

treble clef
la clé de sol
der Violinschlüssel
la clave de sol
la chiave di sol

note
la note
die Note
la nota
la nota

staff
la portée
das Liniensystem
el pentagrama
il pentagramma

bass clef
la clé de fa
der Bassschlüssel
la clave de fa
la chiave di basso

piano • le piano • das Klavier • el piano • il pianoforte

notation • la notation • die Notation • la notación • l'annotazione

overture	sonata	rest	sharp	natural	scale
l'ouverture	la sonate	le silence	la dièse	le bécarre	la gamme
die Ouvertüre	die Sonate	das Pausenzeichen	das Kreuz	das Auflösungszeichen	die Tonleiter
la obertura	la sonata	la pausa	sostenido	natural	la escala
l'ouverture	la sonata	la pausa	il diesis	naturale	la scala
symphony	instruments	pitch	flat	bar	baton
la symphonie	les instruments	le ton	le bémol	la barre de mesure	la baguette
die Symphonie	die Musikinstrumente	die Tonhöhe	das B	der Taktstrich	der Taktstock
la sinfonía	los instrumentos	el tono	bemol	la barra	la batura
la sinfonia	gli strumenti	il tono	il bemolle	la battuta	la bacchetta

english • français • deutsch • español • italiano

woodwind • les bois • die Holzblasinstrumente • el viento-madera • gli strumenti a fiato

piccolo • le piccolo
• die Pikkoloflöte
• el flautín • il piffero

flute • la flûte
traversière • die Querflöte
• la flauta • il flauto

oboe • le hautbois
• die Oboe • el oboe
• l'oboe

English horn • le cor anglais
• das Englischhorn • el corno
inglés • il corno inglese

clarinet • la clarinette
• die Klarinette • el
clarinete • il clarinetto

bass clarinet • la clarinette
basse • die Bassklarinette
• el clarinete bajo
• il clarinetto basso

bassoon • le basson
• das Fagott • el fagote
• il fagotto

double bassoon • le
contrebasson • das
Kontrafagott • el contra-
fagote • il controfagotto

saxophone • le
saxophone • das
Saxophon • el saxofón
• il sassofono

percussion • la percussion • die Schlaginstrumente • la percusión • la percussione

kettledrum • la timbale
• die Kesselpauke • el
timbal • il timpano

gong • le gong • der
Gong • el gong
• il gong

bongos • les bongos
• die Bongos • los
bongos • i bongo

snare drum • la caisse
claire • die kleine
Trommel • el tambor
pequeño • il tamburo
militare

cymbals • les cymbales
• das Becken • los
platillos • i cembali

tambourine
• le tambour
• das Tamburin
• el pandero
• il tamburino

vibraphone • le vibraphone
• das Vibraphon • la marimba
• il vibrafono

triangle
• le triangle
• der Triangel
• el triángulo
• il triangolo

maracas
• les maracas
• die Maracas
• las maracas
• i maracas

brass • les cuivres • die Blechblasinstrumente • el viento-metal • gli ottoni

trumpet • la trompette
• die Trompete • la trompeta
• la tromba

trombone • le trombone • die Posaune
• el trombón de varas • il trombone

French horn • le cor • das
Horn • el corno de caza
• il corno

tuba • le tuba
• die Tuba • la tuba
• la tuba

concert • le concert • das Konzert • el concierto • il concerto

lead singer
le chanteur
der Leadsänger
el vocalista
il cantante

microphone
le microphone
das Mikrophon
el micrófono
il microfono

drummer
le batteur
der Schlagzeuger
el baterista
il batterista

guitarist
le guitariste
der Gitarrist
el guitarrista
il chitarrista

fans
les fans
die Fans
los fans
i fans

speaker
le haut-parleur
der Lautsprecher
la bocina
l'altoparlante

bass guitarist
le bassiste
der Bassgitarrist
el bajista
il bassista

rock concert • le concert de rock • das Rockkonzert • el concierto de rock • il concerto rock

instruments • les instruments • die Instrumente • los instrumentos • gli strumenti

pickup
le pick-up
der Tonabnehmer
la pastilla
il riproduttore acustico

neck
le manche
der Hals
el mástil
il manico

fret
le sillet
der Bund
el traste
il tasto

bridge
le chevalet
der Steg
el puente
il ponte

tuning peg
la cheville
der Wirbel
la clavija
il pirolo

string
la corde
die Saite
la cuerda
la corda

drum
le tambour
die Trommel
el tambor
il tamburo

bass guitar • la basse • die Bassgitarre
• el bajo • il basso

keyboard • le piano électronique • das Keyboard
• el teclado • la tastiera

electric guitar • la guitare électrique
• die elektrische Gitarre • la guitarra
eléctrica • la chitarra elettrica

drum kit • la batterie • das
Schlagzeug • la batería • la batteria

musical styles • les styles de musique • die Musikstile • los estilos musicales • gli stili musicali

jazz • le jazz • der Jazz • el jazz • il jazz

blues • le blues • der Blues • el blues • il blues

punk • la musique punk • die Punkmusik • el punk • il punk

folk music • la musique folk • der Folk • la música folklórica • la musica folk

pop • la pop • der Pop • el pop • il pop

dance • la dance • die Tanzmusik • la música de baile • la musica da ballo

rap • le rap • der Rap • el rap • il rap

heavy metal • la heavy métal • das Heavymetal • el heavy metal • l'heavy metal

classical music • la musique classique • die klassische Musik • la música clásica • la musica classica

song	lyrics	melody	beat	reggae	country	spotlight
la chanson	les paroles	la mélodie	le beat	le reggae	la country	le projecteur
das Lied	der Text	die Melodie	der Beat	der Reggae	die Countrymusic	der Scheinwerfer
la canción	la letra	la melodía	el ritmo	el reggae	la música country	el reflector
la canzone	il testo	la melodia	il ritmo	il reggae	il country	il proiettore

sightseeing • le tourisme • die Besichtigungstour • el turismo • il turismo

tourist
le touriste
der Tourist
el turista
il turista

itinerary
l'itinéraire
die Route
el itinerario
l'itinerario

open-top
à impériale
mit offenem Oberdeck
descubierto
scoperto

This is an official London Sightseeing Bus.

LONDON PRIDE

tour bus • le bus touristique • der Stadtrundfahrtbus • el autobús turístico • il pullman turistico

tour guide
la guide
die Fremdenführerin
la guía turística
la guida turistica

figurine • la statuette • die Figur • la estatuilla • la statuina

guided tour • la tour guidé • die Führung • la visita guiada • la visita guidata

souvenirs • les souvenirs • die Andenken • los recuerdos • i ricordi

tourist attraction • l'attraction touristique • die Touristenattraktion • la atracción turística • il luogo d'interesse turistico

open	guidebook	camcorder	left	Where is…?	I'm lost.
ouvert	le guide	le caméscope	à gauche	Où est…?	Je me suis perdu.
geöffnet	der Reiseführer	der Camcorder	links	Wo ist…?	Ich habe mich verlaufen.
abierto	la guía del viajero	la cámara de vídeo	la izquierda	¿Dónde está…?	Estoy perdido.
aperto	la guida	la videocamera	a sinistra	Dov'è…?	Mi sono perso.
closed	film	camera	right	Can you tell me the way to….?	
fermé	la pellicule	l'appareil photo	à droite	Pour aller à…, s'il vous plaît?	
geschlossen	der Film	die Kamera	rechts	Können Sie mir sagen, wie ich nach… komme?	
cerrado	la película	la cámara fotográfica	la derecha	¿Podría decirme cómo se va a…?	
chiuso	la pellicola	la macchina fotografica	a destra	Mi può dire come si arriva a…?	
admission charge	batteries	directions	straight ahead		
le prix d'entrée	les piles	les directions	tout droit		
das Eintrittsgeld	die Batterien	die Richtungsangaben	geradeaus		
el precio de entrada	las pilas	las indicaciones	recto		
la tariffa d'ingresso	le batterie	le indicazioni	dritto		

english • français • deutsch • español • italiano

attractions • les attractions • die Sehenswürdigkeiten • los lugares de interés • i luoghi d'interesse

painting
le tableau
das Gemälde
el cuadro
il quadro

exhibit
l'objet exposé
das Ausstellungsstück
la muestra
l'oggetto

exhibition • l'exposition
• die Ausstellung • la exposición
• l'esposizione

famous ruin
la ruine célèbre
die berühmte Ruine
la ruina famosa
la rovina famosa

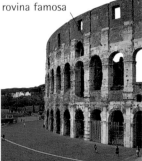

art gallery • le musée d'art
• die Kunstgalerie • la galería
de arte • la galleria d'arte

monument • le monument
• das Monument • el
monumento • il monumento

museum • le musée
• das Museum • el museo
• il museo

historic building • le
monument historique • das
historische Gebäude • el edificio
histórico • l'edificio storico

casino • le casino • das Kasino
• el casino • il casinò

garden • le parc • der Park
• los jardines • i giardini

national park • le parc national • der Nationalpark • el parque
nacional • il parco nazionale

information • l'information • die Information • la información • l'informazione

times
les heures
die Zeiten
las horas
gli orari

floor plan • le plan • der
Grundriss • el plano de la
planta • la pianta del piano

map • le plan • der Stadtplan
• el mapa • la mappa

timetable • l'horaire • der
Fahrplan • el horario
• l'orario

tourist information
• l'information touristique
• die Touristeninformation • la
oficina de información •
l'ufficio informazioni turistiche

outdoor activities • les activités de plein air • die Aktivitäten im Freien • las actividades al aire libre • le attività all'aria aperta

footpath
le sentier
der Fußweg
el sendero
il sentiero

sundial
le cadran solaire
die Sonnenuhr
el reloj de sol
la meridiana

café
le café
das Café
la cafetería
il caffè

park • le parc • der Park • el parque • il parco

grass
la pelouse
das Gras
el pasto
il prato

bench
le banc
die Bank
la banca
la panchina

formal gardens
les jardins à la française
die Gartenanlagen
los jardines clásicos
il giardino all'italiana

roller coaster
les montagnes russes
die Berg-und-Talbahn
la montaña rusa
le montagne russe

fair • la foire • der Jahrmarkt
• la feria • il luna park

amusement park • le parc
d'attractions • der
Vergnügungspark • el parque
de diversiones • il parco a tema

wildlife park • la réserve
• der Safaripark • el safari park
• lo zoosafari

zoo • le zoo • der Zoo
• el zoológico • lo zoo

activities • les activités • die Aktivitäten • las actividades • le attività

cycling • le vélo • das Radfahren • el ciclismo • il ciclismo

jogging • le jogging • das Jogging • el jogging • il footing

skateboarding • la planche à roulette • das Skateboardfahren • la patineta • lo skateboard

rollerblading • le roller • das Inlinerfahren • el patinaje • il pattinaggio

riding trail • la piste cavalière • der Reitweg • el sendero para caballos • il sentiero per cavalli

bird watching • l'observation des oiseaux • das Vogelbeobachten • la ornitología • l'ornitologia

horseback riding • l'équitation • das Reiten • la equitación • l'equitazione

hiking • la randonnée • das Wandern • la caminata • l'escursionismo

hamper • le panier à pique-nique • der Picknickkorb • la canasta • la cesta

picnic • le pique-nique • das Picknick • el picnic • il picnic

---

playground • le terrain de jeux • der Spielplatz • el área de juegos • il parco giochi

sandbox • le bac à sable • der Sandkasten • el cajón de arena • la fossa di sabbia

wading pool • la pataugeoire • das Planschbecken • la alberca de plástico • la piscina gonfiabile

swing • la balançoire • die Schaukel • los columpios • l'altalena

seesaw • la bascule • die Wippe • el subibaja • il bilanciere

slide • le toboggan • die Rutsche • la resbaladilla • lo scivolo

climber • la cage à poules • das Klettergerüst • el changuero • la struttura per arrampicarsi

beach • la plage • der Strand • la playa • la spiaggia

hotel
l'hôtel
das Hotel
el hotel
l'albergo

beach umbrella
le parasol
der Sonnenschirm
la sombrilla
l'ombrellone

beach hut
la cabine de plage
das Strandhäuschen
la caseta
la cabina

sand
le sable
der Sand
la arena
la sabbia

wave
la vague
die Welle
la ola
l'onda

sea
la mer
das Meer
el mar
il mare

beach bag
le sac de plage
die Strandtasche
la bolsa de playa
la borsa da spiaggia

bikini
le bikini
der Bikini
el bikini
il bikini

sunbathe (v) • prendre un bain de soleil • sonnenbaden • asolear • prendere il sole

lifeguard
le maître nageur
der Rettungsschwimmer
el salvavidas
il bagnino

lifeguard tower • la tour de surveillance • der Rettungsturm • la torre de vigilancia • la torre di sorveglianza

windbreak • le pare-vent • der Windschutz • la barrera contra el viento • il paravento

promenade • la promenade • die Promenade • el paseo marítimo • il lungomare

deck chair • le transat • der Liegestuhl • el asoleadero • la sedia a sdraio

sunglasses • les lunettes de soleil • die Sonnenbrille • los lentes obscuros • gli occhiali da sole

sunhat • le chapeau de plage • der Sonnenhut • el sombrero para el sol • il cappello da spiaggia

suntan lotion • la lotion solaire • die Sonnenmilch • el bronceador • la crema abbronzante

sunblock • l'écran total • der Sonnenblock • la crema protectora • la crema protettiva

swimsuit
le maillot de bain
der Badeanzug
el traje de baño
il costume da bagno

shovel
la pelle
der Spaten
la pala
la paletta

pail
le seau
der Eimer
la cubeta
il secchiello

beach ball • le ballon de plage • der Wasserball • la pelota de playa • il pallone da spiaggia

rubber ring • la bouée • der Schwimmreifen • la llanta • la ciambella

sandcastle
le château de sable
die Sandburg
el castillo de arena
il castello di sabbia

beach towel • la serviette de plage • das Strandtuch • la toalla de playa • l'asciugamano da spiaggia

shell
le coquillage
die Muschel
la concha
la conchiglia

camping • le camping • das Camping • el camping • il campeggio

restrooms	waste disposal	showers	electric hook-up
les toilettes	les poubelles	les douches	le branchement électrique
die Toiletten	die Mülleimer	die Duschen	der Stromanschluss
los baños	el contenedor de la basura	las regaderas	el punto eléctrico
i bagni	i rifuti	le docce	la presa di corrente

flysheet	tent peg	guy rope	camper
le double toit	le piquet	la corde	la caravane
das Überdach	der Hering	die Zeltspannleine	der Wohnwagen
el toldo	la estaca	la cuerda	la roulotte
il telo protettivo	il piolo	la corda	la roulotte

campsite • le terrain de camping • der Campingplatz • el camping • il campeggio

camp (v)	site	picnic bench	charcoal
camper	l'emplacement	le banc à pique-nique	le charbon de bois
zelten	der Zeltplatz	die Picknickbank	die Holzkohle
acampar	el lugar	la mesa de picnic	el carbón vegetal
campeggiare	il posteggio	il tavola da picnic	la carbonella
manager's office	pitch a tent (v)	hammock	firelighter
le bureau du chef	monter une tente	le hamac	l'allume-feu
die Campingplatzverwaltung	ein Zelt aufschlagen	die Hängematte	der Feueranzünder
la oficina del director	poner una tienda	la hamaca	la pastilla para fogatas
l'ufficio del direttore	piantare una tenda	l'amaca	l'esca per il fuoco
sites available	tent pole	camper van	light a fire (v)
les emplacements de libre	le mât	l'autocaravane	allumer un feu
Zeltplätze frei	die Zeltstange	das Wohnmobil	ein Feuer machen
hay lugares libres	el tubo de la tienda	el cámper	encender una fogata
le piazzole disponibili	il palo	il camper	accendere un fuoco
full	cot	trailer	campfire
complet	le lit de camp	la remorque	le feu de camp
voll	das Faltbett	der Anhänger	das Lagerfeuer
lleno	el catre de campaña	el remolque	la fogata
completo	il lettino da campeggio	il rimorchio	il fuoco

english • français • deutsch • español • italiano

frame
le cadre
das Gestänge
la estructura
la struttura

ground cloth
le tapis de sol
der Zeltboden
el suelo aislante
il telo isolante

thermos
le thermos
die Thermosflasche
el termo
il thermos

backpack
le sac à dos
der Rucksack
la mochila
lo zaino

water bottle
la bouteille d'eau
die Wasserflasche
la cantimplora
la borraccia

tent • la tente • **das Zelt** • la tienda de campaña • la tenda

insect repellent • le spray contre les insectes • **der Insektenspray** • el repelente de insectos • il repellente per insetti

flashlight • la lampe torche • die Taschenlampe • la linterna • la torcia

mosquito net
la moustiquaire
das Moskitonetz
el mosquitero
la zanzariera

thermal underwear
les sous-vêtements thermiques
die Thermowäsche
la ropa térmica
gli indumenti termici

hiking boots • les chaussures de marche • **die Wanderschuhe** • las botas de trekking • le scarpe da escursionismo

rain clothes • l'imperméable • **die Regenhaut** • la manga • gli indumenti impermeabili

sleeping bag • le sac de couchage • **der Schlafsack** • el saco de dormir • il sacco a pelo

sleeping mat
le tapis de sol
die Schlafmatte
la esterilla
il materassino

camp stove • le réchaud • **der Gasbrenner** • la estufilla • il fornelletto da campeggio

grill • le barbecue • **der Grill** • la parrilla • la griglia per barbecue

air mattress • le matelat pneumatique • **die Luftmatratze** • la colchoneta • il materassino ad aria

home entertainment • les distractions à la maison • die Privatunter-
haltung • el entretenimiento en el hogar • gli intrattenimenti in casa

DVD • le DVD
• die DVD-Platte
• el disco de DVD
• il disco DVD

personal CD player • le
baladeur CD • der Discman
• el discman • il lettore di
CD portatile

mini disc recorder
• l'enregistreur minidisk
• der Minidiskrekorder • la
grabadora de minidisks
• il lettore di mini disk

MP3 player • le baladeur
MP3 • der MP3-Spieler
• el lector de MP3
• il lettore di MP3

DVD player • le lecteur DVD • der
DVD-Spieler • el reproductor de DVD
• il lettore di DVD

record player
le tourne-disque
der Plattenspieler
el tocadiscos
il giradischi

CD player
le lecteur CD
der CD-Spieler
el lector de discos compactos
il lettore di CD

radio
la radio
das Radio
la radio
la radio

amplifier
l'amplificateur
der Verstärker
el amplificador
l'amplificatore

headphones
les écouteurs
die Kopfhörer
los audífonos
le cuffie

stereo rack
l'étagère
das Rack
el mueble
il supporto

speaker
le baffle
die Box
la bocina
l'altoparlante

speaker stand
le support
der Ständer
el pie de la bocina
il supporto per
l'altoparlante

stereo system • la chaîne hi-fi • die Hi-Fi-Anlage
• el equipo de alta fidelidad • l'impianto stereo

videotape
la vidéocassette
die Videokassette
el videocasete
la videocassetta

screen
l'écran
der Bildschirm
la pantalla
lo schermo

eyecup
l'œilleton
die Okularmuschel
el borde del ocular
l'oculare

VCR • le magnétoscope • der Videorekorder • la videocasetera • il videoregistratore

camcorder • le caméscope • der Camcorder • la cámara de video • la videocamera

satellite dish • l'antenne parabolique • die Satellitenschüssel • la antena parabólica • l'antenna parabolica

widescreen television • la télévision 16/9ème • der Breitbildfernseher • la televisión de pantalla panorámica • il televisore a schermo largo

console
la console
das Pult
la consola
la console

fast-forward • l'avance rapide • der Vorlauf • el avance rápido • l'avanzamento veloce

pause
la pause
die Pause
la pausa
la pausa

record
• l'enregistrement
• die Aufnahme
• el botón para grabar • la registrazione

volume
le volume
die Lautstärke
el volumen
il volume

controller
la commande
der Steuerhebel
los controles
il comando

rewind
le retour rapide
der Rücklauf
el botón para rebobinar
il riavvolgimento

play
la lecture
das Abspielen
el play
il play

stop
l'arrêt
der Stop
el stop
lo stop

video game • le jeu vidéo • das Videospiel • el videojuego • il videogioco

remote control • la télécommande • die Fernbedienung • el control remoto • il telecomando

CD le CD die CD-Platte el disco compacto il compact disc	feature film le film der Spielfilm la película il lungometraggio	cable television la télévision par câble das Kabelfernsehen la televisión por cable la televisione via cavo	pay-per-view channel la chaîne à péage der Pay-Kanal el canal de pago por evento il canale a pagamento	turn off the television (v) éteindre la télévision den Fernseher abschalten apagar la televisión spegnere la televisione
cassette tape la cassette die Kassette el casete l'audiocassetta	advertisement la publicité die Werbung el anuncio la pubblicità	programme le programme das Programm el programa il programma	turn on the television (v) allumer la télévision den Fernseher einschalten encender la televisión accendere la televisione	tune the radio (v) régler la radio das Radio einstellen sintonizar la radio sintonizzare la radio
cassette player le lecteur cassettes der Kassettenrekorder la casetera il mangianastri	digital numérique digital digital digitale	change channels (v) changer de chaîne den Kanal wechseln cambiar de canal cambiare canale	watch television (v) regarder la télévision fernsehen ver la televisión guardare la televisione	stereo stéréo stereo estéreo stereo

photography • la photographie • die Fotografie • la fotografía • la fotografia

frame counter
le compteur de vues
der Zähler
el indicador de fotos
il contafotogrammi

flash
le flash
der Blitz
el flash
il flash

aperture dial
le réglage de l'ouverture
der Blendenregler
el obturador
il regolatore di esponsizione

filter • le filtre • der Filter • el filtro • il filtro

shutter release
le déclencheur
der Auslöser
el disparador
il pulsante di scatto

lens cap • le bouchon d'objectif • die Schutzkappe • la tapa del lente • il copriobiettivo

shutter-speed dial
le réglage du temps de pose
die Zeiteinstellscheibe
la rueda de la velocidad
il regolatore del tempo di esposizione

lens
l'objectif
die Linse
el lente
l'obiettivo

SLR camera • l'appareil réflex mono-objectif • die Spiegelreflexkamera • la cámara réflex • la macchina fotografica SLR

flash gun • le flash compact • der Elektronenblitz • el flash electrónico • il lampeggiatore

light meter • le posemètre • der Belichtungsmesser • el fotómetro • l'esposimetro

zoom lens • le zoom • das Zoom • el zoom • lo zoom

tripod • le trépied • das Stativ • el tripié • il treppiede

---

types of camera • les types d'appareils photo • die Fotoapparattypen • los tipos de cámara • i tipi di macchina fotorafica

digital camera • l'appareil numérique • die Digitalkamera • la cámara digital • la macchina fotografica digitale

APS camera • l'appareil photo APS • die Kamera für APS-Film • la cámara APS • la macchina fotografica APS

instant camera • l'appareil instantané • die Sofortbildkamera • la cámara Polaroid • la macchina fotografica instantanea

disposable camera • l'appareil jetable • die Einwegkamera • la cámara desechable • la macchina fotografica usa e getta

photograph (v) • photographier • **fotografieren** • fotografiar • fotografare

film spool
le rouleau de pellicule
die Filmspule
el carrete
il rollino

film • la pellicule • der Film • el rollo • la pellicola

focus (v) • mettre au point • **einstellen** • enfocar • mettere a fuoco

develop (v) • développer • **entwickeln** • revelar • sviluppare

negative • le négatif • **das Negativ** • el negativo • il negativo

landscape • paysage • **quer** • apaisado • orizzontale

portrait • portrait • **hoch** • en formato vertical • verticale

photograph • la photo • **das Foto** • la fotografía • la fotografia

photo album • l'album de photos • **das Fotoalbum** • el álbum de fotos • l'album fotografico

picture frame • le cadre de photo • **der Fotorahmen** • el portarretratos • la cornice

problems • les problèmes • **die Probleme** • los problemas • i difetti

underexposed • sous-exposé • **unterbelichtet** • subexpuesto • sottoesposto

overexposed • surexposé • **überbelichtet** • sobreexpuesto • sovraesposto

out of focus • flou • **unscharf** • desenfocado • sfocato

red eye • la tache rouge • **die Rotfärbung der Augen** • los ojos rojos • l'occhio rosso

viewfinder	print
le viseur	l'épreuve
der Bildsucher	der Abzug
el visor	la foto (revelada)
il mirino	la fotografia (sviluppata)
camera case	mat
le sac d'appareil photo	mat
die Kameratasche	matt
la funda de la cámara	mate
l'astuccio	opaco
exposure	gloss
la pose	brilliant
die Belichtung	Hochglanz-
la exposición	con brillo
l'esposizione	lucido
darkroom	enlargement
la chambre noire	l'agrandissement
die Dunkelkammer	die Vergrößerung
el cuarto oscuro	la ampliación
la camera oscura	l'ingrandimento

I'd like this film processed.
Pourriez-vous faire développer cette pellicule?
Könnten Sie diesen Film entwickeln lassen?
Me gustaría revelar este rollo.
Vorrei far sviluppare questo rollino.

games • les jeux • die Spiele • los juegos • i giochi

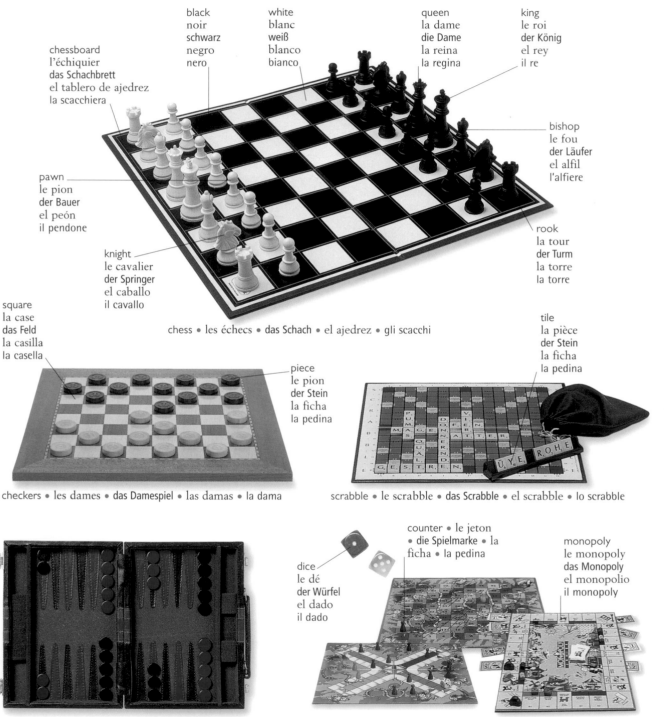

black
noir
schwarz
negro
nero

white
blanc
weiß
blanco
bianco

queen
la dame
die Dame
la reina
la regina

king
le roi
der König
el rey
il re

chessboard
l'échiquier
das Schachbrett
el tablero de ajedrez
la scacchiera

bishop
le fou
der Läufer
el alfil
l'alfiere

pawn
le pion
der Bauer
el peón
il pendone

rook
la tour
der Turm
la torre
la torre

knight
le cavalier
der Springer
el caballo
il cavallo

square
la case
das Feld
la casilla
la casella

tile
la pièce
der Stein
la ficha
la pedina

chess • les échecs • das Schach • el ajedrez • gli scacchi

piece
le pion
der Stein
la ficha
la pedina

checkers • les dames • das Damespiel • las damas • la dama

scrabble • le scrabble • das Scrabble • el scrabble • lo scrabble

counter • le jeton
• die Spielmarke • la
ficha • la pedina

dice
le dé
der Würfel
el dado
il dado

monopoly
le monopoly
das Monopoly
el monopolio
il monopoly

backgammon • le trictrac • das Backgammon
• el backgammon • il tric trac (la tavola reale)

board games • les jeux de société • die Brettspiele • los juegos
de mesa • i giochi da tavolo

english • français • deutsch • español • italiano

dartboard
la cible
die Dartscheibe
la diana
il bersaglio

bullseye
le mille
das Bull's Eye
el blanco
il centro

stamp collecting • la philatélie
• das Briefmarkensammeln
• la filatelia • la filatelia

jigsaw puzzle • le puzzle
• das Puzzle • el rompecabezas
• il puzzle

dominoes • les dominos
• das Domino • el dominó
• il domino

darts • les fléchettes
• das Darts • los dardos
• le freccette

joker
le joker
der Joker
el comodín
il jolly

jack
le valet
der Bube
el joto
il fante

queen
la dame
die Dame
la reina
la regina

king
le roi
der König
el rey
il re

ace • l'as
• das Ass • el as
• l'asso

diamond
le carreau
das Karo
el diamante
il quadro

spade
le pique
das Pik
la espada
la picca

heart
le cœur
das Herz
el corazón
il cuore

club
le trèfle
das Kreuz
el trébol
il fiore

shuffle (v) • battre • mischen
• barajar • mescolare

cards • les cartes • die Karten
• las cartas • le carte

deal (v) • donner • geben
• repartir • distribuire

move	win (v)	loser	point	bridge	Whose turn is it?
le coup	gagner	le perdant	le point	le bridge	C'est à qui de jouer?
der Zug	gewinnen	der Verlierer	der Punkt	das Bridge	Wer ist dran?
el turno	ganar	el perdedor	el punto	el bridge	¿A quién le toca?
la mossa	vincere	il perdente	il punto	il bridge	A chi tocca?
play (v)	winner	game	score	deck of cards	It's your move.
jouer	le gagnant	le jeu	la marque	le jeu de cartes	C'est à toi de jouer.
spielen	der Gewinner	das Spiel	das Spielergebnis	das Kartenspiel	Du bist dran.
jugar	el ganador	la partida	la puntuación	la baraja	Te toca a ti.
giocare	il vincitore	il gioco	il punteggio	il mazzo di carte	Tocca a te.
player	lose (v)	bet	poker	suit	Roll the dice.
le joueur	perdre	le pari	le poker	la couleur	Jette le dé.
der Spieler	verlieren	die Wette	das Poker	die Farbe	Würfle.
el jugador	perder	la apuesta	el póquer	el palo	Tira los dados.
il giocatore	perdere	la scommessa	il poker	il colore	Tira i dadi.

arts and crafts 1 • les arts et métiers 1 • das Kunsthandwerk 1 • las manualidades 1 • arte e artigianato 1

artist
l'artiste peintre
die Künstlerin
la pintora
l'artista

painting
le tableau
das Gemälde
el cuadro
il quadro

easel
le chevalet
die Staffelei
el caballete
il cavalletto

canvas
la toile
die Leinwand
el lienzo
la tela

brush
le pinceau
der Pinsel
el pincel
il pennello

palette
la palette
die Palette
la paleta
la tavolozza

painting • la peinture • die Malerei • la pintura • la pittura

paints • les couleurs • die Farben • las pinturas • la vernice

oil paints • les couleurs à l'huile • die Ölfarben • las pinturas al óleo • i colori ad olio

watercolors • la couleur à l'eau • die Aquarellfarbe • las acuarelas • gli acquarelli

pastels • les pastels • die Pastellstifte • los pasteles • i pastelli

acrylic paint • l'acrylique • die Acrylfarbe • la pintura acrílica • i colori acrilici

poster paint • la gouache • die Plakatfarbe • la témpera • la tempera

colors • les couleurs • die Farben • los colores • i colori

red • rouge • rot • rojo • rosso

blue • bleu • blau • azul • blu

yellow • jaune • gelb • amarillo • giallo

green • vert • grün • verde • verde

orange • orange • orange • naranja • arancione

purple • violet • lila • morado • viola

white • blanc • weiß • blanco • bianco

black • noir • schwarz • negro • nero

gray • gris • grau • gris • grigio

pink • rose • rosa • rosa • rosa

brown • marron • braun • marrón • marrone

indigo • indigo • indigoblau • azul añil • indaco

other crafts • les autres arts • **andere Kunstfertigkeiten** • las otras manualidades • altri lavori artigianali

sketchbook
le carnet à croquis
der Skizzenblock
el bloc de dibujo
il blocco per schizzi

sketch
le croquis
die Skizze
el boceto
lo schizzo

ink
l'encre
die Druckfarbe
la tinta
l'inchiostro

pencil
le crayon
der Bleistift
el lápiz
la matita

charcoal
le fusain
der Kohlestift
el carboncillo
il carboncino

drawing • le dessin • **das Zeichnen** • el dibujo • il disegno

printing • l'imprimerie
• **das Drucken** • la impresión
• la stampa

engraving • la gravure
• **das Gravieren** • el grabado
• l'incisione

stone
la pierre
der Stein
la piedra
la pietra

mallet
le maillet
der Schlegel
el mazo
il martello

chisel
le burin
der Meißel
el cincel
lo scalpello

wood
le bois
das Holz
la madera
il legno

modeling tool
la spatule
das Modellierholz
la herramienta para modelar
l'attrezzo per modellare

sculpting • la sculpture
• **die Bildhauerei** • la
escultura • la scultura

woodworking • la sculpture sur
bois • **die Holzarbeit** • la talla en
madera • la falegnameria

potter's wheel
le tour de potier
die Drehscheibe
el torno de alfarero
il tornio da vasaio

clay
l'argile
der Ton
la arcilla
l'argilla

glue
la colle
der Klebstoff
el pegamento
la colla

cardboard
le carton
die Pappe
la cartulina
il cartone

collage • le collage • **die Collage** • el collage • il collage

pottery • la poterie • **die Töpferei** • la cerámica • la ceramica

jewelry making • la joaillerie
• **die Juwelierarbeit** • la orfebrería
• l'oreficeria

papier-mâché • le papier
mâché • **das Papiermaché** • el
papel maché • la cartapesta

origami • l'origami • **das
Origami** • la papiroflexia
• l'origami

model-making • le modélisme
• **der Modellbau** • el modelismo
• il modellismo

arts and crafts 2 • les arts et métiers 2 • das Kunsthandwerk 2 • las manualidades 2 • arte e artigianato 2

thread guide
le guide de fil
der Fadenleiter
la guía del hilo
il guidafilo

thread reel
la bobine de fil
der Spuler
el carrete de hilo
il rocchetto del filo

balance wheel
le balancier
das Handrad
la rueda de ajuste
la ruota

needle
l'aiguille
die Nadel
la aguja
l'ago

presser foot
le pied-de-biche
der Stoffdrücker
el pie de la aguja
il piedino

stitch selector
le sélecteur de point
der Stichwähler
el selector de puntada
il selezionatore dei punti

needle plate
la platine
die Stichplatte
la placa de la aguja
la piastrina dell'ago

sewing machine • la machine à coudre • die Nähmaschine • la máquina de coser • la macchina da cucire

scissors • les ciseaux
• die Schere • las
tijeras • le forbici

pattern • le patron
• das Schnittmuster
• el patrón • il modello

pincushion
la pelote à épingles
das Nadelkissen
el alfiletero
il puntaspilli

tape measure • le
centimètre • das
Zentimetermaß • la cinta
métrica • il metro

material • le tissu
• der Stoff • la tela
• la stoffa

pin
l'épingle
die Stecknadel
el alfiler
lo spillo

sewing basket • la corbeille à couture • der
Nähkorb • el costurero • la cesta del cucito

thread
le fil
das Garn
el hilo
il filo

eye
l'œillet
die Öse
la hembra
l'occhiello

bobbin • la bobine
• die Spule • la bobina
• la bobina

hook • l'agrafe • der
Haken • el macho
• il gancio

thimble • le dé à
coudre • der Fingerhut
• el dedal • il ditale

tailor's chalk • la craie
de tailleur • die
Schneiderkreide • el
jaboncillo • il gesso

tailor's dummy • le
mannequin • die
Schneiderpuppe • el
maniquí • il manichino

english • français • deutsch • español • italiano

thread (v) • enfiler
• einfädeln • ensartar
• infilare

stitch
le point
der Stich
la puntada
il punto

sew (v) • coudre
• nähen • coser
• cucire

darn (v) • repriser
• stopfen • zurcir
• rammendare

tack (v) • bâtir • **heften**
• hilvanar • imbastire

cut (v) • couper
• schneiden • cortar
• tagliare

needlepoint
• la tapisserie • die
Tapisserie • el bordado
en cañamazo • la
punta dell'ago

embroidery • la
broderie • **die Stickerei**
• el bordado
• il ricamo

crochet hook
le crochet
der Häkelhaken
la aguja de ganchillo
l'uncinetto

crochet • le crochet
• das Häkeln • el
ganchillo • l'uncinetto

macramé • le macramé
• **das Makramee** • el
macramé • il macramè

patchwork
• le patchwork
• **das Patchwork**
• la labor de retales
• il patchwork

lace bobbin • le fuseau
• der Klöppel • el
bolillo • la spoletta

quilting • le ouatage
• **das Wattieren** • el
acolchado • il trapunto

lace-making • la dentelle
• **die Spitzenklöppelei** • la
labor de encaje • la
fabbricazione dei merletti

loom • le métier à
tisser • **der Webstuhl**
• el telar • il telaio

weaving • le tissage
• **die Weberei** • tejer
• la tessitura

knitting needle
l'aiguille à tricoter
die Stricknadel
la aguja de tejer
il ferro da calza

knitting • le tricot • **das Stricken** • la
labor de punto • il lavoro a maglia

yarn
la laine
die Wolle
la lana
la lana

skein • l'écheveau • **der Strang**
• la madeja • la matassa

unpick (v)	nylon
défaire	le nylon
auftrennen	**das Nylon**
descoser	el nailon
scucire	il nailon
fabric	silk
le tissu	la soie
der Stoff	**die Seide**
la tela	la seda
la tela	la seta
cotton	designer
le coton	le styliste
die Baumwolle	**der Modedesigner**
el algodón	el diseñador
il cotone	lo stilista
linen	fashion
le lin	la mode
das Leinen	**die Mode**
el lino	la moda
il lino	la moda
polyester	zipper
le polyester	la fermeture éclair
das Polyester	**der Reißverschluss**
el poliéster	la cremallera
il poliestere	la chiusura lampo

environment
l'environnement
die Umwelt
el medio ambiente
l'ambiente

space • l'espace • der Weltraum • el espacio • lo spazio

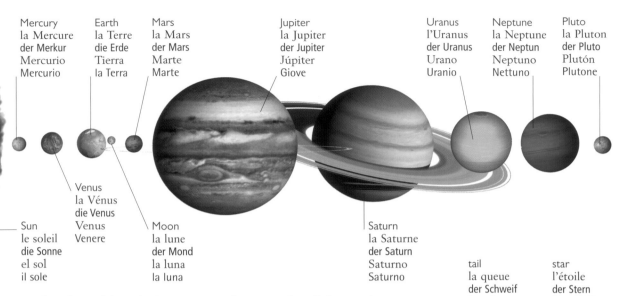

Mercury
la Mercure
der Merkur
Mercurio
Mercurio

Earth
la Terre
die Erde
Tierra
la Terra

Mars
la Mars
der Mars
Marte
Marte

Jupiter
la Jupiter
der Jupiter
Júpiter
Giove

Uranus
l'Uranus
der Uranus
Urano
Uranio

Neptune
la Neptune
der Neptun
Neptuno
Nettuno

Pluto
la Pluton
der Pluto
Plutón
Plutone

Sun
le soleil
die Sonne
el sol
il sole

Venus
la Vénus
die Venus
Venus
Venere

Moon
la lune
der Mond
la luna
la luna

Saturn
la Saturne
der Saturn
Saturno
Saturno

tail
la queue
der Schweif
la cola
la coda

star
l'étoile
der Stern
la estrella
la stella

solar system • le sytème solaire • das Sonnensystem • el sistema solar • il sistema solare

galaxy • la galaxie
• die Galaxie • la galaxia
• la galassia

nebula • la nébuleuse
• der Nebelfleck • la nebulosa
• la nebulosa

asteroid • l'astéroïde
• der Asteroid • el asteroide
• l'asteroide

comet • la comète
• der Komet • el cometa
• la cometa

universe	black hole	full moon
l'univers	le trou noir	la pleine lune
das Universum	das schwarze Loch	der Vollmond
el universo	el agujero negro	la luna llena
l'universo	il buco nero	la luna piena
orbit	planet	new moon
l'orbite	la planète	la nouvelle lune
die Umlaufbahn	der Planet	der Neumond
la órbita	el planeta	la luna nueva
l'orbita	il pianeta	la luna nuova
gravity	meteor	crescent moon
la pesanteur	le météore	le croissant de lune
die Schwerkraft	der Meteor	die Mondsichel
la gravedad	el meteorito	la media luna
la gravità	la meteora	la mezzaluna

eclipse • l'éclipse • die Finsternis • el eclipse • l'eclisse

space exploration • l'exploration spatiale • die Raumforschung • la exploración espacial • l'esplorazione dello spazio

radar
le radar
der Radar
el radar
il radar

space shuttle
la navette spatiale
die Raumfähre
el transbordador espacial
lo shuttle

space suit
le scaphandre spatial
der Raumanzug
el traje espacial
la tuta spaziale

thruster
la fusée d'orientation
die Steuerrakete
el propulsor
il reattore

crew hatch • le
sas d'équipage
• die Besatzungs-
luke • la escotilla
• lo sportello
dell'equipaggio

booster
l'accélérateur
der Booster
el lanzacohetes
il lanciarazzi

astronaut • l'astronaute
• der Astronaut • el
astronauta • l'astronauta

lunar module • le module lunaire • die Mondfähre • el módulo
lunar • il modulo lunare

launch pad • la rampe
de lancement
• die Abschussrampe
• la rampa de
lanzamiento
• la rampa
di lancio

launch • le lancement • der
Abschuss • el lanzamiento •
il lancio

satellite • le satellite • der
Satellit • el satélite • il satellite

space station • la station spatiale • die Raumstation • la estación
espacial • la stazione spaziale

---

astronomy • l'astronomie • die Astronomie • la astronomía • l'astronomia

telescope
le télescope
das Teleskop
el telescopio
il telescopio

tripod
le trépied
das Stativ
el trípode
il treppiede

constellation • la constellation
• das Sternbild • la constelación
• la costellazione

binoculars • les jumelles
• das Fernglas • los prismáticos
• il binocolo

Earth • la terre • die Erde • la Tierra • la Terra

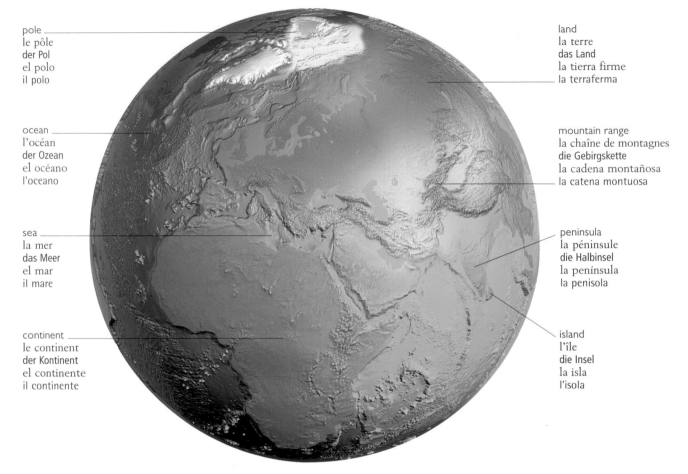

pole
le pôle
der Pol
el polo
il polo

ocean
l'océan
der Ozean
el océano
l'oceano

sea
la mer
das Meer
el mar
il mare

continent
le continent
der Kontinent
el continente
il continente

land
la terre
das Land
la tierra firme
la terraferma

mountain range
la chaîne de montagnes
die Gebirgskette
la cadena montañosa
la catena montuosa

peninsula
la péninsule
die Halbinsel
la península
la penisola

island
l'île
die Insel
la isla
l'isola

atmosphere
l'atmosphère
die Atmosphäre
la atmósfera
l'atmosfera

crust
l'écorce
die Erdkruste
la corteza
la crosta

mantle
le manteau
der Mantel
el manto
il mantello

inner core • le
noyau intérieur
• der innere Kern
• el núcleo
interno • il
nucleo interno

outer core
le noyau extérieur
der äußere Kern
el núcleo externo
il nucleo esterno

planet • la planète • der Planet • el planeta
• il pianeta

section • la section • der Längsschnitt
• la sección • lo spaccato

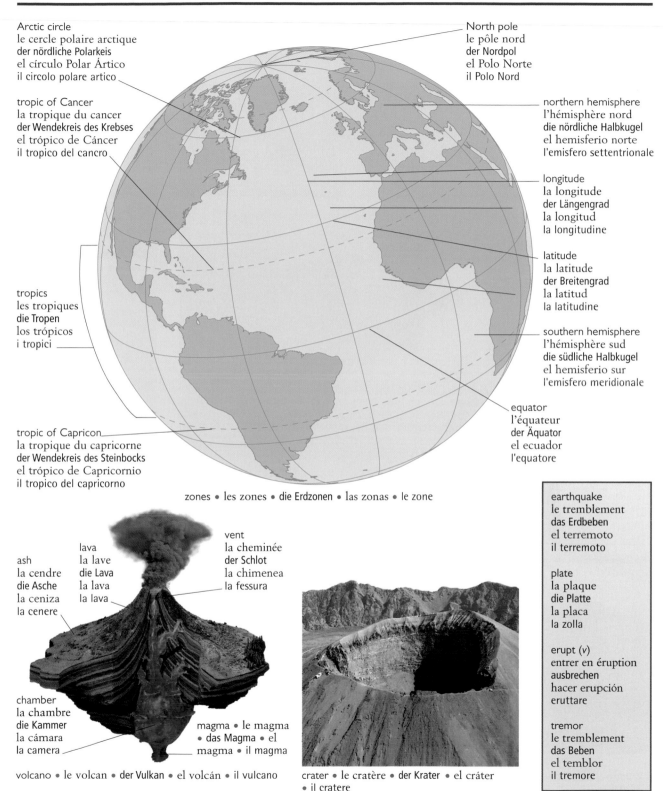

Arctic circle
le cercle polaire arctique
der nördliche Polarkeis
el círculo Polar Ártico
il circolo polare artico

tropic of Cancer
la tropique du cancer
der Wendekreis des Krebses
el trópico de Cáncer
il tropico del cancro

tropics
les tropiques
die Tropen
los trópicos
i tropici

tropic of Capricon
la tropique du capricorne
der Wendekreis des Steinbocks
el trópico de Capricornio
il tropico del capricorno

North pole
le pôle nord
der Nordpol
el Polo Norte
il Polo Nord

northern hemisphere
l'hémisphère nord
die nördliche Halbkugel
el hemisferio norte
l'emisfero settentrionale

longitude
la longitude
der Längengrad
la longitud
la longitudine

latitude
la latitude
der Breitengrad
la latitud
la latitudine

southern hemisphere
l'hémisphère sud
die südliche Halbkugel
el hemisferio sur
l'emisfero meridionale

equator
l'équateur
der Äquator
el ecuador
l'equatore

zones • les zones • die Erdzonen • las zonas • le zone

ash
la cendre
die Asche
la ceniza
la cenere

lava
la lave
die Lava
la lava
la lava

vent
la cheminée
der Schlot
la chimenea
la fessura

chamber
la chambre
die Kammer
la cámara
la camera

magma • le magma
• das Magma • el
magma • il magma

volcano • le volcan • der Vulkan • el volcán • il vulcano

crater • le cratère • der Krater • el cráter
• il cratere

earthquake
le tremblement
das Erdbeben
el terremoto
il terremoto

plate
la plaque
die Platte
la placa
la zolla

erupt (v)
entrer en éruption
ausbrechen
hacer erupción
eruttare

tremor
le tremblement
das Beben
el temblor
il tremore

landscape • le paysage • die Landschaft • el paisaje • il paesaggio

mountain
la montagne
der Berg
la montaña
la montagna

slope
la pente
der Hang
la ladera
la pendice

bank
la rive
das Ufer
la orilla
la riva

river
la rivière
der Fluss
el río
il fiume

rapids
les rapides
die Stromschnellen
los rápidos
le rapide

rocks
les rochers
die Felsen
las rocas
le rocce

glacier • le glacier
• der Gletscher • el glaciar
• il ghiacciaio

valley • la vallée • das Tal
• el valle • la valle

hill • la colline • der Hügel
• la colina • la collina

plateau • le plateau
• das Plateau • la meseta
• l'altipiano

gorge • la gorge • die Schlucht
• el desfiladero • la gola

cave • la caverne • die Höhle
• la cueva • la caverna

english • français • deutsch • español • italiano

plain • la plaine • die Ebene
• la llanura • la pianura

desert • le désert • die Wüste
• el desierto • il deserto

forest • la forêt • der Wald •
el bosque • la foresta

wood • le bois • der Wald
• el bosque • il bosco

rain forest • la forêt tropicale
• der Regenwald • la selva
tropical • la foresta pluviale

swamp • le marais • der
Sumpf • el pantano
• la palude

meadow • le pré • die Wiese
label • el prado • il pascolo

grassland • la prairie
• das Grasland • la pradera
• la prateria

waterfall • la cascade
• der Wasserfall • la cascada
• la cascata

stream • le ruisseau
• der Bach • el arroyo
• il torrente

lake • le lac • der See
• el lago • il lago

geyser • le geyser • der Geysir
• el géiser • il geyser

coast • la côte • die Küste
• la costa • la costa

cliff • la falaise • die Klippe
• el acantilado • la scogliera

coral reef • le récif de corail
• das Korallenriff • el arrecife
de coral • la barriera corallina

estuary • l'estuaire • die
Flussmündung • el estuario
• l'estuario

weather • le temps • das Wetter • el tiempo • il tempo

exosphere
l'exosphère
die Exosphäre
la exosfera
l'esosfera

aurora
l'aurore
das Polarlicht
la aurora
l'aurora

thermosphere
la thermosphère
die Thermosphäre
la termoesfera
la termosfera

ionosphere
l'ionosphère
die Ionosphäre
la ionosfera
la ionosfera

mesosphere
la mésosphère
die Mesosphäre
la mesoesfera
la mesosfera

ultraviolet rays
les rayons ultraviolets
die Ultraviolettstrahlen
los rayos ultravioleta
i raggi ultravioletti

stratosphere
la stratosphère
die Stratosphäre
la estratosfera
la stratosfera

ozone layer
la couche d'ozone
die Ozonschicht
la capa de ozono
lo strato di ozono

troposphere
la troposphère
die Troposphäre
la troposfera
la troposfera

atmosphere • l'atmosphère • die
Atmosphäre • la atmósfera • l'atmosfera

sunshine • le soleil • der Sonnenschein
• el sol • la luce del sole

wind • le vent • der Wind
• el viento • il vento

sleet	shower	hot	dry	windy	I'm hot/cold.
la neige fondue	l'averse	(très) chaud	sec	venteux	J'ai chaud/froid.
der Schneeregen	der Schauer	heiß	trocken	windig	Mir ist heiß/kalt.
el aguanieve	el chubasco	caluroso	seco	ventoso	Tengo calor/frío.
il nevischio	il rovescio	caldo	secco	ventoso	Ho caldo/freddo.
hail	sunny	cold	wet	gale	It's raining.
la grêle	ensoleillé	froid	humide	la tempête	Il pleut.
der Hagel	sonnig	kalt	nass	der Sturm	Es regnet.
el granizo	soleado	frío	lluvioso	el temporal	Está lloviendo.
la grandine	soleggiato	freddo	piovoso	la bufera	Sta piovendo.
thunder	cloudy	warm	humid	temperature	It's … degrees.
le tonnerre	nuageux	chaud	humide	la température	Il fait … degrés.
der Donner	bewölkt	warm	feucht	die Temperatur	Es sind … Grad.
el trueno	nublado	cálido	húmedo	la temperatura	Estamos a … grados.
il tuono	nuvoloso	tiepido	umido	la temperatura	Fa … gradi.

cloud • le nuage • die Wolke • la nube
• la nuvola

rain • la pluie • der Regen • la lluvia
• la pioggia

lightning • l'éclair • der Blitz
• el relámpago • il fulmine

storm • l'orage • das Gewitter
• la tormenta • la tempesta

mist • la brume • der feine Nebel
• la neblina • la foschia

fog • le brouillard • der dichte Nebel
• la niebla • la nebbia

rainbow • l'arc-en-ciel • der Regenbogen
• el arcoiris • l'arcobaleno

icicle • le glaçon • der
Eiszapfen • el carámbano
• il ghiacciolo

snow • la neige • der Schnee
• la nieve • la neve

frost • le givre • der Raureif
• la escarcha • il gelo

ice • la glace • das Eis
• el hielo • il ghiaccio

freeze • le gel • der Frost
• la helada • la gelata

hurricane • l'hurricane
• der Hurrikan • el huracán
• l'uragano

tornado • la tornade
• der Tornado • el tornado
• il tornado

monsoon • la mousson
• der Monsun • el monzón
• il monsone

flood • l'inondation
• die Überschwemmung • la
inundación • l'inondazione

rocks • les roches • das Gestein • las rocas • le rocce

igneous • igné • **eruptiv** • ígneo • igneo

granite • le granit • der Granit • el granito • il granito

obsidian • l'obsidienne • der Obsidian • la obsidiana • l'ossidiana

basalt • le basalte • der Basalt • el basalto • il basalto

pumice • la pierre ponce • der Bimsstein • la piedra pómez • la pomice

sedimentary • sédimentaire • **sedimentär** • sedimentario • sedimentario

sandstone • le grès • der Sandstein • la piedra arenisca • l'arenaria

limestone • le calcaire • der Kalkstein • la piedra caliza • il calcare

chalk • la craie • die Kreide • la tiza • il gesso

flint • le silex • der Feuerstein • el pedernal • la selce

conglomerate • le conglomérat • **das Konglomerat** • el conglomerado • il conglomerato

coal • le charbon • die Kohle • el carbón • il carbone

metamorphic • métamorphique • **metamorph** • metamórfico • metamorfico

slate • l'ardoise • der Schiefer • la pizarra • l'ardesia

schist • le schiste • der Schiefer • el esquisto • lo scisto

gneiss • le gneiss • der Gneis • el gneis • lo gneiss

marble • le marbre • der Marmor • el mármol • il marmo

gems • les gemmes • **die Schmucksteine** • las gemas • le gemme

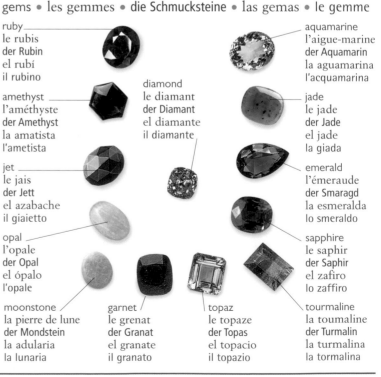

ruby
le rubis
der Rubin
el rubí
il rubino

amethyst
l'améthyste
der Amethyst
la amatista
l'ametista

jet
le jais
der Jett
el azabache
il giaietto

opal
l'opale
der Opal
el ópalo
l'opale

moonstone
la pierre de lune
der Mondstein
la adularia
la lunaria

diamond
le diamant
der Diamant
el diamante
il diamante

garnet
le grenat
der Granat
el granate
il granato

topaz
le topaze
der Topas
el topacio
il topazio

aquamarine
l'aigue-marine
der Aquamarin
la aguamarina
l'acquamarina

jade
le jade
der Jade
el jade
la giada

emerald
l'émeraude
der Smaragd
la esmeralda
lo smeraldo

sapphire
le saphir
der Saphir
el zafiro
lo zaffiro

tourmaline
la toumaline
der Turmalin
la turmalina
la tormalina

minerals • les minéraux • die Mineralien • los minerales • i minerali

quartz • le quartz
• der Quarz • el
cuarzo • il quarzo

mica • le mica
• der Glimmer
• la mica • la mica

sulfur • le soufre
• der Schwefel
• el azufre • lo zolfo

hematite • l'hématite
• der Hämatit • la
hematita • l'ematite

calcite • la calcite
• der Kalzit • la calcita
• la calcite

malachite
• la malachite
• der Malachit
• la malaquita
• la malachite

turquoise • la
turquoise • der Türkis
• la turquesa
• il turchese

onyx • l'onyx
• der Onyx • el ónix
• l'onice

agate • l'agate
• der Achat • el ágata
• l'agate

graphite • le graphite
• der Graphit • el
grafito • la grafite

---

metals • les métaux • die Metalle • los metales • i metalli

gold • l'or • das Gold
• el oro • l'oro

silver • l'argent
• das Silber • la plata
• l'argento

platinum • le platine
• das Platin • el
platino • il platino

nickel • le nickel
• das Nickel • el
níquel • il nichel

iron • le fer • das Eisen
• el hierro • il ferro

copper • le cuivre
• das Kupfer • el cobre
• il rame

tin • l'étain • das
Zinn • el estaño
• lo stagno

aluminum
• l'aluminium • das
Aluminium • el aluminio
• l'alluminio

mercury • le mercure
• das Quecksilber • el
mercurio • il mercurio

zinc • le zinc
• das Zink • el zinc
• lo zinco

---

animals I • les animaux 1 • die Tiere I • los animales 1 • gli animali 1

mammals • les mammifères • die Säugetiere • los mamíferos • i mammiferi

whiskers
les poils
die Schnurrhaare
los bigotes
i baffi

tail
la queue
der Schwanz
la cola
la coda

rabbit • le lapin
• das Kaninchen • el
conejo • il coniglio

hamster • le hamster
• der Hamster • el
hámster • il criceto

mouse • la souris
• die Maus • el ratón
• il topo

rat • le rat • die Ratte
• la rata • il ratto

hedgehog
• le hérisson • der Igel
• el erizo • il riccio

squirrel • l'écureuil
• das Eichhörnchen • la
ardilla • lo scoiattolo

bat • la chauve-souris
• die Fledermaus • el
murciélago • il pipistrello

raccoon • le raton laveur
• der Waschbär • el
mapache • il procione

fox • le renard
• der Fuchs • el zorro
• la volpe

wolf • le loup
• der Wolf • el lobo
• il lupo

puppy
le chiot
der Welpe
el cachorro
il cucciolo

kitten
le chaton
das Kätzchen
el gatito
il gattino

pup
le bébé-phoque
das Junge
la cría
il cucciolo

dog • le chien • der Hund
• el perro • il cane

cat • le chat • die Katze
• el gato • il gatto

otter • la loutre • der Otter
• la nutria • la lontra

seal • le phoque • die Robbe
• la foca • la foca

flipper
la nageoire
die Flosse
la aleta
la pinna

blowhole
l'évent
das Atemloch
el orificio nasal
lo sfiatatoio

dolphin •
le dauphin
der Delphin • el delfin
• il delfino

sea lion • l'otarie
• der Seelöwe • el león
marino • il leone marino

walrus • le morse
• das Walross •
la morsa • il tricheco

whale • la baleine • der Wal
• la ballena • la balena

english • français • deutsch • español • italiano

antler
la ramure
das Geweih
el asta
le corna

mane
la crinière
die Mähne
la crin
la criniera

hoof
le sabot
der Huf
la pezuña
lo zoccolo

hump • la bosse
• der Höcker • la
joroba • la gobba

deer • le cerf • der Hirsch
• el ciervo • il cervo

zebra • le zèbre
• das Zebra • la cebra
• la zebra

giraffe • la girafe
• die Giraffe • la jirafa
• la giraffa

camel • le chameau
• das Kamel • el camello
• il cammello

trunk • la trompe • der Rüssel
• la trompa • la proboscide

tusk
la défense
der Stoßzahn
el colmillo
la zanna

horn • la corne
• das Horn • el
cuerno • il corno

hippopotamus • le
hippopotame • das Nilpferd
• el hipopótamo
• l'ippopotamo

elephant • l'éléphant
• der Elefant • el elefante
• l'elefante

rhinoceros • le rhinocéros
• das Nashorn • el rinoceronte
• il rinoceronte

tiger • le tigre • der Tiger
• el tigre • la tigre

mane
la crinière
die Mähne
la melena
la criniera

lion • le lion • der Löwe
• el león • il leone

monkey • le singe
• der Affe • el chango
• la scimmia

gorilla • le gorille
• der Gorilla • el gorila
• il gorilla

koala • le koala • der Koalabär
• el koala • il koala

pouch
la poche
der Beutel
la bolsa
il marsupio

panda • le panda
• der Pandabär
• el oso panda
• il panda

claw
la griffe
die Klaue
la zarpa
l'artiglio

kangaroo • le kangourou
• das Känguru • el canguro
• il canguro

bear • l'ours
• der Bär • el oso
• l'orso

polar bear • l'ours blanc
• der Eisbär • el oso polar
• l'orso polare

animals 2 • les animaux 2 • die Tiere 2 • los animales 2 • gli animali 2

birds • les oiseaux • die Vögel • las aves • gli uccelli

tail
la queue
der Schwanz
la cola
la coda

canary • le canari
• der Kanarienvogel • el
canario • il canarino

sparrow • le moineau
• der Spatz • el gorrión
• il passero

hummingbird • le
colibri • der Kolibri
• el colibrí • il colibri

swallow • l'hirondelle
• die Schwalbe • la
golondrina • la rondine

crow • le corbeau
• die Krähe • el cuervo
• la cornacchia

falcon • le faucon
(owl)

pigeon • le pigeon
• die Taube • la
paloma • il piccione

woodpecker • le pic
• der Specht • el pájaro
carpintero • il picchio

falcon • le faucon
• der Falke • el halcón
• il falco

owl • la chouette
• die Eule • el búho
• il gufo

gull • la mouette • die
Möwe • la gaviota
• il gabbiano

eagle • l'aigle
• der Adler • el águila
• l'aquila

pelican • le pélican
• der Pelikan • el
pelícano • il pellicano

flamingo • le flamant
• der Flamingo
• el flamenco
• il fenicottero

stork • la cigogne • der
Storch • la cigüeña
• la cicogna

crane • la grue
• der Kranich
• la grulla • la gru

penguin • le pingouin
• der Pinguin • el
pingüino • il pinguino

ostrich • l'autruche
• der Strauß • el
avestruz • lo struzzo

english • français • deutsch • español • italiano

goose • l'oie • die Gans
• la oca • l'oca

swan • le cygne • der Schwan
• el cisne • il cigno

pheasant • le faisan
• der Fasan • el
faisán • il fagiano

peacock • le paon • der Pfau
• el pavo real • il pavone

beak
le bec
der Schnabel
el pico
il becco

turkey • le dindon
• der Truthahn • el guajolote
• il tacchino

feather
la plume
die Feder
la pluma
la piuma

wing
l'aile
der Flügel
el ala
l'ala

claw
la griffe
die Kralle
la garra
l'artiglio

cockatoo
le cacatoès
der Kakadu
la cacatúa
la cacatoa

parrot • le perroquet
• der Papagei • el loro
• il pappagallo

reptiles • les reptiles • die Reptilien • los reptiles
• i rettili

scales • les écailles
• die Schuppen • las
escamas • le scaglie

alligator • l'alligator • der Alligator • el caimán
• l'alligatore

lizard • le lézard • die Eidechse
• el lagarto • la lucertola

iguana • l'iguane
• der Leguan • la iguana
• l'iguana

shell
la carapace
der Panzer
el caparazón
il guscio

turtle • la tortue marine
• die Wasserschildkröte • el
galápago • la testuggine

tortoise • la tortue
• die Schildkröte • la tortuga
• la tartaruga

snake • le serpent
• die Schlange
• la serpiente
• il serpente

snout
le museau
die Schnauze
el hocico
il muso

crocodile • le crocodile
• das Krokodil • el
cocodrilo • il coccodrillo

animals 3 • les animaux 3 • die Tiere 3 • los animales 3 • gli animali 3

amphibians • les amphibiens • die Amphibien • los anfibios • gli anfibi

frog • la grenouille • der Frosch • la rana • la rana

toad • le crapaud • die Kröte • el sapo • il rospo

tadpole • le têtard • die Kaulquappe • el renacuajo • il girino

salamander • la salamandre • der Salamander • la salamandra • la salamandra

---

fish • les poissons • die Fische • los peces • i pesci

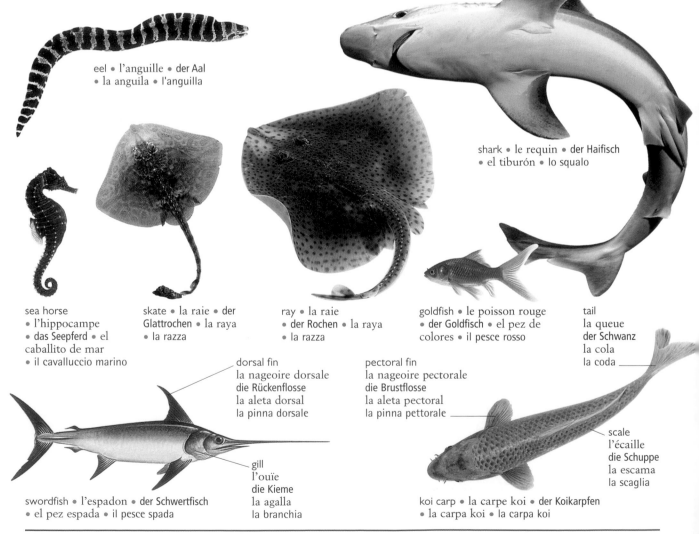

eel • l'anguille • der Aal • la anguila • l'anguilla

shark • le requin • der Haifisch • el tiburón • lo squalo

sea horse • l'hippocampe • das Seepferd • el caballito de mar • il cavalluccio marino

skate • la raie • der Glattrochen • la raya • la razza

ray • la raie • der Rochen • la raya • la razza

goldfish • le poisson rouge • der Goldfisch • el pez de colores • il pesce rosso

tail
la queue
der Schwanz
la cola
la coda

dorsal fin
la nageoire dorsale
die Rückenflosse
la aleta dorsal
la pinna dorsale

pectoral fin
la nageoire pectorale
die Brustflosse
la aleta pectoral
la pinna pettorale

scale
l'écaille
die Schuppe
la escama
la scaglia

gill
l'ouïe
die Kieme
la agalla
la branchia

swordfish • l'espadon • der Schwertfisch • el pez espada • il pesce spada

koi carp • la carpe koi • der Koikarpfen • la carpa koi • la carpa koi

---

invertebrates • les invertébrés • **die Wirbellosen** • los invertebrados • gli invertebrati

ant • la fourmi • **die Ameise** • la hormiga • la formica

termite • la termite • **die Termite** • la termita • la termite

bee • l'abeille • **die Biene** • la abeja • l'ape

wasp • la guêpe • **die Wespe** • la avispa • la vespa

beetle • le scarabée • **der Käfer** • el escarabajo • il coleottero

antenna
l'antenne
der Fühler
la antena
l'antenna

cockroach • le cafard • **der Kakerlak** • la cucaracha • lo scarafaggio

moth • le papillon • **die Motte** • la polilla • la falena

butterfly • le papillon • **der Schmetterling** • la mariposa • la farfalla

cocoon • le cocon • **der Kokon** • el capullo • il bozzolo

caterpillar • la chenille • **die Raupe** • la oruga • il bruco

sting
le dard
der Stachel
el aquijón
il pungiglione

cricket • le grillon • **die Grille** • el grillo • il grillo

grasshopper • la sauterelle • **die Heuschrecke** • el saltamontes • la cavalletta

praying mantis • la mante religieuse • **die Gottesanbeterin** • la mantis religiosa • la mantide religiosa

scorpion • le scorpion • **der Skorpion** • el alacrán • lo scorpione

centipede • le mille-pattes • **der Tausendfüßer** • el ciempiés • il millepiedi

dragonfly • la libellule • **die Libelle** • la libélula • la libellula

fly • la mouche • **die Fliege** • la mosca • la mosca

mosquito • le moustique • **die Stechmücke** • el mosquito • la zanzara

ladybug • la coccinelle • **der Marienkäfer** • la catarina • la coccinella

spider • l'araignée • **die Spinne** • la araña • il ragno

slug • la limace • **die Wegschnecke** • la babosa • la lumaca

snail • l'escargot • **die Schnecke** • el caracol • la chiocciola

worm • le ver • **der Wurm** • el gusano • il verme

starfish • l'étoile de mer • **der Seestern** • la estrella de mar • la stella di mare

mussel • la moule • **die Muschel** • el mejillón • la cozza

crab • le crabe • **der Krebs** • el cangrejo • il granchio

lobster • le homard • **der Hummer** • la langosta • l'aragosta

octopus • la pieuvre • **der Seepolyp** • el pulpo • la piovra

squid • le calmar • **der Tintenfisch** • el calamar • il calamaro

jellyfish • la méduse • **die Qualle** • la medusa • la medusa

plants • les plantes • die Pflanzen • las plantas • le piante

tree • l'arbre • der Baum • el árbol • l'albero

branch
la branche
der Ast
la rama
il ramo

bark
l'écorce
die Rinde
la corteza
la corteccia

leaf
la feuille
das Blatt
la hoja
la foglia

twig
la brindille
der Zweig
la ramita
il ramoscello

willow • le saule
• die Weide • el sauce
• il salice

root
la racine
die Wurzel
la raíz
la radice

trunk
le tronc
der Stamm
el tronco
il tronco

oak • le chêne • die Eiche • el roble • la quercia

poplar • le peuplier
• die Pappel • el álamo
• il pioppo

eucalyptus
• l'eucalyptus • der
Eukalyptus • el
eucalipto • l'eucalipto

larch • le mélèze
• die Lärche • el alerce
• il larice

beech • le hêtre
• die Buche • la haya
• il faggio

birch • le bouleau
• die Birke • el abedul
• la betulla

pine • le pin • die
Kiefer • el pino
• il pino

cedar • le cèdre
• die Zeder • el cedro
• il cedro

maple • l'érable
• der Ahorn • el arce
• l'acero

elm • l'orme • die Ulme
• el olmo • l'olmo

lime • le tilleul
• die Linde • el tilo
• il tiglio

holly • le houx
• die Stechpalme • el
acebo • l'agrifoglio

berry
la baie
die Beere
la baya
la bacca

palm • le palmier
• die Palme • la
palmera • la palma

flowering plant • la plante à fleurs • die blühende Pflanze
• la planta de flor • la pianta da fiori

flower
la fleur
die Blüte
la flor
il fiore

stamen
l'étamine
das Staubgefäß
el estambre
lo stame

petal
le pétale
das Blütenblatt
el pétalo
il petalo

calyx
le calice
der Kelch
el cáliz
il calice

stalk
la tige
der Stängel
el tallo
lo stelo

bud
le bouton
die Knospe
el capullo
il bocciolo

stem
la tige
der Stiel
el tallo
il gambo

buttercup • la renoncule
• der Hahnenfuß
• el ranúnculo
• il ranuncolo

daisy • la pâquerette
• das Gänseblümchen
• la margarita
• la margherita

thistle • le chardon
• die Distel • el cardo
• il cardo

dandelion • le pissenlit
• der Löwenzahn
• el diente de león
• il dente di leone

heather • la bruyère
• das Heidekraut • el
brezo • l'erica

poppy • le coquelicot
• der Klatschmohn • la
amapola • il papavero

foxglove • la digitale
• der Fingerhut
• la dedalera
• la digitale

honeysuckle • le
chèvrefeuille • das
Geißblatt • la madreselva
• il caprifoglio

sunflower
• le tournesol
• die Sonnenblume
• el girasol • il girasole

clover • le trèfle
• der Klee • el trébol
• il trifoglio

bluebells • les jacinthes des
bois • die Sternhyazinthen
• los narcisos silvestres
• i giacinti di bosco

primrose • la
primevère • die
Schlüsselblume • la
prímula • la primula

lupins • les lupins
• die Lupinen • el
lupino • i lupini

nettle • l'ortie
• die Nessel • la ortiga
• l'ortica

town • la ville • die Stadt • la ciudad • la città

street
la rue
die Straße
la calle
la strada

curb
le bord du trottoir
die Bordkante
el borde de la banqueta
il ciglio

street corner
le coin de la rue
die Straßenecke
la esquina
l'angolo della strada

store
le magasin
der Laden
la tienda
il negozio

intersection
le carrefour
die Kreuzung
el crucero
il crocevia

one-way system
la voie à sens
unique • die
Einbahnstraße
• la calle de
sentido único
• il senso unico

sidewalk
le trottoir
der Bürgersteig
la banqueta
il marciapiede

office block
• l'immeuble
de bureaux
• das Bürogebäude
• el edificio de
oficinas • il
complesso di
uffici

apartment block
• l'immeuble
• der Wohnblock
• el edificio de
apartamentos
• il caseggiato

alley
la ruelle
die Gasse
el callejón
il vicolo

parking lot
le parking
der Parkplatz
el estacionamiento
il parcheggio

street sign
le panneau de signalisation
das Straßenschild
la señal de tráfico
il segnale stradale

traffic post
la borne
der Poller
la baliza
la colonnina

street light
le lampadaire
die Straßenlaterne
el farol
il lampione

buildings • les bâtiments • die Gebäude • los edificios • gli edifici

town hall • la mairie • das Rathaus • el palacio municipal • il municipio

library • la bibliothèque • die Bibliothek • la biblioteca • la biblioteca

movie theater • le cinéma • das Kino • el cine • il cinema

theater • le théâtre • das Theater • el teatro • il teatro

university • l'université • die Universität • la universidad • l'università

school • l'école • die Schule • la escuela • la scuola

skyscraper • le gratte-ciel • der Wolkenkratzer • el rascacielos • il grattacielo

areas • les environs • die Wohngegend • las zonas • le zone

industrial park • la zone industrielle • das Industriegebiet • la zona industrial • la zona industriale

city • la ville • die Stadt • la ciudad • la città

suburb • la banlieue • der Vorort • el suburbio • la periferia

village • le village • das Dorf • el pueblo • il villaggio

pedestrian zone la zone piétonnière die Fußgängerzone la zona peatonal la zona pedonale	side street la rue transversale die Seitenstraße la calle lateral la via laterale	manhole la bouche d'égout der Kanalschacht la coladera il tombino	gutter le caniveau der Rinnstein la alcantarilla la cunetta	church l'église die Kirche la iglesia la chiesa
avenue l'avenue die Allee la avenida il viale	square la place der Platz la plaza la piazza	bus stop l'arrêt de bus die Bushaltestelle la parada de autobús la fermata dell'autobus	factory l'usine die Fabrik la fábrica la fabbrica	drain l'égout der Kanal el drenaje il canale di scolo

architecture • l'architecture • die Architektur
• la arquitectura • l'architettura

buildings and structures • les bâtiments et structures • die Gebäude und Strukturen
• los edificios y las estructuras • edifici e strutture

finial
le fleuron
die Kreuzblume
el florón
il pinnacolo

turret
la tourelle
der Mauerturm
el torreón
la torre

spire
la flèche
die Turmspitze
la aguja
la spira

moat
la douve
der Burggraben
el foso
il fossato

gable
le pignon
der Giebel
el frontón
il frontone

dome
le dôme
die Kuppel
la cúpula
la cupola

tower
la tour
der Turm
la torre
la torretta

vault
la voûte
das Gewölbe
la bóveda
la volta

cornice
la corniche
das Gesims
la cornisa
il cornicione

pillar
la colonne
die Säule
la columna
la colonna

skyscraper • le gratte-ciel
• der Wolkenkratzer • el
rascacielos • il grattacielo

castle • le château • die Burg
• el castillo • il castello

church • l'église • die Kirche
• la iglesia • la chiesa

mosque • la mosquée
• die Moschee • la mezquita
• la moschea

temple • le temple
• der Tempel • el templo
• il tempio

synagogue • la synagogue
• die Synagoge • la sinagoga
• la sinagoga

dam • le barrage • der
Staudamm • el embalse
• la diga

bridge • le pont • die Brücke
• el puente • il ponte

cathedral • la cathédrale • die Kathedrale
• la catedral • la cattedrale

styles • les styles • die Baustile • los estilos • gli stili

architrave
l'architrave
der Architrav
el arquitrabe
l'architrave

baroque • baroque • barock • barroco
• barocco

Gothic • gothique • gotisch
• gótico • gotico

Renaissance • Renaissance
• Renaissance- • Renacimiento
• Rinascimento

arch
l'arc
der Bogen
el arco
l'arco

frieze
la frise
der Fries
el friso
il fregio

choir
le chœur
der Chor
el coro
il coro

rococo • rococo • Rokoko- • rococó
• rococò

pediment
le fronton
das Giebeldreieck
el frontón
il frontone

buttress
le contrefort
der Strebepfeiler
el contrafuerte
il contrafforte

neoclassical • néoclassique • klassizistisch
• neoclásico • neoclassico

art nouveau • art nouveau
• der Jugendstil • el estilo
modernista • l'art nouveau

art deco • art déco
• Art-déco- • art decó
• art déco

reference
l'information
die Information
los datos
i dati

time • l'heure • die Uhrzeit • el tiempo • l'ora

minute hand
la grande aiguille
der Minutenzeiger
el minutero
la lancetta dei minuti

hour hand
la petite aiguille
der Stundenzeiger
la manecilla de la hora
la lancetta delle ore

second	now	a quarter of an hour
la seconde	maintenant	un quart d'heure
die Sekunde	jetzt	eine Viertelstunde
el segundo	ahora	un cuarto de hora
il secondo	adesso	un quarto d'ora
minute	later	twenty minutes
la minute	plus tard	vingt minutes
die Minute	später	zwanzig Minuten
el minuto	más tarde	veinte minutos
il minuto	più tardi	venti minuti
hour	half an hour	forty minutes
l'heure	une demi-heure	quarante minutes
die Stunde	eine halbe Stunde	vierzig Minuten
la hora	media hora	cuarenta minutos
l'ora	una mezzora	quaranta minuti

What time is it?
Quelle heure est-il?
Wie spät ist es?
¿Qué hora es?
Che ore sono?

It's three o'clock.
Il est trois heures.
Es ist drei Uhr.
Son las tres en punto.
Sono le tre.

clock • l'horloge • die Uhr • el reloj • l'orologio

five after one • une heure cinq • fünf nach eins • la una y cinco • l'una e cinque

ten after one • une heure dix • zehn nach eins • la una y diez • l'una e dieci

quarter after one • une heure et quart • Viertel nach eins • la una y cuarto • l'una e un quarto

twenty after one • une heure vingt • zwanzig nach eins • la una y veinte • l'una e venti

second hand • la trotteuse • der Sekundenzeiger • el segundero • la lancetta dei secondi

twenty-five after one • une heure vingt-cinq • fünf vor halb zwei • la una y veinticinco • l'una e venticinque

one-thirty • une heure trente • ein Uhr dreißig • la una y media • l'una e trenta

twenty-five to two • deux heures moins vingt-cinq • fünf nach halb zwei • las veinticinco para las dos • le due meno venticinque

twenty to two • deux heures moins vingt • zwanzig vor zwei • las veinte para las dos • le due meno venti

quarter to two • deux heures moins le quart • Viertel vor zwei • el cuarto para las dos • le due meno un quarto

ten to two • deux heures moins dix • zehn vor zwei • las diez para las dos • le due meno dieci

five to two • deux heures moins cinq • fünf vor zwei • las cinco para las dos • le due meno cinque

two o'clock • deux heures • zwei Uhr • las dos en punto • le due

night and day • la nuit et le jour • die Nacht und der Tag • la noche y el día • la notte e il giorno

midnight • le minuit • die Mitternacht • la medianoche • la mezzanotte

sunrise • le lever du soleil • der Sonnenaufgang • el amanecer • il sorgere del sole

dawn • l'aube • die Morgendämmerung • el alba • l'alba

morning • le matin • der Morgen • la mañana • il mattino

sunset • le coucher du soleil • der Sonnenuntergang • el atardecer • il tramonto

noon • le midi • der Mittag • el mediodía • il mezzogiorno

dusk • le crépuscule • die Abenddämmerung • el anochecer • l'imbrunire

evening • le soir • der Abend • la noche • la sera

afternoon • l'après-midi • der Nachmittag • la tarde • il pomeriggio

early	You're early.	Please be on time.	What time does it end?
tôt	Tu es en avance.	Sois à l'heure, s'il te plaît.	Ça finit à quelle heure?
früh	Du bist früh.	Sei bitte pünktlich.	Wann ist es zu Ende?
temprano	Llegas temprano.	Por favor, sé puntual.	¿A qué hora termina?
presto	Sei in anticipo.	Per favore, vieni in orario.	A che ora finisce?
on time	You're late.	I'll see you later.	How long will it last?
à l'heure	Tu es en retard.	À tout à l'heure.	Ça dure combien de temps?
pünktlich	Du hast dich verspätet.	Bis später.	Wie lange dauert es?
puntual	Llegas tarde.	Hasta luego.	¿Cuánto dura?
in orario	Sei in ritardo.	A più tardi.	Quanto durerà?
late	I'll be there soon.	What time does it start?	It's getting late.
tard	J'y arriverai bientôt.	Ça commence à quelle heure?	Il se fait tard.
spät	Ich werde bald dort sein.	Wann fängt es an?	Es ist schon spät.
tarde	Llegaré dentro de poco.	¿A qué hora comienza?	Se está haciendo tarde.
tardi	Arrivo subito.	A che ora inizia?	Si sta facendo tardi.

calendar • le calendrier • der Kalender • el calendario • il calendario

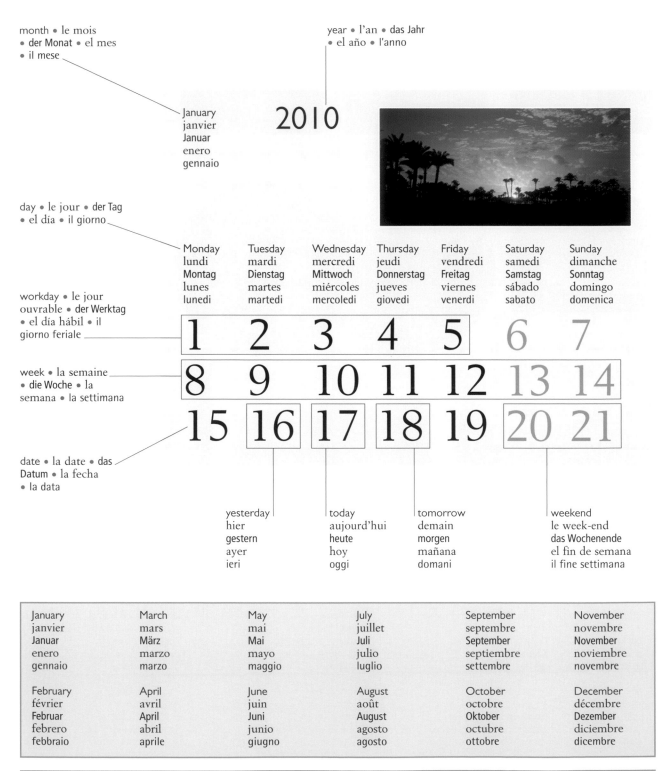

month • le mois
• der Monat • el mes
• il mese

year • l'an • das Jahr
• el año • l'anno

January
janvier
Januar
enero
gennaio

2010

day • le jour • der Tag
• el día • il giorno

Monday	Tuesday	Wednesday	Thursday	Friday	Saturday	Sunday
lundi	mardi	mercredi	jeudi	vendredi	samedi	dimanche
Montag	Dienstag	Mittwoch	Donnerstag	Freitag	Samstag	Sonntag
lunes	martes	miércoles	jueves	viernes	sábado	domingo
lunedi	martedi	mercoledi	giovedi	venerdi	sabato	domenica

workday • le jour
ouvrable • der Werktag
• el día hábil • il
giorno feriale

| 1 | 2 | 3 | 4 | 5 | 6 | 7 |

week • la semaine
• die Woche • la
semana • la settimana

| 8 | 9 | 10 | 11 | 12 | 13 | 14 |

| 15 | 16 | 17 | 18 | 19 | 20 | 21 |

date • la date • das
Datum • la fecha
• la data

yesterday
hier
gestern
ayer
ieri

today
aujourd'hui
heute
hoy
oggi

tomorrow
demain
morgen
mañana
domani

weekend
le week-end
das Wochenende
el fin de semana
il fine settimana

January	March	May	July	September	November
janvier	mars	mai	juillet	septembre	novembre
Januar	März	Mai	Juli	September	November
enero	marzo	mayo	julio	septiembre	noviembre
gennaio	marzo	maggio	luglio	settembre	novembre
February	April	June	August	October	December
février	avril	juin	août	octobre	décembre
Februar	April	Juni	August	Oktober	Dezember
febrero	abril	junio	agosto	octubre	diciembre
febbraio	aprile	giugno	agosto	ottobre	dicembre

years • les ans • die Jahre • los años • gli anni

1900 nineteen hundred • mille neuf cents • **neunzehnhundert** • mil novecientos • millenovecento

1901 nineteen hundred and one • mille neuf cent un • **neunzehnhunderteins** • mil novecientos uno • millenovecentouno

1910 nineteen ten • mille neuf cent dix • **neunzehnhundertzehn** • mil novecientos diez • millenovecentodieci

2000 two thousand • deux mille • **zweitausend** • dos mil • duemila

2001 two thousand and one • deux mille un • **zweitausendeins** • dos mil uno • duemilauno

---

seasons • les saisons • die Jahreszeiten • las estaciones • le stagioni

spring • le printemps
• der Frühling • la primavera
• la primavera

summer • l'été • der Sommer
• el verano • l'estate

fall • l'automne • der Herbst
• el otoño • l'autunno

winter • l'hiver • der Winter
• el invierno • l'inverno

---

century • le siècle • das Jahrhundert • el siglo • il secolo

decade • la décennie • das Jahrzehnt • la década • la decade

millennium • le millénaire • das Jahrtausend • el milenio • il millennio

two weeks • quinze jours • vierzehn Tage • quince días • quindici giorni

this week • cette semaine • diese Woche • esta semana • questa settimana

last week • la semaine dernière • letzte Woche • la semana pasada • la settimana scorsa

next week • la semaine prochaine • nächste Woche • la semana que viene • la settimana prossima

the day before yesterday • avant-hier • vorgestern • anteayer • l'altroieri

the day after tomorrow • après-demain • übermorgen • pasado mañana • il dopodomani

weekly • hebdomadaire • wöchentlich • semanalmente • settimanale

monthly • mensuel • monatlich • mensual • mensile

annual • annuel • jährlich • anual • annuo

What's the date today?
Quelle est la date aujourd'hui?
Welches Datum haben wir heute?
¿Qué día es hoy?
Oggi che giorno è?

It's February seventh, two thousand and two.
C'est le sept février deux mille deux.
Heute ist der siebte Februar zweitausendzwei.
Es el siete de febrero del dos mil dos.
È il sette febbraio, duemiladue.

numbers • les nombres • die Zahlen • los números • i numeri

0   zero • zéro • null • cero • zero

1   one • un • eins • uno • uno

2   two • deux • zwei • dos • due

3   three • trois • drei • tres • tre

4   four • quatre • vier • cuatro • quattro

5   five • cinq • fünf • cinco • cinque

6   six • six • sechs • seis • sei

7   seven • sept • sieben • siete • sette

8   eight • huit • acht • ocho • otto

9   nine • neuf • neun • nueve • nove

10   ten • dix • zehn • diez • dieci

11   eleven • onze • elf • once • undici

12   twelve • douze • zwölf • doce • dodici

13   thirteen • treize • dreizehn • trece • tredici

14   fourteen • quatorze • vierzehn • catorce • quattordici

15   fifteen • quinze • fünfzehn • quince • quindici

16   sixteen • seize • sechzehn • dieciséis • sedici

17   seventeen • dix-sept • siebzehn • diecisiete • diciassette

18   eighteen • dix-huit • achtzehn • dieciocho • diciotto

19   nineteen • dix-neuf • neunzehn • diecinueve • diciannove

20   twenty • vingt • zwanzig • veinte • venti

21   twenty-one • vingt et un • einundzwanzig • veintiuno • ventuno

22   twenty-two • vingt-deux • zweiundzwanzig • veintidós • ventidue

30   thirty • trente • dreißig • treinta • trenta

40   forty • quarante • vierzig • cuarenta • quaranta

50   fifty • cinquante • fünfzig • cincuenta • cinquanta

60   sixty • soixante • sechzig • sesenta • sessanta

70   seventy • soixante-dix • siebzig • setenta • settanta

80   eighty • quatre-vingt • achtzig • ochenta • ottanta

90   ninety • quatre-vingt-dix • neunzig • noventa • novanta

100   one hundred • cent • hundert • cien • cento

110   one hundred and ten • cent dix • hundertzehn • ciento diez • centodieci

200   two hundred • deux cents • zweihundert • doscientos • duecento

300   three hundred • trois cents • dreihundert • trescientos • trecento

400   four hundred • quatre cents • vierhundert • cuatrocientos • quattrocento

500   five hundred • cinq cents • fünfhundert • quinientos • cinquecento

600   six hundred • six cents • sechshundert • seiscientos • seicento

700   seven hundred • sept cents • siebenhundert • setecientos • settecento

800   eight hundred • huit cents • achthundert • ochocientos • ottocento

900   nine hundred • neuf cents • neunhundert • novecientos • novecento

english • français • deutsch • español • italiano

1000
one thousand • mille • **tausend** • mil • mille

10,000
ten thousand • dix mille • **zehntausend** • diez mil • diecimila

20,000
twenty thousand • vingt mille • **zwanzigtausend** • veinte mil • ventimila

50,000
fifty thousand • cinquante mille • **fünfzigtausend** • cincuenta mil • cinquantamila

55,500
fifty-five thousand five hundred • cinqante-cinq mille cinq cents • **fünfundfünfzigtausend-fünfhundert** • cincuenta y cinco mil quinientos • cinquantacinquemilacinquecento

100,000
one hundred thousand • cent mille • **hunderttausend** • cien mil • centomila

1,000,000
one million • un million • **eine Million** • un millón • un milione

1,000,000,000
one billion • un milliard • **eine Milliarde** • mil millones • un miliardo

first • premier • erster • primero • primo

second • deuxième • zweiter • segundo • secondo

third • troisième • dritter • tercero • terzo

fourth • quatrième • **vierter** • cuarto • quarto

fifth • cinquième • **fünfter** • quinto • quinto

sixth • sixième • **sechster** • sexto • sesto

seventh • septième • **siebter** • séptimo • settimo

eighth • huitième • **achter** • octavo • ottavo

ninth • neuvième • **neunter** • noveno • nono

tenth • dixième • **zehnter** • décimo • decimo

eleventh • onzième • **elfter** • undécimo • undicesimo

twelfth • douzième • **zwölfter** • duodécimo • dodicesimo

thirteenth • treizième • **dreizehnter** • decimotercero • tredicesimo

fourteenth • quatorzième • **vierzehnter** • decimocuarto • quattordicesimo

fifteenth • quinzième • **fünfzehnter** • decimoquinto • quindicesimo

sixteenth • seizième • **sechzehnter** • decimosexto • sedicesimo

seventeenth • dix-septième • **siebzehnter** • decimoséptimo • diciassettesimo

eighteenth • dix-huitième • **achtzehnter** • décimo octavo • diciottesimo

nineteenth • dix-neuvième • **neunzehnter** • décimo noveno • diciannovesimo

twentieth • vingtième • **zwanzigster** • vigésimo • ventesimo

twenty-first • vingt et unième • **einundzwanzigster** • vigésimo primero • ventunesimo

twenty-second • vingt-deuxième • **zweiundzwanzigster** • vigésimo segundo • ventiduesimo

twenty-third • vingt-troisième • **dreiundzwanzigster** • vigésimo tercero • ventitreesimo

thirtieth • trentième • **dreißigster** • trigésimo • trentesimo

fortieth • quarantième • **vierzigster** • cuadragésimo • quarantesimo

fiftieth • cinquantième • **fünfzigster** • quincuagésimo • cinquantesimo

sixtieth • soixantième • **sechzigster** • sexagésimo • sessantesimo

seventieth • soixante-dixième • **siebzigster** • septuagésimo • settantesimo

eightieth • quatre-vingtième • **achtzigster** • octogésimo • ottantesimo

ninetieth • quatre-vingt-dixième • **neunzigster** • nonagésimo • novantesimo

one hundredth • centième • **hundertster** • centésimo • centesimo

weights and measures • les poids et mesures • die Maße und Gewichte • los pesos y las medidas • i pesi e le misure

area • la superficie • die Fläche • el área • la superficie

pan • le plateau• die Waagschale • la bandeja • il piatto

square foot
le pied carré
der Quadratfuß
el pie cuadrado
il piede quadro

square meter
le mètre carré
der Quadratmeter
el metro cuadrado
il metro quadro

pound
la livre
das Pfund
la libra
la libbra

kilogram
le kilogramme
das Kilogramm
el kilogramo
il chilogrammo

ounce
l'once
die Unze
la onza
l'oncia

gram
le gramme
das Gramm
el gramo
il grammo

distance • la distance • die Entfernung • la distancia • la distanza

kilometer
le kilomètre
der Kilometer
el kilómetro
il chilometro

mile
le mile
die Meile
la milla
il miglio

scale • la balance • die Waage • la báscula • la bilancia

yard	ton	measure (v)
le yard	la tonne	mesurer
das Yard	die Tonne	messen
la yarda	la tonelada	medir
la iarda	la tonnellata	misurare
meter	milligram	weigh (v)
le mètre	le milligramme	peser
der Meter	das Milligramm	wiegen
el metro	el miligramo	pesar
il metro	il milligrammo	pesare

length • la longueur • die Länge • la longitud • la lunghezza

foot • le pied • der Fuß • el pie • il piede

millimeter • le millimètre • der Millimeter • el milímetro • il millimetro

centimeter • le centimètre • der Zentimeter • el centímetro • il centimetro

inch • le pouce • der Zoll • la pulgada • il pollice

capacity • la capacité • das Fassungsvermögen • la capacidad • la capacità

half-liter • le demi-litre • der halbe Liter • el medio litro • il mezzo litro

pint • la pinte • das Pint • la pinta • la pinta

volume • le volume • das Volumen • el volumen • il volume

milliliter • le millilitre • der Milliliter • el mililitro • il millilitro

measuring cup • le pot gradué • der Messbecher • la jarra graduada • la brocca graduata

liquid measure • la mesure pour les liquides • das Flüssigkeitsmaß • la medida de capacidad • la misura di liquido

gallon
le gallon
die Gallone
el galón
il gallone

quart
deux pintes
das Quart
el cuarto de galón
il quarto di gallone

liter
le litre
der Liter
el litro
il litro

container • le récipient • der Behälter • el recipiente • il contenitore

carton • le carton • die Tüte • el tetrabrik • il cartone

bag • le paquet • das Päckchen • el paquete • il pacchetto

bottle • la bouteille • die Flasche • la botella • il bottiglia

sack • le sac • der Beutel • la bolsa • il sacchetto

tub • le pot • die Dose • la tarrina • la vaschetta

jar • le pot • das Glas • el tarro • il barattolo

can • la boîte • die Dose • la lata • la lattina

tin • la boîte • die Dose • la lata • la scatoletta

spray bottle • le pulvérisateur • die Spritze • el pulverizador • il nebulizzatore

bar
le pain
das Stück
la pastilla
la saponetta

tube • le tube • die Tube • el tubo • il tubetto

roll • le rouleau • die Rolle • el rollo • il rotolo

pack • le paquet • das Päckchen • la cajetilla • il pacchetto

spray can • la bombe • die Sprühdose • el spray • la bomboletta spray

world map • la carte du monde • die Weltkarte • el mapamundi • il mappamondo

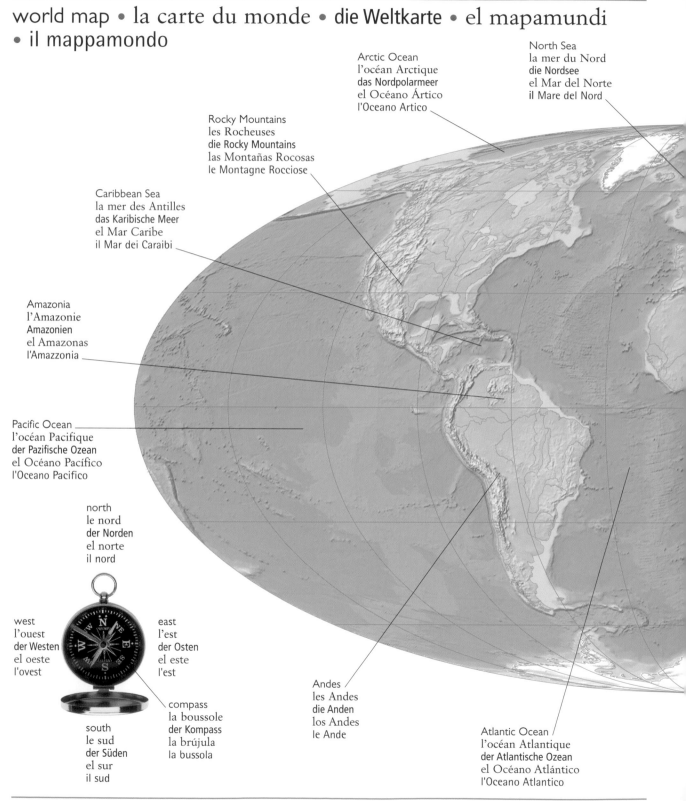

Arctic Ocean
l'océan Arctique
das Nordpolarmeer
el Océano Ártico
l'Oceano Artico

North Sea
la mer du Nord
die Nordsee
el Mar del Norte
il Mare del Nord

Rocky Mountains
les Rocheuses
die Rocky Mountains
las Montañas Rocosas
le Montagne Rocciose

Caribbean Sea
la mer des Antilles
das Karibische Meer
el Mar Caribe
il Mar dei Caraibi

Amazonia
l'Amazonie
Amazonien
el Amazonas
l'Amazzonia

Pacific Ocean
l'océan Pacifique
der Pazifische Ozean
el Océano Pacífico
l'Oceano Pacifico

north
le nord
der Norden
el norte
il nord

west
l'ouest
der Westen
el oeste
l'ovest

east
l'est
der Osten
el este
l'est

compass
la boussole
der Kompass
la brújula
la bussola

south
le sud
der Süden
el sur
il sud

Andes
les Andes
die Anden
los Andes
le Ande

Atlantic Ocean
l'océan Atlantique
der Atlantische Ozean
el Océano Atlántico
l'Oceano Atlantico

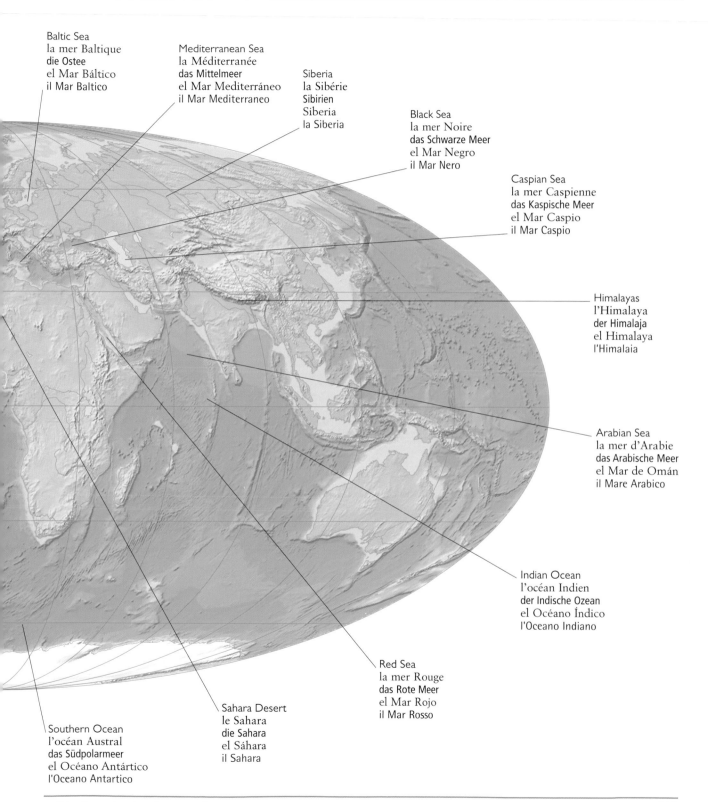

Baltic Sea
la mer Baltique
die Ostee
el Mar Báltico
il Mar Baltico

Mediterranean Sea
la Méditerranée
das Mittelmeer
el Mar Mediterráneo
il Mar Mediterraneo

Siberia
la Sibérie
Sibirien
Siberia
la Siberia

Black Sea
la mer Noire
das Schwarze Meer
el Mar Negro
il Mar Nero

Caspian Sea
la mer Caspienne
das Kaspische Meer
el Mar Caspio
il Mar Caspio

Himalayas
l'Himalaya
der Himalaja
el Himalaya
l'Himalaia

Arabian Sea
la mer d'Arabie
das Arabische Meer
el Mar de Omán
il Mare Arabico

Indian Ocean
l'océan Indien
der Indische Ozean
el Océano Índico
l'Oceano Indiano

Red Sea
la mer Rouge
das Rote Meer
el Mar Rojo
il Mar Rosso

Sahara Desert
le Sahara
die Sahara
el Sáhara
il Sahara

Southern Ocean
l'océan Austral
das Südpolarmeer
el Océano Antártico
l'Oceano Antartico

North and Central America • l'Amérique du Nord et centrale • Nord- und Mittelamerika • América del Norte y Central • l'America del Nord e Centrale

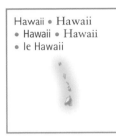

Hawaii • Hawaii
• Hawaii • Hawaii
• le Hawaii

1 Alaska • l'Alaska • Alaska • Alaska • l'Alaska
2 Canada • le Canada • Kanada • Canadá • il Canada
3 Greenland • le Groenland • Grönland • Groenlandia • la Groenlandia
4 United States of America • les États-Unis d'Amérique • die Vereinigten Staten von Amerika • Estados Unidos de América • gli Stati Uniti d'America
5 Mexico • le Mexique • Mexiko • México • il Messico
6 Guatemala • le Guatemala • Guatemala • Guatemala • il Guatemala
7 Belize • le Bélize • Belize • Belice • il Belize
8 El Salvador • Le Salvador • El Salvador • El Salvador • l'El Salvador
9 Honduras • le Honduras • Honduras • Honduras • l'Honduras
10 Nicaragua • le Nicaragua • Nicaragua • Nicaragua • il Nicaragua
11 Costa Rica • le Costa Rica • Costa Rica • Costa Rica • il Costa Rica
12 Panama • le Panama • Panama • Panamá • il Panama
13 Cuba • Cuba • Kuba • Cuba • Cuba
14 Bahamas • les Bahamas • die Bahamas • Bahamas • le Bahamas
15 Jamaica • la Jamaïque • Jamaika • Jamaica • la Giamaica
16 Haiti • Haïti • Haiti • Haití • Haiti
17 Dominican Republic • la République dominicaine • die Dominikanische Republik • República Dominicana • la Repubblica Dominicana
18 Puerto Rico • la Porto Rico • Puerto Rico • Puerto Rico • Puerto Rico
19 Barbados • la Barbade • Barbados • Barbados • Barbados
20 Trinidad and Tobago • la Trinité-et-Tobago • Trinidad und Tobago • Trinidad y Tobago • Trinidad e Tobago
21 St. Kitts and Nevis • Saint-Kitts-et-Nevis • Saint Kitts und Nevis • Saint Kitts y Nevis • Saint Kitts-Nevis
22 Antigua and Barbuda • Antigua-et-Barbuda • Antigua und Barbuda • Antigua y Barbuda • Antigua e Barbuda
23 Dominica • la Dominique • Dominica • Dominica • Dominica
24 St. Lucia • Sainte-Lucie • Saint Lucia • Santa Lucía • Saint Lucia
25 St. Vincent and the Grenadines • Saint-Vincent-et-les-Grenadines • Saint Vinzent und die Grenadinen • San Vicente y las Granadinas • Saint Vincent e Grenadine
26 Grenada • la Grenade • Grenada • Granada • Grenada

South America • l'Amérique du Sud • Südamerika • América del Sur • l'America del Sud

1 Venezuela • le Venezuela • **Venezuela** • Venezuela • il Venezuela

2 Colombia • la Colombie • **Kolumbien** • Colombia • la Colombia

3 Ecuador • l'Équateur • **Ecuador** • Ecuador • l'Ecuador

4 Peru • le Pérou • **Peru** • Perú • il Perù

5 Galápagos Islands • les îles Galapagos • **die Galapagosinseln** • las Islas Galápagos • le Isola Galapagos

6 Guyana • la Guyane • **Guyana** • Guyana • la Guyana

7 Suriname • le Surinam • **Suriname** • Suriname • il Suriname

8 French Guiana • la Guyane française • **Französisch-Guayana** • la Guayana Francesa • la Guyana Francese

9 Brazil • le Brésil • **Brasilien** • Brasil • il Brasile

10 Bolivia • la Bolivie • **Bolivien** • Bolivia • la Bolivia

11 Chile • le Chili • **Chile** • Chile • il Cile

12 Argentina • l'Argentine • **Argentinien** • Argentina • l'Argentina

13 Paraguay • le Paraguay • **Paraguay** • Paraguay • il Paraguay

14 Uruguay • l'Uruguay • **Uruguay** • Uruguay • l'Uruguay

15 Falkland Islands • les îles Malouines • **die Falklandinseln** • las Malvinas • le Isola Falkland

continent	province	zone
le continent	la province	la zone
der Kontinent	die Provinz	die Zone
el continente	la provincia	la zona
il continente	la provincia	la zona
country	territory	district
le pays	le territoire	le district
das Land	das Territorium	der Bezirk
el país	el territorio	el distrito
il paese	il territorio	il distretto
nation	principality	region
la nation	la principauté	la région
die Nation	das Fürstentum	die Region
la nación	el principado	la región
la nazione	il principato	la regione
state	colony	capital
l'État	la colonie	la capitale
der Staat	die Kolonie	die Hauptstadt
el estado	la colonia	la capital
lo stato	la colonia	la capitale

Europe • l'Europe • Europa • Europa • l'Europa

1 Ireland • l'Irlande • Irland • Irlanda • l'Irlanda

2 United Kingdom • le Royaume-Uni • das Vereinigte Königreich • Reino Unido • il Regno Unito

3 Portugal • le Portugal • Portugal • Portugal • il Portogallo

4 Spain • l'Espagne • Spanien • España • la Spagna

5 Balearic Islands • les Baléares • die Balearen • las Islas Baleares • le Isole Baleari

6 Andorra • l'Andorre • Andorra • Andorra • Andorra

7 France • la France • Frankreich • Francia • la Francia

8 Belgium • la Belgique • Belgien • Bélgica • il Belgio

9 Netherlands • les Pays-Bas • die Niederlande • los Países Bajos • i Paesi Bassi

10 Luxembourg • le Luxembourg • Luxemburg • Luxemburgo • il Lussemburgo

11 Germany • l'Allemagne • Deutschland • Alemania • la Germania

12 Denmark • le Danemark • Dänemark • Dinamarca • la Danimarca

13 Norway • la Norvège • Norwegen • Noruega • la Norvegia

14 Sweden • la Suède • Schweden • Suecia • la Svezia

15 Finland • la Finlande • Finnland • Finlandia • la Finlandia

16 Estonia • l'Estonie • Estland • Estonia • l'Estonia

17 Latvia • la Lettonie • Lettland • Letonia • la Lettonia

18 Lithuania • la Lituanie • Litauen • Lituania • la Lituania

19 Kaliningrad • Kaliningrad • Kaliningrad • Kaliningrado • Kaliningrad

20 Poland • la Pologne • Polen • Polonia • la Polonia

21 Czech Republic • la République tchèque • die Tschechische Republik • República Checa • la Repubblica Ceca

22 Austria • l'Autriche • Österreich • Austria • l'Austria

23 Liechtenstein • le Liechtenstein • Liechtenstein • Liechtenstein • il Liechtenstein

24 Switzerland • la Suisse • die Schweiz • Suiza • la Svizzera

25 Italy • l'Italie • Italien • Italia • l'Italia

26 Monaco • Monaco • Monaco • Mónaco • Monaco

27 Corsica • la Corse • Korsika • Córcega • la Corsica

28 Sardinia • la Sardaigne • Sardinien • Cerdeña • la Sardegna

29 San Marino • le Saint-Marin • San Marino • San Marino • San Marino

30 Vatican City • la Cité du Vatican • die Vatikanstadt • la Ciudad del Vaticano • la Città del Vaticano

31 Sicily • la Sicile • Sizilien • Sicilia • la Sicilia

32 Malta • Malte • Malta • Malta • Malta

33 Slovenia • la Slovénie • Slowenien • Eslovenia • la Slovenia

34 Croatia • la Croatie • Kroatien • Croacia • la Croazia

35 Hungary • la Hongrie • Ungarn • Hungría • l'Ungheria

36 Slovakia • la Slovaquie • die Slowakei • Eslovaquia • la Slovacchia

37 Ukraine • l'Ukraine • die Ukraine • Ucrania • l'Ucraina

38 Belarus • la Bélarus • Weißrussland • Belarús • la Bielorussia

39 Moldova • la Moldavie • Moldawien • Moldavia • la Moldavia

40 Romania • la Roumanie • Rumänien • Rumanía • la Romania

41 Yugoslavia • la Yougoslavie • Jugoslawien • Yugoslavia • la Jugoslavia

42 Bosnia and Herzogovina • la Bosnie-Herzégovine • Bosnien und Herzegowina • Bosnia y Herzegovina • la Bosnia ed Erzegovina

43 Albania • l'Albanie • Albanien • Albania • l'Albania

44 Macedonia • la Macédonie • Mazedonien • Macedonia • la Macedonia

45 Bulgaria • la Bulgarie • Bulgarien • Bulgaria • la Bulgaria

46 Greece • la Grèce • Griechenland • Grecia • la Grecia

47 Turkey • la Turquie • die Türkei • Turquía • la Turchia

48 Cyprus • Chypre • Zypern • Chipre • Cipro

Africa • l'Afrique • Afrika • África • l'Africa

30 Somalia • la Somalie • Somalia • Somalia • la Somalia

31 Kenya • le Kenya • Kenia • Kenya • il Kenya

32 Uganda • l'Ouganda • Uganda • Uganda • l'Uganda

33 Central African Republic • la République centrafricaine • die Zentralafrikanische Republik • República Centroafricana • la Repubblica Centrafricana

34 Gabon • le Gabon • Gabun • Gabón • il Gabon

35 Congo • le Congo • Kongo • Congo • il Congo

36 Cabinda • Cabinda • Kabinda • Cabinda • Cabinda

37 Democratic Republic of the Congo • la République démocratique du Congo • die Demokratische Republik Kongo • República Democrática del Congo • la Repubblica Democratica del Congo

38 Rwanda • le Rwanda • Ruanda • Rwanda • il Ruanda

39 Burundi • le Burundi • Burundi • Burundi • il Burundi

40 Tanzania • la Tanzanie • Tansania • Tanzania • la Tanzania

41 Mozambique • le Mozambique • Mosambik • Mozambique • il Mozambico

42 Malawi • le Malawi • Malawi • Malawi • il Malawi

43 Zambia • la Zambie • Sambia • Zambia • lo Zambia

44 Angola • l'Angola • Angola • Angola • l'Angola

45 Namibia • la Namibie • Namibia • Namibia • la Namibia

46 Botswana • le Botswana • Botsuana • Botswana • il Botswana

47 Zimbabwe • le Zimbabwe • Simbabwe • Zimbabwe • lo Zimbabwe

48 South Africa • l'Afrique du Sud • Südafrika • Sudáfrica • il Sud Africa

49 Lesotho • le Lesotho • Lesotho • Lesotho • il Lesotho

50 Swaziland • le Swaziland • Swasiland • Swazilandia • lo Swaziland

51 Comoros • les Comores • die Komoren • Comoros • le Comore

52 Madagascar • Madagascar • Madagaskar • Madagascar • il Madagascar

53 Mauritius • l'île Maurice • Mauritius • Mauricio • la Mauritania

1 Morocco • le Maroc • Marokko • Marruecos • il Marocco

2 Western Sahara • le Sahara occidental • Westsahara • Sáhara Occidental • il Sahara Occidentale

3 Mauritania • la Mauritanie • Mauretanien • Mauritania • la Mauritania

4 Senegal • le Sénégal • Senegal • Senegal • il Senegal

5 Gambia • la Gambie • Gambia • Gambia • il Gambia

6 Guinea-Bissau • la Guinée-Bissau • Guinea-Bissau • Guinea-Bissau • la Guinea-Bissau

7 Guinea • la Guinée • Guinea • Guinea • la Guinea

8 Sierra Leone • la Sierra Leone • Sierra Leone • Sierra Leona • Sierra Leone

9 Liberia • le Libéria • Liberia • Liberia • la Liberia

10 Ivory Coast • la Côte d'Ivoire • Elfenbeinküste • Costa de Marfil • la Costa d'Avorio

11 Burkina Faso • le Burkina • Burkina • Burquina Faso • il Burkina Faso

12 Mali • le Mali • Mali • Malí • il Mali

13 Algeria • l'Algérie • Algerien • Argelia • l'Algeria

14 Tunisia • la Tunisie • Tunesien • Túnez • la Tunisia

15 Libya • la Libye • Libyen • Libia • la Libia

16 Niger • le Niger • Niger • Níger • il Niger

17 Ghana • le Ghana • Ghana • Ghana • il Ghana

18 Togo • le Togo • Togo • Togo • il Togo

19 Benin • le Bénin • Benin • Benin • il Benin

20 Nigeria • le Nigéria • Nigeria • Nigeria • la Nigeria

21 São Tomé and Principe • Sao Tomé-et-Principe • São Tomé und Príncipe • Santo Tomé y Príncipe • São Tomé e Príncipe

22 Equatorial Guinea • la Guinée équatoriale • Äquatorialguinea • Guinea Ecuatorial • la Guinea Equatoriale

23 Cameroon • le Cameroun • Kamerun • Camerún • il Camerun

24 Chad • le Tchad • Tschad • Chad • il Ciad

25 Egypt • l'Égypte • Ägypten • Egipto • l'Egitto

26 Sudan • le Soudan • der Sudan • Sudán • il Sudan

27 Eritrea • l'Érythrée • Eritrea • Eritrea • l'Eritrea

28 Djibouti • Djibouti • Dschibuti • Djibouti • Gibuti

29 Ethiopia • l'Éthiopie • Äthiopien • Etiopía • l'Etiopia

Asia • l'Asie • Asien • Asia • l'Asia

1 Russian Federation • la Fédération de Russie • die Russische Föderation • Federación Rusa • la Federazione Russa

2 Georgia • la Géorgie • Georgien • Georgia • la Georgia

3 Armenia • l'Arménie • Armenien • Armenia • l'Armenia

4 Azerbaijan • l'Azerbaïdjan • Aserbaidschan • Azerbaiyán • l'Azerbaigian

5 Iran • l'Iran • der Iran • Irán • l'Iran

6 Iraq • l'Irak • der Irak • Iraq • l'Iraq

7 Syria • la Syrie • Syrien • Siria • la Siria

8 Lebanon • le Liban • der Libanon • Líbano • il Libano

9 Israel • Israël • Israel • Israel • l'Israele

10 Jordan • la Jordanie • Jordanien • Jordania • la Giordania

11 Saudi Arabia • l'Arabie Saoudite • Saudi-Arabien • Arabia Saudita • l'Arabia Saudita

12 Kuwait • le Koweït • Kuwait • Kuwait • il Kuwait

13 Qatar • le Qatar • Katar • Qatar • il Qatar

14 United Arab Emirates • les Émirats arabes unis • Vereinigte Arabische Emirate • Emiratos Árabes Unidos • gli Emirati Arabi Uniti

15 Oman • l'Oman • Oman • Omán • l'Oman

16 Yemen • le Yémen • der Jemen • Yemen • lo Yemen

17 Kazakhstan • le Kasakhastan • Kasachstan • Kazajstán • il Kazakistan

18 Uzbekistan • l'Ouzbékistan • Usbekistan • Uzbekistán • l'Uzbekistan

19 Turkmenistan • le Turkmenistan • Turkmenistan • Turkmenistán • il Turkmenistan

20 Afghanistan • l'Afghanistan • Afghanistan • Afganistán • l'Afghanistan

21 Tajikistan • le Tadjikistan • Tadschikistan • Tayikistán • il Tagikistan

22 Kyrgyzstan • le Kirghizistan • Kirgisistan • Kirguistán • il Kirghizistan

23 Pakistan • le Pakistan • Pakistan • Pakistán • il Pakistan

24 India • l'Inde • Indien • India • l'India

25 Maldives • les Maldives • die Malediven • Maldivas • le Maldive

26 Sri Lanka • Sri Lanka • Sri Lanka • Sri Lanka • lo Sri Lanka

27 China • la Chine • China • China • la Cina

28 Mongolia • la Mongolie • die Mongolei • Mongolia • la Mongolia

29 North Korea • la Corée du Nord • Nordkorea • Corea del Norte • la Corea del Nord

30 South Korea • la Corée du Sud • Südkorea • Corea del Sur • la Corea del Sud

31 Japan • le Japon • Japan • Japón • il Giappone

32 Nepal • le Népal • Nepal • Nepal • il Nepal

33 Bhutan • le Bhoutan • Bhutan • Bhutan • il Bhutan

34 Bangladesh • le Bangladesh • Bangladecsh • Bangladesh • il Bangladesh

35 Burma (Myanmar) • la Birmanie (le Myanmar) • Birma (Myanmar) • Birmania (Myanmar) • la Birmania (il Myanmar)

36 Thailand • la Thaïlande • Thailand • Tailandia • la Tailandia

37 Laos • le Laos • Laos • Laos • il Laos

38 Viet Nam • le Vietnam • Vietnam • Viet Nam • il Vietnam

Australasia • l'Australasie • Australien und Ozeanien • Australasia • l'Oceania

1 Australia • l'Australie • Australien • Australia • l'Australia
2 Tasmania • la Tasmanie • Tasmanien • Tasmania • la Tasmania
3 New Zealand • la Nouvelle-Zélande • Neuseeland • Nueva Zelandia • la Nuova Zelanda

39 Cambodia • le Cambodge • Kambodscha • Camboya • la Cambogia
40 Malaysia • la Malaisie • Malaysia • Malasia • la Malaysia
41 Singapore • Singapour • Singapur • Singapur • Singapore
42 Indonesia • l'Indonésie • Indonesien • Indonesia • l'Indonesia
43 Brunei • le Brunei • Brunei • Brunei • Brunei
44 Philippines • les Philippines • die Philippinen • Filipinas • le Filippine
45 Taiwan • Taiwan • Taiwan • Taiwán • Taiwan
46 East Timor • le Timor oriental • Ost-Timor • Timor Oriental • Timor Est
47 Papua New Guinea • la Papouasie-Nouvelle-Guinée • Papua-Neuguinea • Papua Nueva Guinea • la Papua Nuova Guinea
48 Solomon Islands • les îles Saloman • die Salomonen • Islas Salomón • le Isole Salomone
49 Vanuatu • Vanuatu • Vanuatu • Vanuatu • Vanuatu
50 Fiji • Fidji • Fidschi • Fiji • Figi

particles and antonyms • particules et antonymes • Partikeln und Antonyme • partículas y antónimos • particelle e antonimi

to	from	through	around
à	de	à travers	autour de
zu, nach	von, aus	durch	um
a, hacia	de, desde	a través de	alrededor de
a	da	attraverso	attorno
over	under	on top of	beside
au-dessus de	sous	sur	à côté de
über	unter	auf	neben
encima de	debajo de	encima de	al lado de
sopra	sotto	in cima	accanto
in front of	behind	between	opposite
devant	derrière	entre	en face de
vor	hinter	zwischen	gegenüber
delante de	detrás de	entre	en frente de
davanti	dietro	tra	di fronte
onto	into	near	far
sur	dans	près de	loin de
auf	in	nahe	weit
sobre	dentro de	cerca	lejos
sopra	dentro	vicino	lontano
in	out	with	without
dans	dehors	avec	sans
in	aus	mit	ohne
en	fuera	con	sin
dentro	fuori	con	senza
above	below	before	after
au-dessus de	au-dessous de	avant	après
über	unter	vor	nach
sobre	bajo	antes	después
sopra	sotto	prima	dopo
inside	outside	by	until
à l'intérieur de	à l'extérieur de	avant	jusqu'à
innerhalb	außerhalb	bis	bis
dentro	fuera	antes de	hasta
all'interno	all'esterno	entro	fino
up	down	for	toward
en haut	en bas	pour	vers
hinauf	hinunter	für	zu
arriba	abajo	para	hacia
su	giù	per	verso
at	beyond	along	across
à	au-delà de	le long de	à travers
an, bei	jenseits	entlang	über
en	más allá de	por	al otro lado de
a	oltre	lungo	attraverso

english • français • deutsch • español • italiano

No smoking
Défense de fumer
Rauchen verboten
Prohibido fumar
Vietato fumare

Out of order
En panne
Außer Betrieb
Fuera de servicio
Guasto

Opening times
Heures d'ouverture
Öffnungszeiten
Horario de apertura
Orario di apertura

Free admission
Entrée gratuite
Eintritt frei
Entrada libre
Ingresso libero

Knock before entering
Frappez avant d'entrer
Bitte anklopfen
Llame antes de entrar
Bussare prima di entrare

Keep off the grass
Défense de marcher sur la pelouse
Betreten des Rasens verboten
Prohibido pisar el pasto
Non calpestare l'erba

help • assistance • Hilfe • ayuda • aiuto

Can you help me?
Pouvez-vous m'aider?
Können Sie mir helfen?
¿Me puede ayudar?
Mi può aiutare?

I don't understand.
Je ne comprends pas.
Ich verstehe nicht.
No entiendo.
Non capisco

I don't know.
Je ne sais pas.
Ich weiß nicht.
No lo sé.
Non lo so

Do you speak English, French…?
Vous parlez anglais, français…?
Sprechen Sie Englisch, Französisch…?
¿Habla inglés, francés…?
Parla inglese, francese…?

I speak English, Spanish…
Je parle anglais, espagnol…
Ich spreche Englisch, Spanisch…
Hablo inglés, español…
Parlo inglese, spagnolo…

Please speak more slowly.
Parlez moins vite, s'il vous plaît.
Sprechen Sie bitte langsamer.
Hable más despacio, por favor.
Parli più lentamente.

Please write it down for me.
Écrivez-le pour moi, s'il vous plaît.
Schreiben Sie es bitte für mich auf.
¿Me lo puede escribir?
Me lo scriva, per favore.

I have lost…
J'ai perdu…
Ich habe… verloren
He perdido…
Ho perso…

directions • directions • Richtungsangaben • indicaciones • indicazioni

I am lost.
Je me suis perdu.
Ich habe mich verlaufen.
Estoy perdido.
Mi sono perso/a.

Where is the…?
Où est le/la…?
Wo ist der/die/das…?
¿Dónde está el/la…?
Dov'è il/la…?

Where is the nearest…?
Où est le/la…le/la plus proche?
Wo ist der/die/das nächste…?
¿Dónde está el/la… más cercano/a?
Dov'è il/la … più vicino/a?

Where are the toilets?
Où sont les toilettes?
Wo sind die Toiletten?
¿Dónde están los baños?
Dov'è il bagno?

How do I get to…?
Pour aller à…?
Wie komme ich nach…?
¿Cómo voy a…?
Come si arriva a…?

To the right
À droite
Nach rechts
A la derecha
A destra

To the left.
À gauche
Nach links
A la izquierda
A sinistra

Straight ahead
Tout droit
Geradeaus
Todo recto
Sempre dritto

How far is…?
C'est loin…?
Wie weit ist…?
¿A qué distancia está…?
Quant'è lontano…?

accommodation • logement • Unterkunft • alojamiento • alloggio

I have a reservation.
J'ai réservé une chambre.
Ich habe ein Zimmer reserviert.
Tengo una reservación.
Ho una prenotazione.

What time is breakfast?
Le petit déjeuner est à quelle heure?
Wann gibt es Frühstück?
¿A qué hora es el desayuno?
A che ora è la colazione?

Where is the dining room?
Où est la salle à manger?
Wo ist der Speisesaal?
¿Dónde está el comedor?
Dov'è la sala da pranzo?

eating and drinking • nourriture et boissons • Essen und Trinken • comida y bebida • cibo e bevande

Cheers!
À la vôtre!
Zum Wohl!
¡Salud!
Salute!

It's delicious/awful.
C'est délicieux/terrible.
Es ist köstlich/scheußlich.
Está buenísimo/malísimo.
È buonissimo/disgustoso.

I don't drink/smoke.
Je ne bois/fume pas.
Ich trinke/rauche nicht.
Yo no bebo/fumo.
Non bevo/fumo.

I don't eat meat.
Je ne mange pas de la viande.
Ich esse kein Fleisch.
Yo no como carne.
Non mangio la carne.

No more for me, thank you.
Je n'en veux plus, merci.
Nichts mehr, danke.
Ya no más, gracias.
Per me basta, grazie.

May I have some more?
Encore un peu, s'il vous plaît.
Könnte ich noch etwas mehr haben?
¿Puedo repetir?
Posso prenderne ancora?

May we have the check?
L'addition, s'il vous plaît.
Wir möchten bitte zahlen.
¿Me trae la cuenta?
Il conto, per favore.

Can I have a receipt?
Je voudrais un reçu.
Ich hätte gerne eine Quittung.
¿Me da un recibo?
Mi dà una ricevuta?

No-smoking area
Partie non-fumeurs
Nichtraucherbereich
Área de no fumar
Area riservata i non fumatori

English index • index anglais • englisches Register • índice inglés • indice inglese

english

english

english

E

dusk 305
dust cloth 77
dust v 77
dustpan 77
duty-free store 213
DVD 269
DVD player 268
dyed 39
dynamo 207

eagle 292
ear 14
Ear Nose and Throat 49
early
earring 36
Earth 280, 282
earthenware dish 69
earthquake 283
easel 174, 274
east 312
East Timor 319
Easter 27
easy 321
easy-to-cook 130
eat in 154
eat v 64
eating 75
eau de toilette 41
eaves 58
éclair 140
eclipse 280
economics 169
economy class 211
Ecuador 315
eczema 44
Edam 142
edge 246
editor 191
eel 294
egg 20
egg white 137
eggcup 65, 137
eggplant 125
eggs 137
Egypt 317
eight 308
eight hundred 308
eighteen 308
eighteenth 309
eighth 309
eightieth 309
eighty 308
ejaculatory duct 21
El Salvador 314
elbow 13
electric blanket 71
electric drill 78
electric guitar 258
electric meter 60
electric razor 73
electric shock 46
electric train 208
electrical goods 107
electrical tape 81
electrician 188
electricity 60
electronics 105
elephant 291
elevator 59, 100, 104
eleven 308
eleventh 309
elliptical trainer 250
elm 296
email 98, 177
email account 177

email address 177
embarrassed 25
embossed paper 83
embroidery 277
embryo 52
emerald 288
emergency 46
emergency exit 210
emergency lever 209
emergency phone 195
emergency room 48
emergency services 94
emigrate v 26
emotions 25
employee 24
employer 24
empty 321
enamel 50
encore 255
encyclopedia 163
end 321
end zone 220
endive 123
endline 226
endocrine 19
endocrinology 49
engaged couple 24
engine 202, 204, 208, 210
engine room 214
engineering 169
English breakfast 157
English garden 84
English horn 257
english mustard 135
engraving v 275
enlarge v 172
enlargement 271
entrance 59
entrance ramp 194
envelope 98, 173
environment 280
epidural 52
epiglottis 19
epilepsy 44
episiotomy 52
equals 165
equation 165
equator 283
equipment 165
equipment 233, 238
Equitorial Guinea 317
equity 97
eraser 163
Eritrea 317
erupt v 283
escalator 104
esophagus 19
espresso 148
essay 163
essential oils 55
estate agent 189
Estonia 316
estuary 285
Ethiopia 317
eucalyptus 296
Europe 316
evening 305
evening dress 34
events 243, 247
evergreen 86
evidence 181
examination 163
excess baggage 212
exchange rate 97
excited 25
excuse me 322

executive 174
exercise bike 250
exercises 251
exfoliate v 41
exhaust pipe 203, 204
exhibit v 261
exhibition 261
exit 210
exit ramp 194
exosphere 286
expectant 52
experiment 166
expiration date 109
exposure 271
extend v 251
extension cord 78
exterior 198
extra time 223
extraction 50
eye 14, 51, 244, 276
eye dropper 109
eye drops 109
eye shadow 40
eye test 51
eyebrow 14, 51
eyebrow brush 40
eyebrow pencil 40
eyecup 269
eyelash 14, 51
eyelet 37
eyelid 51
eyeliner 40
eyepiece 167

F

fabric 277
fabric conditioner 76
face 14
face cream 73
face mask 225
face pack 41
face powder 40
face-off circle 224
facial 41
facial composite 181
factory 299
faint v 25, 44
fair 41, 262
fairway 232
falcon 292
Falkland Islands 315
fall 237
fall 31, 307
fall in love v 26
Fallopian tube 20
family 22
famous ruin 261
fan 60, 202
fan belt 203
fans 258
far 320
fare 197, 209
farm 182, 183, 184
farmer 182, 189
farmhouse 182
farmland 182
farmyard 182
farsighted 51
fashion 277
fast 321
fast food 154
fast food restaurant 154
fast-forward 269
fat 119, 321
fat-free 137
fat-free milk 136

father 22
father-in-law 23
faucet 61, 66
fault 230
fava bean 122
fava beans 131
fax 98, 172
fax machine 172
feather 293
feature film 269
February 306
feed v 183
feijoa 128
female 12, 20
feminine hygiene 108
femur 17
fence 85, 182, 243
fencing 249
feng shui 55
fennel 122, 133
fennel seeds 133
fenugreek 132
fern 86
ferry terminal 216
ferryboat 215, 216
fertilization 20
fertilize v 91
fertilizer 91
festivals 27
fetus 52
fever 44
fiancé 24
fiancée 24
fiber 127
fibula 17
field 182, 222, 228, 234
field hockey 224
field v 225, 229
fifteen 308
fifteenth 309
fifth 309
fiftieth 309
fifty 308
fifty five thousand, five
    hundred 309
fifty thousand 309
fig 129
fighter plane 211
figure skating 247
figurine 260
Fiji 319
filament 60
file 81, 172, 177
filing cabinet 172
fill v 82
filler 83
fillet 119, 121
filleted 121
filling 50, 140, 155
film 260, 271
film chamber 270
film set 179
film spool 271
filo dough 140
filter 270
filter coffee 148
filter paper 167
fin 210
finance 97
financial advisor 97
fingerprint 94
finial 300
finish line 234
Finland 316
fire 95
fire alarm 95

fire department 95
fire engine 95
fire escape 95
fire extinguisher 95
fire station 95
firefighters 95
firelighter 266
fireman 189
fireplace 63
firm 124
first 309
first aid 47
first aid kit 47
fish 107, 120, 294
fish and chips 155
fish counter 114
fish farm 183
fish seller 120
fish spatula 68
fisherman 189
fishhook 244
fishing 244, 245
fishing boat 217
fishing license 245
fishing port 217
fishing rod 244
fishmonger 188
fist 15, 237
fitness 250
fitting room 104
five 308
five hundred 308
flag 221, 232
flageolet beans 131
flakes 132
flamingo 292
flan pan 69
flare 240
flash 270
flash gun 270
flashlight 267
flat 256
flat race 243
flat tire 203, 207
flatbread 139
flavored oil 134
flax 184
fleece 74
flesh 127, 129
flex v 251
flight attendant 190
flight attendant 210
flight number 213
flint 288
flipchart 174
flip-flop 37
flipper 239, 290
float 244
float ball 61
flock 183
flood 287
floor 58, 62, 71
floor exercises 235
floor plan 261
florentine 141
floret 122
florist 110, 188
floss v 50
flours 138
flower 297
flowerbed 85, 90
flowering plant 297
flowering shrub 87
flowers 110
flu 44
flute 139, 257

english

english

english

english

english

english

english

V

vacation 212
vacuum cleaner 77, 188
vagina 20
valance 71
valley 284
valve 207
vanilla 132
vanity table 71
Vanuatu 319
varnish 79, 83
vas deferens 21
vase 63, 111
Vatican City 316
vault 235, 300
VCR 269
veal 118
vegetable garden 85, 182
vegetable oil 135
vegetables 107, 122, 124
veggie burger 155
veil 35
vein 19
venetian blind 63
Venezuela 315
venison 118
vent 283
ventilation hood 66
Venus 280
verdict 181
vest 33
vet 189
vibraphone 257
video game 269
video phone 99
videotape 269
Viet Nam 318
viewfinder 271
village 299
vine 183
vinegar 135, 142
vineyard 183
vintage 199
viola 256
violin 256
virus 44
visa 213
vise 78
vision 51
visiting hours 48
visor 205
vitamins 108
v-neck 33
vocal cords 19
vodka 145
vodka and orange 151
voice message 99
volcano 283
volley 231
volleyball 227

voltage 60
volume 165, 179, 269, 311
vomit v 44

W

waders 244
wading pool 263
waffles 157
waist 12
waistband 35
waiting room 45
waitress 191
wake up v 71
walk 243
walking boot 37
wall 58, 186, 222
wall light 62
wallet 37
wallpaper 82, 177
wallpaper brush 82
wallpaper paste 82
wallpaper v 82
walnut 129
walnut oil 134
walrus 290
ward 48
wardrobe 70
warehouse 216
warm 286
warm up v 251
warm-up suit 31, 32
warrant 180
wash v 38, 77
washer 80
washer fluid reservoir 202
washer-dryer 76
washing machine 76
wasp 295
waste disposal 61, 266
waste disposal unit 61
wastebasket 172
watch 36
watch television v 269
water 144, 238
water bottle 206, 267
water chamber 61
water chestnut 124
water garden 84
water hazard 232
water heater 61
water jet 95
water plant 86
water polo 239
water ski 241
water sports 241
water v 90, 183
watercolors 274
watercress 123
waterfall 285
watering 89

watering can 89
watermelon 127
waterskier 241
waterskiing 241
wave 241, 264
wavelength 179
wax 41
weak 321
weather 286
weaving 277
website 177
wedding 26. 35
wedding cake 141
wedding dress 35
wedding reception 26
wedge 233
Wednesday 306
weed killer 91
weed v 91
weeds 86
week 306
weekend 306
weekly 307
weigh v 310
weight 166
weight bar 251
weight belt 239
weight training 251
west 312
Western 255
Western sahara 317
wet 286, 321
wet wipe 75, 108
wetsuit 239
whale 290
wheat 130, 184
wheel 198, 207
wheel lugs 203
wheelbarrow 88
wheelchair 48
wheelchair access 197
whiplash 46
whipped cream 137
whipped cream 157
whipping cream 137
whisk 68
whisk v 67
whiskers 290
whiskey 145
white 39, 145, 272, 274
white bread 139
white chocolate 113
white currant 127
white flour 138
white meat 118
white rice 130
whole 129, 132
whole milk 136
whole-grain 131
wholegrain mustard 135

whole-wheat bread 139
whole-wheat flour 138
wicket 225
wicket-keeper 225
wide 321
widescreen television 269
width 165
wife 22
wig 39
wild rice 130
wildlife park 262
willow 296
win v 273
wind 241, 286
windbreak 265
windbreaker 33
windlass 214
window 58, 96, 98, 177, 186,
  197, 209, 210
windpipe 18
windshield 198, 205
windshield wiper 198
windshield wiper fluid 199
windsurfer 241
windsurfing 241
windy 286
wine 145, 151
wine glass 65
wine list 152
wine vinegar 135
wing 119, 210, 293
wings 254
winner 273
winter 31, 307
winter sports 247
wipe v 77
wire 79
wire cutter 80
wire stripper 81
wires 60
with 320
withdrawal slip 96
without 320
witness 180
wok 69
wolf 290
woman 23
womb 52
women's clothing 34
womenswear 105
wood 79, 233, 275, 285
wood bits 80
wood glue 78
wood shavings 78
wooden spoon 68
woodpecker 292
woodstain 79
woodwind 257
woodworking 275
work 172

work bowl 66, 69
workbench 78
workday 306
workshop 78
world map 312
worm 295
worried 25
wound 46
wrap 155
wrapping 111
wreath 111
wrench 80
wrestling 236
wrinkle 15
wrist 13, 15
wristband 230
writ 180
write v 162

X

x-ray 48
x-ray film 50
x-ray machine 212
x-ray viewer 45

Y

yacht 215
yam 125
yard 310
yarn 277
yatch 240
yawn v 25
year 163, 306
yeast 138
yellow 274
yellow card 223
Yemen 318
yes 322
yesterday 306
yoga 54
yogurt 137
yolk 137, 157
young cabbage 123
you're welcome 322
Yugoslavia 316

Z

Zambia 317
zebra 291
zero 308
zest 126
Zimbabwe 317
zinc 289
zip code 98
zipper 277
zone 315
zones 283
zoo 262
zoology 169
zoom lens 270
zucchini 125

French index • index français • französisches Register • índice francés • indice francese

français

français

français

français

français

français

français

français

français

français

français

français

français

français

German index • index allemand • deutsches Register • índice alemán • indice tedesco

deutsch

deutsch

deutsch

deutsch

deutsch

deutsch

english • français • deutsch • español • italiano

deutsch

deutsch

deutsch

deutsch

deutsch

español

español

español

español

español

español

español

español

español

español

Italian index • index italien • italienisches Register • índice italiano • indice italiano

italiano

italiano

italiano

italiano

italiano

italiano

italiano

italiano

italiano

italiano

italiano

italiano

acknowledgments • remerciements • Dank • agradecimientos • ringraziamenti

DORLING KINDERSLEY would like to thank Tracey Miles and Christine Lacey for design assistance, Georgina Garner for editorial and administrative help, Sonia Gavira, Polly Boyd, and Cathy Meeus for editorial help, and Claire Bowers for compiling the DK picture credits.

The publisher would like to thank the following for their kind permission to reproduce their photographs:
Abbreviations key:
t=top, b=bottom, r=right, l=left, c=center

Abode: 62; **Action Plus:** 224bc; **alamy.com:** 154t; **A.T. Willett** 287bcl; Michael Foyle 184bl; Stock Connection 287bcr; **Allsport/Getty Images:** 238cl; **Alvey and Towers:** 209 acr, 215bcl, 215bcr, 241cr; **Peter Anderson:** 188cbr, 271br. **Anthony Blake Photo Library:** Charlie Stebbings 114cl; John Sims 114tcl; **Andyalte:** 98tl; **apple mac computers:** 268tcr; **Arcaid:** John Edward Linden 301bl; Martine Hamilton Knight, Architects: Chapman Taylor Partners, 213cl; Richard Bryant 301br; **Argos:** 41tcl, 66cbl, 66cl, 66br, 66bcl, 69cl, 70bcl, 71t, 77tl, 269tc, 270tl; **Axiom:** Eitan Simanor 105bcr; Ian Cumming 104; Vicki Couchman 148cr; **Beken Of Cowes Ltd:** 215cbc; **Bosch:** 76tcr, 76tc, 76tcl; **Camera Press:** 27c, 38tr, 256t, 257cr; Barry J. Holmes 148tr; Jane Hanger 159cr; Mary Germanou 259bc; **Corbis:** 78b; Anna Clopet 247tr; Bettmann 181tl, 181tr; Bo Zauders 156t; Bob Rowan 152bl; Bob Winsett 247cbl; Brian Bailey 247br; Carl and Ann Purcell 162l; Chris Rainer 247ctl; ChromoSohm Inc. 179tr; Craig Aurness 215bl; David H.Wells 249cbr; Dennis Marsico 274bl; Dimitri Lundt 236bc; Duomo 211tl; Gail Mooney 277ctcr; George Lepp 248c; Gunter Marx 248cr; Jack Fields 210b; Jack Hollingsworth 231bl; Jacqui Hurst 277cbr; James L. Amos 247bl, 191ctr, 220bcr; Jan Butchofsky 277cbc; Johnathan Blair 243cr; Jon Feingersh 153tr; Jose F. Poblete 191br; Jose Luis Pelaez.Inc 153tc, 175tl; Karl Weatherly 220bl, 247tcr; Kelly Mooney Photography 259tl; Kevin Fleming 249bc; Kevin R. Morris 105tr, 243tl, 243tc; Kim Sayer 249tcr; Lynn Goldsmith 258t; Macduff Everton 231bcl; Mark Gibson 249bl; Mark L. Stephenson 249tcl; Michael Pole 115tr; Michael S. Yamashita 247ctcl; Mike King 247cbl; Neil Rabinowitz 214br; Owen Franken 112t; Pablo Corral 115bc; Paul A.

Sounders 169br, 249ctcl; Paul J. Sutton 224c, 224br; Peter Turnley 105tcr; Phil Schermeister 227b, 248tr; R. W Jones 309; R.W. Jones 175tr; Richard Hutchings 168b; Rick Doyle 241ctr; Robert Holmes 97br, 277ctc; Roger Ressmeyer 169tr; Russ Schleipman 229; Steve Raymer 168cr; The Purcell Team 211ctr; Tim Wright 178; Vince Streano 194t; Wally McNamee 220br, 220bcl, 224bl; Yann Arhus-Bertrand 249tl; **Dixons:** 270cl, 270cr, 270bl, 270bcl, 270bcr, 270ccr; **Education Photos:** John Walmsley 26tl; **Empics Ltd:** Adam Day 236br; Andy Heading 243c; Steve White 249cbc; **Getty Images:** 48bcl, 100t, 114bcr, 154bl, 287tr; 94tr; **Dennis Gilbert:** 106tc; **Hulsta:** 70t; **Ideal Standard Ltd:** 72r; **The Image Bank/Getty Images:** 58; **Impact Photos:** Eliza Armstrong 115cr; John Arthur 190tl; Philip Achache 246t; **The Interior Archive:** Henry Wilson, Alfie's Market 114bl; Luke White, Architect: David Mikhail, 59tl; Simon Upton, Architect: Phillippe Starck, St Martins Lane Hotel 100bcr, 100b; **Jason Hawkes Aerial Photography:** 216t; **Dan Johnson:** 26cbl, 35r; **Kos Pictures Source:** 215cbl, 240tc, 240tr; David Williams 216b; **Lebrecht Collection:** Kate Mount 169bc; **MP Visual.com:** Mark Swallow 202t; **NASA:** 280cr, 280ccl, 281tl; **P&O Princess Cruises:** 214bl; **P A Photos:** 181br; **The Photographers' Library:** 186bl, 186bc, 186t; **Plain and Simple Kitchens:** 66t; **Powerstock Photolibrary:** 169tl, 256t, 287tc; **Rail Images:** 208c, 208 cbl, 209br; **Red Consultancy:** Odeon cinemas 257br; **Redferns:** 259br; Nigel Crane 259c; **Rex Features:** 106br, 259tc, 259tr, 259bl, 280b; Charles Ommaney 114tcr; J.F.F Whitehead 243cl; Patrick Barth 101tl; Patrick Frilet 189cbl; Scott Wiseman 287bl; **Royalty Free Images:** Getty Images/Eyewire 154bl; **Science & Society Picture Library:** Science Museum 202b; **Skyscan:** 168t, 182c, 298; Quick UK Ltd 212; **Sony:** 268bc; **Robert Streeter:** 154br; **Neil Sutherland:** 82tr, 83tl, 90t, 118, 188ctr, 196tl, 196tr, 299cl, 299bl; **The Travel Library:** Stuart Black 264t; **Travelex:** 97cl; **Vauxhall:** Technik 198t, 199tl, 199tr, 199cl, 199cr, 199ctcl, 199ctcr, 199tcl, 199tcr, 200; **View Pictures:** Dennis Gilbert, Architects: ACDP Consulting, 106t; Dennis Gilbert, Chris Wilkinson Architects, 209tr; Peter Cook, Architects: Nicholas Crimshaw and partners, 208t; **Betty Walton:** 185br;

Colin Walton: 2, 4, 7, 9, 10, 28, 42, 56, 92, 95c, 99tl, 99tcl, 102, 116, 120t, 138t, 146, 150t, 160, 170, 191ctcl, 192, 218, 252, 260br, 260l, 261tr, 261c, 261ctr, 271cbl, 271cbr, 271ctl, 278, 287br, 302, 401.

DK PICTURE LIBRARY:
Akhil Bahkshi; Patrick Baldwin; Geoff Brightling; British Museum; John Bulmer; Andrew Butler; Joe Cornish; Brian Cosgrove; Andy Crawford and Kit Hougton; Philip Dowell; Alistair Duncan; Gables; Bob Gathany; Norman Hollands; Kew Gardens; Peter James Kindersley; Vladimir Kozlik; Sam Lloyd; London Northern Bus Company Ltd; Lucky Luke Licensing; Tracy Morgan; David Murray and Jules Selmes; Musée Vivant du Cheval, France; Museum of Broadcast Communications; Museum of Natural History; NASA; National History Museum; Norfolk Rural Life Museum; Stephen Oliver; RNLI; Royal Ballet School; Guy Ryecart; Science Museum; Neil Setchfield; Ross Simms and the Winchcombe Folk Police Museum; Singapore Symphony Orchestra; Smart Museum of Art; Tony Souter; Erik Svensson and Jeppe Wikstrom; Sam Tree of Keygrove Marketing Ltd; Barrie Watts; Alan Williams; Jerry Young.

Additional Photography by Colin Walton.

Colin Walton would like to thank:
A&A News, Uckfield; Abbey Music, Tunbridge Wells; Arena Mens Clothing, Tunbridge Wells; Burrells of Tunbridge Wells; Gary at Di Marco's; Jeremy's Home Store, Tunbridge Wells; Noakes of Tunbridge Wells; Ottakar's, Tunbridge Wells; Selby's of Uckfield; Sevenoaks Sound and Vision; Westfield, Royal Victoria Place, Tunbridge Wells.

Front jacket image © Volkswagen